THE ILLUSTRATED SLAVE

THE ILLUSTRATED
SLAVE

Empathy, Graphic Narrative,
and the Visual Culture of the Transatlantic
Abolition Movement, 1800–1852

Martha J. Cutter

THE UNIVERSITY OF GEORGIA PRESS
ATHENS

A Sarah Mills Hodge Fund Publication

This publication is made possible in part through a grant from the Hodge Foundation in memory of its founder, Sarah Mills Hodge, who devoted her life to the relief and education of African Americans in Savannah, Georgia.

© 2017 by the University of Georgia Press
Athens, Georgia 30602
www.ugapress.org
All rights reserved
Designed by Erin Kirk New
Set in Adobe Caslon Pro
Printed and bound by Thomson-Shore, Inc.
The paper in this book meets the guidelines for
permanence and durability of the Committee on
Production Guidelines for Book Longevity of the
Council on Library Resources.

Most University of Georgia Press titles are
available from popular e-book vendors.

Printed in the United States of America

17 18 19 20 21 C 5 4 3 2 1

Library of Congress Cataloging-in-Publication Data

Names: Cutter, Martha J., author.
  Title: The illustrated slave : empathy, graphic narrative, and the
  visual of the transatlantic abolition movement, 1800–1852 /
  Martha J. Cutter.
Description: Athens, Georgia : The University of Georgia Press, [2017]
  | Includes bibliographical references and index.
Identifiers: LCCN 2016055420| ISBN 9780820351162 (hardback : alk.
  paper) | ISBN 9780820351155 (ebook)
Subjects: LCSH: Slaves—United States—Illustrations. | Slavery—
  United States—Illustrations. | American literature—African
  American authors—History and criticism. | American literature—
  19th century—History and criticism. | Slavery in literature. |
  Antislavery movements in literature.
Classification: LCC PS217. S55 C87 2017 | DDC 810.9/352625—dc23
  LC record available at https://lccn.loc.gov/2016055420

CONTENTS

ACKNOWLEDGMENTS

Most of the chapters in this book have been deftly read and commented on by friends and colleagues at numerous universities. I list them in no particular order and sincerely thank them for their care with my ideas. They are Augusta Rohrbach, Sharon Harris, John Ernest, Alan Rice, Joycelyn Moody, Chris Vials, Shawn Salvant, Kate Capshaw, Jerry Phillips, Cassandra Jackson, Michael Gill, Kathy Knapp, Anna Mae Duane, Chris Clark, Jeffrey Ogbar, Patrick Hogan, Fiona Vernal, and Jeannine De Lombard. Thanks as well to Alexis Boylan and Shirley Samuels for feedback on both the manuscript and on the cover design. I owe a particular debt of gratitude to Cathy Schlund-Vials, who read many of these chapters in draft form and offered unstinting advice and praise; I cannot imagine a better colleague and friend. I also thank the members of the UConn Humanities Institute (UCHI) in 2014–2015, who heard many parts of this book and offered feedback: Rachel L. Greenblatt, Joseph McAlhany, Fakhreddin Azimi, Frank Costigliola, Fiona Somerset, Gordon Fraser, Christina Henderson, and Beata Moskal. A special thanks to UCHI's director, Michael Lynch, and associate director, Brendan Kane, for feedback and the fellowship that allowed me to complete this manuscript, and to the previous director, Sharon Harris, for help with my UCHI application. I also express my gratitude to the anonymous readers from the University of Georgia Press for revision suggestions and especially to Walter Biggins for his enthusiasm about this project. Special thanks also go to Rebecca Norton, production editor at the University of Georgia Press, for her incredible patience, and to Kip Keller, freelance editor, for careful copyediting and manuscript suggestions. For help with archival research on Henry Box Brown and feedback on the chapter about him, I thank the following people: Jeffrey Ruggles, Rory Rennick, Heather Murray, Karolyn Smartz-Frost, Mary Chapman, Linda Cobon, Guylaine Petrin, Michael Lynch, Brendan Kane, and librarians at Toronto Public Library (especially Irena Lewycka). Thanks as well to Michelle Maloney-Mangold for proofreading and research assistance, and to Rebecca Rumbo for proofreading and intellectual feedback. Laura A. Wright came in at the last minute to help with citation checking; I am extremely grateful for her care and diligence. The interlibrary loan staff at the University of Connecticut went above and beyond the call of duty in obtaining rare archival manuscripts and facilitating my research, and librarians and archivists at the Library Company of Philadelphia, the New-York Historical Society, the American Antiquarian Society in Worcester (Massachusetts), the Archives of Ontario, and Toronto General Hospital were also extremely helpful. A special debt is owed to David K. Frasier of the Lilly Library for helping me obtain high-resolution JPEGs of Amelia Opie's *The Black Man's Lament*. I also owe a huge thanks to Melanie Hepburn for assisting me in the massive amount of paperwork required to pay permission fees and engage in archival work.

I must also thank the University of Connecticut's English Department for giving me a sabbatical in the spring of 2012 to work on this book, and Veronica Makowsky for taking over my editorial duties at *MELUS* so that I could write during this sabbatical. I deeply thank the chair of the English Department, Robert Hasenfratz, for giving me release time from teaching while I completed the book. At the University of Connecticut, I am especially grateful to the Africana Studies Institute and Melina Pappademos, the Felberbaum Family Fund, FIRE (Fund for Interdisciplinary Research), and the Office of the Vice President for Research, as well as the Humanities Institute, for grants that helped pay for archival research and other manuscript costs. I also thank the CLAS Book Support Committee for subvention funding.

For permission to use images in this book and for providing TIFFs of images, I thank Mike Caveney; Celia Caust-Ellenbogen and Swarthmore College; Timothy Rohe and the Redwood Library and Athenaeum; the Houghton Library (Harvard University); the Library Company of Philadelphia; the American Antiquarian Society; the Moorland-Spingarn Research Center, Howard University; Yale University; the Library of Congress; the National Portrait Gallery, Smithsonian Institution; Wilmer Wilson IV and the Connersmith Gallery; Elliott Banfield and the *New York Sun*; Glenn Ligon, Regen Projects, and the Hirshhorn Museum and Sculpture Garden, Smithsonian Institution; and Kara Walker, Scott Briscoe, and Sikkema Jenkins & Co. An earlier version of chapter 3 was published in *ESQ: A Journal of the American Renaissance* 60, no. 3 (2014): 371–411, copyright 2017 by the Board of Regents of Washington State University, and I thank the editors and readers for helpful feedback and permission to reprint. Brief excerpts of chapter 5 were published in *Common-Place: The Journal of Early American Life* 16, no. 1 (2015), and I thank Anna Mae Duane and Walter Woodward for suggested revisions.

On a more personal note, I thank my parents for supporting my work as a scholar all these many years. I thank all the students who have listened to me discuss this work, especially those in my graduate seminar "Visual Rhetoric and Social Change" in the fall of 2013. Last but certainly not least, I thank my partner, Peter Linehan, who has listened to my ideas patiently for years now, cooked food and taken care of the dogs while I wrote, driven me back and forth to archives and libraries across the United States and Canada, taken photographs for my research, and never complained about any of this.

This book is dedicated to Terry Rowden and Cathy J. Schlund-Vials. Terry, my great friend and colleague, has offered me invaluable feedback on my work throughout my career—more, certainly, than I have ever given him. I also thank my colleague and best friend Cathy Schlund-Vials, who has metaphorically held my hand more times than I can count when I needed to have faith that this manuscript would ultimately be completed. The generous mind and spirit of these two friends is an inspiration and a true gift for which I am eternally thankful.

PREFACE

To understand it, one must needs experience it, or imagine himself in similar circumstances.
—Frederick Douglass (108)

This project began while I was working on a book about black-white racial passing and reading Moses Roper's *A Narrative of the Adventures and Escape of Moses Roper, from American Slavery*, first published in 1837 in England and republished in the United States and England in 1838. What first caught my eye was Roper's ability to pass in a variety of ways: for "white" (which his skin color allowed), for Native American (which his mother might have been), and for a free citizen (which he certainly was not). On a second reading, however, I became fascinated by the fact that Roper's narrative had illustrations—four of them in 1838 and five by 1840. Most critics have evaluated the text negatively in our own era, but few scholars, with the exception of Marcus Wood, have paid any attention to the illustrations. Even Wood fails to spend much time on how the graphic content interacts with Roper's written account to form a specific rhetorical argument about the subjectivity of the enslaved, the relationship of the enslaved to the viewer, and the concomitant demand for freedom.

Roper's text is probably the first illustrated narrative written by a U.S. born slave, but more importantly, it is a significant but overlooked document in the archive of antislavery visual culture, one that attempts to shift readers toward abolitionist action through the mobilization of *both* words and pictures working synchronically to create intersubjectivity (shared cognition and affective states)[1] and what I term "parallel empathy"—empathy that asserts concordance between a viewing reader and the enslaved. The politics of Roper's text seems more radical, and the argument made by its words and pictures more challenging, to his readers than that in *Uncle Tom's Cabin* (1852), which relies on pity and on what I term in this book "hierarchical empathy" for the "lowly" enslaved. I wondered whether there were other illustrated books that attempted to challenge the rhetoric of pathos, pity, and voyeurism common in abolitionist visual and written discourse, ones that might personify a mode of empathy in which the enslaved and the viewing self could not be disentangled.

This book attempts to answer this question. It has two primary goals. The first is to analyze some of the more innovative works in the archive of antislavery graphic illustrated books published before *Uncle Tom's Cabin*, using tools from graphic narrative theory and visual rhetoric studies to assess how these works formulate arguments through the symbiotic interrelationship between words and pictures. In this study, I use the term "graphic illustrated book" or "graphic narrative" to suggest precisely that words and pictures work synergistically, making the overall effect more than the sum of the parts, and the empathetic spark more than words or pictures alone might engender. Of late, much has been written about abolitionist art and visual culture, yet there has been little systematic investigation of the graphic illustrated book, at least until the appearance of Harriet Beecher Stowe's *Uncle Tom's Cabin*, published in 1852 with six illustrations. Yet across diverse genres—travelogues, slave narratives, long-form poems, sentimental novels, children's books, and antislavery semiautobiographical memoirs—illustrated books were first used extensively by the antislavery movement in the early nineteenth century; certain technical changes in wood engraving and printing, discussed in the introduction, made the use of illustrations within a printed text more economically feasible during these years. I have found many illustrated antislavery books written in the first half of the nineteenth century by blacks and whites, men and women, free and formerly enslaved. My first objective in this book is to assess the cultural and political work that some of the more innovative of these texts perform.

A second intent is to analyze the politics of empathy and agency represented in these works. As many critics have noted, in the nineteenth century the spectacle of enslaved torture—of what was termed "sentimental wounding"—often positioned the enslaved as "erotic objects of sympathy rather than subjects in their own rights" (Noble, "Ecstasies of Sentimental Wounding," 296) and fueled an "allure of bondage" that replicated physical enslavement (Sánchez-Eppler, *Touching Liberty*, 25). Karen Halttunen argues that spectatorial sympathy—a sympathy between the viewer and the enslaved stirred through sight—might have been pleasurable to the viewer because it "liberally mingled pleasure with vicarious pain," creating a sort of pleasing anguish that was very close to the pornography of pain, which first developed in the early nineteenth century ("Humanitarianism and Pornography," 317). Some of the works I examine use a mode of spectatorial sympathy that mingles pleasure with vicarious pain. Yet there are also moments when these books try to *shift* a reader's horizon of expectations by portraying the enslaved as possessing both power over the tools of oppression and modes of agency; they also mobilize a politics of empathy and intersubjectivity that attempts to move *beyond* spectatorial sympathy by pushing a viewer to see the enslaved as connected with his or her own subjectivity, on terms of parity and equality.

Marcus Wood has made the controversial argument that "the suffering of . . . another will always be out of bounds and beyond recovery" and that therefore belief in the "aesthetically healing powers of empathetic fiction" is something of a crime (*Slavery, Empathy, and Pornography*, 36). I am more interested in what kinds of textual structures embedded in antislavery graphic illustrated books might figure forth the *symbolic* crossing of borders between self and other, the reading viewer and the enslaved. Using data on the facilitation of empathy, I focus on textual structures embedded within these texts that are meant to erode the gap between self and other, the spectator and the spectated. Further, some of these graphic books seem to be in pursuit of a mode of reading that seeks not to "recover" the trauma of enslavement but to fill this self-other gap with a new meaning, with an alternative message about the subjectivity of the enslaved and his or her relationship to the viewing reader. In such works, then, we can also see strands of what the historian Manisha Sinha recently termed a radical, interracial movement within abolition that viewed slavery as a transnational problem of human rights and took insurgent steps to overturn it, one of which included "the attempt to evoke radical empathy" from those who read (and saw visual images within) abolitionist publications (*Slave's Cause*, 1, 339, 4).

I do not intend to be ahistorical in my use of the term "empathy," which was coined in the early part of the twentieth century.[2] Yet as discussed in the book as a whole, at times the emotional and cognitive response that these texts seem to demand from the viewing reader includes a condition that today is termed empathy, defined in its most basic form by the *Collins English Dictionary* as "the power of understanding and imaginatively entering into another person's feelings." As early as 1759, Adam Smith broke with previous thinkers about morality to argue (in *The Theory of Moral Sentiments*) that sympathy operates through a mirroring process in which a spectator imaginatively reconstructs the experience of the person he watches: "Though our brother is on the rack, as long as we ourselves are at our ease, our senses will never inform us of what he suffers. . . . It is by the imagination only that we can form any conception of what are his sensations. . . . By the imagination, we place ourselves in his situation" (3). The ability imaginatively to place "ourselves in [another's] situation" is figured as a mode of empathy, but was generally called sympathy in the eighteenth and nineteenth centuries. Frederick Douglass evokes a similar process when he writes: "To understand it, one must needs experience it, or imagine himself in similar circumstances" (*Narrative of the Life*, 108). By imagination, Douglass seems to believe, an individual may place himself or herself in similar circumstances and so come to some degree of comprehension of occurrences not directly experienced. Such an imaginative, empathetic mode attempts to translate the viewer *beyond* spectatorial sympathy by undermining cognitive, affective, and visual barriers separating the enslaved, viewed other from the free, viewing subject.

Numerous critics have argued that portrayals of the enslaved within abolitionist art and visual culture, in particular, cordon off a white viewing subject from that of the black, abject, viewed body; in so doing, these depictions short-circuit the process of imagining oneself in similar circumstances, of empathy. Many abolitionist texts did not, in the words of Barbara Hochman, "ask the readers to collapse the distance between themselves and the objects of their sympathy," because they believed that a "proper sense of white separateness was crucial to benevolent feelings and actions" *("Uncle Tom's Cabin,"* 26). But perhaps illustration located within a narrative—a type of graphic story—accesses a more radical experiential paradigm. In what ways might words on a page be combined with text to move readers toward certain prosocial ends or actions more effectively than pictures or words alone? How can narrative text (stories, captions, titles, and speech bubbles) braid itself around pictures to forward innovative antislavery arguments that visual elements alone might not be able to present? A picture alone might be ambiguous, but a narrative twined around a picture heightens the author's ability to advance an argument that entails psychological energy moving between individuals—to facilitate, in other words, mutual understanding instead of only pity for the plight of the enslaved. The polyphonic story told between words and pictures, in turn, might generate more readerly empathy than words or pictures alone, because, as some studies of empathy have suggested, complex, or "writerly," works that force readers to struggle to make meaning and understand different perspectives tend to increase reader participation with the text, as well as empathy itself (Kidd and Castano, "Reading Literary Fiction," 378; Bruner, *Actual Minds,* 25).

The crucial role of visualization in the process of creating an understanding of enslavement was recognized in the nineteenth century.[3] Some abolitionists believed that a specific collaboration between words and graphic images was essential to promoting a more powerful interaction between the enslaved individual and a reader. Charles C. Green, the author of a book-length antislavery illustrated poem called *The Nubian Slave* (1845), wrote: "The application of Pictorial Art to Moral Truth is capable of producing a great, and as yet, almost untried force, which the Friends of Human Freedom have now an opportunity to test" ("Prospectus," 4). Sometimes Green implanted figures of enslaved and tortured bodies into words themselves, literally blurring demarcations separating the pictorial from the lexical; in the illustration here, for example, the slave's body intercedes in the word "Unhappy" between the letters *U* and *N* (see figure oo.1). Green's huge book—twenty inches wide and thirteen inches tall, or almost three and a half feet wide when spread open—contains full-page illustrations; the huge size seems to ask a reader to linger over some images, to inhabit them for a while.

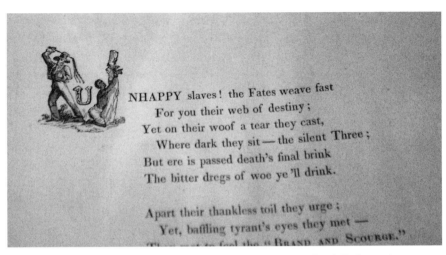

FIGURE 00.2 From Charles C. Green, *The Nubian Slave* (1845). Lithograph.
American Antiquarian Society.

As noted, many critics have argued that antislavery discourse—and illustrations in particular—merely replicates physical slavery by allowing a viewer to scopically surveil and other the enslaved, and we can certainly see such a practice in the image above from Green's text. Yet I tell a somewhat more nuanced story in this study about how *some* graphic illustrated books combine narrative—the power of storytelling— with pictures to attempt to shift viewers toward parity and empathy with the enslaved. In a speech in May 1849, William Lloyd Garrison argued that the antislavery movement's greatest difficulty was "an unwillingness to see in the form and face of the slave, a man." Garrison audaciously urges abolitionists to use their own embodied experiences—as husbands, fathers, and humans—to place themselves into the situation of the enslaved: "The moment we recognize in [the enslaved] a child of God, one like ourselves, all difficulties vanish. . . . The moment we make the case of the slave our own; for instance, as husbands whose wives are ready for the public auction block, whose children are to be put in the scales to be sold by the pound to the highest bidders, that moment we cease to have any fault to find with those who plead the cause of the southern slave." Garrison uses a highly visual language—one that entails seeing and recognizing the abolitionist's self in the enslaved—to notate this process. Graphic illustrated books, I argue, were crucial and important instruments for achieving what Garrison sought— seeing "in the form and face of the slave" a human being.

In the works I analyze, the illustrations, which range from five pictures in a volume to as many as twenty-three, were created by someone other than the author, and the illustrator is often unknown; they were also sometimes taken from other sources. How does this feature of the books affect the antislavery argument being generated? In a discussion of children's picture books, Perry Nodelman notes that words and pictures often exist in an ironic relationship to each other: "The objective conclusion we reach by perusing the pictures conflicts interestingly with the viewpoint demanded by the words" (*Words about Pictures*, 234). Most picture books display, to some degree, irony in this sense, but irony is at its height when illustrations are inserted into a text by a hand other than the original author or editor. Nodelman also theorizes that pictures generally focus on "key events rather than on the fluid connection of one action with the next," whereas we rely on narration to tell us "what happens" (240), to (as it were) connect the dots between the pictures and create a narrative or story. Pictures often are a string of moments frozen in time with nothing between them, but narration in illustrated books often tells us the story of what these images are supposed to mean. I suggest, then, that the words of the narrative—which frequently focus on the equality, resilience, and resourcefulness of the enslaved—might push a reader toward certain fairly specific interpretations of the illustrations, interpretations in which the line between the enslaved and a free viewing subject is partially dismantled. Taken together, the words and the pictures in many abolitionist texts often enforce an argument that the enslaved should be free not because slavery hurts the pained body of the enslaved (which it does) or because it wounds the psyche (which it also does), but because the enslaved are coequal human beings, with agency, power, and resourcefulness to feel this pain and work toward its end.

For some critics, the idea of the enslaved possessing any degree of agency or control over their lives or narratives is extremely problematic. Some abolitionists forced the fugitive to bear witness to the "truth" about slavery—but a truth that had already been theorized and crafted in a particular way by abolitionist discourse, which often then packaged and sold these narratives. Therefore, "before the slave ever speaks," contends Dwight McBride, "we know the slave; we know what his or her experience is, and we know how to read that experience" (*Impossible Witnesses*, 5). Fugitives often occupied a liminal space within transatlantic culture—although no longer in physical bondage, they had to recount continually the terms of their psychic and physical enslavement for abolitionist purposes. Even more profoundly, the enslaved situation may seem to preclude an articulation of subjectivity. Saidiya Hartman has asked: "How is it possible to think 'agency' when the slave's very condition of being or social existence is defined as a state of determinate negation? In other words, what are the constituents of agency when one's social condition is defined by negation and personhood refigured in the fetishized and fungible terms of object of property?" (*Scenes of Subjection*, 52). Hartman answers this question in part by hypothesizing that certain performances and practices may "exploit and exceed the constraints of domination" (54). I am most interested in examining those performances and practices of representation that exploit and exceed the constraints of domination in these illustrated antislavery books' imaging of torture, enslavement, modes of agency, and freedom.

One nexus of debate and signification concerning agency in these works centers on the meaning of the term "slave," and so I am attentive to its relevant visual and verbal connotations. This textual debate about the agency of the enslaved in the nineteenth century connects with an important recent discussion concerning the connotative and political implications of the use of the term "slave" in scholarship about the antebellum period. Scholars such as Deborah Gray White (*Ar'n't I a Woman*, 8) and Daina Ramey Berry (*"Swing the Sickle,"* 167) refrain from using the word whenever possible, because it is said to connote a permanent status of subjugation, an unchanging fact. Such scholars instead prefer the term "enslaved," which emphasizes a process of subjugation, one with a specific teleology and duration, a condition into which a person is put by slave owners, rather than an evident and unchanging fact.[4] On the other hand, the historian David Blight has argued against using the term "enslaved": "Slave is the historically accurate term. . . . American slaves knew they had been 'enslaved' by someone or some process. They didn't choose the condition. Why can't we muster the same strength they did and leave the historical language alone in its accuracy?" Blight insists that the term slave is accurate, and does not connote an unchanging fact (comment).

To signal my understanding of this debate and my agreement that in a contemporary time period it is beneficial to challenge the idea that the enslaved were static individuals, I employ the word "enslaved" when possible, and especially when gesturing toward a wider theoretical debate about the meaning of enslavement as a whole. But because this study is a historical one about how people explicitly labeled "slaves" resisted and took agency within the discursive and visual landscape of this nomenclature, and about how some writers resignified and challenged the idea of slave abjection and otherness from inside a visual and discursive terrain in which the enslaved were already pejoratively labeled, I use the term "slave" at times, most notably in the title of this book. In the works I consider, "slave" can signify the articulation of a critique that works against the dominant discourse, rejecting its tenets but not its explicit nomenclature. In other words, some authors in my study consciously employ the term to challenge its explicit denial of personhood and agency.

Use of the word "slave" in the title of this book also highlights an interpretive struggle during the first half of the nineteenth century over the nature of enslavement and its visual rhetoric. The historian David Waldstreicher fears that the use of terms such as "enslaved persons" may "cover over the contest over the nature of enslavement and its languages that occurred in the past" (comment). Indeed, as depicted in illustrated works, slaves were used to elucidate many ideologies, some of which entailed otherness and a permanent state of abjection. Yet some of the works I discuss turn this meaning of the word "slave" back on itself, using the term not to illustrate the superiority of the white man and the slave's permanent abject status, but his or her resistance to this status. "You have seen how a man was made a slave," writes Frederick Douglass in a famous phrase, "you shall see how a slave was made a man" (*Narrative of the Life*, 65–66). Douglass emphasizes that enslavement is a process, and he uses "slave" in this sentence and in the title of his 1845 autobiography to signal that the term must be resignified, twisted to acknowledge an articulation of agency and selfhood from inside the discursive paradigm of "slave." Within both pro- and antislavery visual culture, there was a contest about the meaning of slavery and the status of the enslaved, and many of the graphic illustrated books I assess engaged in this contest, not by inventing a new term or avoiding the word "slave" (although some did), but by employing this term in a radically altered fashion. Ultimately, like Douglass, the authors I study demonstrate that the illustrated slave is also finally and foremost an illustrated man (or woman)—one whose body has been inscribed with a static message of abnegation and otherness, but who contests this inscription through a visual rhetoric that emphasizes a configuration of slave resistance and agency.

Not all the authors discussed here destabilize the scopic power of a viewer and of antislavery visual politics or depict a visual configuration of enslaved resistance to abjection. But I am most attentive to how the archive of antislavery graphic books written before 1852 complicates the argument that many critics have made about abolitionist visual culture—a culture that has almost always been read as engaged in an indiscriminate denial of power and subjectivity to the viewed object, the enslaved body. Some early books endeavor to use words and pictures to integrate a reader into the text in a structure of equality; they also represent the enslaved as manipulating a configuration of subjectivity that emphasizes psychical resistance to torture, torment, and abasement. If, as Robyn Wiegman has noted, the "visible" operates "as the primary vehicle for making race 'real' in the United States" (*American Anatomies*, 21), then it is crucial to study the way this literary genre intervenes in the political and social representation of the visible meaning of enslaved racial subjectivity. These graphic illustrated books tell us much about how antislavery writers conceptualized a powerful interactive effect that interwoven words and pictures could have on a reading viewer, who ultimately might come to feel his or her concordance with the illustrated slave.

THE ILLUSTRATED SLAVE

FIGURE 0.1 White jasper medallion for the Society for the Abolition of the Slave Trade, modeled by William Hackwood, made at Josiah Wedgwood's factory, Etruria, Staffordshire, England, c. 1787. Copyright Victoria and Albert Museum no. 414:1304-1885. Used with permission.

Introduction

Visualizing Slavery and Slave Torture

In 1787 Josiah Wedgwood, the famous pottery crafter and Nonconformist, issued a beautiful jasperware medallion with an applied relief of a kneeling enslaved man and the inscription "Am I Not a Man and a Brother?" (see figure o.1). The image was loosely modeled on that of the seal for the Committee for the Abolition of the Slave Trade, founded in that same year by Thomas Clarkson. But whereas Clarkson's image was flat and somewhat harsh in outline, Wedgwood turned the image into an elegant three-dimensional picture of the heavily chained supplicant slave's suffering, as he begs for help from powers situated, visually and metaphorically, above his kneeling figure. Wedgwood intuited that the icon could be made into an appealingly stylish piece of high art, and the public was quick to take notice. As Clarkson recounts, the image soon became part of everyday culture and fashion: "Some had them [antislavery medallions] inlaid in gold on the lid of their snuff-boxes. Of the ladies, several wore them in bracelets, and others had them fitted up in an ornamental manner as pins for their hair. At length the taste for wearing them became general, and thus fashion . . . was seen for once in the honourable office of promoting the cause of justice and humanity and freedom" (*History of the Rise*, 191–92). The image was emblazoned in gold on white china and in green on an enamel patch box—symbols now not only of suffering but of elegance and taste (see figures o.2 and o.3; color images 1 and 2).

In some of these representations, the question mark at the end of the motto is removed, but what remains unchanged are the spatial hierarchy and the caption, in which the enslaved seeks validation of his unfinished humanity in the only words that appear in the image: "Am I Not a Man and a Brother." In most

FIGURE 0.2 Abolitionist sugar bowl, purchased at the Philadelphia Anti-Slavery Fair by Josiah Quincy, c. 1836–1861. Courtesy of the Friends Historical Library of Swarthmore College. Used with permission.

FIGURE 0.3 Patch box with abolitionist motif, "Am I not a Man and a Brother." South Staffordshire, c. 1790. Enamel on copper. Accession number 1987. 212. 3; International Slavery Museum, Liverpool. Used with permission.

drawings of this supplicant slave, the implied horizon line situates the enslaved figure slightly below the horizon; a viewer's glance therefore tends to fall slightly downward onto the abject body in the foreground, which is much larger than anything else.[1] Viewers' sight lines are drawn to the heavily chained body of the downcast slave as he begs for freedom from a disembodied presence located outside the picture frame and above him. In each representation, the enlarged figure in the foreground (wearing little more than what appears to be an infantilizing diaper) attracts attention, so the enslaved seems to become wholly a body; even when the shallow and flat background contains significant symbols (such as huts or a slave ship), these details are small and do not compel attention in the same way that the slave's aching and supplicant body does.

The image of the kneeling, supplicant slave crossed the Atlantic to the United States. Around 1800, the New-Jersey Society for Promoting the Abolition of Slavery created a certificate of membership that shows a well-dressed white man gesturing toward the same naked and chained supplicant slave while holding a Bible opened to Isaiah 61:1, which reads, "He came to proclaim liberty to the captives, and the opening of the prison to them that are bound." As if to bless this example of white benevolence toward the enslaved, beams from Heaven shine down upon the pair through an aperture in the clouds (see figure 0.4).

The image was later remodeled in ways allowing for the possibility of more than mere abject subjectivity. As Sharon Patton notes, the New York Anti-Slavery Society sponsored the African American engraver Patrick Reason to study engraving techniques in London. In 1839, Reason copied Wedgwood's image in a copper engraving, but modified its composition (see figure 0.5). Patton argues that Reason produced an image that "plays both to the sentimentalism and to African-Americans' view of themselves as intelligent people, not bondsmen" (*African-American Art*, 77–78). The enslaved man's face is turned more toward the front of the image, and he is more fully clothed in Reason's image. Yet he still does not look directly at the viewer, and the question of whether the slave is a man and a brother remains for a viewer to answer. The pleading, supplicant slave is still on his knees and in chains, with his hands clasped in prayer in front of him. Reason went on to construct images of African Americans as tasteful, dignified, literate subjects (as in his 1849 portrait of Henry Bibb).[2] Yet the enslaved man depicted in this 1839 remodeling of the supplicant slave image seems unsure whether he is "a man and a brother"; he still looks to someone or something outside the frame that can convert his abject and othered status into subjectivity.

This body reflects what Mikhail Bakhtin might call a grotesque or low body, "unfinished" and "open to the outside world" (*Rabelais*, 26). Peter Stallybrass and

FIGURE 0.4 Membership certificate from the New-Jersey Society Promoting the Abolition of Slavery, c. 1800. Stipple engraving. Courtesy of the Library Company of Philadelphia. Used with permission.

FIGURE 0.5 Patrick Reason, "Am
I Not a Man and a Brother" (1839).
Copper engraving. Collection of
the Moorland-Spingarn Center,
Howard University, Washington,
D.C. Used with permission.

Allon White argue for a reading of the body in which "high discourses" of the
classical, finished, closed body are "structured in relation to the debasements and
degradations" of low discourse and bodies (*Politics and Poetics*, 3), and we may view
such a politics of the body at work in Reason's image. The viewer's perspective is
directed at an object of exchange within cultural discourse, one who pleads for a
granting of his unfinished subjectivity and in so doing affirms a viewer's status
as a subject who is finished, closed, separate, and not debased or commodified.
Psychologists have theorized that empathy may be a response to an "over-inclusive
kin recognition" in which kinship becomes more metaphorical than literal and so
may lead to helping behavior for larger groups of people than one's own kinship
network (Park, Schaller, and Van Vugt, "Human Kin Recognition," 225–26). In the
image by Reason, one can see the attempt to mobilize a kinship relationship (of
brotherhood), even as the formation of this sentiment as a question (Am I not
your brother?) may fail to mobilize fully a politics of overinclusive kinship and an
empathy that could lead to assisting actions.

By way of contrast, we might look at the remodeling of this icon on the title
page of the radical British abolitionist Elizabeth Heyrick's pamphlet *Immediate,
Not Gradual Abolition* (1824) (see figure 0.6). In this wood engraving, the enslaved
individual is standing, having broken free of his chains; he looks out of the image

directly at the viewer, insisting on a literal or metaphorical kinship: "I Am a Man, Your Brother."[3] A Bible verse functions as a caption that attempts to erase the line separating the viewing Christian spectator from the (black) viewed "pagan" object, by emphasizing that enslaved and free, black and white, the viewed and the viewer, are all made by God and share one common humanity: "He hath made of one blood all nations of men."[4] Because the man's head, shoulders, and torso are above the horizon line of the picture and because he looks directly at the viewer, the viewer's attention is drawn to his glance. We are placed on the same level as the man who has broken free of his chains; we see him, I think, just at the moment when he sees us.

The illustration to Heyrick's popular and widely reprinted pamphlet clearly draws on the iconic power of the original image and its particular meaning— that slavery was criminal and should be abolished. Yet Heyrick struggles to shift her reader away from thinking of the enslaved as solely an abject, disempowered other. Her text's visual rhetoric—the argument made by its words and pictures together—redeploys the icon of the supplicant slave in the service of a differ- ent argument for ending slavery: all men, as partakers of a common humanity, are capable of attaining freedom and subjectivity, and even of fighting for their right to freedom. While still relegating the body of the enslaved in some ways to the realm of the primitive (the man is half naked, and his features are rather unfinished), the image attempts to structure a reading—a social experience of the image—in which the enslaved have the potential to invade the consciousness of the subject through a visual rhetoric in which they refuse a low status; the image imposes a counterview in which the slave *is* a man and a brother, connected with the humanity of the white viewer on a parallel plane, rather than structuring the downward glance that allows the white person to claim subjectivity through pro- cesses of othering and abjection. In the pamphlet, Heyrick grounds her appeal in a practice not of pity for the other but of intersubjectivity with the enslaved— and in a common humanity between the enslaved and the British populace; she writes that "hundreds of thousands of *human beings* continue to be disinherited of those inherent rights of humanity, without which, life becomes a curse instead of a blessing," all so that a "few noble lords and honourable gentlemen may experience no privation of expensive luxury,—no contraction of profuse expenditure,—no curtailment of state and equipage" (19, emphasis added). She specifically indicates here that the high and noble subject is created through debasement of someone who is viewed as other yet possesses all the "inherent rights of humanity."[5]

These illustrations demonstrate that a visual rhetoric composed of lexical and pictorial elements was developing rapidly in the early nineteenth century to

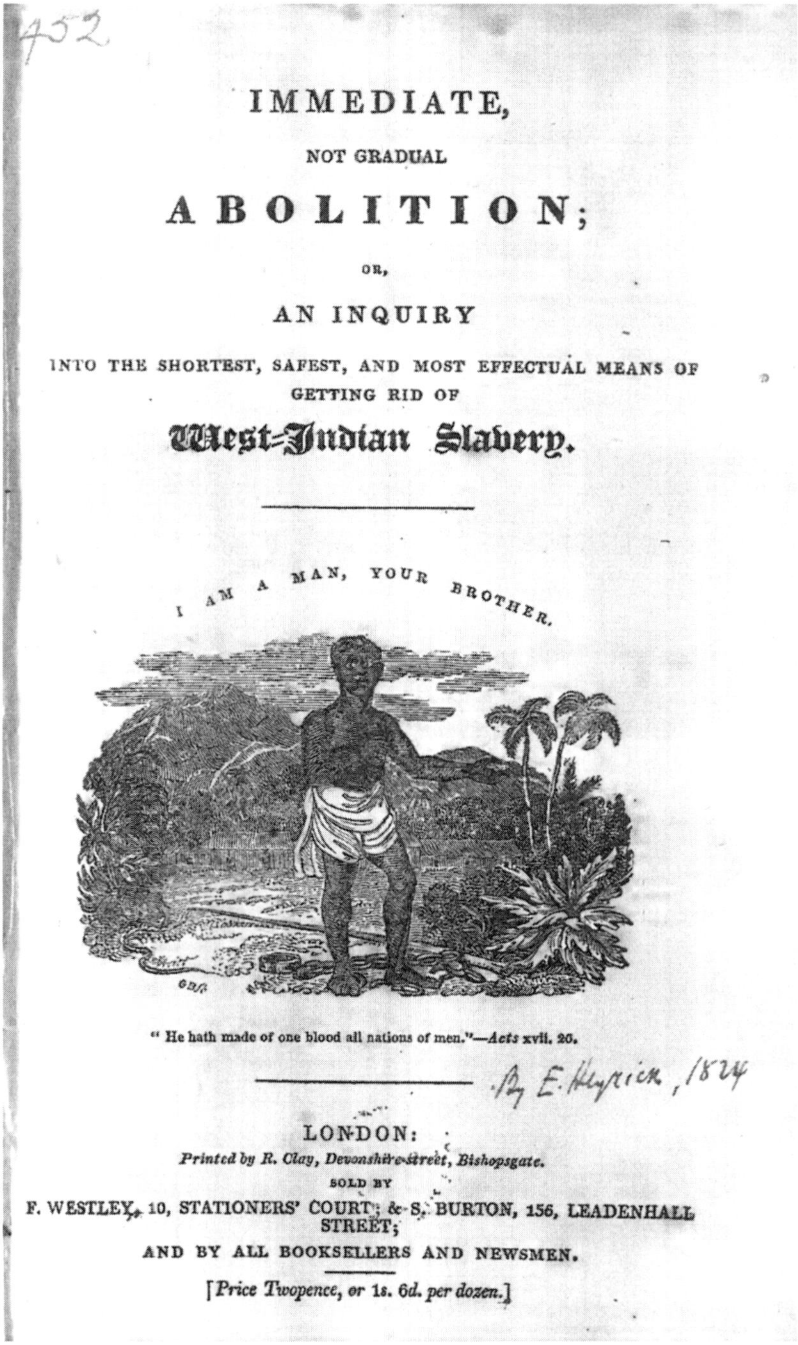

IMMEDIATE,

NOT GRADUAL

ABOLITION;

OR,

AN INQUIRY

INTO THE SHORTEST, SAFEST, AND MOST EFFECTUAL MEANS OF
GETTING RID OF

West=Indian Slavery.

I AM A MAN, YOUR BROTHER.

" He hath made of one blood all nations of men."—*Acts* xvii. 26.

By E. Heyrick, 1824

LONDON:
Printed by R. Clay, Devonshire-street, Bishopsgate.
SOLD BY
F. WESTLEY, 10, STATIONERS' COURT; &. S. BURTON, 156, LEADENHALL
STREET;
AND BY ALL BOOKSELLERS AND NEWSMEN.

[*Price Twopence, or* 1s. 6d. *per dozen.*]

FIGURE 0.6 Title page vignette, Elizabeth Heyrick, *Immediate Not Gradual Abolition* (1824). Wood engraving. Google Books.

support antislavery agendas. They also delineate how visual-verbal representations of the enslaved body were employed to articulate different structures of feeling, which notate discrete types of social and political abolitionist arguments. At times, the image and its caption structure a hierarchical reading in which the viewer enables or creates the humanity and freedom of the enslaved. In other instances, the Wedgwood image is repurposed as a semantic figure that directly confronts a viewer, via horizontal imaging, with the truth that men and women were enslaved by other men and women. In this second structure of feeling, the figure argues for the immediate end of slavery by suggesting similarity and equality—a type of parallel argument in which a viewer is encouraged to move toward an intersubjective or shared understanding of the graphic violence of enslavement enacted upon coequal human beings.

As the circulation of the Wedgwood image implies, abolition was a multimedia and multimodal political movement that relied heavily on visual technologies. Some of the newly emerging visual technologies used in the first half of the nineteenth century included daguerreotypes, lithographs, ambrotypes, tintypes, photographs, cartes de visite, dioramas, and panoramas; these techniques, along with well-established ones such as woodcuts and copper engravings, were used with performance modes such as stage shows and songs to further antislavery arguments. I examine in particular one facet of antislavery visual rhetoric: the illustrated books that emerged from 1800 to 1852 crafted by African American and Anglo-American authors on both sides of the Atlantic.[6] Like Heyrick's pamphlet, some of these early illustrated books formulate a mechanism whereby political change might occur not through a hierarchical and vertical structure, in which an elevated viewer lifts the chains off the (black) downtrodden slave (as seen in the first Wedgwood design), but through a horizontal, intersubjective perspective in which a viewer realizes that he or she cannot be disentangled from the enslaved individual—that the slave is not radically different from the viewing self, and vice versa. Some illustrated books invoke for their audience the familiar horrors of slavery—torture, whipping, beating, and abasement—to suggest not only the need to end slavery, but also an alternative configuration of the relationship between the viewed and the viewer. In works by authors spanning and transcending specific religious affiliations (the ones discussed in this study were Quaker, Baptist, Unitarian, Presbyterian, and nondenominational), we see a construction of the enslaved body not exclusively as an object of sympathy but also as one having parity with the viewing subject.[7]

"Methodologically," comments Raymond Williams, a "'structure of feeling' is a cultural hypothesis, actually derived from attempts to understand such elements and their connections in a generation or period" (*Marxism and Literature*, 132–33). For Williams, a structure of feeling may precede the formation of new ideology and be a reaction to a previous one (134), yet because works of art are experienced by readers or viewers in a present-tense moment, a structure of feeling is an ongoing social process. The idea of a structure of feeling, he notes, can be related to semantic figures, which are often the "very first indication that such a new structure is forming" (133). The semantic and visual figure of the enslaved body was used by some abolitionists to denote an ideological process in which the enslaved were, in effect, dehumanized, as critics such as Marcus Wood have argued.[8] Yet other scholars, such as Cassandra Jackson, have noted that while the image of the black wounded body (whether enslaved or free) is rooted in specific histories of oppression in the United States and elsewhere, this wounding also represents a "specular moment" that "mediates power relations between seers and the seen." Jackson argues that in this specular moment, "the exchange is not so much static as fluid," and she posits that in such exchanges "the viewed can retain agency" (*Violence, Visual Culture*, 3). In many instances, it is hard to know whether the viewed retained agency, but one project of this book is to understand how visual culture—in particular, graphic illustrated books—uses the semantic figure of the enslaved body to create a specular moment that stages an exchange between the viewed and the viewer in which the enslaved are portrayed as achieving or retaining some degree of agency. In so doing, these works create new structures of feeling for abolitionism, since they move the viewer toward parity with an agentive body represented in a fluid specular moment.

My study assesses the structures of abolitionist feeling—of both affect and cognition joined "in a living and related continuity" (Williams, *Marxism and Literature*, 132)—in early graphic illustrated books about slavery written by authors popular in their own time but mostly forgotten in ours, such as Thomas Branagan, Amelia Opie, George Bourne, Moses Roper, Lydia Maria Child, Henry Bibb, and Henry Box Brown. The texts authored by these writers and illustrated by often unknown artists contain visual and verbal structures that attempt to blur lines separating the enslaved from the free, the spectacle from the spectator. They did not always succeed in this endeavor, but my argument is that (like the illustration and rhetoric in Heyrick's pamphlet) such texts configure processes of similitude between the viewer and the viewed so that the "low" body of the slave becomes connected with (rather than separate from) the "high" discourse of white empowered subjectivity. I analyze instances in which these books, in the affective and cognitive processes they foster, diverge from the dominant abjection present in much abolitionist visual culture. The alternative reading or viewing protocols they enable through structures of feeling are embedded within their visual rhetoric. I analyze how these texts attempt to structure a new social experience in which the enslaved bodies portrayed possess some degree of similarity with a reader and in so doing encourage intersubjectivity, defined here as a state of mutual understanding in a relationship of parity.[9]

Throughout this book, I make a distinction between two strategies for empathy mobilized within illustrated antislavery works: parallel empathy and hierarchical empathy. Empathy has been defined in many ways, but I define it here as a cognitive and emotional process in which perception of the state of pain in another person leads the perceiver to feel similar emotions; the viewing subject and the viewed pained object become entangled, entwined, and coterminous. Empathy may lead to vicarious introspection and a spiraling process between self and other in which one comes to understand that but for the luck of birthplace, wealth, or skin color, the other could be the viewing self. This mode of empathy does not erase differences between self and other, but viewers come to an understanding that these differences are incidental and superficial rather than integral to enslaved personhood.

As illustrated by the discussion of the Wedgwood icon, the mode of empathy most common in abolitionist artwork and visual texts relies on hierarchy: the idea that the pained body and psyche of the enslaved is a low, unfinished, disabled, childlike, or in some way inferior entity that needs the help and mediation of the white viewer, who is separated within the text or artwork from the viewed. This hierarchical mode of empathy relies on a viewer's pity for the enslaved, who possesses only an unfinished and open selfhood, rather than the finished and closed selfhood of the viewer. I contrast this mode of hierarchal empathy with a more parallel and in some ways more radical form of empathy that relies on similarity between the enslaved person and the viewing subject; the enslaved person is seen as a conspecific, and the connection between the self and the other is emphasized over figuration of division and difference. The viewer and the enslaved are brought into some degree of concordance by this mode of parallel empathy. These modes of empathy can and do overlap within some visual texts. But a parallel mode of empathy, the creators of early illustrated antislavery books seem to believe, may be more effective in moving a viewer beyond receptivity to another's pain (common in hierarchical empathy) toward specific, tailored helping actions (such as stopping a whipping) or larger, prosocial ones (for instance, joining an abolitionist movement or becoming part of the Underground Railroad). At least, that seems to be the theory behind this second, more conformational mode of empathy, in which the viewing reader is asked to see the pained body or psyche of the enslaved as not an other for whom they can feel pity, but a self that could also potentially be whipped, tortured, or emotionally traumatized. This parallel mode of empathy may lead, at times, to introspection (reflection on the self and the self's place in the world) rather than only pity; it may also lead to a sense of the ambiguity of the lifeworld of the enslaved—a consciousness that some aspects of enslaved experience cannot in fact be represented or comprehended, and remain outside a viewer's realm of understanding. (See the appendix for a schematization of these two modes of empathy.)[10]

Criticism has focused on many aspects of the visual culture of abolition, but the archive of antislavery illustrated books that appeared before *Uncle Tom's Cabin* (1852) has been virtually ignored. And yet in many ways, these early books laid the technical foundation for the visual and cultural transatlantic phenomenon that was Stowe's famous novel, analyzed in the last chapter of this book. Like Stowe's text, these illustrated books can be seen as early forms of graphic narrative used for a political purpose. Yet some of these early graphic illustrated books contain features that contest the scopic regime of slavery; the creators of these works sometimes embed within the visual rhetoric a narrative about not only enslaved torture, but also resistance to the social regulation of enslaved bodies and the technologies of power that lead to specific modes of power relations and object relations—specific modes of both subjugation (for the enslaved) and subjectivity (for the modern subject). Using tools from graphic narrative theory and visual rhetoric to analyze these books, I argue that they sometimes suggest ways that the enslaved might representationally wield a power over their own bodies and subjectivities officially denied by the epistemological-juridical formation of slaveholding society and law, and that they sometimes contain elements that encourage a viewing reader to move beyond passive spectatorship toward active resistance to slavery's sociopolitical regime. These early graphic illustrated books circulated transatlantically and went through many printings; it is therefore crucial to understand how they functioned as instruments of propaganda designed to create a particular affective or cognitive impact on a viewing reader.[11]

In this book, I frequently refer to the "reader" or the "viewer." In most cases, we know little about the readership of the texts I discuss; where reviews are available, I have introduced them, but they represent just one aspect of readership. Many of the texts appear to have in mind as their primary audience a reader who would need to be convinced of the equality of the enslaved—a white reader, in other words. Yet we might hypothesize that the texts appealed to a diverse readership of blacks and whites, and men and women. There was an active black reading public in this period; for example, William Lloyd Garrison's antislavery newspaper the

Liberator (1831–65) had a circulation in 1834 of about 3,000, and three-quarters of the subscribers were African Americans (Ripley, introduction, 9). Lara Langer Cohen and Jordan Alexander Stein note that in "antebellum America, African Americans figured prominently in literary production both on the page (as writing subjects as well as subjects of writing) and off (as readers, editors, printers, engravers, compositors, papermakers, librarians, and so on)" (introduction, 3). Moreover, as Robert Fanuzzi has argued, one goal of abolitionist print publications in the 1830s was the "formation of a reading public composed of the enslaved, the free blacks of the North, and the women of the abolition movement" (*Abolition's Public Sphere*, 1). Narratives by former slaves were reviewed in journals with a large black readership such as the *Liberator* and Frederick Douglass's *North Star* (1847–51). Beginning in the early nineteenth century, free blacks in the North realized the need to create their own opportunities to become readers. Elizabeth McHenry has documented how literary societies in particular fostered "the development of a literate [black] population" and in so doing furthered the "evolution of a black public sphere and a politically conscious society" (*Forgotten Readers*, 3). The graphic illustrated books discussed in this study, then, might primarily have been intended for white readers, yet they appear as well to have had in mind a secondary audience composed of a literate black population.

Antislavery illustrated books seem to have been trained on what I call the "man or woman in the middle": a reader (whether U.S. or British, male or female) who might have had antislavery leanings but had not yet made up his or her mind about abolition. The focus of these texts appears to have been to shift such readers toward active abolitionism by changing what theorists of readership have called their "horizon of expectations." The reader-response theorist Hans Robert Jauss argues that works of literature evoke for readers a specific "horizon of expectations and rules familiar from earlier texts, which are then varied, corrected, altered, or even just reproduced" (*Aesthetic of Reception*, 23). This horizon, created by the social milieu, views, and ideology of the audience, can be shifted by the negation of familiar experiences or "by raising newly articulated experiences to the level of consciousness" (25). The works in this study may begin by evoking for a reader the familiar horizon of expectations for antislavery representations of the enslaved, in which the enslaved are an unfinished, low self for whom a reader should feel only pity. Yet at some point this horizon of expectations is shifted, and a new idea is raised to the level of consciousness—the idea that a reader and the enslaved are connected in a relationship of parity, similarity, and concordance, rather than disconnected through inequality, dissimilarity, and difference. There may be, for example, a visual moment in which the abject body of the enslaved is departicularized and comes to resemble the viewer's body. Or the narrative may fleetingly but deliberately create ambiguity about whose body, precisely, is being tortured, represented, or spoken. These instances momentarily break the structure of the specular moment, allowing for a new articulation of experience in which the viewing reader and the viewed object are temporarily intermingled, equalized, or united. The focus of many of these texts is to transport a reader beyond spectatorship into action through revisions of the specular scene lying at the heart of much abolitionist discourse.

The ability to empathize, cognitive studies have shown, is related to mirror neurons in the brain, and is frequently intensely visual; as András Sajó notes, "In the case of processing pain the firsthand experience of pain and the observation of others in pain shows important similarities in the neural circuits involved" (*Constitutional Sentiments*, 3).[12] The symbiotic relationship that illustrated books create between words and drawings is meant to enable not only compassion for the plight of the enslaved, but also, at times, the capacity to mirror the thoughts, emotions, and experience of others. Graphic narrative theory—which attends to how projection of a self into another body or world operates visually and linguistically—is therefore particularly well suited to explain how such a process of identification might function. Visual rhetoric study, on the other hand, provides tools for understanding the specific structures of argumentation embedded in an illustrated work that might create a particular affect or cognitive process. But before examining the graphic and rhetorical techniques used by illustrated antislavery books to portray torture and bodily pain that might create empathy, it is necessary to investigate how power operates on the body in culture in a more general way.

The Microtheater and Fable of the Visual Slave

As seen in the above discussion of the Wedgwood medallion, enslaved persons were often reduced to what Michael Chaney refers to as an "object of commodification" as well as to a (potentially) permanent status as a "subject of subjection" (*Fugitive Vision*, 6). Graphic illustrated books at times perpetuate a vision of the slave as always-already an object of subjection within visual culture, yet in some places we find (in Chaney's words) "the subtle but meaningful trace of a visual field contrary to the one established by the twin hegemonies of abolition and slavery" (9). What might these traces of resistance to slave torture and debasement look like? How might resistance to the discourse of the supplicant slave be performed by a text's visual rhetoric?

In discussing a time before the birth of the modern prison, Michel Foucault writes about the many "theaters of punishment" that might have existed:

> At the crossroads, in the gardens, at the side of roads being repaired or bridges built, in workshops open to all, in the depths of mines that may be visited, will be hundreds of tiny theaters of punishment. Each crime will have its law; each criminal his punishment. It will be a visible punishment, a punishment that tells all, that explains, justifies itself, convicts. . . . But the essential point, in all these real or magnified severities, is that they should all, according to a strict economy, teach a lesson: that each punishment should be a fable. (*Discipline and Punish*, 113)

Foucault argues for the "disappearance of punishment as a spectacle" (8) in the years 1760–1840, a point that most observers of enslavement would certainly dispute. Yet his argument about the "tiny theaters of [visible] punishment" aptly fits the transatlantic regime of enslavement and its visual texts, in which "each punishment should be a fable."[13] If, *pace* Foucault, every picture of punishment tells a story, what function does the visual serve within these books and within the regimes of torture depicted—for masters, those involved in the slave trade, viewers, abolitionists, and the enslaved themselves? The psychic goals of the visual representation of torture may include spectacle, containment of threat, creation of a docile body, voyeurism, sexual or sadomasochistic pleasure, and the creation of pity, sympathy, or empathy. Political goals, too, are embedded in these visual tableaux, including a desire to ameliorate, terminate, or sustain slavery, and the presentation of an enslaved body as either part of a social pact or political entity or as separate from it. Most radically, some of these texts employ illustrations that confuse the body of a reader with that of the enslaved or portray bodies that resist the imposed and intended purpose of the technology of punishment; in so doing, these texts move toward a visual rhetoric in which enslaved bodies are not categorically equated with debasement and punishment.

The exercise of power on a body is a strategy. Such power is manifested as a network of relations constantly in tension; the attempt to create a docile, punished body is therefore a "perpetual battle," and the power to regulate this body is something "exercised rather than possessed" (Foucault, *Discipline and Punish*, 26). The books discussed in this study use scenes of enslaved torture to make manifest the network of relations between masters and slaves, the interconnections between spectators and black (viewed) objects, and the perpetual battle for psychic power inscribed within enslaved bodies. These works sometimes marshal visual texts to suggest how the enslaved might manifest strategies of control over the social relations that govern their status. As Foucault notes, social relations of power are not univocal; they manifest as "innumerable points of confrontation [and] focuses of instability," each with its own possibility for "an at least temporary inversion of the power relations" (27). It is these "temporary inversion[s] of the power relations" that I am concerned with here. I am particularly attentive to how sight, hearing, and touch might be used as foci of instability and confrontation. Martin Jay observes that "vision is normally crossed with the other senses, but it can be artificially separated out" (*Downcast Eyes*, 4). Throughout this book, I suggest that these illustrations refuse to separate eyesight from other senses in their manipulation of visual rhetoric; in so doing, they attempt to make a wide appeal to an affective sensorium of experience.

Simon Gikandi has commented that although slavery is one of the informing conditions of modern identity, it is often "confined to a shadow existence on the margins of the discourse of cultured subjects" (*Slavery and Taste*, 29). The books I consider use forms of visual rhetoric to contest this discursive and figural containment of the slave's body, its relegation to a mere shadow that informs the modern subject. These texts sometimes refuse to quarantine the material body of the slave within the shadows or margins of rhetoric; they represent bodies as physical entities but also as signs of culture that can be used figurally or semiotically to impugn the dominant culture's relegation of these bodies to the realm of the silent, disempowered, abject, unfree noncitizen.

As several critics (including Gikandi) have noted, reading the slave's presence, as well as his or her materiality and agency, is a complex problem. We can salvage only fragments of the past, the invisible and the phantasmal, as Saidiya Hartman discovers in *Lose Your Mother* (2007). Dror Wahrman contends that what we recover from the past are only "unself-conscious *traces*" or "unintended *marks*" (*Making of the Modern Self*, xv; emphasis added). Hortense Spillers comments that most slaves existed outside discourse proper, and notes the slave's fall or "descent into the loss of communicative forces" ("Mama's Baby," 69). Yet visual texts written by the formerly enslaved contain more than an "unintended mark" of the past. The deliberate marks and traces of the past, as I show with Roper, Bibb, and Brown, are deliberate and work toward a certain end—the creation of a visual figuration of enslaved agency designed to generate a specific cognitive and affective response of parallel empathy in a nineteenth-century reader. The texts created by these individuals—all of whom had a great deal of control over the terms of textual production[14]—consciously marshal their visual and discursive performance toward a presentation of tropes of resistance that begin to nullify the erasure of their presence within the dominant culture. Antislavery writers, too, attempted not only to contrive what Toni Morrison calls black surrogacy—a real or fabricated Africanist presence crucial to their own sense of subjectivity and voice (*Playing in the Dark*, 13)—but also to investigate methods through which the enslaved might be shown enacting formations of their own voice and self-control. The graphic illustrated

books of writers such as Thomas Branagan, George Bourne, Amelia Opie, and
Lydia Maria Child are sometimes embedded with reading protocols or structures
of affect and modes of cognition that encourage readers to become empathetic
and intersubjective viewers rather than (merely) passive spectators of the slave's
plight. This study describes textual structures that might enable viewers' antipathy
to the scopic regime of slavery, as well as figurations of the enslaved's will to power
within a particular visual rhetoric.

The phrase "visual rhetoric" is employed here because I am interested in looking at how semiotic systems—the visual, the linguistic, the rhetorical, and the
sensory—intersect within these texts to create structures of affect and cognition
that go beyond a single form of rhetoric to attempt to compel a viewer toward
some specific emotion, thought, or action. Sonja Foss describes visual rhetoric as
"the study of visual imagery within the discipline of rhetoric" ("Theory of Visual
Rhetoric," 141) and goes on to note that objects become part of a visual rhetoric when they have three characteristics: "the image must be symbolic, involve
human intervention, and be presented to an audience for the purpose of com-
municating with that audience" (144). Michael Charlton comments that "while
both visual rhetoric and semiotics are interested in the production, transmission, and interpretation of 'signs' in the visual sphere, visual rhetoric insists that
these 'signs' carry with them some potential for activation—that is, an explicit or
implicit intent to produce an alteration of viewpoint or action on the viewer, even
if this intent is subverted or problematized by other elements" ("Visual Rhetoric,"
115). The term encompasses visual and verbal structures of affect and cognition
within texts that work synchronically to activate a reader's consciousness toward a
specific antislavery goal.

Technological developments in the early nineteenth century abetted the creation of forms of visual rhetoric that fostered an interaction between words and
text, and so drew readers more consciously into their diegetic universe. Georgia
Barnhill sees 1825 as a key dividing line between old and new ways of producing images for pictorial printing; by then, "steel replaced copper as the metal
upon which some engravings were made; stereotyping improved the durability
of woodcuts; and an entirely new printmaking process, lithography, originated
in Europe at the end of the eighteenth century, became commercially useful and
viable" ("Transformations in Pictorial Printing," 426). These changes were particularly dramatic in the United States, where a professional class of artists arose and
created what Barnhill calls "a far more accessible visual culture" (424) that flooded
homes with "images in all formats" (436). Moreover, in the United States in the
1830s, as Phillip Lapsansky points out, "newly introduced steam-powered presses

in major urban centers drove publishing capacity up and costs down" ("Graphic Discord," 202). These decades saw U.S. publishers both copying images from British publications and employing engraved, lithographed, or woodcut prints of their own. Antislavery writers took advantage of these changes, flooding the U.S. market with illustrated pamphlets, books, and broadsides that complemented and competed with antislavery illustrated work from England.

Most specifically for the purposes of this study, it was not until the early 1820s and 1830s that new techniques in wood engraving allowed for the creation of inexpensive texts in which images and words could appear together and be easily reproduced. The English engraver Thomas Bewick was a leading figure in this change; at the end of the eighteenth century, he began using an engraver's tool—a burin—on ends of hardwood to create thin, delicate lines and improve the durability of his compositions. Bewick's techniques were quickly adapted by the talented U.S. wood engraver Alexander Anderson, who was the first U.S. artist to reach a mass audience (Rainey, "Wood Engraving in America," 12; Richter, *Prints*, 114–19). The wood was hard enough "to withstand many thousands of impressions on a press," and these blocks produced relief prints "that could be set directly onto a plate alongside of typeface" (O'Donnell, "Book and Periodical Illustration," 145). For the first time, printers could create thousands of copies of illustrated pages with little loss of quality. This period also saw the invention of the printing stereotype (1811) and the electrotype (1841), which meant that subsequent editions of a text could be created quickly and inexpensively and that type did not have to be reset from scratch (Fink, "Book Publishing," 151). Papermaking became faster and cheaper in the early 1830s, which drove down the cost of printing on the newly invented steam-powered press (Fink, "Book Publishing," 150; Rainey, "Wood Engraving in America," 18). This conjunction of new wood engraving methods and mechanized printing, along with the popularity of illustrated books such as Charles Dickens's *Pickwick Papers* (serialized in 1836), led to a rapid expansion in the number of illustrated books published in the 1830s (Rainey, "Wood Engraving in America," 16; J. Cohen, *Charles Dickens*, 4). By the mid-nineteenth century, wood engravers rivaled their copperplate counterparts in skill and technique, but their works were much cheaper to produce and reproduce. Most importantly, by the 1820s wood engravings could be printed inexpensively along with typographical characters, allowing for "a high-quality image to appear on the same page as the text" (M. Samuels, "Illustrated History Book," 239). These technological and commercial developments in printing facilitated the growth and development of the illustrated book.

There could nonetheless be a profound disconnection between the author of an illustrated book, the artist who drew the engravings or illustrations, and the

engraver who realized them. This study therefore views these books as collabora-
tive to some degree. Indeed, because the texts were illustrated by often unknown
artists, and because illustrations were sometimes taken from other print sources
in an elaborate process of citation, reprinting and adapting them (frequently with
changes), we need to view these graphic illustrated books as exhibiting a form of
what Augusta Rohrbach has called "bricolage" ("Shadow and Substance," 84)—of
assemblage and collaboration. They represent what Lara Langer Cohen and Jordan
Alexander Stein term, in their study of print culture, a collective endeavor in which
authorship is only one part of the story (introduction, 15), even if a large part. My
study insists that because word and image appear on the same page (and often
in cooperation with each other), simultaneous levels of discourse are accessed—
the verbal and the pictorial—to create meaning for a reader or viewer, activating
experiences that are aural, oral, pictorial, and sensory. Some of these books render
an enslaved person as a kind of everyman or everywoman figure whose suffering
represents the debasement of both white and black individuals in the face of a
dehumanizing and degrading regime of torture—the 250-plus-year history of the
slave trade. This is not a straightforward process, however, and it sometimes fails
to create bodies that are anything other than abject. Yet in some graphic illustrated
books, traces of an insubordinate and intersubjective perspective are encoded; in
some books we see the "perpetual battle" for power over enslaved corporeality,
rather than only the finished product (the docile body). Specific modes of resistance to the scopic regime of enslavement performed through a visual rhetorical
matrix therefore are examined in greater detail below.

Visualizing Slavery, Pain, and Enslaved Insubordination

This book analyzes visual and verbal structures used to represent something that
has often been said to be beyond language—the pain of torture. As Elaine Scarry
has noted, pain exceeds and yet vanishes out of language (*The Body in Pain*). The
writers discussed in this book do not seek to represent the feeling of torture
(which may be beyond language); rather, they use graphic illustrated books to
script meanings into the void that is pain. The meanings inserted into this void
vary, entailing debasement, fear, and horror as well as resistance, willfulness, and
at times a certain kind of empowerment in the face of dehumanization. We must
also be sensitive to the fact that by reproducing these dehumanizing illustrations,
we may become, as Frederick Douglass notes about his watching of his aunt's
beating, both "a witness and a participant" (*Narrative of the Life*, 6). By viewing
these image-texts, we may replicate a politics of looking in which the empowered

viewer gazes at the dehumanized and tortured object; for this reason alone, certain critics have avoided reproducing even verbal descriptions of torture, much less the illustrations themselves.[15] Yet our line of vision must be drawn back to the interaction between words and pictures. While the images at times participate in an aesthetic of the status quo, the words may subvert this aesthetic and formulate an alternative form of redress. Or, conversely, the images may contain affective properties or cognitive formations that attempt to short-circuit the binary of empowered and gazing subject over disempowered and tortured object. Some of these illustrations attempt to make the white torturer the object of the gaze, or turn scopic power on the white bystander who does nothing in the face of this spectacle. In short, recognizing the horror of representing torture is not enough; torture must be examined as something that writers, both black and white, sometimes used to renovate dominant social scripts of white identity formation and transcode the subjectivity of the enslaved.

In an analysis of enslaved modes of resistance to abasement, Gikandi asks, "How does one write of the space of enslavement as both a radical form of debasement, the site of undoing identity, and a place where new modes of being, new identities, were constructed, elaborated, and represented in an altered public sphere?" (205–6). I suggest that the visual can be a place where new modes of power (for both the viewed, abject other and the viewing, empowered subject) might be constructed within a public sphere that was altered specifically by the discourse of antislavery itself. Some of these books figure structures of resistance on the part of a reader or the enslaved that refuse to contain the slave's body within an epistemological-juridical formation that Foucault calls "both a productive body and a subjected body" (Discipline and Punish, 26). Textual structures of affective or cognitive resistance entail figuration of a refusal to embrace abjection, an unwillingness to remain enchained (either literally or figuratively), an opposition to remaining silent or docile, and a repudiation, on the part of a viewing subject within the illustration, of complicity with these surveillant regimes of terror. These texts therefore visually and rhetorically model the enslaved's resistance to dehumanization, but also contain structures of affect and cognition that enable a viewer (or a prosthetic viewing presence) to become resistant to the torture being enacted on the bodies of the enslaved.

Much has been written about the reputed power of sentimental texts to move readers toward resistance to enslavement, and about the emotional or political efficacy of the use of sympathy in protesting slavery.[16] It is certainly true that by the 1820s and 1830s, as Elizabeth Clark has shown, with the cresting of the Second Great Awakening (1790–1840), many people identified morality with feeling rather

than with rational thought ("'Sacred Rights of the Weak,'" 477)—a construct that
abolitionists across a broad spectrum of religious and political beliefs were able
to use. Many sentimental texts have, as Jane Tompkins notes, "designs upon their
audience, in the sense of wanting to make people think and act in a particular way" (*Sensational Designs*, xi). Some sentimental texts sought to evoke action
rather than only sympathy, as Elizabeth Dillon notes ("Sentimental Aesthetics,"
515). Dillon calls this a "sentimental aesthetic," and at times I refer to this aesthetic
as well as to its extremely problematic attempt to empower white bodies toward
action through the specific abjection of the black (enslaved) body. It is clear, however, that by the 1820s and 1830s a sentimental aesthetic was not considered to be a
private emotion, limited to the domestic sphere, bur instead to act "in conjunction
with the problem of the body" and, as Shirley Samuels argues, to figure forth "how
social, political, racial and gendered meanings are determined through their different embodiment" (introduction, 5).

I consider the question of sentimentality later in more detail in relationship to
specific texts (such as John Gabriel Stedman's *Narrative* and Lydia Maria Child's
Joanna). In the book as a whole, I look at a different question: what visual structures do graphic illustrated books contain that might impel an interpretation in
which the enslaved are not sequestered from the free viewing subject? Advocates
of sentimentality have discussed the reputed power of sentimental texts to close
gaps between the enslaved and a reader, but many of these sentimental texts commence by assuming that fundamental barriers exist. This book suggests a more
radical mode of imagining (pictorially and textually) the relationship between
subjectivities than that generally thought to be present in sentimentalism. This
mode of imagining blurs the line between self and other, so the body and psyche
of the enslaved cannot be disentangled from those of the viewing self; parity and
similarity are forwarded through emotional investment in a particular scene of
(for example) family separation or enslaved torture, and an insistence that a reader
feel this pain in his or her own body or heart. The objective is to apprehend interconnections between self and other, which can generate identity transformation or
conversion on the part of a viewer, radical emotional alterations, and activist col-
laborative actions. The reading protocols in some of these texts may also focalize a
momentary convergence between two subjects, one that does not erase differences
but shifts a reader toward a mode of intersubjectivity with the enslaved.

The first of the textual structures deployed to move a viewer toward intersubjectivity is the placement of words in relation to a particular illustration. Do images
stand alone? Is there text above them, below them, or surrounding them? Do the
pictures have a frame box around them, and if so, what is the nature of the frame

or margins? Where is the caption, and how much space does it take up? At what points are images discordant with the text (and vice versa), and how does this discrepancy affect interpretation? Most importantly, how do words and images used together interpellate a reader, ask, demand, or entreat that he or she enter the ideology of the text and of the antislavery movement? In regard to early illustrated antislavery books, the placement of the images on the page is virtually ignored in the little extant criticism of these texts, yet examining images and text together generates new modes of assessing the structures of cognition and affect of a text. It is also crucial to pay attention to the way in which focalizing features such as light or margins are used, sight lines are drawn, and verbal components (captions, speech balloons, italics, and so on) interact within these visual texts to drive readers toward certain emotional states, cognitive processes, or actions. In addition, some of these works contain prosthetic observing presences that resist the spectacle of violence; these figures function as an affective formation that strives to impel a reader into the text and represents an impetus for the possibility of a viewer's resistance to slavery as an optical and political regime.

Visual structures within the texts may also blur bodies, and the distinction between a subject and an object, allowing a viewer to move toward identification and intersubjectivity. As the psychologist Mark Davis illustrates, most definitions of empathy include "the transformation of the observed experiences of another person into a response within the self." Empathy thereby becomes the "psychological process that at least temporarily *unites* the social entities of self and other" ("Empathy," 20). Davis considers empathy to have both affective and cognitive elements; that is, empathy can evoke both emotional states and mental (or intellectual) processes. Experiments in social psychology have emphasized that an empathic response of concern, helpful social behavior, perspective taking, and the creation of an interdependent self-construct are enabled by an overlapping of cognitive structures between self and other (36, 37). Many of the works I consider attempt to activate within a reader not only affective responses but also cognitive processes that enable a parallel mode of empathy and intersubjectivity. One consistent structure (beyond their visuality) is a modeling of processes of emotional and cognitive similarity and equality between the enslaved and the free, the viewed and the viewer.[17]

These texts also encourage what Raymond Williams calls active readings. Works of art, Williams contends, must be made present in a reader's mind through "specifically active 'readings'" (*Marxism and Literature*, 129). Structures of feeling embedded within texts make such active readings possible: "We are then defining these elements as a 'structure': as a set, with specific internal relations, at once interlocking and in tension" (132). He notes that such structures of feeling notate a "social experience still in process," one with its own specific hierarchies (132). The visual and linguistic features of some graphic illustrated books demand an active type of reading that sometimes subverts the mechanisms of power scripted onto enslaved bodies. In so doing they attempt to construct a new abolitionist reading of the enslaved, a structure of feeling in which a semantic figure (the enslaved body) comes to have meaning as a subjectified presence rather than an abjectified (subhuman) absence. For Williams, a structure of feeling is specifically a mode of social formation, "explicit and recognizable in specific kinds of art, which is distinguishable from other social and semantic formations by its articulation of presence" (135).

A viewer also may be impelled to understand the need for redress, defined by Saidiya Hartman as a way of "operating [the pained body] in and against the demands of the system, negotiating the disciplinary harness of the body, and counterinvesting in the body as a site of possibility" (*Scenes of Subjection*, 51). It has been noted that abolitionist artwork functions generally by rendering enslaved bodies as sexualized, submissive, and subservient, and that there was an explosion of voyeuristic or erotic images treating enslaved abuse in the 1830s (Lasser, "Voyeuristic Abolitionism," 92).[18] Many of these artworks are discussed in subsequent chapters. This study argues, however, that the visual rhetoric of some graphic illustrated books at times countervails this tendency by investing the bodies depicted with modes of agency, grace, empowerment, and voice. These early illustrated books therefore are critical for understanding the transatlantic movement for the liberation of enslaved people, as well as the way in which cognitive or affective modes of parallel or hierarchical empathy may be enabled by rhetorical practices.

Graphic Narrative and Visual Rhetoric in Early Illustrated Antislavery Books

Barbara Lacey argues that "the pictorial element [of images of African Americans] provides new information, contends with or subverts the verbal meaning, and creates a dialectic with the text" ("Visual Images of Blacks," 137). My study uses concepts from graphic narrative theory involving the manipulation of captioning, speech bubbles, frames (or their lack), page layout, projection, splash pages, and crossover characters to develop a new methodology with which to analyze how pictorial elements of abolitionist visual culture might contend with, support, or undermine textual meaning, as well as how such features might interpellate a reader. I highlight graphic features of the text that might promote certain types of interpretive practices and certain modes of parallel empathy. More specifically, I argue for an active reading and viewing protocol embedded within these texts that moves between words and pictures to create antislavery meaning. Linguistically, this reading protocol may entail directly confronting a viewer ("How would you feel if your wife and children were sold?"); modeling modes of active resistance (for example, stopping a whipping, signing a petition to end the slave trade, or becoming an abolitionist); narrating actions indicating that the enslaved are not an other but a human subject (for example, by figuring the enslaved as husbands, wives, mothers, fathers, Christians, citizens); and portraying enslaved bodies as having types of agency (to escape, to refuse to be defined by the master's system of ideology, to resist in other ways). Visually, this active reading protocol may entail portraying bodies that meet the gaze of a viewer; structuring enslaved bodies in parallel lines of equality (and not as low bodies) with free bodies; representing bodies that are whole, not rent by torture; depicting bodies that have physical or emotional poise and integrity; visually entangling white and black bodies (the enslaved body may look like the free one); and employing modes of visual symbolism (religious, trickster, or magical) that allow the enslaved to appear to transcend the master's imagining of them.

Beyond these active reading and viewing protocols, it is crucial to consider how illustrations make arguments that might move a viewer toward some sort of action. How can we analyze the nature of a viewer's affective or cognitive response to antislavery illustrations—as endorsing enslavement, identifying with the enslaved and agreeing to work for the end of slavery, or indicating some range of behavior between these poles? To answer this intricate question, I start by attending to a number of structures of affect and cognition within these texts that allow them to function as visual rhetoric directed toward a particular end. We can examine, for example, how lightness and darkness and the planes or regions of the illustration attract a viewer's eyes to particular details (or obscure others). What is in the foreground and background of the illustration? How does a horizon or implied horizon create perspective lines that place a viewer above, below, or in line with the image? What is sharply in focus and what is blurry? In what types of spaces are the illustrations set? Because slavery was a highly scopic regime of control over the enslaved body, I attend closely to how a reader's gaze might be positioned in regard to these bodies; I scrutinize what the people in the drawing are looking at, who is looking at them, and what vantage a reader might take on these processes of looking. I examine prosthetic apparatuses of vision and eyesight, such as pictures within pictures, mirrors, and visual or lexical symbolizations of eyes, which might direct a reader's own eyes toward particular features of the visual text. Shifting among these details, I attempt to understand what affective or cognitive state is evoked by a particular illustration, and whether this state agrees with the intent of the written text. Of particular interest are visual formations that subvert distinctions between the viewing (empowered) subject and the viewed (black, abject) body and create transitory textual moments when the viewer's gaze or perspective might become intersubjective or shared.

This study develops Roberts Braden's theory that there is often a visual-verbal symbiosis in rhetoric that produces "a stronger message" than either words or pictures alone ("Visualizing the Verbal," 161). Maureen Goggin comments that "when images and words appear together in one discursive space, they operate synergistically" ("Visual Rhetoric," 88). J. Anthony Blair observes that "many so-called 'visual' arguments are in fact mixtures of visual and verbal communication" and that "verbal content can (and often does) function to disambiguate [visual arguments] or make them sufficiently precise" ("Rhetoric of Visual Arguments," 47). The majority of texts I discuss in this book avoid visual-verbal discontinuity, and their lexical-visual combinations tend to work together to forward and support the text's antislavery agenda. The arguments made on the visual and verbal levels have as their goal the attempt to alter the perspective of reading viewers, to move them toward abolitionist goals, feelings, beliefs, or actions. One avenue for the activation of a reader is the realm of the senses, since the text's apparatus attempts to force readers into an understanding of slavery that is visual, physical, and sensory as well as intellectual.

Blair's concept of visual argument facilitates comprehension of the mechanisms that texts employ to forward an argument and challenge a reader to take specific actions. Blair contends that arguments are generally used to change the audience's attitudes, intentions, or behavior; arguers do this "first by appealing to commitments their audience already has, and, second, by showing (or alleging) that these beliefs, attitudes or behavior also commit that audience to accept the modified or new belief, attitude or conduct being advanced" ("Rhetoric of Visual Arguments," 47). In Blair's formulation, an antislavery argument might begin by stating verbally that all people deserve freedom; it might then use illustrations to imply that the enslaved are human beings; this conjunction could then promote the unstated or stated conclusion that all enslaved people should be set free. Individuals who argued for slavery's end knew what many advertisers today comprehend: effective arguments operate on several modalities at once, and these modalities can include the visual, the verbal, the sensory, the emotional, the political, the intellectual, and the psychological realms. Blair states that visual arguments "are typically *enthymemes*—arguments with gaps left to be filled in by the participation of the audience" (52). It is here that graphic narrative theory crosses with visual rhetorical studies: both consider features of visual texts that might attempt to impel a reader to complete a story in a particular way. I am not arguing that we always know what a reader felt or saw when reading an illustrated book, nor whether a reader's behavior or thinking changed when the book ended. But delineating the structures of affect and cognition within the visual rhetoric forwards comprehension of places where readers might project themselves into these arguments, and how verbal and visual rhetorical features of text might promote various antislavery responses, actions, or changes in belief structure.

Graphic Illustrated Books and the Visual Culture of Abolition: An Overview

Antislavery illustrated books had their origins in earlier visual forms that circulated between England and the United States. I therefore begin this study with a chapter that examines visual works published from 1793 to 1812 that are not illustrated antislavery books but created a technical foundation on which later writers built. Chapter 1 begins with a visual text that is ambiguous in its antislavery stance, John Gabriel Stedman's wildly popular illustrated travelogue *Narrative of a Five Years' Expedition, against the Revolted Negroes of Surinam* (1796). The chapter then discusses works that are clearer in their abolitionist politics yet still partially leave intact the scopic regime of enslavement: *Remarks on the Methods of Procuring Slaves* (1793), a British broadside containing twelve illustrations; Alexander Anderson's revision of this broadside under the title *Injured Humanity: Being a Representation of What the Unhappy Children of Africa Endure from Those Who Call Themselves Christians* (ca. 1805–7); the anonymous pamphlet *Mirror of Misery* (1807, 1811, 1814); and the Irish American writer Thomas Branagan's epic antislavery poem *The Penitential Tyrant* (1805, 1807). I end the chapter with a brief discussion of William Elmes's "Adventures of Johnny Newcome" (1812), a colored satirical six-panel cartoon set in the West Indies and featuring (in one panel) drawings of the torture of enslaved individuals. These works contain visual and verbal features that later writers incorporated and transformed, and I argue that in them we can see a movement toward the genre of the antislavery illustrated narrative, a graphic story that uses the synergistic operation of words and pictures to attempt to create a mode of empathy.

In chapter 2, I consider two graphic illustrated books from the 1820s and 1830s that have received little scholarly attention: the British abolitionist Amelia Opie's *The Black Man's Lament; Or, How to Make Sugar* (1826), a children's book with color illustrations, and the radical U.S. Presbyterian minister George Bourne's profusely illustrated *Picture of Slavery in the United States of America* (1834), published both in

the United States and England. Both texts labor to break from the mode of hierarchical empathy present in most abolitionist antislavery illustration and embed
structures of affect and cognition that implicate a reader intersubjectively in the
illustrative content of the texts. Opie's book, I argue, like Stowe's *Uncle Tom's Cabin*
(published twenty-five years later) uses the figure of the child to propel the adult
reader into accepting an antislavery ideology; the audience for the book is both
the child and the adult who might read it to the child. Bourne's text, intended for
adults, primarily uses its captions as liminal spaces where new modes of identification between a reader and an enslaved individual, the viewer and the viewed, can
be essayed. Both works contain resistant metavisual presences—figures within the
illustration that stare back defiantly at the viewer in a mode of envisioning that
seeks to contest the scopic order of the master's regime of enslavement.

Chapter 3 concerns an extraordinary but little analyzed example of transatlantic visual culture that symbolically transforms enslaved bodies by investing them
with voice, authority, and an alternative configuration of being. Moses Roper (c.
1815–1891) was a U.S.-born fugitive slave whose *A Narrative of the Adventures and
Escape of Moses Roper, from American Slavery*, printed in London in 1837 and in the
United States in the following year, was extremely popular in both countries. The
1838 British edition was probably the first illustrated slave narrative with original
graphic materials ever published by U.S.-born slave; I therefore devote an entire
chapter to this work. Roper's visual and verbal rhetoric productively indicts slavery
because its violence is both written onto the enslaved body and rescripted through
religious metaphor (which ultimately turns the physical experiences of torture into
metaphysical or spiritual events). Further, the narrative astutely entangles the body
of the tortured enslaved individual with that of a white viewing reader in order to
further what cognitive scientists have called simulation—the production of mental or physical states that match the mental or physical states of others (Gallese
and Sinigaglia, "What Is So Special," 512).

Chapter 4 investigates the methods that two authors from the 1830s and 1840s
used to repurpose illustrations from earlier texts and to revise the visual rhetoric in
circulation about enslaved masculinity and femininity. I begin with the abolitionist
publication by Lydia Maria Child of a book based on Stedman's famous *Narrative*:
the 1838 publication (forty-two years after the original text) of excerpts from it
titled *Narrative of Joanna: An Emancipated Slave, of Surinam* (1838).[19] While critics
such as Jenny Sharpe have noted the movement of Joanna—Stedman's mixed-race
mistress—from text to text (see Sharpe, *Ghosts of Slavery*), I examine changes in
the visual rhetoric that surrounds her and ask what purpose this crossover character served within abolitionist visual culture of the late 1830s, particularly in regard

to the abolitionists' frequent need to configure women as pathetic, abject, or sexual victims of slavery. I compare this text's verbal and visual rhetoric with that in Henry Bibb's *Narrative of the Life and Adventures of Henry Bibb, an American Slave, Written by Himself* (1849). Bibb's illustrations likewise attempt to reassess paradigms of enslaved African American masculinity and femininity. More importantly, the text transgresses the affective and cognitive content of earlier abolitionist illustrations through subversive replacement and displacement. Bibb's text also contains original illustrations by Thomas Strong depicting acts of resistance on the part of the enslaved. The text therefore attempts to undermine the ideology of slavery and slave torture visually and rhetorically and to contest the functioning of abolitionist graphic narrative systems that presented this ideology; at times, Bibb implies that the experience of enslavement is in fact beyond representation.

The final chapter attends to modes of visual rhetoric surrounding enslaved bodies from 1849 to 1859 by scrutinizing two pivotal artists from the period. It assesses the treatment of visual and verbal rhetoric in the first published print edition of Stowe's phenomenally popular novel *Uncle Tom's Cabin* (1852), which contained six illustrations, as well as the visual materials surrounding the infamous escape from slavery of Henry Box Brown, who mailed himself from the South to the North, and from slavery to freedom, in a large postal crate. His narrative about this event was published by an amanuensis in 1849 in the United States and republished in 1851 in England. Beginning in 1850, Brown toured the United States and Britain with an illustrated panorama consisting of canvases sewn together and displayed on a huge vertical spool called *Henry Box Brown's Mirror of Slavery*. An examination of materials associated with Brown's narratives and his performance modes (which ultimately also included playwriting, acting, mesmerism, and magic) demonstrates that competing strategies of visual representations of slavery, enslaved bodies, and enslaved agency existed in both the United Kingdom and the United States in these years. Stowe's text visually triangulates empathy between a viewer, a white on-screen presence, and the enslaved; it also instills a message of enslaved passivity, stasis, and suffering, or removes the enslaved from U.S. territory. The visual materials surrounding Henry Box Brown, on the other hand (which continued to be generated into the late 1870s), attempt to implant a sense of an enslaved individual's movement, agency, and ability to resurrect, and even magically transform and transmute, himself.[20] While Brown never entirely evaded the legacy of his enslavement, his narratives and his work in magic and mesmerism carved new roads and routes into and out of the visual realm of slavery, suggesting ways it could become a permeable and open performative space.

The epilogue considers some recent artworks that revive images of enslaved people present in earlier graphic illustrated books, such as Glenn Ligon's artistic homage to Henry Box Brown, titled *To Disembark* (1994), and Kara Walker's panoramic art piece *The End of Uncle Tom and the Grand Allegorical Tableau of Eva in Heaven* (1995). In conjunction with a brief discussion of Quentin Tarantino's *Django Unchained* (2012) and Steve McQueen's *12 Years a Slave* (2013), I ask why slavery continues to spawn a visual culture all its own, and I argue for a movement toward a type of empathy that is more ironic and self-reflexive than that found in earlier visual works.

Slavery was a fundamentally scopic regime of terror that relied on the gaze to enact much of its sovereignty, as critics such as Maurice Wallace have explicated (see his *Constructing the Black Masculine*). Readers of graphic illustrated books about slavery might, then, reside in a brutal universe where only one person—a surveillant, authorized viewer—has the power to speak, act, and gaze. Yet in the hands of some people subjected to this scopic regime, and of some who were free dissenters, visual rhetoric delineated structures for parallel empathy and a cognitive and affective response of resistance on the part of the enslaved, a reader, or a viewer. When visual rhetoric obscures the lines between the enslaved object and the viewing subject, power may seem to flow differently, across and between bodies and subjectivities, as it flows across and between words and pictures that cannot be disentangled from each other.[21] This book investigates how visual and verbal technologies used in the rhetoric of enslavement were sometimes deployed to produce a novel diegetic universe. In the virtual and perhaps imaginary universe depicted in some graphic illustrated books, enslaved individuals had the power to speak, look, and act, and readers had the power to participate in the making of this phantasmal world, which perhaps would ultimately transcend the pages of the text.

1

Precursors

Picturing the Story of Slavery in Broadsides, Pamphlets, and
Early Illustrated Graphic Works about Slavery, 1793–1812

In 1793, *Remarks on the Methods of Procuring Slaves, with a Short Account of Their Treatment in the West Indies*, an anonymous illustrated broadside, appeared in London. It presents a vividly realistic account of the tortures of slavery, which included branding with irons, shackles, flogging, log yokes, the cruel separation of families, and mouthpieces and collars used to prevent suicide by dirt eating. Other visual texts about slavery were already in circulation, such as the infamous *Description of a Slave Ship* (1789), which was reprinted in various forms more than ten thousand times between March and April 1789 in the United States, Britain, and other locations (see figure 1.1).[1] Unlike *Description of a Slave Ship*, whose only explanatory text is below the image, *Remarks* (discussed later in this chapter) contains twelve woodcuts, running down the left and right sides in evenly spaced columns; each illustration includes a caption echoing the words of the narrative text. *Remarks* therefore moves toward the idea of a graphic narrative that uses words and pictures to create an argument against slavery and achieves meaning specifically through this fructifying interrelationship. Many of these images (perhaps created by James Poupard)[2] became famous in the abolition movement and were pirated, excerpted, and republished in different formats for more than thirty-five years on both sides of the Atlantic.[3]

To lay the historical and technical groundwork for the development of the graphic illustrated book about slavery that occurred from 1820 to 1852, this chapter examines the circulation and flow of the images and text in *Remarks* within three other abolitionist publications: Alexander Anderson's broadside *Injured Humanity: Being a Representation of What the Unhappy Children of Africa Endure*

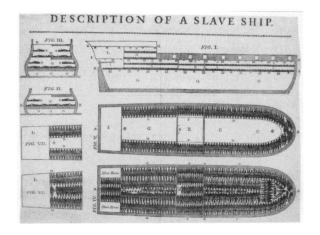

FIGURE I.I
Description of a Slave Ship
(London: James Philips,
1789). Copper engraving.
Courtesy of the Harvard
University Library
(Houghton).

from Those Who Call Themselves Christians (ca. 1805–7), the anonymous pamphlet *Mirror of Misery* (1807, 1811, 1814), and Thomas Branagan's epic antislavery poem *The Penitential Tyrant* (1805, 1807).

This chapter begins, however, by contrasting these explicitly abolitionist documents with John Gabriel Stedman's widely popular *Narrative of a Five Years' Expedition against the Revolted Negroes of Surinam* (1796). Stedman's travelogue was published in 1796 in a volume that contained eighty "elegant engravings from drawings made by the author," some of which were etched by William Blake. Many were later excerpted, printed, and reprinted in many other formats. Although not an antislavery book per se, this text is perhaps the first illustrated book that dealt with enslaved torture systematically, so it is worth close examination. Nicholas Mirzoeff argues that "the ordering of slavery was a combination of violent enforcement and visual surveillance that sustained the new colonial order of things" (*The Right to Look*, 49–50). The first published edition of Stedman's *Narrative* waffles, weaves, and equivocates, but ultimately uses its visual rhetoric (its words and pictures) to enact a mode of visual surveillance that sequesters enslaved individuals within the status of the subhuman. Although Blake's powerful engravings have a visual agenda patently sympathetic to the enslaved, Stedman's narrative and his use of captioning and other linguistic modes domesticate the illustrations in the text as a whole, ultimately telling a story in which the torture of slavery is ameliorated not through emancipation of the enslaved but through reform of the masters. The other, more explicitly abolitionist texts discussed in this chapter, Branagan's in particular, strive to create a counterpolitics of visuality; they attempt to shift a reader's horizon of expectations away from the idea of a perpetually debased, enslaved other situated outside the domain of full human subjectivity toward an understanding of the intersubjective connection between oppressor and oppressed, and the concomitant need for liberation of the enslaved.

Because these works were frequently reprinted in the United States and Europe, they created a technical base on which later graphic illustrated books about slavery would build. The texts discussed in this chapter illuminate how rapidly images flowed between genres and geographic locations within early abolitionist discourse, around and across the Atlantic Ocean. Sentimental rhetoric is an aspect of the circulation of these texts. Some critics have argued that sentimentalism depends on an experimental extension of complete humanity to classes of figures from whom it has been withheld, such as the enslaved (Fisher, *Hard Facts*, 99, 92). This chapter analyzes how these texts struggle to move beyond sentimentalism through affective or cognitive textual and visual modes that incite readerly identification and intersubjectivity. More specifically, some of these works contain metavisual components that notate and implicate the process of seeing and being seen. In so doing, they attempt not to extend selfhood to the oppressed, across the pages of the book, but instead to erode the line separating the viewer from the viewed. These early texts do not entirely dissolve the boundary between a reader and an enslaved individual, but they do attempt to drive a viewer toward intersubjective introspection and parallel empathy[4]—toward a sense that the viewer and the viewed cannot be easily disentangled from each other.

Historical Overview: Slavery and Abolition, 1793–1812

The last decade of the eighteenth century can be characterized as the first era in which abolitionists made significant gains globally, especially in England and its colonies. The time period 1793–1812 is therefore crucial for the illustrated works under discussion in this chapter, for they entered into fraught terrain where worldwide opinion was gradually shifting from the ameliorant position (slavery could be retained if it was made more humane) to the abolitionist one (it should be ended, either immediately or gradually). This period culminated in two crucial victories for abolitionists in the United States and Britain: in 1807, Parliament passed the Abolition of the Slave Trade Act, abolishing slave trading in the British Empire; and in the United States in 1808, the Act Prohibiting Importation of Slaves took effect, outlawing the slave trade between Africa and the United States (importation nonetheless went on for many years from other places and also from Africa illegally). The 1807 British law was a significant decision that enabled many later laws to be passed, leading to the end, in 1834, of enslavement in British colonies.[5]

The historical backdrop of this period is also composed of the ironic formation of the United States (in 1776) as a new political entity in which "all men are created equal," although legal practices such as slavery and genocide against indigenous peoples patently violated this rhetoric. Yet the main focus of abolitionism did not shift to the United States until the 1820s, when the battle in England and other parts of Europe could be considered, for the most part, safely won, and when the slave-holding states seemed to be gaining the majority in the United States.[6]

In the last decade of the eighteenth century and the first decade of the nineteenth, international efforts to end slavery in Europe and parts of North America were largely successful. In 1792, Denmark-Norway declared the transatlantic slave trade illegal after 1803; in 1793, Upper Canada abolished the importation of slaves; in 1794, France abolished slavery in all its possessions;[7] and serfdom was abolished in Prussia in 1807. In Mexico, comprehensive steps to end slavery were passed in 1810; Spain abolished slavery at home and in all of its colonies except Cuba, Puerto Rico, and Santo Domingo in 1811; and in Chile, the 1811 "Freedom of Wombs" act was passed, which set free the children of slaves born on Chilean territory, regardless of whether their parents were slaves. By 1811, the worldwide tide appeared to turn against enslavement, although the United States certainly lagged behind this effort, and the number of slave-holding states increased until 1845.[8]

Many modes of visual culture participated in these shifts, and important works of art enshrined and forwarded an abolitionist agenda. An 1808 decorative plate by Henry Moses commemorating the abolition of the slave trade shows a personified Britannia trampling the chains of slavery as Justice looks on. Alexander Rippingille's painting *To the Friends of Negro Emancipation* celebrates the abolition of slavery in the British Empire in 1834. Some of those involved in abolition in Britain, such as Thomas Clarkson, used visual materials such as maps, broadsides, and illustrations in their struggles to forward an abolitionist agenda.[9] Illustrated texts reflected and in some instances advanced these political struggles over whether (and how) to combat slavery, confirming or undermining the highly scopic order of slavery itself.

Apotropaic Images and Pornotroping in Stedman's
Narrative of a Five Years' Expedition to Surinam

Stedman's illustrated book *Narrative of a Five Years' Expedition* was widely admired, translated into many languages, and extensively excerpted and reprinted. Even today it remains a source of fascination for scholars and artists, as Dustin Kennedy has shown ("Going Viral," 1).[10] It is therefore crucial to consider it as a text that forms a backdrop and counterpoint to abolitionist graphic illustrated books in a later period; as discussed in chapter 4, as late as 1838 the abolitionist Lydia Maria Child used it as the basis for *Narrative of Joanna: An Emancipated Slave, of Surinam.*

Stedman was a British-Dutch soldier who served in the Dutch-controlled colony of Surinam from 1772 to 1777 as part of a force attempting to quell rebel Maroon communities.[11] Plantations there were reputed to have some of the most inhumane conditions anywhere in the world, and slavery was not abolished in the colony until 1873. Moreover, for more than a hundred years before the publication of Stedman's book it had been portrayed as a "literary space for the presentation of extremes of violence and interracial sexuality focused on plantation slavery" (Wood, *Slavery, Empathy, and Pornography*, 96). The 1796 edition of Stedman's narrative is based on journals he kept while in Surinam. He gave edited copies of the journals to his publisher, who hired someone else to reedit them; upon publication, Stedman claimed his work had been spoiled.[12] The 1796 publication is the one that circulated (with minor corrections), and the one that the popular imagination knew as Stedman's text for almost two hundred years. To acknowledge the "collectively produced" (Kennedy, "Going Viral," 3) voice that narrates the work, I employ the term "Stedman's narrator" or "persona" when referring to the 1796 edition.[13]

Mirzoeff argues that modern ways of seeing emerged out of slavery: "The ordering of slavery was a combination of violent enforcement and visualized surveillance that sustained a new colonial order of things" (*The Right to Look*, 49–50). This "plantation complex" (1660–1860) granted the right to look to the overseer and his representatives while literally or symbolically blinding the enslaved; slavery functioned in part through the "removal of the right to look" (7) and by insisting that the tortured object is always-already the object of the gaze. As a discursive practice, visuality first "classifies [groups] by naming" them, then "separates the groups so classified as a means of social organization," and finally "makes this separated classification seem right and hence aesthetic" (3). The 1796 Stedman narrative classifies, separates, and aestheticizes the enslaved bodies it portrays. The text also employs apotropaic images meant to rivet a reader (rather than compel action), along with sensualized and violent pornotroping (in which female bodies become sources of visual fascination yet are also irreducibly marked as powerless others) that might be pleasurable to some reading viewers.[14]

In short, the visual rhetoric of this narrative often denies anything beyond abject, low subjectivity to the bodies it portrays. In so doing, it may impede empathetic identification with the enslaved. Numerous studies of empathy have argued that it tends to increase when individuals perceive another person in terms of similarity (perceived overlap between subject and object) and familiarity (subjects have previous experience with the object) (Preston and de Waal, "Empathy," 3). Stephanie Preston and Frans de Waal argue that "the more interrelated the subject and object, the more the subject will attend to the event, the more their similar representations will be activated, and the more likely a response" (5). The visual rhetoric of Stedman's text usually defamiliarizes the body of the enslaved, portraying it as one that has no interrelationship to a viewer's own body. In so doing, the text short-circuits the empathetic response that a viewer might have for the enslaved, as well as any reaction to the pictures other than horror, paralysis, and stupefaction.

The engravings for this text—based on sketches Stedman drew—are piercingly beautiful yet also raw and macabre, as in the illustration captioned "A Negro hung alive by the Ribs to a Gallows" (see figure 1.2; color image 3). William Blake was the engraver of this illustration, and his black-and-white composition allows the subject's facial expression to be viewed and delineates the sculpted muscles of the tortured man's body with careful grace. The blood dripping in lacy lines down from the hook, through the bones of the ribs, and onto the bones on the ground creates a strong vertical axis through the center of the picture that draws a viewer's eyes upward and downward, in parallel with the vertical line of the gallows (the longest line in the picture). The grace of the balanced and delicate body is counterpoised by the horror of the image as a whole. Yet the violently tortured, enslaved body appears to lack any kind of agency—the victim looks away from the viewer with hollow eyes and appears to be only a symbolization of torture and pain.

As discussed earlier, visual rhetoric may function through enthymemes, unstated arguments. What are the possible unstated arguments a viewer might find in this image? Mark Canuel notes that in this illustration, "Blake will not give his readers a clear answer to the obvious question that arises here: who is the unrepresented agent of the death? His point is not to provide the answer but to ask the reader to interrogate the possible suspects that widen out into larger and larger circles of responsibility: the slavers sailing away in their ships, the plantation owners, the reader herself" (*Shadow of Death*, 154). Raphael Hoermann similarly argues that Blake heightens Stedman's gothic horrors by adding items not listed in Stedman's text, such as skulls and a broken femur ("'A Very Hell of Horrors,'" 22). For Alan Rice, these bone fragments evoke the remains of a "cannibal meal that relates to white abuse rather than black savagery" (*Radical Narratives*, 139). Blake's antislavery views were strongly influenced by Stedman's descriptions of the brutality of slavery, and his illustration attempts to instill horror at the fate of the enslaved, and sympathy for their plight.[15] But does the engraving, when read within its intended

A Negro hung alive by the Ribs to a Gallows.

FIGURE 1.2 William Blake, "A Negro hung alive by the Ribs to a Gallows," illustration for John Gabriel Stedman, *Narrative of a Five Years' Expedition* (1796). Copperplate engraving.

context (Stedman's narrative), indeed attempt to move a viewer toward a mode of parallel empathetic identification?[16]

When the picture is closely scrutinized, it becomes evident that its affective characteristics, when placed within the narrative context, erode the humanity of the man being tortured and maintain a cognitive estrangement between the viewing reader and the spectacle of the viewed subject. The tortured man, for example, lacks a name in the caption; he is simply a "Negro hung alive"—although it is clear from the skulls in the foreground and background what the final outcome of this particular form of state-sanctioned torture will be. Moreover, viewers' eyes may slide away from the gaunt gaze (which does not confront us) and become fastened on the hook itself, the instrument of torture. A structure of affect or readerly empathy might entail any of the following: giving the man a name; showing (within the illustration) a viewer's horror in the face of such trauma; or presenting an unruly person who in one way or another resists this torture. But all such features are absent. No textual characteristics would motivate a reader to become emotionally or cognitively implicated in the picture. We may gaze in horror, rather than *sharing* this experience.

The surrounding narrative text likewise scrupulously separates the viewer from the viewed. It thereby corroborates the horizon of expectations of a reader who would tend to see this abject body as alienated from his or her own subjectivity and corporeality. First of all, the body of the enslaved is apparently so dissimilar from a viewer's body that it cannot feel pain:

> I saw a black man suspended alive from a gallows by the ribs, between which, with a knife, was first made an incision, and then clinched an iron hook with a chain: in this manner he kept alive three days, hanging with his head and feet downwards, and catching with his tongue the drops of water (it being in the rainy season) that were flowing down his bloated breast. Notwithstanding all this, he never complained, and even upbraided a negro for crying while he was flogged below the gallows. (Stedman, *Narrative of a Five Years' Expedition*, 64)[17]

Not only is this man's body impervious to suffering, but he even upbraids other blacks for crying out against their agony. Perhaps this is a show of some sort of heroism that Stedman's narrator admires, but it turns the body into something almost superhuman. In so doing, the text further removes this body from the viewer's own body, which can and would suffer pain if tortured in this way.

The litany of gruesome and brutal torture methods that this passage scrupulously and almost lovingly delineates (64–65) creates little structure of affect for intersubjectivity with the enslaved body. Instead, I suggest that the narrator's response of petrifaction is meant to stand in for that of a reader's: "I was petrified at the inhuman detail; and breaking away with execrations from this diabolical scene of laceration, made the best of my way home to my own lodgings" (64). W. J. T. Mitchell refers to images that have an "apotropaic" or "Medusa" effect, in which "the figures [in an image] seem paralyzed by the awful spectacle" of what they see (*Picture Theory*, 78). Stedman's narrator often draws attention to how the spectacle of torture freezes him into inaction. Studies in the field of empathy using neuroimaging data suggest that fearful facial expressions may "act as unconditioned aversive stimuli to encourage conspecifics to avoid the object/action that elicited the response" (Blair and Perschardt, "Empathy," 27), and such an avoidance effect is clearly at work here, as the persona turns away. Perhaps a reader, too, after staring in horror, turns away from this fearful spectacle. A mode of paralysis rather than prosocial action is foregrounded.

Stedman's narrative invokes Medusa specifically in a long delineation of the execution and death of Neptune, an enslaved man,[18] yet again the focus is on the narrator's stupefaction (see figure 1.3). The torture is described vividly and in detail, yet Stedman's persona focuses on his own response: "I imagined him dead, and felt happy" (383). Moreover, the torture is again presented as visually apotropaic; when the narrator encounters Neptune's skull several hours later, propped up on a stick, he thinks the head is "nodding to me backwards and forwards," and he is "rivetted to the ground" (384). When he investigates this "wonderful phænomenon," he discovers that a vulture has just flown away and struck the skull with his talons, causing it to seem to nod. He then digresses into a long compensatory passage that features an explication of the differences between vultures and eagles, and the species of eagles that inhabit Surinam (384–85).[19] Indeed, the narrative often draws a reader away from the torture depicted in the illustrations, by lapsing into a multitude of explicit details about Surinam's fauna and flora. The narrator's description of torture metaphorically blinds Neptune (his eyes have been picked out by the vulture), and the illustrations in Stedman's text as a whole generally show tortured persons looking away from a viewer. The narrator here perhaps models an affective response, but one that entails noninterference and readerly identification only with a subject already imagined as dead.

The visual rhetoric of the illustration of Neptune by Blake (see figure 1.3) also at times appears to curtail identificatory structures and hinder rather than advance an empathetic reaction. For example, the caption once again neglects to state the name of the individual, presenting instead in pretty, cursive handwriting an objective and matter-of-fact label: "The Execution of Breaking on the Rack." The predominant sight line is the black man doing the torturing, with his upraised implement and

The Execution of Breaking on the Rack.

FIGURE 1.3 William Blake, "The Execution of Breaking on the Rack,"
illustration for John Gabriel Stedman, *Narrative of a Five Years' Expedition* (1796).
Copperplate engraving.

plucking. A reader's sight line might be drawn to the women's breasts (with their protruding nipples), which are presented mid picture and so attract attention, since the upper frame of each engraving contains few visual features other than the bodies of the women. The bodies are large and sexually alluring, encouraging scopic surveillance and visual as well as aesthetic pleasure. Based on Stedman's sketches, these images disturbingly and casually lay out the nude or seminude female body for inspection, torture, or national symbolism. The plate captioned "Europe Supported by Africa and America" (fig. 1.4D) intimates that both nonwhite and white female bodies are subject to degrees of surveillance and pornotroping.

Most disconcerting, perhaps, is the illustration labeled "Flagellation of a Female Samboe Slave" (fig. 1.4C), in which the tortured female form is the recipient of explicit scopic voyeurism (at least three male figures stare at her nearly nude posterior). Simon Gikandi observes that the torture of enslaved women leads to "the conclusion that the female subject has been selected as the conduit through which violence could be sensualized or even eroticized" (*Slavery and Taste*, 185), and this is apparent in this figure. As the woman hangs delicately from a tree branch like some strange fruit, with her toes just barely touching the ground, she appears to be almost dancing (see figure 1.5). Clearly, something animates her body—but is it pain or something else? Her mouth is open in an oval, but we do not know what sound she is emitting. The trunk and branch of the tree creep delicately along the left side and top of the image, as if embracing the woman and providing a decorative bricolage half border that softens the hard outline of the rectangular frame, turning the image into an art object that depicts suffering but offers no subjectivity for the viewed, an aesthetic set piece. The woman is foregrounded, and her immense nude form stands in opposition to the diminutive African male slaves in the background, who are also naked but hold whips and stare at her naked body. A reader provides a vantage point that closes the panopticonic structure of surveillance. As Marcus Wood asserts, "Staring front on at an almost naked and physically magnificent young woman, who is pushed right up against the viewer, it is hard not to become compromised" (*Blind Memory*, 236). A reader cannot help gazing directly onto this enlarged and naked spectacle of a tortured, enslaved female.[22]

The narrator's reaction to this spectacle of feminine torture is more active than his response to male torture. He describes her thus: "A beautiful Samboe girl of about eighteen, tied up by both arms to a tree, as naked as she came into the world, and lacerated in such a shocking manner by the whips of two negro-drivers, that she was from her neck to her ankles literally dyed with blood. It was after she had received two hundred lashes that I perceived her, with her head hanging

FIGURE I.5
William Blake, "Flagellation of a
Female Samboe Slave," illustration for
John Gabriel Stedman, *Narrative of a
Five Years' Expedition* (1796).
Copperplate engraving.

downwards, a most affecting spectacle" (177). If Stedman's narrator sees this girl
only after she was lacerated from head to toe by two hundred lashes, it might
be hard for him to know that she is a "beautiful Samboe girl"; violent beatings
habitually interfere with being comely. But he sees her as beautiful in her pain
and—all covered in blood and gore—as a most "affecting spectacle." He describes
this woman as being as "naked as she came into the world," whereas Blake's illustration puts a few rags on her bloody body and shields her genitalia from a full
frontal view; yet the illustration also specifically inserts the black men who point
at her into the image. So both text and image (in varying ways) make her a voyeuristic spectacle of enslaved sexuality and erotic torture. Stedman's persona is so
moved by the spectacle of the bondage of this lacerated beauty that he tries to
intervene and have the girl cut down, only to learn that the overseer doubles the
punishment inflicted on slaves when a stranger tries to interfere with them; so the
poor "Samboe girl" receives an additional two hundred lashes. Stedman's narrator
thus has no alternative, he claims, but "to run to my boat, and leave the detestable
monster, like a beast of prey, to enjoy his bloody feast, till he was glutted" (178).
Resistance to torture is futile, it seems.

Of course, the narrator does have other alternatives: he could attack the overseer, lodge a protest of some sort with his captain, or simply cut the woman down

despite the overseer's directives. Instead, as a compensatory gesture, he resolves to have nothing more to do with overseers and then abruptly segues into detailed discussion of the term "Samboe": "A Samboe is between a mulatto and a black, being of a deep copper-coloured complexion, with dark hair, the curls in large ringlets. These slaves, both male and female, are generally handsome" (178). The narrator easily slides away from the violence of this scene into classification, separation, and aestheticization of this woman; in so doing, he moves her out of the sphere of empathy and interrelationship and into the realm of otherness. Moreover, tortured women, unlike the men, have no speech; as Mario Klarer notes, "[Stedman] never endows the female victims with a voice. They all seemingly bear their pain with complete passivity" ("Humanitarian Pornography," 564). This further obstructs intersubjectivity because, as Alex Gillespie has noted, speech itself is intersubjective and dependent on the possibility of a self that communicates with another to integrate different perspectives within the social field ("Intersubjective Nature of Symbols," 30). To move a person out of the sphere of language is therefore to hinder the possibility of a process of empathetic interrelationship.

Yet not all women in this text lack voice or the possibility of empathetic identification. Most famously, Stedman became involved with a Surinamese enslaved woman named Joanna, and it is here that the narrator is dragged violently between, on the one hand, scopic surveillance, classification, and aestheticization of this beautiful mulatto body, and on the other a desire to create affective or cognitive visual and lexical structures that might shift a reader into empathetic interrelationship with her.[23] When Stedman's narrator first meets Joanna, he is captivated by her beauty and grace, but also by what he views as her incipient sexuality (she is fifteen at the time):

> Rather taller than the middle size, she was possessed of the most elegant shape that nature can exhibit, moving her well-formed limbs with more than common gracefulness. . . . Round her neck, her arms, and her ankles, she wore gold chains, rings, and medals: while a shawl of India muslin, the end of which was elegantly thrown over her polished shoulders, gracefully covered part of her lovely bosom: a petticoat of rich chintz alone completed her apparel. . . . The figure and appearance of this charming creature could not but attract my particular attention, as they did indeed that of all who beheld her. (52–53)

Joanna is a "charming creature"—a beautiful *object*. She is gazed upon, sexualized, and pornotroped, not only in her beauty and her only partially covered breasts, but also by the "gold chains, rings, and medals" that she wears—for indeed, "chains" and "rings" have a double meaning, being both jewelry and instruments of torture, sexual bondage, and enslavement.

Jenny Sharpe reads Stedman's Joanna as a "nurturing native" who depicts "the unique position concubines occupied within slavery" (*Ghosts of Slavery*, 51), which could be a movement into an incipient form of empathy, since it entails interdependency. Yet the pictorial portrait of Joanna (see figure 1.6) is not modeled as diverging from those of other enslaved women, who are represented as being outside the realm of familiarity, similarity, and intersubjectivity. Indeed, Joanna's portrait is arranged within the text between images of tortured enslaved women to whom she bears both physical and symbolic resemblance as part of a continuum of enslaved, bound, and beaten beauty. Like the "Female Samboe" (see figure 1.5), Joanna is a huge body, taking up more than three-quarters of the height of the frame, and the illustration by Francesco Bartolozzi creates a direct sight line to Joanna's perky, upturned breast by placing it almost exactly in the center of the frame, as a sort of bull's-eye, suggesting that her ineluctable sexual power renders inoperable any other mode through which a reading viewer might comprehend her. The chains around Joanna's ankles visually echo the bonds around the enslaved woman "with a weight chained to her ankle" (see figure 1.4A), and her half-clothed form foreshadows the half-clothed and bloody form of the "Female Samboe" being flagellated (see figure 1.5). Indeed, although engraved by separate illustrators (Blake and Bartolozzi) the African women in these plates look remarkably similar to one another, perhaps because they were based on Stedman's own sketches of female bodies, including Stedman's sketches of his mistress, Joanna. These female bodies seem exchangeable and interchangeable, but also profoundly marked by their blackness, irresistible sexuality, and (most importantly) otherness.

As Sharpe also observes, Bartolozzi's engraving of Joanna collapses time, for she is fifteen here, but in the lower-right corner a small image of her stands with the four-year-old son she had with Stedman (*Ghosts of Slavery*, 54), and in the lower-left corner there is a small picture of the house they lived happily in for several years. Despite these accoutrements of cozy domesticity, the visual and linguistic rhetoric of the text as a whole objectifies her as a not quite fully human subject. As Wood argues in *Slavery, Empathy, and Pornography*, "Joanna exists on the sexual and race borderline between black and white, wanton and demure, civilized and barbarian" (129); she also stands in a liminal space between the poor, tortured "Samboe girl" described above and empowered white European women such as Mrs. Godefroy, who eventually purchases Joanna. Perhaps this is why Joanna's illustration is the only one that has two captions—the one in the table of contents, which is objective and distant ("A mulatto woman"), and the one that names her on the illustration ("Joanna") and attempts to reinstate her humanity. Yet within the text, Stedman's narrator constantly reduces her to a possession—calling her "*his* inestimable Joanna" (155)—and naming her price of 2,000 florins (200 pounds

FIGURE 1.6 Francesco Bartolozzi, "Joanna," illustration for
John Gabriel Stedman, *Narrative of a Five Years' Expedition* (1796).
Copperplate engraving.

sterling) (260). Stedman's ownership of Joanna is only symbolic, however; his persona purchases and frees one of his male slaves—Quacco—but the fine object that is Joanna has a price that is too high for him to afford (353).

As Stedman's persona tells the story, Mrs. Godefroy buys Joanna to be her servant, meaning to set her free. But Joanna refuses to accept this freedom, wanting instead to pay her debt to Mrs. Godefroy, and in so doing evidently accepting her status as an object to be bought and sold. She therefore remains in Surinam with her son (named Johnny) when Stedman leaves. Mary Louise Pratt reads this "transracial romance" as one in which Joanna refuses to assimilate into European culture (*Imperial Eyes*, 96). But the text narrates only how Stedman's narrator *represents* her refusal (326). In Holland, Stedman marries a white woman and starts a family with her (Kennedy, "Going Viral," 12). Back in Surinam, Joanna languishes for five more years and then dies in 1782; at the time Stedman leaves her, she is nineteen, making her only twenty-four upon her death.[24]

Stedman's 1796 text attempts at times to portray Joanna as not like the poor tortured Samboe girl, but the text's verbal and visual rhetoric keeps her within the stereotype of the tragic mulatto—always-already sexualized, always-already a thing, and always-already doomed. Joanna's tortures are more emotional than physical, but she too suffers, especially when Stedman's narrator leaves: "Joanna . . . was unable to utter one word!!! . . . She bowed her head, and motionless sunk in the arms of her adopted mother" (427). This sentimental rhetoric is the text's last first-hand portrayal of Joanna—and soon this symbolic death is followed by an actual one (439). Stedman's gaze defines Joanna, and as Mirzoeff reminds us, visuality is a "discursive practice that has material effects" (*The Right to Look*, 3). In this case, the material effect of the text's visual and verbal rendering of Joanna means that there is no narration of her—indeed, no existence for her—once Stedman leaves her behind in Surinam. The process of empathy is impaired here, since she is never endowed with features such as self-possession, speech, or a form of resistance to enslavement, which might move her beyond the realm of the object of pathos.

The narrative as a whole vividly and dramatically represents the torture of enslaved men and women, and perhaps this is why the text appealed to some abolitionists. Yet enslaved persons are often portrayed as being outside the sphere of full human subjectivity. They are beaten and raped with impunity (370) and "loaded with irons, and chained to everlasting torment" (57); they are "scarcely animated automatons" (111) who are "almost degenerated into . . . brute[s]" (179); they are driven to commit suicide by eating dirt (368) or leaping into cauldrons of fire (373). Stedman's narrative presence refuses to model processes of sameness and identification that might lead to empathy. He refuses to say that slavery as a system is wrong or that other men (and women) just like him are kept enslaved. Instead, he suggests that slavery needs "impartial regulations" pertaining to work hours, punishment, and food; if such regulations are enforced, the "master will look with pleasure on his sable subject as his children," and "the negroes will bless the day their ancestors did first set foot on [South] *American* ground" (419). In this quotation, the "master" is kept separate from the low, abject, and childlike Negroes who need and even "bless" his regulation. As Helen Thomas observes, Stedman declared that he was opposed to men like Thomas Clarkson (*Romanticism and Slave Narratives*, 128), and his text "oscillates tenuously between his concern for the negro slaves . . . and the ideological forces determining his presence in Surinam as a Scots Brigade lieutenant sent to quell the insurrection [of slaves]" (127). His text remains more committed to the propagation of forms of scopic and actual enslavement than to dismantling the ideologies that subtend these formations.

In the end, Stedman's illustrated text, finished in 1791 and published in 1796, uses its sight lines, visual ordering, and narrative proper to encourage the contemplation of shocking spectacles and the closing off of this horror from a viewer's own subjectivity; it does not attempt to move a viewer toward tailored helping actions (such as stopping a whipping) or prosocial behavior (such as becoming an abolitionist). One reviewer specifically notes that the text "will not only afford much amusement, but suggest to the contemplative mind matter for important *reflections*" (*Analytical Review*, review, 225, emphasis added); the focus is on amusement and reflection, not action. A number of other reviews focused on Stedman's portrayal of animals specific to Surinam, such as the vampire bat, which appears to have afforded U.S. readers an unironic spectacle of fascination.[25] If empathy is "the psychological process that at least temporarily *unites* the separate social entities of self and other" (M. Davis, "Empathy," 20), Stedman's narrative rarely presents this merger with any degree of either cognitive or affective intensity; textual structures rigorously segregate the enslaved (who are always classified, gazed at, and othered) from the white narrator. The text's cataloguing, description, mapping, and illustrating therefore mainly serve the purpose of suggesting ways that slavery might be made better, while its basic order of violent visual surveillance and othering of enslaved bodies remains intact.

Counterorders: From *Remarks on the Methods of Procuring Slaves* (1793) to *The Mirror of Misery* (1807)

As previously noted, *Remarks on the Methods of Procuring Slaves* appeared in 1793 (see figure 1.7).[26] To some extent, the images on this broadside are crude and seem to present primitive and abject bodies. Yet the visual rhetoric subtly attempts to shift a reader's horizon of expectations by complicating the separation between a viewer and the "low" enslaved other present in a text such as Stedman's. For example, in the narrative accompanying figure 5, we are told, "In none of the sales is any care taken to prevent the separation of relatives and friends, but Husbands and Wives, Parents and Children, fig 5, are parted with as much unconcern as Sheep and Lambs by the Butcher." Such a statement syntactically undermines the containment of the enslaved within the discourse of otherness, for it first calls them "relatives and friends, husbands and wives, [and] parents and children" before denoting how the white "Butcher" creates his own subjectivity through the debasement of these persons, viewing them as only so many "sheep and lambs"; it cites, in short, the process whereby a human being (a conspecific) is turned into a thing, a possession, something outside the pale of full humanity, but posits that the humanity of the individual precedes this process of debasement.

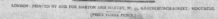

FIGURE 1.7 *Remarks on the Methods of Procuring Slaves.*
Broadside with twelve woodcuts, London, 1793.
Courtesy of the Harvard Library (Houghton).

The illustration referred to by this passage ("fig 5") is designed to make clear that humans are subjected to this treatment: it shows a man and woman being whipped as they weep and embrace while a young child clings to its mother's side (see figure 1.8). This illustration was reused in several other abolitionist publications as the first in a sequence of images, so it seems to have been judged to be effective in telling the graphic story of slavery. The captions on the broadside, more emotional than the text proper, are designed to elicit readerly empathy. For example, the caption to figure 5 reads, "The Husband and Wife, after being sold to different purchasers, violently separated—probably never to see each other more!"; the exclamation point functions as an affective lexical structure designed to propel readers into moral indignation. It also contravenes the "Butcher's" treatment of these bodies as "sheep and lambs," for they are shown to be human and capable of feeling emotional and physical pain. The bodies in the foreground of the frame—the mother, father, and child—huddle together and block out (in part) the body of the white master, with his upraised whip. The scopic focus here is on raw human torment, in the site of an unframed illustration meant to reach out of the page to a reader. A viewer cannot see, for instance, the breasts of the woman (as in Stedman's illustrations), but can clearly discern the outlines of the small child, who clings sorrowfully to the mother's side, and the despair evident in the embracing figures of the husband and wife being violently separated. Like Stedman's illustrations, these images tend to present enslaved bodies as disempowered, as "poor victims" (figure 12 on the broadside). But they also try to abrogate the surveillant order of slavery by arguing, through visual rhetoric, that humans—not as *homo sacer* or bestial objects—are caught in slavery's vicious and ruinous yoke and turned into objects by its merciless processes.

The Husband and Wife, after being sold to different purchasers, violently separated—probably never to see each other more!

FIGURE 1.8 Figure 5 from *Remarks on the Methods of Procuring Slaves* (1793). Courtesy of the Harvard Library (Houghton).

The broadside attempts to open spaces where intersubjective sensory experiences might be located. Some floggings, for example, are said to tear the skin so deep that "*you* may lay your finger in the wounds, and are such as no time can erase" (paragraph twelve, emphasis added). In using the phrase "you may lay your finger in the wounds," the broadside attempts to compel a reader to engage in sensory participation and in what theorists of empathy have called "embodied simulation"—the reuse of mental states and processes involving representations that have a bodily format (Gallese and Sinigaglia, "What Is So Special?," 515).[27] The text of the broadside uses the body of the viewer—and again, the image of the viewer's own hand—to exhort viewing readers to end any involvement in the slave trade: "Let now every honest man *lay his hand on his* breast, and ferociously reflect whether he is justified in countenancing such barbarities; or whether he ought not to reject with horror, the smallest participation in such infernal transactions" (paragraph 26, emphasis added). The hand that has laid its finger in the wound that "no time can erase"—that metaphorically has been bloodied with the enslaved's blood—is now laid on the breast of the man who becomes an abolitionist, in a strange sort of metaphorical blood pact to end slavery. The hand of a reader, which might be holding the broadside itself, may come to function as a cognitive and affective template for intersubjectivity and prosocial action.

In addition, the work attempts to script intersubjectivity and empathy through active reading protocols, both in the above quotations and in the document as a whole. As theorists of graphic narrative might be quick to notice, the broadside does not present a distinct "reading route" (Groensteen, *System of Comics*, 59) through the page. A reader's eyes are expected to move in several directions: down the text (from top to bottom and left to right) as it is being read, and back and forth across the text when following the images (from fig. 1 on the left to fig. 2 on the right, back to fig. 3 on the left and then to fig. 4 on the right, and so on). Moreover, when readers first confront the page, they may have no idea where to start. Figures 1 and 2 are higher horizontally on the page than the text proper, and compete with the document's title for our attention, so we may be tempted to start there, but when we sweep our eyes back to the left to continue reading, we encounter a block of text that interferes with this even sweep and blocks our access to figure 3. Unlike Stedman's text, which encourages readers to gaze on the aestheticized images, a reader of the broadside must create his or her own reading route and engage in what Raymond Williams would call a specifically active reading practice (*Marxism and Literature*, 129) that perhaps makes a reader not only a consumer of the text but also its intellectual producer or cocreator.[28] Such an active mode of reading might more thoroughly integrate a reader into the text and into an intersubjective perspective of the bodies represented; a reader is not allowed to be a passive voyeur of the suffering of the enslaved.

Whether or not the 1793 broadside created empathy for the enslaved, it must have been seen as an effective abolitionist document in raising awareness about enslaved torture, because it was reproduced quickly in a number of formats, locations, and languages. Just one year later, it crossed the ocean to the United States, where it was translated into German and reprinted by the apothecary Tobias Hirte under the title *Sclaven-Handel* (Slave trade). About a decade later—sometime between 1805 and 1808[29]—a substantially altered version of the document was created by the U.S. wood engraver Alexander Anderson under the title *Injured Humanity: Being a Representation of What the Unhappy Children of Africa Endure from Those Who Call Themselves Christians* (see figure 1.9). From the very title—*Injured Humanity*—Anderson insists that the enslaved are part of human-kind and also that their suffering is the fulcrum upon which some Christians erect their subjectivity. The title cries out in capital letters to CHRISTIANS to understand and end this unholy suffering; in so doing it seeks to directly inter-pellate a viewer who is religious yet still condones slavery. The title eliminates the reference to the West Indies; by this deletion, Anderson's broadside creates a visual text that could be used by abolitionists anywhere to protest the grave inhumanity of slavery. And yet it also engages in a hierarchical mode of empathy when it calls the enslaved the "unhappy children of Africa"—the enslaved are lesser persons who need the help of the adult reader, a formulation that Harriet Beecher Stowe will reuse in *Uncle Tom's Cabin*, in which enslaved blacks fre-quently are configured as a childlike race.

As with the 1793 broadside, readers must be active producers of the text, and move back and forth between words and pictures to create meaning. Yet Anderson's broadside guides the reading viewer a bit more than the earlier broadside. Anderson's text sorts the images from the 1793 broadside, condenses them from twelve to seven, and encloses the narrative in a text box that separates it from the images and creates a more controlled space of narrative exegesis within the center of the document. Perhaps most interestingly, the broadside as a whole is bounded by a decorative border composed of flowers, stems, and leaves. This border is more than aesthetic; if looked at carefully, the leaves and flowers appear to spell out the word "no" over and over again in a verbal caption that may provide a kind of lexical scream in response to the horror of the action being depicted (see figure 1.10). As Will Eisner notes, frames can "make an effort to generate the reader's own reaction to the action and thus create emotional involvement" (*Comics and Sequential Art*, 59), and Anderson was fond of putting ornate and highly metaphorical frames around his images.[30]

FIGURE 1.9 Alexander Anderson, *Injured Humanity*,
ca. 1805–8. Wood engraving and letterpress broadside.
Courtesy of the American Antiquarian Society.

FIGURE 1.10 Detail, Alexander Anderson, *Injured Humanity*. The flowers and stems appear to spell out the word "no" over and over again. Courtesy of the American Antiquarian Society.

Visual rhetoric often contains "arguments with gaps left to be filled in by the participation of the audience" (J. A. Blair, *Rhetoric of Visual Arguments*, 52), and the border here promotes a specific form of participation for the audience: horror and resistance to slavery, but also a loud, repeated, and resounding verbal no to the existence of the system as a whole.

The broadside as a whole contains more cognitive and affective constructions that facilitate empathy between the enslaved and the viewer than either Stedman's text or the 1793 broadside. For example, it opens (top left) with an image more moving than the first one in the 1793 *Remarks*—the image of the husband and wife embracing as they are sold to separate owners (figure 5 in the 1793 *Remarks*); this image has been slightly remodeled and now becomes the first figure. Opening with this illustration creates symmetry, because the broadside begins and ends with images that would be readily legible to a U.S. or British audience: depictions of black men and women being beaten by white masters. The officious figure numbers of the 1793 broadside have been removed from the text, and the words of the captions are wrapped carefully around the images, so the words begin to flow into the pictures and interweave with the narrative. Unlike Stedman's text, which often justifies the torture of slavery by referring to "complicated crimes" (383) committed by slaves and which mainly eschews showing white men beating them,[31] *Injured Humanity*, in its first two images, shows well-dressed white men beating or branding slaves; it therefore places the blame for torture squarely on the white master or overseer and creates a visual structure in which scopic focus is directed at white men who are part of the spectacle of enslaved torment.[32]

By starting with the image of the husband and wife parting and the crying child, Anderson's broadside strives to create an affective process that shifts a viewer toward empathy with the enslaved. Yet the cobbled-together nature of the broadside (with sections interpolated from other works) ensures that cognitive gaps between the enslaved and the viewer remain. For example, language such as "A front and profile view of an African's head, with mouth-piece and necklace" (right column, panel 2) separates the viewed African from the viewing subject, and an overly clinical tone at times impedes an understanding that humans are being tortured. Yet this document attempts to show the ways that human beings are transformed into objects that can be bought, sold, and tortured, and to show that their human subjectivity precedes this technological process.

The images from the 1793 broadside were also reused in the anonymous 1807 pamphlet *The Mirror of Misery; or, Tyranny Exposed*, also printed and sold by Samuel Wood, and reissued with these same images in 1811 and 1814. Well aware of its status as a visual and rhetorical text, the 1807 edition of *The Mirror of Misery* contains on its title page an imprint of the famous Wedgwood seal and motto. *The Mirror of Misery* reuses all the images in Anderson's document, along with excerpts from *An Abstract of the Evidence Delivered Before a Select Committee of the House of Commons* (1791). At times, however, it also creates full pages to focalize these images—what graphic narrative theorists refer to as "splash pages"—with no captions or text to interfere with the shock of the visual (see figure 1.11). By leaving some images standing alone and surrounding others with text, *Mirror of Misery* remakes the original broadside. Yet does an illustration such as the one shown in figure 1.11 create empathy within a reader? Its very nakedness on the page seems to encourage horror rather than an intersubjective understanding that this self is also a reader and that a reader is (or could become) this self. This image seems to seal off the pain of the enslaved within the implements of torture themselves (the mask, the spurs, the headpiece), never indicating that the bodily pain inflicted could be a reader's own.

More crucial for an understanding of the illustrated antislavery book's elaboration of a practice of empathy, however, is how the narrative proper of *The Mirror of Misery* places illustrations on the same page with text, and how the narrative

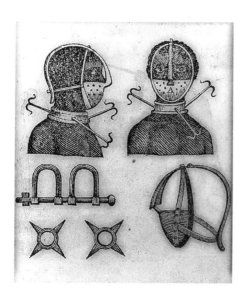

FIGURE 1.11
Mirror of Misery (1807), 19. Pamphlet
with wood engravings. America's
Historical Imprints, Readex.

enfolds these images. In so doing, it attempts to create a story about the enslaved that would draw in a reader as he or she turns the pages of the pamphlet (see figure 1.12). Here a nearly full-page image is sandwiched between two passages of text. It should be noted that the authors of this pamphlet reorder and resequence both text and images from the 1793 broadside to create new meaning. This work may be the inception of an illustrated antislavery graphic narrative that symbiotically interweaves words and pictures. The text below the image carries over onto the next page, where a reader finds more text and the next image (see figure 1.13). Thus, *The Mirror of Misery* crudely attempts to create a type of graphic narrative. Furthermore, while Anderson's initial image (see figure 1.12) is still the start of the visual text, from there the pamphlet uses the images in an order entirely different from that of either the 1793 or the 1805–8 broadside to try to tell a visual-rhetorical story of slavery. It has been recently theorized that stories increase empathy because they enable readers to construct complex representations of others' states of mind (Kidd and Castano, "Reading Literary Fiction," 377). Moving these images into a narrative format, then, may be an attempt to make them matter to a reader in a new way.

DESCRIPTIVE PLATES.

The husband and wife, after being sold to different purchasers, violently separated; probably never to see each other more.

The manner of yoking the slaves by the Mandingo-s, or African slave merchants, who usually march annually in eight or ten

16

parties, from the river Gambia to Bambarra; each party having from one hundred to one hundred and fifty slaves.

The Log-Yokes are made of the roots of trees, so heavy as to make it extremely difficult for the persons who wear them to walk, much more to escape or run away.

Where the roads lie through woods, the captives are made to travel several hundred miles with logs hung from their necks, as described in the plate.

FIGURE 1.12 *Mirror of Misery* (1807), 15.
America's Historical Imprints, Readex.

FIGURE 1.13 *Mirror of Misery* (1807), 16.
America's Historical Imprints, Readex.

Furthermore, at times *The Mirror of Misery* attempts to transport a (white) reader into some form of intersubjectivity with the enslaved body. For example, the pamphlet ends with a woodcut that chains the Wedgwood antislavery icon to an image of a white man, a debtor (see figure 1.14). "Am I not a Man and a Brother?" is replaced by the motto "Liberty Suspended but Will Be Restored." The authors of *The Mirror of Misery* here repurpose the emblem of the masthead of a newspaper published in 1800 by William Keteltas from a debtor's prison in New York: the *Forlorn Hope* (see Mann, *Republic of Debtors*, 110–11). In reusing Keteltas's image, the authors of this pamphlet attempt to blur the distinction between a free, visualizing, white subject and an enslaved, visualized, black object of the gaze. The philosopher Edmund Husserl posited a theory of intersubjectivity in which for a person to be able to put himself or herself into someone else's shoes (or in this case, chains) and simulate his or her experience (in this case, enslavement), the person must assume that the world-experience of the other person in some way coincides with his or her own world-experience (*Cartesian Meditations*, 127–28). The image in figure 1.14 seeks to foster a similarity of world-experience by implying that the chains of the enslaved could be those of the white man; in so doing, it promotes or stages an embodied simulation meant to position the white viewer in the shoes of the enslaved. Yet intersubjectivity may be impeded by the fact that the black enslaved man is on his knees, and he faces away from the enslaved debtor, who looks down on him. The image affectively structures a reader's (downward) glance as he or she watches the (white) debtor watching the enslaved man. This image therefore aims to create intersubjectivity, but ultimately may enforce a hierarchical relationship of white corporeal and visual power.

Perhaps a more efficacious structure for intersubjectivity in the work is the title, *The Mirror of Misery*, which asks readers to propel themselves into the world-experience of the narrative. Mirrors, of course, reflect the misery that slavery inflicts on the enslaved, but if the pamphlet is in some sense a mirror (a prosthetic object that functions as a synecdoche for vision and viewing) that a reader holds in his or her hands, then a reader might be encouraged to see himself or herself in these illustrations. As readers read the pamphlet, they are encouraged toward a form of intersubjectivity in which the self and other are conjoined through what Husserl would call "repeated presentations" (*Cartesian Meditations*, 125–27). The mirror of the text does not annihilate the actual distinction between free viewer and enslaved other, since the viewer is still in a position of power. But it attempts to create repeated representations of parity so that viewers might see themselves in the mirrored image of the other's world-experience.

In short, the anonymous authors of *The Mirror of Misery* use a mode of graphic narrative to shift a reader away from being merely an observer of the story into

48

" Slow o'er the smooth ocean she glides,
     As the mist that hangs light on the wave,
And fondly her lover she chides,
     That lingers so long from his grave :
" Oh, Maratan ! haste thee," she cries,
     " Here the reign of oppression is o'er,
The tyrant is robb'd of his prize,
     And Adela sorrows no more."

" Now sinking amidst the dim ray,
     Her form seems to fade to my view ;
Oh ! stay thee—my Adela, stay—
     She beckons, and I must pursue.
To-morrow the White man in vain,
     Shall proudly account me his slave ;
My shackles I'll plunge in the main,
     And rush to the realms of the brave."

LIBERTY SUSPENDED BUT WILL BE RESTORED.

FIGURE I.14 *Mirror of* Misery (1807), 48.
America's Historical Imprints, Readex.

a type of embodied participation. Thomas Branagan's *The Penitential Tyrant; or, Slave Trader Reformed: A Pathetic Poem, in Four Cantos* (1807) also strives to foster intersubjectivity between the viewer and the viewed. But Branagan begins by crafting a more expansive verbal story through which graphic images can be activated as visual rhetoric, in an attempt to transport a reader into a process of empathetic identification.

"Cast Your Bodily Eyes upon the Instruments of Torture": The Structure of
In-Visioning in Branagan's *The Penitential Tyrant* (1807)

Branagan's 1807 edition of *The Penitential Tyrant* moves close to being a graphic
narrative about slavery in that its images are consciously incorporated in such a
way as to produce echoes between them and the narrative text. Branagan (1774–
1843), an Irish-born author, was involved in the slave trade, and at the age of sixteen he became an overseer on a plantation in Antigua. Overcome by the horror
of the slave trade, he converted to Protestantism and settled in Philadelphia (in
roughly 1798 or 1799), where he "struggled for over 30 years to convince Americans
to abandon slavery" (Tomek, "'From Motives of Generosity,'" 121).[33] He recounts
these experiences in *The Penitential Tyrant*, a multigenre work containing a short
biography of an enslaved man (Joseph), an autobiographical essay, political essays
on slavery by others, a long autobiographical narrative poem by Branagan telling of his transformation, and the illustrations present in *The Mirror of Misery*.[34]
In other works, Branagan lists numerous barriers to empathy between blacks
and whites (see his *Serious Remonstrances*, 43, 103), yet in the 1807 version of *The
Penitential Tyrant*, he attempts to put a reader into the shoes of the enslaved and
to make a reader feel with all of his or her senses, and with both mind and body,
what the enslaved experience.

Branagan's text begins with a new illustration—one created specifically for the
1807 version of his work—that visually models his transition: we see him reaching
out to a figure that embodies liberty and turning away from the ship in the background, which seems to be a slave ship (see figure 1.15).[35] The two enslaved individuals in the background watch the central male figure as he reaches out to Liberty—
perhaps implying that they too have a gaze that can look, as well as be looked at
by others. Phillip Lapsansky argues that this image puts whites into the pose of
the supplicant slave and is meant to represent "abolitionists pleading the slave's
cause" ("Graphic Discord," 206).[36] It should be noted, however, that the figures of
the enslaved are small and in the background, and the pictorial focus is placed on
the white man's activity to enact abolition. Yet the text as a whole, which begins
and ends with images, strives to create a rhetorical and visual structure whereby a
reader's horizon of expectations is transformed not only into antislavery action but
also into a mode of parallel empathy with the enslaved.

For both the enslaved and the slave trader, Branagan implies again and again,
slavery is a gory business, but also one in which the tortured bodies are linked to
that of the torturer, as the opening to canto 2 makes clear:

FIGURE 1.15 David Edwin, frontispiece to Thomas Branagan, *Penitential Tyrant* (1807). Copper engraving. America's Historical Imprints, Readex.

I saw the thousands, thousands, thousands slain,
On their primeval, their parental plain;
Their lacerated limbs, with chains opprest,
Their minds, alas! with mighty woes distrest!
Each body mangled, scourged in every part,
While sighs and groans burst from each swelling heart!
I saw in tides of tears their sorrows flow,
And still new anguish added to their woe;
Shade after shade before my eyes arose,
All wailing with unutterable woes!
. . . .
I saw the phantoms, which too well I know
And while I look'd, [my] tears began to flow.
(71–72)

Jonathan Crary has argued that in the early nineteenth century, there was a falling away from visual technologies, such as the camera obscura, that implied a fixed relation between "internal sensation and external signs," and there was a concomitant blurring of the boundaries between the exterior world and internal perceptions (*Techniques of the Observer*, 24). The complicated set of visual images in Branagan's poem muddles such boundaries. He interweaves the physical landscape with the torment of those being enslaved, and moves toward signifying a cognitive overlap between self and other when he connects his internal torment about the part he played in the slave trade with externalized signs of suffering that he sees in slavery. The slave overseer, the enslaved, and the slave owner are interlinked in a circle of horror. This passage evokes a bodily sensorium—of sound (sighs and groans), feeling (tears), and sight ("I saw" is repeated over and over). Here Branagan is in the sensorium, modeling his embodied response to the picture of enslavement ("And while I look'd, [my] tears began to flow"). Foreshadowing how Stowe's *Uncle Tom's Cabin* (1852) will encourage readers to shed tears over the plight of the enslaved, Branagan uses embodied simulation to delineate an appropriate reader reaction to the horrific scenes.

This narrative strategy is problematic in many ways. Branagan did not in fact suffer these horrors, and tears do not always compel a reader to action, as James Baldwin argues in "Everybody's Protest Novel" in regard to *Uncle Tom's Cabin*. Yet the text endeavors to transform readers' positioning in relation to these scenes of torture, specifically through the example of Branagan himself, who saw these scenes of torture, empathized with the enslaved, and moved into antislavery activity. Whereas Stedman's narrative persona was always just outside the scenes he describes, Branagan the eyewitness, the horrified and petrified observer, attempts to place a reader into the sensorium of enslaved torture, as he was placed. In so doing, he tries to smudge the lines between the slaveholder and the enslaved, and between the viewing subject and the object of the gaze. That his message was understood to some degree is evidenced by reviews of *The Penitential Tyrant*; one notes that "the [wood] Cuts will serve to show the horrid barbarity of Man to Man," but that the treatise as a whole, written by a "person formerly concerned in this nefarious business of enslaving his fellow men," will also "show the salutary effects of conscience when submitted to the mind of man" (*Mercantile Advertiser*, "Just Published"). Like Branagan's conscience, which impelled him into antislavery action, the conscience of the reading viewer is supposed to induce movement into abolitionist action after the book has been viewed and read and after man's "horrid barbarity" to other men has been comprehended.

Branagan takes on the responsibility not only of "feeling rightly" (317), as Stowe put it forty-five years later, but also of using his book and its illustrations to end slavery.[37] He thereby models an active mode of intersubjectivity and parallel empathy. After one particularly intense vision of suffering and gore (72), he hears enslaved people calling out to him: "You promis'd in that penitential hour, / Our wrongs t'exhibit, and our tyrants' power" (73). Invoking the idea of the enslaved demanding an "exhibition" of wrongs, Branagan struggles to revise the scopic regime of slavery, which visually supports (*pace* Stedman) a colonial order; here, visuality is meant to undermine the tyrants' power, and the enslaved are given a voice of political protest. Moreover, it is the enslaved people's "wrongs" (not their bodies) that are "exhibited." Branagan also may attempt to create a counterorder of visuality by asking a reader to imagine slavery differently:

> I would also request the reader . . . not only to keep his mind's eye upon the intellectual picture I have delineated, but also to *cast his bodily eyes upon the instruments of torture . . . In order that he may be capable of drawing a right conclusion, I would particularly recommend him to draw a picture himself* (some leisure moment), not of the multitude of sad groups of wretched Africans . . . [but] of a single slave from the millions now in slavery: let him read, in his emaciated and woe-worn face, a brief and striking history of his misfortunes, of his antecedent subjugation and subsequent degradation. (230–31, emphasis added)

In asking a reader to cast his or her bodily eyes on the "instruments of torture" but then to move beyond them to the human individual, he endeavors to transfer a reader's focus away from torture and onto the tortured yet fully human person. The specific affective structure here is a reader's body—his or her eyes, which act as a mirror to the enslaved individual's suffering. Branagan also asks a reader to "draw a picture," not of a disembodied mass, but of a "single slave." He puts a reader into the role of creating affective images, and he yokes external, sensory experiences to internal perception so that a reader will feel the harm done to a particularized individual. In drawing attention to the artifice of enslaved visuality by asking a reader to "draw a picture" of an enslaved person, he also creates a brief metavisual moment in which a reader may contemplate not only the horror of slavery, but in addition his or her representational power both within its scopic reign and also (possibly) outside it.

Branagan's main rhetorical argument seems to be that slavery is a harm done to other human beings; thus, it must also be ended by humans. To make this argument, he creates other textual characteristics that enable affective and cognitive overlap between a reader and the enslaved. For example, he gestures toward a time when slaveholders and "friends of slavery" will "feel our brother's grief, our brother's woe; / Feel sympathetic love for all our race, / And circle mankind in one kind embrace" (130). In using the term "brother," he implies that the enslaved are part of the human race and therefore deserve "sympathetic love," love that not only extends humanity to the enslaved but also begins to undermine barriers between the other and the self. Such a world of "sympathetic love" for all "mankind" is not portrayed in Branagan's text. Yet by using present tense he attempts to bring it into being—to enact it narratively. He asks readers to feel the history of slavery not only intellectually but also bodily by placing readers' corporeal forms within the sensorium of slavery and enslaved torment.

In *The Penitential Tyrant*, as in *The Mirror of Misery*, the images from *Remarks on the Methods of Procuring Slaves* are reframed and reorganized. On pages 255–56, Branagan presents all the verbal prose from *Remarks*. On pages 266–74, he redeploys each of the images from the broadside, page by page, picture by picture, allowing them to be read as a somewhat coherent graphic narrative text. Most of the pages have captions and illustrations, although full-text and splash pages (pages with a single image) are also used. Like *The Mirror of Misery*, *The Penitential Tyrant* groups the images so that they form a coherent narrative, beginning with the separation of families (presumably in Africa) and proceeding through several forms of torture. Branagan's text, however, unlike either of the broadsides, ends with an image of branding on the breast (274), perhaps indicating arrival in the United States, where the captives are "purchased by the planters" (see figure 1.16).

What do we make of Branagan's closing his text with this image? Unframed images such as this one reach out of the page to a reader, encouraging a reader to project himself or herself into the diegetic space. And some of the enslaved figures appear to be looking directly at a reader; the man on the far left (in particular) appears to be staring out of the picture at something or someone—the reading viewer, perhaps? Moreover, in this enlarged version of the image, fully half the frame is taken up by the white master doing the branding, so the white slave owner may also become the subject of scopic surveillance. Indeed, because he is the tallest figure in the illustration, a viewer's eyes might first be drawn to the slave owner and then to the enslaved figures. Branagan's text puts the focus squarely on the one doing the torturing, even as it encourages a reader to see himself or herself in the person looking back at the viewer, positing a mode of potential resistance to slavery's torturous regime.

Marcus Wood comments that Branagan's "most significant contribution to the abolition movement was his ability to show the uses to which wood engravings could be put" and that "what he wrote is not, perhaps, as important as the manner in which he published it" (*Poetry of Slavery*, 425). And it is true that in other works Branagan endorsed colonization and articulated viewpoints against intermarriage

FIGURE 1.16 Thomas Branagan,
Penitential Tyrant (1807), 274.
America's Historical Imprints,
Readex.

(*Serious Remonstrances,* 43, 103). Yet what Wood and other critics have elided is the manner in which *The Penitential Tyrant* fashions a protocol for how readers should decipher graphic images of enslaved torture, images that might encourage a certain type of emotional and physical contagion between blacks and whites. Branagan's text formulates an affective and cognitive mode for reading these engravings, along with an entire story that buttresses their signification. *The Penitential Tyrant* envisions an affective sensorium formed not only from the intellectual (internal) eye of a reader, but also from a reader's (external) "bodily eyes." In so doing, Branagan's work tries to transmigrate a reader into a mode of embodied simulation in which empathy and intersubjectivity are enhanced through the reuse of a reader's mental states and physical processes. When readers finally encounter the descriptive plates on pages 267–74, they have been prepared by affective and cognitive modes presented early in the text to see an overlap between enslaved bodies and their own corporeality. Finally, perhaps in these images readers see not a disembodied, abject other, but their own (potential) identity, reflected back in the gaze of an enslaved, yet also resistant and particularized, human being.

Conclusion

In an essay on comic modes, Joseph Witek contends that cartoons are rooted stylistically in two distinct traditions of visual representation: caricature, which has as its basic principle simplification or exaggeration, and realistic illustration, which relies on verisimilitude and the re-creation of accurate physical appearances ("Comics Modes," 28). Although most caricature during the period discussed in this chapter supported a proslavery agenda,[38] I end by turning to a six-panel cartoon that employs this comic mode to criticize the visual order of slavery. Attributed to William Elmes, "Adventures of Johnny Newcome" (1812) contains a strong ironic and ludic quality that might be assessed in light of Branagan's evocation of a world where we experience the pain of all (including the enslaved) who are aggregated in "the circle of mankind" (see figure 1.17; color image 4). Elmes fashioned a hand-colored engraving with a great deal of graphic complexity. We can see his use of emerging visual technologies such as words on the same page as pictures, the symbolization of motion (in the first panel, Johnny's hat pops off as he looks at the land), and vibrant pigments. The first three panels evoke the notion of the West Indies as a kind of paradise: Johnny lands on the shore and becomes enamored of the land and the "Nymphs bathing" (panel 3); like Stedman, he enjoys the physical charms of the local beauties.[39] Yet in the first three panels, it is also evident that Johnny uses his vision to create a colonial order, gazing on every item he encounters—the land, the stores, and the women—and claiming them. Panel 3 is particularly clear in this regard as Johnny trains his monocle on the women, visually pinning or penetrating them with his patriarchal and colonizing gaze.

By panel 4, Johnny has become the lord and master of all he surveys. He is carried on a sort of litter and fanned furiously by the natives, who seem to be starving, judging by the way the man in panel 5 gulps his food surreptitiously behind Johnny's back. Moreover, a sinister note is introduced in panels 4 and 5, where we see Johnny carrying a gun. In panel 5, he even uses one of the locals as a gun rest while he practices his shooting and watches "the sports of the field." Perhaps this man is not as steady in this hazardous task as Johnny would like, for in panel 6 we see this same man (in yellow trunks) being whipped by Johnny, with the sarcastic caption, "Johnny Preachee and Flogee Poor Mungo." In panel 6, in a scene that suggests a latent homoeroticism, Johnny happily smokes his pipe, eats his food, and almost delicately dangles his phallic whip over the enlarged posterior of Mungo. We see Elmes using caricature to portray this realm as a despoiled Eden, ruled over by an idiot king whose power resides mainly in his guns and whips.

FIGURE I.17 William Elmes, "Adventures of Johnny Newcome" (1812), plate 1.
Hand-colored engraved cartoon. Courtesy of Yale University.

There is no countertheater of visuality in Elmes, but there is a deep sense that the colonial order is ludic, idiotic, and hypocritical.

The early visual texts discussed in this chapter approach in various ways the subject of how one envisions the colonial order of slavery and enslaved torture. Some texts—such as those by Stedman and Elmes—seem to imply that this order is eternal and unchanging. Others—such as the broadsides and *The Penitential Tyrant*—are more critical of the scopic colonial order and attempt to imagine a space where it ceases. But even these texts at times confirm a scopic order in which the enslaved are abject bodies, separate and separated from an empowered subject. It remained for later authors to portray how empathy and agency might be signified in subjugated bodies—bodies that are blurred with a viewing subject. Illustrated graphic stories in various configurations continued to be pivotal to this enterprise as the scripting of affective and cognitive modes of intersubjectivity was negotiated within the visual rhetoric of the antislavery movement.

2

"These Loathsome Pictures Shall Be Published"

Reconfigurations of the Optical Regime of Transatlantic Slavery in Amelia Opie's *The Black Man's Lament* (1826) and George Bourne's *Picture of Slavery in the United States of America* (1834)

In 1827 and 1828, Captain Basil Hall (1788–1844)—a British officer from Scotland whose feats included commanding Royal Navy vessels on hazardous scientific and diplomatic missions, exploring Java in 1813, and interviewing Napoleon on St. Helena in 1817—traveled through North America, using a camera lucida to make illustrations. Patented in 1806 by William Hyde Wollaston, the camera lucida uses prisms that create optical superimpositions of objects onto the surface on which the artist draws, allowing the artist to trace accurate outlines of them. Hall's crisp illustrations made with the camera lucida, such as "Two Slave Drivers and a Backwoodsman with His Rifle," seem almost ethnographic in focus (see figure 2.1). The two slave drivers appear to be well dressed and well fed. A diminutive whip on the left-hand side of the frame alludes to enslaved torture, but it coils upward, as if stuck in the waistband of the slave driver's trousers; its circular shape creates a visual echo of the hat in the man's left hand, making the whip seem to be nothing more than part of the man's costume—not something to be used. The slave driver on the right has no whip and is attired in a long frock coat more suggestive of gentility than enslavement. Indeed, it takes a moment to realize that the individuals on the left and right are enslaved.[1]

This visual text portrays slavery as something of a munificent institution. It might also support political rhetoric from the period that called slavery a legitimate and benevolent substitute for the alleged cruelty of freedom.[2] Hall's description of the image hints that he favors such a view; for example, he states, "The figure on the left was a Black man in charge of a plantation in South Carolina. . . . I did not suppose it was possible that a negro in the situation of a slave-driver could be so much like

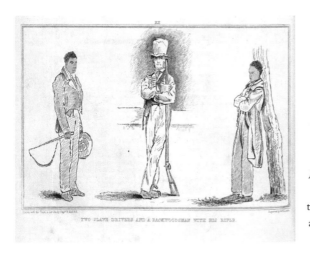

FIGURE 2.1 *Basil Hall's Forty Etchings, from Sketches made with the Camera Lucida, in North America, in 1827 and 1828* (1829). Wood engraving with the caption "Two Slave Drivers and a Backwoodsman with his Rifle." Library of Congress.

a gentleman." Hall describes the camera lucida as a visual aid that enabled him to capture external visual objects—to communicate "truth," "correct representations," and "correct outlines" of the people and places he saw (i). For Hall, the camera lucida acted as a model of how observation leads to truths about the external world and the status of the enslaved.

Yet as early as 1810, the supposition that visual apparatuses and vision itself convey objective and external truths was being questioned. Following up on hypotheses of Johann von Goethe, for example, in 1818 the scientist Johann Purkinje conducted a series of experiments to show that eyes were not passive objects but subjective participants in the production of visual meaning; the results of these experiments were published in his *Contributions to the Knowledge of Vision in its Subjective Aspect* (1819).[3] Moreover, as Peter Brownlee notes, the discipline of ophthalmology developed in the first decades of the nineteenth century; in studying eye diseases and changes in vision, "scientists and philosophers were awakening to the possibilities of an individualized and bodily formulation of vision . . . [that] conceived vision produced by the eyes as a phenomenon always *in process*" ("'The Economy of the Eyes,'" 57). This evolving paradigm of vision, visual processes, and the relationship between external and internal sight was used carefully by some abolitionist visual texts, which attempt to put a viewer's perceptual experiences into the picture (so to speak).

As elucidated in the introduction, changes in print and visual technology in the 1820s and 1830s led to low-cost methods of putting images on the same page as text and less expensive printing techniques overall. These developments facilitated a rapid proliferation of texts featuring pictorial representations of enslaved individuals and of illustrated books about enslavement. The changes meant that authors could easily appropriate codes from other semiotic systems, beyond narrative language, such as art and color. Yet as several critics have noted, and as discussed in chapter 1, some of these texts replicate a politics of the gaze in which enslaved individuals are the abject, subhuman other within a colonialist visual order that grants subjectivity and power to a free, white viewer.[4]

This chapter argues that Amelia Opie's colored, graphic illustrated book for children *The Black Man's Lament; or, How To Make Sugar* (1826) and George Bourne's illustrated antislavery work *Picture of Slavery in the United States of America* (1834) endeavor to shift a reader's horizon of expectations away from passive spectatorship of abject bodies to abolitionist action on behalf of humanized and paralleled subjects. In making use of newly emerging visual technologies borrowed from media such as painting, captioning, and printmaking, these visual texts mobilize transmedial ways of *seeing* the torture of slavery. In addition, they incorporate some of these new ideas about the repositioning of the origins of vision and a viewer's role in creating images in order to attempt to implicate a reader within these texts and their arguments. I chose these works because they use visually complex methods to promote readerly identification and intersubjectivity with the enslaved, and also because they introduce technical visual innovations into the structure of the graphic illustrated book.[5] I do not contend that these books always succeed in using their visual rhetoric to create a parallel (rather than a hierarchical) mode of empathy.[6] I maintain, however, that these texts manifest an attempt to equalize the viewer and the viewed through direct referencing of the process of visualization and through reading protocols that seek to amalgamate a viewer into the visual rhetoric of the text. These texts at times coerce reading viewers toward abolition with prosthetic viewing presences who ask not only for visual sympathy, but also for nonhierarchical empathetic standpoints that might lead to seditious actions.[7]

Historical Overview: Slavery and Abolition, 1820–1835

As discussed in chapter 1, during the late eighteenth and early nineteenth centuries, abolitionists secured significant victories worldwide. Yet in 1826, when Amelia Opie published *The Black Man's Lament*, Britain had not emancipated its enslaved population; although the ban on the slave trade had been in effect since 1808, slaves continued to be held, bought, and sold in Britain's colonies. The West Indies was a particularly important location for the slave trade because it produced a vast amount of a popular crop—sugar (Marshall, *Eighteenth Century*, 422–23).

Abolition societies organized boycotts of sugar and other slave-produced products, and Opie's book can be understood as part of the visual culture that argued for these boycotts. Children, in particular, were urged to deny themselves sugar in order to undermine the slave trade (Drescher, *Abolition*, 221).

Britain had to pass, in 1833, the Slavery Abolition Act, which became law one year later, in order to end slavery officially throughout the empire. The law did not apply to Ceylon, St. Helena, or territories held by the East India Company; these exceptions were eliminated in 1843 (Morgan, *Slavery and the British Empire*, 191). After 1834, Britain increasingly turned its attention to international efforts to end the slave trade. In 1839, for example, the British and Foreign Anti-Slavery Society (BFASS) attempted to pressure governments to enforce the suppression of the slave trade by declaring slave traders pirates. Perhaps most importantly for the purposes of this study, the BFASS was crucial to the interconnection between U.S. and British antislavery interests; according to Kenneth Morgan, it "supported abolitionists in the United States, welcomed American guests to Britain, and sponsored visits to America" (201). The publication of Bourne's *Picture of American Slavery* (1834) in both the United States and Europe (Glasgow) was facilitated by comprehension that abolitionist struggles needed to be fought internationally.

Bourne was a leading advocate of immediate abolition in the United States, and the urgency of his focus can been seen when it is placed in its historical context. In the 1820s and 1830s, the number of slave-holding states increased, and the lines of battle between antislavery and proslavery states calcified. According to Seymour Drescher, progress on gradual emancipation in the United States had virtually ceased by the 1820s (*Abolition*, 145). Moreover, the Missouri Compromise of 1820, which admitted Missouri as a slave state and Maine as a free one, set a precedent in which states were admitted into the Union in pairs so that a balance between states in which slavery was legal and those in which it had been outlawed would be preserved. Many historians therefore view the Missouri Compromise as an act that led directly to the Civil War (Dooley, "Missouri Compromise," 349–50).

Bitter conflicts also developed in the United States in the 1820s and 1830s between those who favored gradual abolition and those, such as Bourne, who argued for the immediate end of slavery, with no reparations paid to slaveholders (Rodriguez, "Gradualism," 319). Those who argued for immediate abolition also took pains to insist on the status of African Americans as citizens who had the legal right to remain in the United States, a point that also emerges in Bourne's text. The works discussed in this chapter further indicate that if claims for freedom and citizenship were not heeded, dire results might occur—a point congruent with the historical backdrop of the period. Fear of slave insurrections was significant in these decades. In the United States, revolts were led by Gabriel Prosser (1800), Charles Deslondes (1811), Denmark Vesey (1822), Nat Turner (1831), and others. The publication of David Walker's incendiary *Appeal* (1829) was also an important historical event; Walker was one of the earliest writers not only to demand immediate abolition but also to urge slaves to rebel en masse against their masters.

Indeed, with the growing chasm between those on opposite sides of these issues—but especially over immediate versus gradual emancipation—graphic images showing enslaved torture took on special urgency. U.S. abolitionists became more and more convinced that visual images might be key to enacting immediate change. As Phillip Lapsansky notes, in 1835 the American Anti-Slavery Society published over a million pieces of literature (a ninefold increase over previous years), and many of these tracts featured visual materials ("Graphic Discord," 202). This outburst in print and visual culture had as its goal not only to portray enslaved torment but also to relieve it. Within this paradigm, engravings of cruelty were meant to act as a visual spark or catalyst for sympathy. Opie and Bourne both attempt to draw on these historical debates and to use their visual texts as a trigger for their readers' sympathy. At times they also try to reconfigure these debates so that the cognitive and affective separation between the suffering, enslaved body and the empathetic viewer is eroded or undermined, and direct dissent against slavery is facilitated.

Amelia Opie and the Visual Technologies of the Graphic Illustrated Book for Children

Scholars may be familiar with abolitionist works for children (some of which were illustrated) published from the 1840s to 1860s, such as the *Anti-Slavery Alphabet* (1846). But Opie's *The Black Man's Lament* (1826), containing fifteen hand-colored copperplate engravings in twenty-four pages, precedes these works by at least twenty years. It is thus one of the earliest and most elaborate graphic illustrated books for children exclusively devoted to an antislavery topic.[8] I consider Opie's work in particular because it had a double audience of adults (who might read the book to children) and children; one clear emphasis of the work as a whole is to galvanize the adult white reader into action through the child's example. Opie's book imagines the child as a subject with agency—not necessarily a citizen, but someone who will eventually grow into citizenship and be able to enact social change. Opie forwards the idea that the child's example could motivate an adult reader; during this period, as Holly Keller argues, the child was viewed as both a symbolic "teacher and redeemer" ("Juvenile Antislavery Narrative," 87). Opie's envisioning of the child as a proto-political subject who inspires adult action may also have enabled the cultural work of a text such as *Uncle Tom's Cabin*, which takes a similar approach to the function of children like Little Eva. Writing before the rise of Juvenile Abolition societies in the late 1830s (see De Rosa, *Domestic Abolitionism*, 110–14), Opie foreshadows how, in later years, the child became a unique catalyst and model for social change.

Opie (1769–1853) was a well-known British abolitionist and the author of seven novels, one play, three volumes of poetry, and seven collections of tales from 1790 to 1830 (Eberle, "'Tales of Truth?,'" 72). Her work was popular both in England and the United States (De Rosa, "Amelia Anderson Opie," 1). Considered something of a grande dame of abolition, she was one of only four women present at the first World Anti-Slavery Convention, which met in London in 1840. Some recent scholars have placed her works within the tradition of British romantic antislavery writing, yet critics have not situated her writing within the tradition of the early antislavery illustrated book.[9] There is no information about the illustrator for *The Black Man's Lament*. A similar style of illustration is used in an 1826 reprint of William Cowper's poem "The Negro's Complaint" (1788), so it appears that the firm Harvey and Darton (which published both books) employed an illustrator competent at working with individual texts to shape images that augment each poem's diegesis.[10]

The Black Man's Lament commences with an illustration that specifically instructs a reader about the status of the child as a proto-political subject and uses a mode of empathy that is more hierarchical than parallel (see figure 2.2; color image 5). This drawing refers to a political subject—a petition for the abolition of the slave trade; the illustration makes clear that the child on the left is inscribing his name on the petition: his pen touches the page.[11] The verse on this page works with the picture to grant white children's agency within the political sphere of abolition; the narrator addresses her "plaintive ditty" to "children dear" so that their souls might be moved not only to pity but to trying to "*end* the griefs you hear." The italicized text strives to propel the children (and perhaps more surreptitiously, the adult) into action. "Emotions pervade all social life, social movements included," notes the sociologist James Jasper. "Without them, there might be no social action at all" ("Emotions of Protest," 398). Opie uses an affective process even in this first verse, referring to "tender hearts" and describing her poem as a "plaintive ditty," to attempt to compel social engagement. In her study of pain and humanitarianism in this time period, Abruzzo comments, "Moral philosophers and ministers tried to rescue sympathy from any hint of association with passive sentiment. . . . Moralists still praised the sympathetic souls who spilled tears over

suffering victims—but only so long as such tears were merely a prelude to benevolent *action* to relive the suffering" (*Polemical Pain*, 123). We can see this move into
action in the child's signing of the petition; this is a deed of political empowerment designed to relieve the suffering of the enslaved through participation in the
abolition movement.[12]

But visual sight lines of the illustration draw focus to the free white adult.
Because he is the tallest and most dominant figure, and because he stands foregrounded in the exact center of the picture, with the long vertical line of a tree
branch that extends over his head and almost seems to point at him, a viewer may
look at this man first, before scrutinizing the child or the supplicant slave. The
half-naked enslaved man also attracts a viewer's focus, but the illustration's composition places greater optical emphasis on the white adult, the man in the middle,

COME, listen to my plaintive ditty,
    Ye tender hearts, and children dear!
And, should it move your souls to pity,
    Oh! try to *end* the griefs you hear.

FIGURE 2.2 Amelia Opie,
The Black Man's Lament (1826),
first illustrated page. Copperplate
engraving and watercolor.
Courtesy of the Lilly Library,
Bloomington, Indiana.

so to speak, whose role is somewhat ambiguous. He seems to be clasping the petition so that the children can sign it, yet visually and symbolically he contributes to enslavement by physically holding the manacled slave—exhibit A—in place; he does not, for example, unchain the slave, a power the adult would have if he owned the slave or had bought him to set him free. Interestingly, the man in the middle is elegantly dressed in blue breeches, a white button-up shirt, and a red jacket. Red, white, and blue: these are colors that might not be lost on a U.S. viewer, and they recur in many images in the text that feature overseers whipping slaves. A visual pantomime of a sort is underway here: the children sign the petition, and the slave appears to be speaking to and reaching out to the children, yet the man in the middle (who has the most social power) does nothing, and in fact looks away from the enslaved man. The optical focus of the illustration therefore is placed as much on the adult and his inaction as on the enslaved man or the children.

The written text attempts to compel the children's souls into feeling "pity" for the enslaved, which suggests a mode of hierarchal empathy—a viewing of the enslaved man as an other in need of the children's rescue, a point the illustration visually replicates as the manacled and supplicant slave holds out his chained hands to the children. The illustration triangulates empathy through the white children; if they can feel empathy for the enslaved and sign a petition for abolition, a person reading the book should be compelled to do so also.[13] The text as a whole, however, strives to shift a reader's horizon of expectations beyond this mode of indirect and hierarchical empathy, of spectatorial sympathy, into a mode of parallel empathy. For example, by calling the poem *The Black Man's Lament; or, How To Make Sugar*, Opie focuses on the enslaved person's subjectivity as a man, and on the capitalist and technological processes that undergird enslavement (the making of sugar). The work takes care to show that the condition of freedom precedes enslavement by tracing the technological processes used to tear the black man from his homeland and make him into a slave (4). Elsewhere in the book, blacks are described as "freemen / forc'd from Negro land" (7) and "black men and women" (9); the text uses the term "slave" only two times. This rhetoric lays the groundwork for a construction of affective and cognitive parity (rather than only hierarchy) that is forwarded lexically and visually in other parts of the text.

To further underlie this conception of parity, the African bodies, once enslaved, are visualized sometimes as fully clothed and not tortured, unlike many of the texts discussed in chapter 1. In figure 2.3 (and color image 6), a muscular man dressed in a tunic and skirt of bright colors inspects the blossoming land. He is framed by tall sugarcane plants in full bloom; unfettered and free (visually), he holds an implement of cultivation (a scythe). Opie's illustrator portrays him in a moment of calmness and beauty; he also seems to be employing a panoramic perspective as he surveys the land. Unlike Basil Hall's narrative, however, Opie's words make the grave trauma of enslavement verbally apparent. We are told that the Negro "toils, and bleeds, and *dies*" for the sugarcane plant (4), and that slavery makes "the Black man's woes" and "the White man's crimes" (3).

Visually, the pages of the book are often set up like the one shown in figure 2.3. There is usually a colored illustration carefully framed at the top and surrounded by a generous margin, a caption below it, a short dash rule separating the illustration from the narrative, and then a quatrain of narrative poetry. The rule establishes an orderly visual boundary between the poetic text and the illustration, as does the framing of this image and the wide borders on either side of the page. The diction is

THE BLACK MAN'S LAMENT.   3

SUGAR-CANE.

There is a *beauteous plant* *, that grows
    In western India's sultry clime,
Which makes, alas! the Black man's woes,
    And also makes the White man's crime.

* " A field of canes, when standing in the month of November, when it is in arrow or full blossom, (says Beckford, in his descriptive account of the Island of Jamaica,) is one of the most beautiful productions that the pen or pencil can possibly describe. It, in common, rises from three to eight feet, or more, in height; a difference

FIGURE 2.3 Amelia Opie, *The Black Man's Lament* (1826), 3. Copperplate engraving and watercolor. Courtesy of the Lilly Library, Bloomington, Indiana.

generally appropriate for children, with direct language and few compound words. Opie employs long meter, often used for hymns: quatrains arranged in an *abab* rhyme scheme in iambic tetrameter; there is little enjambment, making the poetry easy to follow. What is unusual about page 3 (seen in figure 2.3), however, is that it contains a lengthy footnote about the sugarcane plant, which is perhaps a bit too technical for young children and in fact extends to page 4. This footnote speaks to Opie's double audience of children and adults, and also slightly distorts the visual aesthetic arrangement of the page, perhaps suggesting that slavery as a subject undermines the artworks that attempt to contain it. Moreover, as the text progresses, this neat symmetrical arrangement on the page becomes more and more disordered: pages 17–19 have two quatrains of poetry each, and pages 21–25 have only poetic text and no illustrations. The pictures are first eroded (as the poetry takes over) and then totally effaced. The illustrations may pull a reader into the text at first, but then they vanish, leaving us to confront the black man's soliloquy and his dialogue with his captors, which completely take over the text on pages 4–25. A heterodiegetic narrator—a narrator external to the world of the text—introduces and concludes the work, but the main poem is communicated directly by a homodiegetic narrator—a black man who has been enslaved for sugar production in the West Indies.

As discussed in previous chapters, many abolitionist images about the experience of enslavement circulated from text to text, and in Opie's book an image of African bodies closely packed into the hull of a ship echoes the famous Clarkson illustration of the slave ship *Brooks* (*History of the Rise, Progress, and Accomplishment of the Abolition of the African Slave-Trade*, 6), with which she was certainly familiar (Opie and Clarkson had worked together on abolition projects). Moreover, like other abolitionist publications, *The Black Man's Lament* contains illustrations of enslaved torture. The depiction on page 5 is probably the most violent one in the text. It takes place in Africa and corresponds closely to the image repeated on abolition broadsides of the husband and wife being mercilessly parted from each other while a child clings to its mother's side, discussed in chapter 1 (see figure 2.4; color image 7). The quatrain below this image emphasizes the deep wound of family destruction that precedes the middle passage:

> From parents, brethren's fond embrace;
> From tender wife, and child to tear;
> Then in a darksome ship to place,
> Pack'd close, like bales of cotton there.

Yet even in this depiction of torture, Opie's text attempts to forward intersubjectivity by referring to the stolen man not as a slave but a person with parents,

THE BLACK MAN'S LAMENT.   5

TORN FROM HIS FRIENDS.

From parents, brethren's fond embrace;
  From tender wife, and child to tear;
Then in a darksome ship to place,
  Pack'd close, like bales of cotton there.

FIGURE 2.4 Amelia Opie,
The Black Man's Lament (1826), 5.
Copperplate engraving and
watercolor. Courtesy of the Lilly
Library, Bloomington, Indiana.

friends, a tender wife, and children. Yet he is treated like a product—a bale of cotton—and packed close in a "darksome ship." In other words, the poem shows how the enslaved is turned into a commodity, but also indicates that a human subjectivity precedes this metamorphosis.

The drawing is filled with a violent kinetic energy, and we can almost hear the woman's beseeching voice and the child's cry, see the movement of the clubs as they descend, and feel the hands that roughly wrench the father away from his family. The illustration uses these mechanisms to structure an affective response, what Jasper terms a moral shock ("Emotions of Protest," 409) that may create a type of framing in which the "passion for justice is fueled by anger over existing injustice" (414). The small child in the foreground contributes to the anger a reader might feel on viewing this illustration; unlike the flat, undifferentiated child portrayed in the broadsides, (see chapter 1), this one is three-dimensional, plump and nourished. He or she is also portrayed dynamically, in movement, caught by the illustration with one foot on the ground and one in the air, as if having just been dragged away from the father by the mother. Pineapples in the illustration contribute to the framing of the scene as an injustice; they function in ironic contrast to the main action because in many locales pineapples symbolize hospitality, and perhaps they were being offered to the white men as a gesture of friendship.[14]

Technologies developed during the first decades of the nineteenth century such as the thaumatrope, phenakistoscope, and kaleidoscope allowed pictures and images to become mobile in some way. The kaleidoscope, for example, was invented in 1815; the phenakistoscope, an early animation device, was invented in 1833. Opie's text uses the concept of pictorial mobility to elicit, manage, and transform the viewer's emotions—key aspects of recruitment into any social movement, as Francesca Polletta and Edwin Amenta have demonstrated ("Second That Emotion?," 309–10). This extremely vivid and mobile illustration has a mosaic-like structure, composed of at least ten color tones (pink, purple, blue, orange, white, brown, yellow, red, tan, and green), and achieves a dramatic effect of fragmentation, movement, and motile dynamism. In the specific content of the illustration, this print is like abolitionist documents such as the broadsides discussed in chapter 1: it shows torture and the separation of families. Yet in its visual methodology, such as its use of color and symbolization of movement to connote the fragmentation and destruction that enslavement fosters, it is unlike early antislavery visual works. Sonja Foss argues that visual images appeal to readers when they employ a "novel technical aspect" that "violates viewers' expectations"; this violation then functions "both to sustain interest in the image and to decontextualize it" ("Construction of Appeal," 215). The mosaic of pastel colors in this image and the symbolization of movement might attract a reader's attention but then violate his or her expectations (the colors and movement do not symbolize joy but disruption and violence). The brightness of the image is further decontextualized by the language, which refers to the "darksome" place of the slave ship's hold.

As previously discussed, enslaved women were a frequent source of abolitionist and nonabolitionist art, yet Opie's images of women bear some significant differences from such traditional representations. Visual culture from this period tended to portray nude or seminude enslaved women who represent figures of irresistible sexuality but are also emblems of general powerlessness (Spillers, "Mama's Baby," 67). Opie's text does depict a seminude and supplicant woman being tortured (see figure 2.4). Yet other illustrations struggle to move a reader beyond sexualized or voyeuristic viewing. For example, the text appears to go to great lengths to

show that enslaved women have the capacity for both self-possession and meaningful work; they are not, in other words, merely decorative figures on which to
hang voyeuristic fantasies of white (masculine) sexuality and empowerment. In
figure 2.5, the woman is fully and decorously clothed in a (pink) topcoat and a
white skirt; she helps plant the sugarcane by holding the extra top shoots for the
enslaved man to place in the furrows. Most importantly, she carefully watches the
man planting the sugarcane, as if she wishes to learn how to perform this labor.
She is a figure of bodily integrity and control, not a flayed or decimated corporeality that has been broken open, such as the women portrayed in Stedman's imaging
of enslaved torture. The possibility of torture is evident in the overseer's whip, of
course, but it is important that Opie's illustration focuses not on beaten bodies but
on laboring ones. Abruzzo comments that after 1808, graphic details of torture

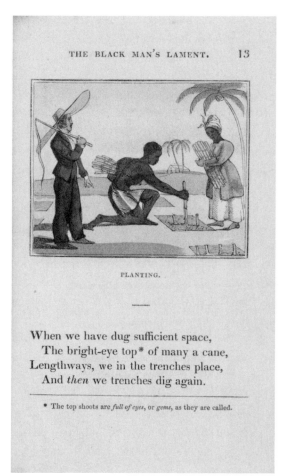

THE BLACK MAN'S LAMENT.   13

PLANTING.

When we have dug sufficient space,
    The bright-eye top* of many a cane,
Lengthways, we in the trenches place,
    And *then* we trenches dig again.

* The top shoots are *full of eyes*, or *gems*, as they are called.

FIGURE 2.5 Amelia Opie,
The Black Man's Lament (1826), 13.
Copperplate engraving and
watercolor. Courtesy of the Lilly
Library Bloomington, Indiana.

took on more importance in the drive to ban the slave trade and that "with each decade, antislavery imagery grew more explicit, detailed, and gruesome" (*Polemical Pain*, 88). Opie's text mainly eschews the use of voyeuristic scenes of sadomasochistic torment, forwarding instead scenes of bodily integrity.

Such scenes emphasize, as well, the potentiality of formerly enslaved persons, once emancipated, to contribute meaningfully to local or national economies. There was significant debate during this time period about whether emancipation might produce a large group of people unfit to work without a master telling them what to do (Newman, *Freedom's Prophet*, 203; Painter, *Exodusters*, ix). In figure 2.5, the enslaved labor diligently and carefully without being whipped as the complacent overseer (again in red, white, and blue) lazily looks on their efforts. "The top shoots are *full of eyes*," warns the footnote, as if alluding to prosthetic eyes that might implicate a viewer in the picture, but certainly incriminate the lazy overseer, who himself engages in no physical work. "Pictures are things that have been marked with all the stigmata of personhood and animation: they exhibit both physical and virtual bodies; they speak to us, sometimes literally, sometimes figuratively," W. J. T. Mitchell states (*What Do Pictures Want?*, 30). The images in this text, marked with literal and metaphorical eyes as well as with other "stigmata of personhood" (such as bodies), seem to ask a reader (perhaps) not to bury his or her eyes in the ground in the way that the "bright eye-top[s]" of the cane are laid into the trenches. The illustrations seem to implore the viewer to use his or her eyes to apprehend the trauma of slavery, but also to perceive the resilience, intelligence, and industriousness of the enslaved.

Furthermore, the drawings in Opie's text diverge from more traditional images of enslavement in which the enslaved lack the right to look. In an ongoing debate about the ways in which white abolitionist women writers portrayed the enslaved, some critics have argued that these writers enfranchised themselves as reforming subjects only by depicting subhuman objects (abject enslaved bodies).[15] Yet some critics have argued for a less compromised form of representation. Moira Ferguson, for example, even in noting how "Europe speaks for Africa," argues that some radical writers "endowed Africans who lived inside and outside their prose with more of a subject than a subjected status" (*Subject to Others*, 163). Ferguson does not discuss Opie's illustrated poem, yet we can see this subject status being formulated, since the work's visual rhetoric insists on an enslaved person who gazes, speaks, and acts, a person who in some ways is parallel to a viewer. Page 9, for example, depicts enslaved individuals on the verge of being tortured as the overseer (dressed in blue breeches, a white buttoned shirt, and a red coat, the colors of which echo the man in the middle of the opening scene) raises his whip menacingly (see figure

2.6; color image 8). Although the overseer stands in the background of the picture, he appears to be at least as large as the slaves in the foreground, and he takes up roughly one-third of the pictorial space. This foreshortening of perspective may at first draw a viewer's eyes to him, directing scopic surveillance to the man who tortures rather than only to the slaves. The foreshortening also suggests the overseer's attempt to dominate the landscape and all that he sees around him, both by his whip and by visually pinning the slaves to their task.

Does this attempt to dominate the slaves and the landscape work? Most of the enslaved workers look away from the overseer, and away from a viewer; the half-naked man in the front of the line, for example, puts up no visual resistance to the master's scopic dominance. Crucially, Opie's illustrator portrays a man in the center of the line (in a long azure robe) who looks out *at readers* as if contesting

THE BLACK MAN'S LAMENT.   9

STANDING IN LINES, WITH THE DRIVER BEHIND.

They bid black men and women stand
  In lines, the drivers in the rear :
Poor Negroes hold a *hoe* in hand,
  But they the wicked cart-whip bear.

FIGURE 2.6 Amelia Opie,
The Black Man's Lament (1826), 9.
Copperplate engraving and
watercolor. Courtesy of the Lilly
Library, Bloomington, Indiana.

the scopic dominance of the overseer with another envisioning presence, as if asking the reading viewer to refuse the overseer's order of vision. The overseer or the half-naked man in front might first draw a viewer's eyes, but this man's azure robe is the longest and most vibrant block of color in the print. It may thus cause a reader's eyes to linger on the man in the robe, who appears to be looking back at a viewer, asserting what Mirzoeff would call the right to look. By looking at a viewer and away from the overseer, this man may function as a sort of visual conduit or route into the picture for a reader—a technique that Bourne also used—and as a sort of prosthetic eye for a possible oppositional viewing. By looking back at the viewer, he may imply that the enslaved person can suspend, at least momentarily, the master's ability to dominate him; his mode of visioning may also try to implicate readers in a type of civil contract (to borrow terms from Ariella Azoulay's book on photography) that assumes the existence of a hypothetical spectator who could be moved toward indignation or anger by such images (*Civil Contract*, 22).

Opie's text therefore scrutinizes the subject of vision itself—how it is created, shared, and objectified. Peter John Brownlee contends that "a widely held discussion over the nature of vision was conducted in the first half of the nineteenth century" as "conceptions of vision became written in the human body and across the surfaces of an assortment of objects particularly attendant to *the eyes of human observers*" ("'The Economy of the Eyes,'" 18, emphasis added), such as mirrors, pictures, and reflective surfaces. Opie's illustrations leave traces of the process of seeing in order to focalize questions of how vision functions as either a mode of white dominance or a possible mode of resistance to the slaveholder's panoptic power. In figure 2.6, the enslaved look nothing like the huddled, forlorn bodies in Stedman's narrative, the broadsides, or Elmes's *Adventures of Johnny Newcome* (discussed in chapter 1). The bodies in Opie's text are arranged in a neat line, and while the man in the front is only partially clothed, other figures are fully attired in what seems to be the illustrator's conception of traditional Afro-Caribbean dress.

Opie's portrayal of enslaved Africans can be compared with that present in images on the frontispiece and title page of another early, much-reprinted children's book about slavery—*Dazee, Or the Re-Captured Negro* (1821), written by Mary Martha Sherwood (see figure 2.7). Published five years before Opie's book, this work relies on existing iconography to make its argument. Dazee is a literal replication of the Wedgwood supplicant slave, repurposed and repackaged but with unchanged features. The enslaved African in Sherwood's text is the recipient of the gaze of both the individual in the image (on the left of the frontispiece) and of a reader. The enslaved African does not return the gaze of a reader, nor does his imprimatur contest the dominant scopic order of slavery in any way.

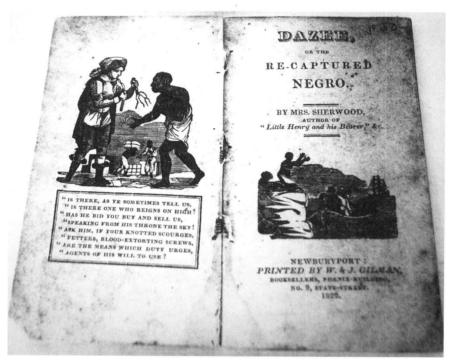

FIGURE 2.7   Mary Martha Sherwood, *Dazee, Or the Recaptured Negro*,
2nd ed. (Newburyport, Mass.: Gilman, 1822). Wood engraving.
Courtesy of the Library Company of Philadelphia.

Opie's book, by contrast, takes care to depict distinctive (rather than stereotypical) persons, unbroken corporealities that can assert a mode of ocular resistance.
Again and again her illustrations depict men and (sometimes) women who appear
to be staring away from the action of the scene and back at the viewer (pages 1,
4, and 17). In discussing photographs in which the individual looks at the viewer,
Azoulay argues that such images may formulate a series of questions: "Why are
these men, women, children, and families looking at me? . . . At whom, precisely,
did they seek to look—was it truly at me? And why? What am I supposed to do
with their look? What is the foundation of the gaze I might turn back toward
them?" (*Civil Contract*, 18). She argues that this looking back may gesture toward
a realm in which relationships between the viewed and the viewer are mediated
not by the dominant power but instead by a type of civil contract that presupposes
or perhaps imagines a new conceptual framework of partnership and solidarity
between the oppressed and the viewer (23). This partnership may be virtual or
symbolic (rather than actual and localized). Because many images in Opie's text
feature enslaved individuals who look back at the viewer, her text may be gesturing

to a hypothetical community of readers who can understand the political content of this gesture and respond to it with something like solidarity.

Opie's text also attempts to create a configuration of oppositional viewing and reading lexically. Her text manipulates first-person discourse to seem to allow enslaved figures within the pictures and the narrative to speak, thereby forwarding a type of rhetorical and linguistic resistance to enslavement as well as a mode of intersubjectivity. As previously noted, speech is intersubjective and presupposes a listener who can understand the needs and claims of the speaker (Gillespie, "Intersubjective Nature of Symbols," 30). On pages 4–25 of the poem—in thirty-two of the poem's thirty-eight quatrains—a black man speaks of his experience of enslavement. As Roxanne Eberle has noted, the text begins with the (presumably) white narrator's voice, which validates the truth of the black man's experiences in its final lines ("'Tales of Truth?,'" 25). In the nineteenth century, a white voice was frequently used to authorize a narrative by an African American; perhaps Opie adheres to this tradition. More importantly, however, the black man is a vocal, interlocutory, intelligent subject. For example, an Englishman rather abruptly and somewhat doltishly steps into the poem to compare the lot of slaves to that of "peasant[s]" and asks: "Thou wouldst not, sure, have Negroes play?" to which the black man voices a cogent rejoinder: peasants are not flogged "almost to death" (21), fettered like "beasts of prey," starved, or deprived of their families (22); the white man makes no response. The black man, in other words, wins the argument.

This litany of suffering in the speaker's first-person discourse narratively enacts the tortures on the broadsides discussed in the preceding chapter, so it is striking that Opie's illustrator mainly chooses not to dramatize them in pictures, with a few exceptions. Instead, the text generally allows the enslaved a form of nonscopic textual redress that places the black speaker within a societal body rather than outside it. He is human and has the same desires (for home, wife, and children) as other men:

> But Englishmen can work
> Whene'er they like, and stop for breath;
> No driver dares, like any Turk,
> Flog peasants on almost to death.
> . . . .
> He has a cottage, he a wife;
> If child he has, that child is free.
> I am depriv'd of married life,
> And my poor child were *slave* like me.
> (21–22)

Physical tortures, while certainly difficult to bear, are not the cruelest part of the enslavement. Instead, the passage focuses on the enslaved man's psychological torment when he is deprived of a wife, children who are free, and a home. Perhaps to focalize empathy, the poem returns to the idea of the enslaved child at its end ("and my poor child were *slave* like me"). Opie places enslaved persons within the crucial social sphere of familial life and attempts to foster intersubjectivity through the representation of mental states that might match those of viewers. Like Stowe twenty-five years later, Opie hopes her reader, bonded parentally with the child to whom he or she might be reading the book, might be able to imagine what it would be like to be the parent of an enslaved child.

Other passages move toward embodied simulation, the "reuse of mental states and processes involving representations that have a bodily format" (Gallese and Sinigaglia, "What Is So Special," 515), by trying to place the white man into the sensorium of enslaved torture; the black man wishes he could make "White men . . . feel" the black man's "miseries" (22). The black man longs for an intersubjective sharing of embodied experience (in this case, pain). Yet this sharing of pain ultimately is not enough, and the text attempts to transport a viewer beyond sentimentalism's sadomasochistic discourse through a focus on action. Toward the end of the poem, Opie's black man hints at a possible escape from torture for the enslaved body. After learning about Christianity, he tries to wait patiently for freedom, yet ultimately he is not content to anticipate only a heavenly salvation:

> Yet still, at times, with fear I shrink;
> For, when with sense of injury prest,
> I burn with rage! And *then* I think
> I ne'er can *gain* that place of rest.
> (25)

Anne K. Mellor argues that the poem shows the enslaved man repressing his anger ("Am I Not a Woman," 324).[16] Yet these lines—the last ones the black man speaks in the poem—hint at a rage that persists beyond the end of the poem and prevents a Christlike turning of the other cheek ("I burn with rage!"). Given the number of slave rebellions in this period, this reference to rage may be a coded reference to insurrection. And what does the black man mean when he says that he never can gain "that place of rest"? Does he refer specifically to heaven, or something else? As discussed in chapter 3, Moses Roper fuses the idea of Christian redemption with an enslaved body that is always agentive and running away from, or out of, slavery. The black man's rage in Opie's text may denote that he can never fully embrace Christianity and might instead embrace bloody insurrection. Opie refuses to display what Moira Ferguson calls a "homogenous conceptualization of Africans as pious converts" or as "silent or silenced individuals . . . who must always remain 'under control'" (*Subject to Others*, 4). Her text portrays the opposite of the colonial discourse of enslaved, Christianized passivity, a "shadowy textual presence" (5) that includes the potential rebellion of slaves against this colonial discourse.

This distinctive diatribe against redemption, accompanied by an articulation of potential enslaved rebellion, is set off by a white man who wonders why slaves cannot work for themselves after they have performed work for the master (23). This white interrogative voice is given a quatrain on pages 21 and 23. This is not the discourse of the narrator, who speaks with more compassion. Perhaps this is the voice of someone who is not yet sure where he stands on immediate abolition—or someone who might become an abolitionist. Physical and emotional sensation, the text adumbrates, are vital to this movement into abolition, and the text attempts to transport a reader into embodied simulation, making readers "*feel*" the wrongs of slavery (4) in their bodies and psyches. Opie's text strives to coerce viewing readers of various ages toward an intersubjective apprehension of enslaved torture and into antislavery action through such embodiments of physical and mental sensation, and through independent, intelligent, particularized, interlocutory characters with whom a reader might identify.

Given Crary's notion of a "freeing up of vision" in the 1820s, as well as experiments with vision and perception by scientists such as Purkinje that established (in 1818) the subjective and physiological character of vision itself, we might conceive of Opie's text as attempting a kaleidoscopic form of seeing meant to loosen abolitionist images of enslaved torture through the use of color, movement, and an awareness of the sensory and intersubjective, embodied character of eyesight. Although the images on the broadsides discussed in chapter 1 move from text to text, they are fixed and immobile, dark and rigid in their forms and formations. But Opie's kaleidoscopic text cuts and recuts these images, shakes them, remakes them, and mobilizes them, as well as adding innovative ones that hint at an insubordinate mode of visualization and even physical rebellion against the colonial order on the part of the enslaved. The text includes visual technologies such as prosthetic and resistant viewing presences that attempt to integrate a viewer within these images and impel a reader toward defiant standpoints and actions, toward a new (perhaps virtual) community of readers based in a configuration of partnership and solidarity. The work's visual rhetoric therefore advances the technologies of the graphic illustrated book about slavery, urging that a viewer understand reading as a protocol for provoking people into modes of political action that exploit processes initiating from within their own hands, bodies, minds, and, most especially, eyes.

Jack's Back: The Sensorium of Enslaved Torture in George Bourne's
Picture of Slavery in the United States of America

Toward the end of George Bourne's long antislavery screed *Picture of Slavery in the United States of America* (1834), a word-picture gives a visceral apprehension of the torture of slavery and foreshadows the carte de visite and photograph of a formerly enslaved man named Gordon, which was used by abolitionists in the 1860s:

> The above citizen Jack had become free in divine providence; but his back was a transcendent curiosity. From his neck to his loins, it appeared in furrows like a ploughed field, and the whole quality unimpressible and hard. . . . I asked the brother, how his back could possibly have attained such an extraordinary character? His reply was, "Master . . . used to take the hickory sticks and the cow-skins; first he would whip the flesh up, then he would beat it downwards, and when he was tired, he would put on the salt, pepper, mustard and vinegar. So he followed on, till he made my back just as you see it." I inquired, "How did you get free?" His answer was uttered with great devotional sensibility. "The Lord in heaven knows how that was done; Jack could never find out; but it is safely recorded, and now Jack will have his wife and children free too." (117)

The complicated visual, cultural, and abolitionist work that Bourne sets out to do in *Picture of Slavery* is embodied by this passage. A reader can perhaps see and feel the scourging of the back of "citizen Jack," but she or he also might hear a type of resistance in the idea of Jack's escape and his determination to free his wife and children. Yet what mostly makes Jack's back a "transcendent curiosity" is that it is both a visual and a physical representation of the fact that slavery in the United States endured; by the 1830s, it too had hardened into "furrows" and "raised rows" that were resisting "feeling and softness"—any degree of human compassion. Bourne walks the line, here, as he often does in this text, between portraying the enslaved as a human being with desires for family, home, and love, and delineating the persistent sadomasochism and dehumanization of slavery that has turned this body into an abject other. Bourne often uses a storytelling mode—as in the above passage—to create narratives about particular experiences (rather than mere facts). Some theorists of empathy recently have argued that stories may lead to increases in empathy and helping behavior through the specific method of emotional transportation—when a reader becomes transported into (or lost in) a story (see Johnson, "Transportation into a Story"; and Bal and Veltkamp, "How Does

Fiction Reading"). Bourne's text sometimes falls into a factual mode in which slaves are merely brutalized and abject bodies; yet analysis of its visual rhetoric and its use of storytelling techniques demonstrates an attempt to release the bodies portrayed into resistance and activism and shift a reader's horizon of expectations toward defiant standpoints and parallel empathy with the enslaved.

Bourne (1780–1845) was an influential British-born antislavery editor, writer, and Presbyterian minister who settled in Virginia in 1804. He was a founder of the American Anti-Slavery Society, worked tirelessly at developing a U.S.-based Protestant alliance of churches, and often is credited with being the first U.S. abolitionist to argue for immediate emancipation of all U.S. slaves without compensation to owners. His controversial stance on this issue ultimately caused his expulsion from the Presbyterian Church.[17] *The Book and Slavery Irreconcilable* (1816) is Bourne's best-known (unillustrated) work, described by David Brion Davis as "the most radical abolitionist tract yet to appear in the United States—a work which attacked the complicity of the churches in the sin of slavery, which rejected the palliative of colonization, and which demanded nothing less than total and immediate emancipation" (*Problem of Slavery*, 200). Bourne's graphic illustrated book *Picture of Slavery* appears to have been moderately successful; it was printed and reprinted in the United States in 1834 and 1838 and in the United Kingdom (in Glasgow) in 1835 and 1838. It participated in the "explosion of print and visual culture" in the 1830s that "allowed slavery's critics to re-create the immediacy of both enslaved suffering and the corresponding obligation to relieve it" (Abruzzo, *Polemical Pain*, 138).

According to Julie L. Mellby, Bourne's text contains "wood engravings designed by H. A. Munson (born 1814) and G. W. Flagg (1816–1897), carved on wood by Munson" ("Picture of Slavery"). Since some illustrations are not signed, it is difficult to verify this information; what is clear is that Bourne's illustrators created images that mainly work to extend his narrative's meanings. Carol Lasser has argued that *Picture of Slavery* has a strong scopic—even voyeuristic—regime of surveillance to which it subjects enslaved bodies ("Voyeuristic Abolitionism").[18] When Bourne's work is set against some other chronicles of enslaved torture, this would at first appear to be the case. For instance, Bourne describes "women and girls" who are often "scourged in rotation, not for any real, alleged, or even pretended fault, but merely for the sake of example" (99); such examples allow the overseer "to gratify lust" (99) whenever he feels like doing so. The whippings themselves perform a violent type of penetration of female enslaved bodies: "K. the builder was awakened at a very early hour in the morning, by a piteous moaning and shrieking, which harrowed his soul. He arose and quickly dressed himself; and following the sound, at length discovered a colored woman naked to the loins, tied by the neck to the rail of a fence, and her feet similarly pinioned below; while S. was lacerating her with the cowskin or hickory rod in his hand. K. instantly commanded the brute to desist. A long and severe altercation ensued" (99). The naked and bound woman, moaning and shrieking, might fulfill some viewers' voyeuristic and sadomasochistic fantasies. This voyeuristic mode of viewing, however, may be interrupted when K. commands "the brute" (the owner) to stop the beating.

Moreover, the illustration of this whipping, and illustrations of whippings in the text in general, frustrate an attempt to read the text solely through a sexually voyeuristic mode. Instead, the illustrations and their captions inculcate a social process of viewing the bodies portrayed as political subjects with whom a reader should feel parity or empathy. For example, when a viewing reader looks at the wood engraving delineating this passage, his or her eyes perhaps first focus on the master but then are drawn upward by the print's lines (the beams of light emanating from the sun rising in the east on the right side of the print) toward the figure on the hill, who appears to be looking at the viewer, not at the spectacle of enslaved torture (see figure 2.8). A reader may look first, then, at the man with the upraised arm who surveils the master or at the master himself in the foreground, rather than at the slave being beaten. The standing figure in the background with right arm upraised recurs in a number of illustrations and sets up the visual echoes between illustrations that are a key feature of illustrated books and graphic narrative. In this particular instance, this figure, known as "K." in the text, perhaps metamorphoses the narrating persona himself, a homodiegetic narrator, who is forced to witness, and forces us to witness, this brutal beating.[19] Yet what we witness is not eroticized. The woman may be "naked to the loins" (99), but we do not see her breasts, as we did in Stedman's illustrations of women, nor is the implication that either K. or the overseer are viewing them, as is the case in some other abolitionist prints. In fact, her arms tied to the post block a view of her chest. The rising sun casts a pool of light on the master, but the woman is mostly in shadow; the light functions as a sensory diegetic image—a part of the environment or actual world being shown—but it also (in a technique that the illustrator later refines) draws attention to the inhumanity of the slaveholder's action by literally spotlighting him. A house in the backdrop of the picture perhaps alludes to the domestic sphere and to this woman's (possible) status as a wife or mother.

The overseer is dressed in black (heavy-handed symbolism for his evil role), while K. and the woman wear lighter-colored clothing. The trees and bushes that surround the sides and part of the top of the image give it an almost decorative second frame that stands in opposition to the harsher outlines of the rectangular

Flogging American Women.   Page 28,

FIGURE 2.8 "Flogging
American Women," from
George Bourne, *Picture of
American Slavery* (1834).
Wood engraving. New
York Public Library Digital
Collections.

frame but also in some ways invites a reader into the image. In a discussion of
comics, Scott McCloud theorizes that when a face is drawn as "an empty shell"
with a lack of particularity in features, it "enables us to travel in another realm"
because we project ourselves into this face and so become part of the image
(*Understanding Comics*, 36). The overall style of this naturalistic wood engraving
is not particularly delineated, and the expression on the woman's face is difficult
to read; the whipping master does not even face the viewer. It therefore seems
that readers are most likely to project themselves into the empty shell of K.; K.'s
resistance may provide a visual transport into the text and into a social model of
direct opposition to slavery. Unlike Stedman's narrator, K. is successful (after a
long argument with S.) in ending the whipping (100); moreover, he intercedes
on behalf of another woman, telling S., "Strike the girl again, and I will fell you

to the earth" (100). K. comments to S., "How would you like to see your wife and daughters, tormented as you do these women?" (101); he here rather boldly tries to use the bodies of the master's own wife and daughters to force the slaveholder into some degree of intersubjective parallel empathy.

As discussed in chapter 1, Husserl posits a theory of intersubjectivity in which a person can put himself or herself into someone else's shoes (or in this case, chains) and simulate his or her experience (in this case, enslavement) only by assuming that the world-experience of the other person in some way coincides with his or her own world-experience (*Cartesian Meditations*, 127–28). K. seems to be trying to force S. to see similarity between his own world-experience and that of the enslaved. The verbal rhetoric—the words of the caption and the narrative—disambiguates the illustration and draws out its enthymeme, or unstated argument: slavery is a crime enacted on corporealities that are intersubjectively connected with white bodies, a crime that must be stopped. The verbal rhetoric may encourage a reader to place himself or herself within the sphere of the enslaved ("how would *you* like to see *your* wife or daughter tormented?") as it attempts to drive a viewer beyond this mode of empathetic identification toward specific tailored helping actions.

Noting that punishment and torture are often objects of representation, Foucault argues that the role of the criminal in punishment is usually to reactivate "the signifying system of the code." Individual corrections must therefore guarantee "the process of redefining the individual as subject of law, through the reinforcement of the system of signs and representations that they circulate" (*Discipline and Punish*, 128). Bourne's text circulates a radically different system of signs regarding punishment, one in which the enslaved individual is neither criminalized nor a criminal, and the punishment is excessive and unjustified. Moreover, Bourne refuses to use his illustrations to coerce his viewer into passivity or acceptance of these punishments. As Foucault also notes, "The exercise of discipline presupposes a mechanism *that coerces by means of observation*; an apparatus in which the techniques that make it possible to see induce effects of power" (170–71, emphasis added). Yet Bourne's text often contains a subversive metavisual observer like K., who sees the harm of torture and resists it; in so doing, the text suggests mechanisms whereby a viewer of the illustration might specifically repudiate the effects of power on the enslaved body. Moreover, a reader who does project himself or herself into K. (as McCloud suggests) would be encouraged to raise a hand against slavery. Bourne therefore moves one step beyond the civil contract that Opie creates between the viewing reader and the viewed object; he models within his text a movement from observation of torture into resistant actions that might terminate it.

Beyond a radical metaviewing presence, Bourne's text uses captioning insurgently to undercut the opposition between the torturer and the tortured, enslaved, degraded body. The caption to this illustration—"Flogging American Women"— stands in a liminal space between the picture and the narrative proper and negotiates a realm in which the enslaved are granted a type of (at least) linguistic redress. They are not beasts of burden or breeders but "American Women." This drawing can be compared with a contemporaneous illustration that appeared on the cover of the October 1835 issue of the *Anti-slavery Record*, which is captioned "The Flogging of Females" (see figure 2.9). This caption is not as clear in intention as Bourne's, for it uses the generic term "females" rather than "American women." Moreover, "The Flogging of Females" enables scopic and voyeuristic power to reside with viewers; at least four people in the image look on this woman's torture, and a reader could complete the panopticonic structure of enslaved surveillance by looking directly at this woman's bare breasts, which face outward in the picture and are not shielded by her arms. The man in the background looks amused by the whipping, and the individuals on the right—two adults and a young child, presumably slaves forced to watch the whipping as a lesson—weep but cannot intervene. There is no suggestion of physical or psychological resistance or any contestation of the master's mode of ocular supremacy.

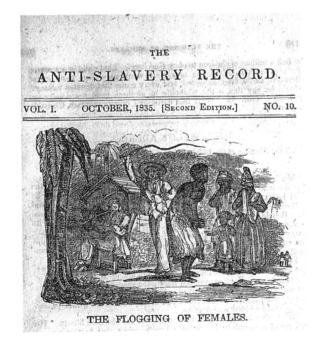

FIGURE 2.9 "The Flogging of Females," *Anti-slavery Record*, October 1835. Wood engraving. New York Public Library Digital Collections.

Bourne's text, conversely, uses captioning to delimit the optical regime of slavery and shift a reader toward identificatory practices. The captions listed in the table of contents exploit terms with strong personal or legal valences for the enslaved: "woman," "family," "girls," "citizens," and "a boy." The captions generally (as with Opie) refuse to label the enslaved as slaves; the one caption that employs this moniker ("A Slave Plantation," [94]) does not refer to slaves qua slaves but to the commercial realm of production. Thierry Groensteen contends that the content of captions is more than informational; it often functions as a type of "voiceover" that "encloses a form of speech, that of the explicit narrator (who can be the principal narrator or the delegated narrator)" (*System of Comics*, 128). In the captions, Bourne perhaps speaks to a reader most directly about his textual intentions. The captions entrench enslaved people within the body politic of the United States; this is especially evident in the captions "Exchanging Citizens for Horses" (106) and "Torturing American Citizens" (129). Enslaved men and women were not citizens with legal rights, and even states in which slavery was illegal often refused to extend to free blacks all rights associated with full legal citizenship, such as voting, serving on juries, or testifying in court (see Horton, "Weevils in the Wheat," and Gross, *What Blood Won't Tell*). Yet these captions lexically grant black enslaved bodies a status as nominal "citizens," a status they did not have by law in the world outside the text.

A caption such as "Ladies Whipping Girls" (109) linguistically blurs the binary that is supposed to separate enslaved (abject) objects from empowered (human) subjects. Like "Flogging American Women," the picture "Ladies Whipping Girls" uses visual technologies that put a surveillant lens on whites who whip their slaves, but in this instance the focus is on a woman who tortures another woman. In this drawing, the sky is almost entirely overcast with clouds, as if a storm is arriving, but the whipping white female stands in a small pool of light that might come from a break in the clouds (see figure 2.10). The black woman might be the object of the gaze, but we can make out few physical details concerning her. The white woman, conversely, is almost spotlighted. Indeed, as one reviewer from the period notes with incredulity, the lady stands in an "elegant" outfit "inflicting chastisement on a half-naked negro woman, with a horse-whip almost as large as herself, which she flourishes with Jehu-like dexterity" (*New York Spectator*, "An Atrocious Publication," 3). Randy Duncan has made a distinction in visual texts between sensory diegetic images (parts of the external world) and hermeneutic images, which reflect the author's commentary and convey "the underlying meaning of the story" ("Image Functions," 46). As examples, he uses a raincloud that appears over a character's head in a cartoon to symbolize a bad mood or a spotlight drawn in an illustration that connotes the glow someone feels when she or he is being praised. Both these items might be drawn realistically, but they do not actually exist in the world being pictured and are therefore figurative or metaphorical. The light shining on the "lady" in figure 2.10 may be a hermeneutic image, for it seems too large to come from the small break in the clouds. Duncan comments, "When a particular hermeneutic image—or some slight variation on that image—appears repeatedly, it becomes a visual motif. . . . Those images usually provide important clues to the meaning the author hopes to convey" (47). Some of the illustrations in Bourne's text employ a visual motif that directs light onto the flagellator rather than the flagellant, conveying an alternative to the scopic surveillance of the enslaved body.

Ladies Whipping Girls.   Page 109.

FIGURE 2.10 "Ladies Whipping Girls," from George Bourne, *Picture of American Slavery* (1834). Wood engraving. Courtesy of the Library Company of Philadelphia.

The image in figure 2.10 refers to text on page 105, in which a church member named Mrs. H. boasts that she is "the best hand to whip a 'wench'" in all that county. After brutally flaying enslaved women on Sunday morning, she "would sprinkle them with the usual mixture of salt, vinegar, &c., leave them fastened, exposed to the sun and flies, [and] walk to the church," where she sat "as demure as a popish nun" (105). Bourne's illustration backtracks the action in order to portray her in the act of brutally beating another woman. Her arm curves backward, and the deadly-looking whip is raised above her head so that it can rain down with force on the huddled woman. Branches or roots on the ground creep toward the white woman, as if symbolizing her engulfment in this regime of terror, and the tiny house in the background suggests just how far she has strayed from the domestic sphere, in which (in theory) she is supposed to be a force of virtue and morality. The trees and plants look wild and unkempt; they take up at least two-thirds of the diegetic space of the drawing, as if symbolizing how slavery has placed white women within savage and overgrown territory. The sexualized "anti-slavery writings of the 1830s," notes Lasser, might have shocked audiences yet also fostered "humane identification with the victims of such brutality, linking in particular white women and women of color in . . . 'the bonds of womanhood'" ("Voyeuristic Abolitionism," 93). Here, however, violent brutality indicates that the so-called bonds between women are tenuous, even fictitious.

Moreover, Bourne's text accentuates how both white men and white women are corrupted by slavery's power, as another image of enslaved torture—"Torturing American Citizens"—reveals. Examining this image without the text that surrounds it, a reader might be tempted to argue that like many other abolitionist illustrations, it makes an argument for the end of slavery precisely by visually subjugating the African American bodies it attempts to empower (see figure 2.11). My point here, however, as throughout this book, is that authors of graphic illustrated books used multiple rhetorical and visual modes (such as the picture, its caption, and the narrative itself) to redirect the viewing reader's focus and drive him or her toward a particular argument about the wrongness of slavery that often entailed empathetic understanding of the situation of the enslaved. For example, no matter how visually abject this body seems, it is still labeled by the caption, the narrative voiceover, as an " American Citizen." In the text as a whole, Bourne uses the word "citizen" over and over again to describe slaves (it is deployed at least one hundred times) and often counterposes it with terms such as "citizen man-stealer" or "citizen-thief" to erode verbal distinctions between black and white citizens. In so doing, he forwards a practice of intersubjectivity in which it may become increasingly difficult to disentangle the enslaved from the citizen proper.

Torturing American Citizens.   Page 129.

FIGURE 2.11 "Torturing
American Citizens," from
George Bourne, *Picture of
American Slavery* (1834).
Wood engraving. New
York Public Library Digital
Collections.

Crucially, the caption lexically contests a separation of the "citizen" from the
enslaved. Page duBois has noted how the practice of torture plays a role in sta-
bilizing the binary of citizen versus slave (*Torture and Truth*, 41); she argues that
the slave is a person who can be tortured legally, and the one doing the torture
is the citizen. The caption for figure 2.11 troubles such a binarism. It does not
grant full citizenship rights to the enslaved, but it configures them as cognitively
and affectively connected with citizens. Scholars have argued that citizenship in
U.S. political discourse as well as in abolitionist rhetoric could entail rights that
might fall far short of full national citizenship. Jeannine DeLombard notes, for
example, that the "few African Americans who did manage to attain recognition

as state citizens in places like New York and Massachusetts found their access to a broader national citizenship (however ill-defined) stubbornly blocked" (*Shadow of the Gallows*, 52). Bourne is aware of this, for he refers to laws of slavery being enshrined not only in "the slave-driver's code" but also "in our federal ungodly legislation" (120). Historians and legal theorists have shown that only whites were seen as being capable of attaining full citizenship rights on a federal level, and whiteness itself was a highly contentious issue (see Gross, *What Blood Won't Tell*; Haney López, "Social Construction of Race"; Jacobson, *Whiteness*). So Bourne's use of the term "citizen" in this caption does not mean that he declares blacks to be equal to whites in legal rights. Yet at least rhetorically they are not *homo sacer*, like those in Stedman's text—they are "American Citizens." Bourne subtly counters the idea that slaves are noncitizens by asserting that U.S. "civil institutions are professedly established upon their conformity with the word of God, and the fundamental principles of the social compact, as they are declared in the Bills of Rights adopted by the several states" (38). The Bill of Rights (approved in 1791) guaranteed a number of personal freedoms on a federal level, and these rights were gradually extended to the state level over time. Bourne refers, then, to a document that ultimately granted broader citizenship rights, on the federal and state levels, to many nonwhites.

Returning to the image, we can see that the visual focus of figure 2.11 is not so much the (enslaved) "American Citizen" but the (white) free citizen-torturer, who stands in the middle of the picture and is again the first visual hook to attract a reader's attention, with his upraised whip. A reader's eyes then might travel down to the (black) U.S. citizen on the ground, who is tied firmly to a tree trunk; a cat is bound tightly to the man's back. Although the enslaved man being tortured is in the foreground, it is difficult to notice these details. The torturer, on the other hand, clearly has an expression of anger on his face, and his carefully delineated clothing includes a top hat and a vest. The clarity of these details, as well as the upraised whip, tends to attract a viewer's eyes away from the figure on the ground.

The torturer stands above his victim and seems thereby to have achieved a sort of visual superiority. As Teresa Goddu comments, while the slave is "literally tied to the landscape and always embedded in it," the slaveholder has access to an "aerial view," establishing his visual and literal power as "perspectival" and panoramic ("Antislavery's Panoramic Perspective," 18). The description of this image, however, attempts to deconstruct this hierarchy, and it is therefore crucial to consider the symbiotic message achieved by the words and illustration together. The passage is narrated by a white man born in Virginia, "amid slaves" (128), who has become an ardent abolitionist:

When I was a boy . . . on a short ramble from my father's house, I encountered a neighboring farmer, who had a coloured citizen tied to a large log or a tree lying on the ground. The man was lying on his face uncovered, from his neck downwards. His driver had been lacerating him most mercilessly, until his back was one entire mass of blood and flesh cut up in pieces, which were commingled and slowly amalgamating together. To complete the tortures of his writhing victim, who could scarcely move on account of the tightness with which his hands, neck, and feet were bound to the tree, the citizen-flayer caught a large cat, and so fastened the animal, that in endeavoring to get lose, the cat's talons continually tore the slave's already gory back, until the villain's vengeance was glutted; when he released the cat, administered the usual plaster, salt, pepper, vinegar, &c., and ordered the son of anguish to resume his labor. (129–30)

A storytelling mode is blatantly deployed here, one that might move a reader into a process of embodied simulation and empathy. From the nostalgic and bucolic "when I was a boy. . . . on a short ramble," the passage segues abruptly into the gory and multisensory moral shock of the description of the torture of the "coloured citizen." A reader might feel the whip, hear the cries of the man and the cat, and see the bloody torn-up back in which "blood and flesh" are "slowly amalgamating together" (130). One can imagine the effect that this moral shock might have had on a young boy, and indeed the boy instantly becomes "the resolute and unalterable enemy of slavery, in every degree" (129). Like Opie, Bourne envisions the child as a proto-political subject who will grow into adult antislavery action and also inspire adults to become abolitionists.

Moreover, the picture of this terrible torture, rather than causing the viewing presence to freeze or turn away, as we saw with Stedman's text, compels the young boy to action—he becomes an antislavery orator. In a detailed study of the role of transformative emotions in abolition movements, Michael P. Young comments that some forms of contentious politics "present a fundamental link between transformation of the self and transformation of society, an immediate relation between the two that is not only thought but felt"; such movements, "operating on the sentiments of those they hope to influence, . . . mobilize around institutions much closer to the spheres of intimacy than the agencies of power." In such cases, "identity transformations or conversions, understood as radical and emotional alterations of the self, are constitutive of radical collective action" ("Revolution of the Soul," 105). In the above passage, we can see Bourne's narrator modeling and simulating for a reader an affective and cognitive transformation of the self that will (he hopes) lead to radical collective action. The individual discussed transmits this "eye salve"—"with which in junior life his eyes had been anointed" (128)—to Bourne, who then conveys this picture in order to propel a reader into abolitionist action. "Eye salve" refers to an ointment for the eyes, and Bourne may have had in mind the biblical passage from Revelation 3:18, "Anoint thine eyes with eye salve, that thou mayst see" or the famous hymn by John Henry Newton (1725–1807) published in 1779, "Amazing Grace," with its line "Was blind but now I see," which specifically notates how seeing the real harm of slavery—an embodied experience—can foment abolitionism. Bourne calls the narrating individual in his text a "graphical portrayer" (129)—he describes in words what the text pictures in its illustration—and his words are supposed to have the same affective result as the pictures, propelling a reading viewer toward antislavery work.

Beyond its use of affective and cognitive mechanisms for empathy within the visual and rhetorical stories of torture, Bourne's text contains a number of illustrations of slave auctions and sales that blur the binary between the viewed black, bestial object and the viewing, presumably white subject; this blurring is achieved by positioning enslaved bodies in liminal or off-center spaces, or even by omitting them from the drawing. "Selling Females by the pound" (see figure 2.12), for example, visually moves the enslaved body away from the center of focus in order to facilitate a confrontation with another metaviewing presence. This framed image places the woman being sold "by the pound" on the far left, almost out of a reader's view. A reader looks into the frame at another figure—possibly K.—and also at the back and profile views of the three men involved in this transaction (presumably the owner, the buyer, and the dealer). They each take up a large portion of the image, as do the scale and the weights, leaving just a small slice of visual space, perhaps one-eighth of the picture, for the woman. More than half the woodcut is given over to the sky and the low-lying dark clouds that seem to be massing on the horizon, which literally foreshadow rain but also may symbolize a future storm between North and South over slavery. This ominous image does not remove the enslaved woman from the structure of panopticonic surveillance, yet it does force viewers to gaze on those who are witnesses to these transactions, and witnesses to the system of slavery, yet do nothing to stop it. A viewer might again project himself or herself into the somewhat undifferentiated but appalled face of the man who looks from inside the picture out at a reader. If, following Mitchell, we see this picture as a model and constitutive stigmatism for the visual process itself, we might say that it tries to teach us to see the harm of slavery differently: it wants us to be appalled by the infernal transactions and to focus on those who perpetuate the system rather than on those who are its victims.

The incident that follows this illustration indicates once again that people must move beyond being appalled by such visual spectacles and into antislavery action. This passage tells of a northern Baptist minister who journeys through the South.

Selling Females by the pound.   Page 88.

FIGURE 2.12 "Selling Females by the pound," from George Bourne, *Picture of American Slavery* (1834). Wood engraving. New York Public Library Digital Collections.

His southern hosts have mapped out a tour for him, but he diverges from it to interview the enslaved and hear directly about their conditions. Ultimately, he becomes convinced of the horror of slavery, which he then "detail[s] . . . to his brethren in Philadelphia." "Men may travel to the south, and so far as slavery is concerned may continue in a dead sleep until they return; but wakeful and inquiring persons may *witness* in every varying occurrence, such facts as these," comments Bourne (91, emphasis added). Textual focus begins with the misery of the enslaved population but ultimately ends with the (northern) white man's movement into political and antislavery action after he has seen or witnessed such facts. Bourne recommends an active, engaged form of touring, traveling, and envisioning that will end with antislavery activism.

In addition, Bourne's text features illustrations of auctions that disrupt a textual focus on enslaved bodies as well as the politics of who is the object of the gaze and who the gazing subject. In "Auction at Richmond," for example, although the person being sold is in the center of the picture, the point of focus becomes the auctioneer himself, who stands with an upraised right arm and gavel (see figure 2.13). The enslaved man being sold is (from within the illustration) the subject of panopticonic surveillance, surrounded on all sides by (presumably white) observing viewers (other figures—presumably slaves—sit in a circle outside the bidders, with downcast eyes). But from outside the drawing, a reader's eyes are drawn

Auction at Richmond.   Page 111.

FIGURE 2.13 "Auction at Richmond," from George Bourne,
Picture of American Slavery (1834). Wood engraving.
New York Public Library Digital Collections.

upward to the auctioneer with raised hand, who recalls K. (who in figure 2.8 raises his hand to stop a beating) and the overseer in figure 2.11, who raises his right arm to whip an enslaved man. Bourne's illustrator plays with the focus of the picture, but also blurs the distinction between those who torture and those who do nothing to stop it. The double frame of the picture contains two additional, smaller frames within it—rectangular boxes within the overall rectangular box of the picture—namely, window frames to the left and right of the auctioneer. The light from these windows is a sensory diegetic image that spotlights the auctioneer and draws a viewer's attention even more emphatically to him.

According to Maurie McInnis, "Auction at Richmond" "established certain pictorial conventions that nearly twenty years later [an illustrator such as Eyre] Crowe was still using" (*Slaves Waiting for Sale*, 45). Bourne endeavors to create affective and cognitive processes for intersubjectivity and parallel empathy through the word pictures he draws of auctions. Again and again, he underscores both the humanity of the enslaved and the fact that this humanity and citizenship cannot be disentangled from that of the (white) slave owner: "The crimson auction flag announces that the blood and bones of *American citizens* are publicly to be vended! Here, half covered with rags, and loaded with chains, *human beings* are driven together in crowds, and by beings *calling themselves human*, are sold and bought" (111, emphasis added). The narrator uses affective language to exhort and compel a reader to share in the sorrows of enslaved human beings and to experience their torment: because the enslaved are described as families, husbands, wives and children who all feel "love," "woe," and "wild despair" upon separation (111), it becomes much more difficult to assume a hierarchical, panoramic, or panopticonic perspective of distant visualization. The rhetoric attempts to persuade a reader to envision or in-vision the scene—to feel the pain in his or her own flesh and to experience intersubjectivity with these individuals as he or she "draws near" (111) them.

The text pointedly contrasts the wretchedness of the spectacle of the sale of human beings with the heartlessness of the auctioneer: "From this vivid portraiture, it appears that at those auctions for slaves, all family bonds, and every relation of domestic life are severed without compunction or remorse; and the wailings of the wretched and hopeless children of despotism and savageness only furnish amusement to the obdurate flint-hearted soul-traders. Parents and children, and lovers; and associates in misery, whose cohabitation has been their only solace in privations, stripes, chains, disease, and starvation, are separated to glut the avarice, or to satiate the prodigality of the licentious slave-driver. Is he a just man?" (113). This multisensory passage—which blurs vision, sound, and feeling in a type of synesthesia—begins with a focus on the abject enslaved individual, but ends with a hard and sharp rhetorical turn to the "licentious slave-driver" in the abrupt and staccato phrase: "Is he a just man?" As in the illustrations, Bourne here strives to shift attention linguistically onto the individual creating enslavement—in this case, the slave driver. Like Opie, Bourne makes manifest that the slave driver and the enslaved are bound to each other by a common humanity—an idea that came under assault in the mid-1830s as scientists shifted from monogenesis (common descent of races) to polygenesis (separate descent of races).[20]

Interrelationship between the races, rather than biological separation or difference, is made even more patent in illustrations that feature either racial passing (such as "Tanning a Boy," in which a white boy is stained black and sold into slavery) or racial "amalgamation." For example, interconnectivity between the races is made manifest in the print "Family Amalgamation among the Menstealers" (see figure 2.14). "You put up at the Tavern of some Major or Colonel of 70 years of age; presently you are astonished to find yourself attended by a tawdrily dressed girl who appears as the tavernkeeper's daughter; as conceited, and vain, and empty as a magpie; with two or more waiters nearly or quite naked, manifestly her own brothers or sisters, only with a differently tinged skin," Bourne blandly informs his readers (91–92). The repeated use of "you" is meant to intercalate a reader into the reading experience and indeed into the story of the picture itself. If empathy is a double movement, a circular or spiraling process between a self and another in which an individual comes to understand another's pain by vicariously reflecting on his or her own pain, as Louis Agosta has suggested ("Empathy and Intersubjectivity," 43, 48), then we can see Bourne encouraging readers to open up their experiences imaginatively and produce within them a possible space for identification with the enslaved.

The picture delineates "family amalgamation," since the enslaved young black woman who waits on the table in the front of the picture is (presumably) the daughter of the man who is sitting on the left and pontificating. But both black children are meant to look similar to their (white) brother and sister. Once again, white and black bodies are intersubjectively amalgamated and blurred, a tactic that tends to increase empathy by the use of similarity and familiarity. Across numerous studies of empathetic behavior, "the most robust findings . . . are for familiarity or similarity of the subject with the object," write Stephanie Preston and Frans de Waal ("Empathy," 16). In addition, familiarity and similarity may enable the emotional expression of the subject and object to converge, leading to a movement from perception to action. If, as Ivy Wilson has noted, African Americans in visual culture often function strategically to organize spaces around centers (which whites occupy) and margins (where black figures are often placed) and delimit

Family Amalgamation among the Men-stealers.   Page 91.

FIGURE 2.14 "Family Amalgamation among the Men-stealers,"
from George Bourne, *Picture of American Slavery* (1834). Wood engraving.
New York Public Library Digital Collections.

boundaries (*Specters of Democracy*, 107–8, 125), this illustration is unusual in that it is
not clear that African Americans are the constitutive outside of the white interior
space or psyche. The illustration's architectural space seems to box the entire family
into one space, rather than leaving the mixed-race children outside what Wilson
terms the realms of social interaction (108).

Curiously, the illustration refuses to sustain any point of focus, either on the
"man-stealer" or on his white and black family. A viewer's gaze might circle the table
and circle the illustration in search of meaning. Groensteen comments that when
a reader views visual texts, the eye "slides, within the hyperframe, along the surface
of the plane of the page; it always arrives, and in a justified manner, from another
point situated within the plane" (*System of Comics*, 48). Yet this double-framed
image with its wide margins seems to frustrate a viewer's ability to arrive "in a
justified manner" from another point situated within the plane. A framed picture
on the back right wall—presumably of the family's patriarch—functions as an

ironic contrast to the present scene: it highlights how the family, which might be proud of its "pure bloodlines," has in fact become more mixed than pure. This framed picture—a picture within a picture, and so a metapicture—stands next to a large mirror, which reflects light in a blurry white patch. The mirror is also a type of metapicture, and though it does not reflect back an actual viewer's image (as a real mirror would), by carefully inserting it into the picture, Bourne's illustrator asks a reader to reflect on his or her culpability within this scene. On the far left, large embroidered screens picture churches and houses, again adding a degree of self-referentiality to this metapicture but also frustrating the eye's ability to achieve a point of focus within the illustration.

Goddu postulates that antislavery visual culture uses a panoramic perspective to convert "Northern viewers to its cause by presenting in its mirror of slavery a reflection of their own empowered subjectivity" ("Antislavery's Panoramic Perspective," 13). But how does a viewer process images such as this one, which appears to disallow a panoramic or fixed perspective and instead creates a mirroring that might be regulated by the claustrophobic private familial space of amalgamation and enslavement? The drawing alludes to technologies of vision (such as mirrors and mirroring) and of picture production (such as painting and tapestry making) to accentuate the artifice of this illustration, but also to place readers into the delimited and confining domain of the text's graphic representational space. How can readers take what Goddu calls "visual possession" (13) of an enslaved individual when they may see themselves in the picture, either mirrored back or looking back? Seizing "the slaveholder's panoptic viewpoint" (12), which would facilitate an empowered and benevolent reinforcement of the northern white readers' social position and political power, might prove difficult for them. Instead, processes of vision emanating from within the picture impel readers to enter its provenance and be altered by the visual modes and symbolic structures it deploys.

Reviews of Bourne's *Picture of Slavery* were mixed. Abolitionist publications advocated that it should be "read and prayed over, by every disciple of Christ" (*Liberator*, "Bourne's Picture" 200), while proslavery publications suggested that it was "atrocious" and "embellished with sundry wood cuts and etchings . . . representing the imagined horrors of slavery" (*New York Spectator*, "An Atrocious Publication"). Gradualist writers seemed to feel that the book lacked "sufficient authority" to prove its points and that "men who have been for many years eyewitnesses of the condition of slaves . . . [would] contradict the testimony of Mr. Bourne" about these atrocities ("Picture of Slavery," 113). Bourne's prosthetic eyes and metaviewing presences within the picture were regarded as less than reliable. Bourne seemed aware that the pictures were "loathsome" (97) and perhaps not believable—and that despite all his precautions, they might debase the individuals portrayed, whom he hoped to free, both visually and legally.

Yet because Bourne yearned to banish "the thralldom of American citizens," he remarks in the text, "However otherwise objectionable, these loathsome pictures shall be published to excite universal indignation; and then the loud demand for the death of this atrocious monster of sin and uncleanness [slavery] will be uttered in a voice of thunder" (97). Bourne imagines that the publication of "loathsome pictures" will enact clear and specific goals: the awakening of reading viewers into abolition, and the end of enslavement. Bourne's images, with their dark and roiling clouds, present an almost apocalyptic vision of slavery. Yet he holds open the possibility of a great revelation of the evil and a wondrous awakening as the "eye-salve" of his pictures unblinds readers or viewers and motivates them toward action. This diegetic space of awakening and action is generally not represented in the text or its images (with the possible exception of the conversion of the man born in Virginia into antislavery activity). Bourne instead gestures to a nondiegetic realm outside the text where the blinded will see, and the citizen-flayer will become aware of his all-too-human intersubjective connection with the citizen-slave.

Conclusion: *Slave Market of America* (1836)

In 1836, the American Anti-Slavery Society issued a broadside condemning the sale and keeping of slaves in the District of Columbia, home of the U.S. Capitol and the White House (see figure 2.15). At the top of the broadside are three contrasting scenes. On the left is an image of white men reading the Declaration of Independence, with the caption "The Land of the Free"; in the drawing on the far right, slaves are led past the Capitol by a slave overseer, with the caption "The Home of the Oppressed." Between these images is a map of Washington, D.C., onto which is superimposed the Wedgwood image of the enchained slave and an image of a fleeing enslaved man, with a poster that reads "$200 Reward." This carefully crafted broadside, part of the petition campaign of 1835–36 led by Theodore Dwight Weld, clearly shows the irony of enslavement in the very capital of the so-called Land of the Free.

Nevertheless, the careful framing of images on the page and the wide margins between them seem to affirm a visual order in which abject black bodies remain disconnected from empowered white ones.[21] Scopic focus is directed at enslaved bodies or at African Americans who are attempting to flee from slavery, yet nowhere in this image do we see the point enunciated in Opie's book that African people have a subjectivity that precedes enslavement or the blurring between

FIGURE 2.15 William Dorr, *Slave Market of America.*
American Anti-Slavery Society, 1836. Letterpress with nine
wood engravings. Library of Congress.

white and black subjectivity delineated in Bourne's text. *Slave Market of America* is a brilliant document in the way it uses visual and verbal technologies to unhinge the dominant political rhetoric of the nation—that the United States is truly the land of the free. But it stops short of forwarding the more radical viewpoints promoted by Bourne's and Opie's texts. Bourne and Opie use visual and narrative technologies to shift a viewer's horizon of expectations toward another rhetorical and pictorial imagining of the political and social relationship between enslaved black bodies and white ones. In this alternative visual rhetoric, this new civil contract between the viewer and the viewed, the margin or boundary separating the enslaved from the empowered and gazing citizen is eroded. A reader is forced to see the "colored citizen" and the "citizen-flayer" as parallel and interconnected. Both types of people are bodies of a nation that has not yet fully committed itself to the end of an order that artificially separates people into hierarchical categories of slave and master, the viewed other and the viewing subject. Both texts labor to create an order of visual rhetoric that drives readers away from spectatorship or passivity into parallel empathy, abolitionist action, and even outright revolution against slavery as a social, political, and visual formation.

Entering and Exiting the Sensorium
of Slave Torture

A Narrative of the Adventures and Escape of Moses Roper,
from American Slavery (1837, 1838) and the Visual Culture of the
Slave's Body in the Transatlantic Abolition Movement

Torture endeavors to dehumanize and render powerless its subjects. It also intends to shred human dignity and condense a person to a body in pain or even to an animal that cannot articulate its torment. As Elaine Scarry famously observed, physical pain habitually entails a "shattering of language," and a tortured individual is degraded into a state "anterior to language, to the sounds and cries a human being makes before language is learned" (*The Body in Pain*, 4). More recently, Idelber Avelar has pointed to how "torture may lead to a trauma that eventually buries the subject into silence altogether" (*Letter of Violence*, 45). Therefore, the brutalization of enslaved individuals, when represented in British and U.S. abolitionist rhetoric from the nineteenth century, presents a distinct paradox, since these bodies must be spoken of in such a way that political change might be enacted. Within this context, as numerous critics have maintained, formerly enslaved narrators struggled to script messages onto the tortured body not only of pain, but also of modes of agency and voice, to move from being contained within the corporeal and silent realm (as tortured objects that were seen and read) into the verbal and spoken one.[1]

Previous chapters examined the ways in which graphic illustrated books by white, free writers use visual rhetoric—an argument formulated through a synergistic relationship between words and pictures—to endeavor to undermine the separation often made within abolitionist visual culture between the enslaved object and the viewing subject, and to shift a reader's horizon of expectations towards intersubjectivity and empathetic identification through visual-verbal modes involving similarity, familiarity, embodied simulation, prosthetic viewing presences, and storytelling techniques. Moses Roper's *A Narrative of the Adventures and Escape of Moses Roper, from American Slavery* (1837, 1838) contains four illustrations in the 1838 version and five in its 1840 edition. It therefore is perhaps the first illustrated graphic narrative written by a former slave.[2] Because it was reviewed positively and sold well on both sides of the Atlantic for over a decade, this chapter focuses exclusively on this narrative.[3] I examine how this text's visual rhetoric scripts modes of agency and voice that a reading viewer could understand as originating within enslaved bodies themselves. For Foucault, social relations of power are not static; instead they figure forth numerous points of confrontation and foci of instability, each of which may have its own potential for "an at least temporary inversion of the power relations" (*Discipline and Punish*, 27). Roper's text dramatizes points at which the technology of power over the enslaved body breaks down, and asserts a paradigm for enslaved subjectivity that overturns the power relations the master attempted to enact. His text also provocatively blurs the boundaries between white and black bodies, and (ultimately) between white and black readers.

In the 1830s, as the historian Elizabeth Clark notes, "gruesome tribulations of the body became a staple of antislavery literature" ("Sacred Rights of the Weak," 465). This public discourse about pain and suffering at times divested these corporealties of social or political agency. Indeed, as Marcus Wood has shown through a detailed examination of images of enslaved torture, and as previous chapters have argued, visual culture often rendered enslaved African Americans as abject and silent victims. Roper's work has not received much positive critical assessment, yet a meticulous evaluation of the text's visual and verbal technologies demonstrates that it deviates from this replication of the scopic and disciplinary regime of slavery by situating torture within a larger teleological framework.[4] The narrative creates an eclectic and syncretic version of salvation that encompasses torture, spiritual transcendence of this torture through resistance and voice, and ultimately forgiveness of the master-torturer. Roper's text delicately layers patterns of Christian symbolism that invoke martyrdom and even crucifixion onto and over a resistant and active enslaved body; in so doing, it enacts a radical form of Christian salvation that involves putting one's fate in the hands of God but one's feet in the position of running away from, or out of, slavery.[5]

Roper's narrative as a whole depicts modes of agency and subjectivity that move beyond the master's system of representation. Slave narratives were, of course, written for particular purposes and audiences, and their discourse was often tightly controlled by white abolitionists. Yet Roper had a large degree of control over the successive versions of his text, adding material about his own life after slavery, deleting an "authenticating" letter from one of his sponsors, and expanding the amount of visual content. The longest version of Roper's narrative, the 1848 edition, appears to have been self-published. I contend, then, that Roper is most interested in using his visual rhetoric to depict a representation of an enslaved mode of agency. In so doing, Roper, like other slave narrators described by Sinha, creates "an authentic, original, and independent critique of slaveholding" (Sinha, *Slave's Cause*, 421) that could act as a potent antislavery document. An analysis of the narrative's rhetorical depiction of physical torment shows that the text reworks religious tropes to grant the enslaved body power over its own suffering; in so doing, it encourages a reader to enter the sensorium that was slave torture. The last part of this chapter situates the text's illustrations within transatlantic abolitionist visual culture to show how the narrative's visual rhetoric encourages readers to exit the sensorium of torture and attain an understanding of an enslaved body that was more metaphysical than physical, more transcendent and spiritual than debased. Enslaved bodies were indeed almost crucified on the "cross" of U.S. slavery, but spiritually as well as physically they arose to run again. Yet because the body that the work depicts is anybody—and indeed, any body (whether male, female, white, black, free, or enslaved)—it becomes difficult to scopically surveil and other this body, which may become enmeshed with a reader's own corporeality. This overlapping of corporealities strives to shift a reader's horizon of expectations toward a parallel mode of empathy founded on similarity and parity rather than difference and hierarchy.[6]

Textual Production of the First Antislavery Graphic Narrative

Roper's text is not discussed in detail by many scholars. It may therefore be helpful to first give some information about Roper's narrative itself and the conditions of its textual production. The main trajectory of the text is as follows: Roper, a very light-skinned slave, attempts to escape from slavery in Caswell, North Carolina, often by passing for white or Indian. He is caught and beaten. He runs away again, is beaten again, and so on. Finally, he escapes to England, where he learns to read and write, converts to Christianity, becomes a well-known abolitionist speaker, and writes his text. Not narrated in the 1838 text is his later life: Roper married a Bristol woman named Anne Stephen Price and had two children. He moved to Canada in 1844, returned to Europe several times, and finally came back to the United States sometime after 1861. At that point, he seems to have abandoned his

British wife and children and to have taken on the life of an itinerant lecturer and preacher until his death in 1891.[7]

The text that Roper wrote went through many editions, yet there is little information about the illustrations. The publisher of the 1837 and 1838 editions, listed as Darton, Harvey, and Darton, was a Quaker firm better known for publishing didactic children's books (it published Opie's *The Black Man's Lament*, as noted in chapter 2). It also published a limited number of antislavery texts for adults, in keeping with an adamant opposition to slavery. Perhaps the publisher helped Roper find an illustrator; it is clear that Roper's illustrations have a specificity that enhances and extends the meaning of the narrative. Many illustrations of slaves in newspapers and other publications were "stock"—generic images that could be placed into almost any narrative and in fact moved between narratives (see Wood, *Blind Memory*, fig. 3.8, 90). The images in Roper's narrative, on the other hand, collaborate with the narrative to fructify and expand its meanings.

As mentioned, Roper exercised increasing authorial control over successive editions of the text. In the first edition, a letter from the Reverend Thomas Price, one of Roper's British sponsors, introduces the text, but later editions eliminate it; Roper introduces the book himself. Roper thus emphasizes his authorial independence by breaking with a formal convention of fugitive slave narratives in which well-known white abolitionists typically "authorize" an African American's autobiographical account. The 1840 edition (still published by Darton, Harvey, and Darton) includes a fine sketch of Roper as the frontispiece, another introductory device that puts the text back into his own narrative voice. Moreover, when Roper self-published the text (in 1848), under the longer title *Narrative of the Adventures and Escape of Moses Roper, from American Slavery: With an Appendix, Containing a List of Places Visited by the Author in Great Britain and Ireland and the British Isles; and Other Matter*, he retained all the illustrations from the 1838 and 1840 versions, with only minor changes to them; this suggests that the illustrations were satisfactory to his sense of the text's implications. By 1848, Darton, Harvey, and Darton are not listed on the title page, but the title page does contain a reference to "Thirty-Six Thousand," which may be a notation of how many copies the narrative had sold up to this juncture. Roper had estimated in 1844 that 30,000 copies had sold. If that was the case, the narrative was still selling at the rate of about 1,500 volumes a year more than a decade after its original publication, suggesting its longevity and popularity within the antislavery movement, which may well have contributed to Roper's ability to control the placement of illustrations, distribution of the book, and revisions to the 1837 narrative text.

Entering and Exiting the Sensorium of Physical Pain

In all versions of the narrative, Roper intimates that the grave torture he endured under slavery might be unbelievable to a reader unfamiliar with the "peculiar institution." As he states in his preface to the first edition, "The general narrative, I am aware, may seem to many of my readers, and especially to those who have not been before put in possession of the actual features of this accursed system, somewhat at variance with the dictates of humanity. But the facts related here do not come before the reader unsubstantiated by collateral evidence" (xi). His narrative exhibits the visual and physical proofs against slavery—the "collateral evidence"—to make slavery visceral and sensory, even as he creates a figurative enslaved corporeality that cannot be contained within this rhetoric. In so doing, he repudiates what Scarry terms the "language-destroying" and "unmaking" or self-deconstructive aspects of torture (*The Body in Pain*, 19) in favor of a more agentive approach toward pain that attempts to "invent linguistic structures that will reach and accommodate this area of experience" (6). He repeatedly hails a reader, asking him or her to understand how his subjectivity was not unmade by torture.

In part, Roper's narrative repudiates the self-deconstructive aspects of torture by pressing them back into language and by attempting to share psychic comprehension of torture intersubjectively with a reader. After one escape attempt, for example, Roper comments, "[My master] gave me five hundred lashes on my bare back. This may appear incredible, but the marks which they left at present remain on my body, a standing testimony to the truth of this statement of his severity" (13).[8] Roper directly interpellates a reader by incorporating his or her response of (possible) incredulity; he adds that "the reader will see" that such severe tortures are of "no possible use" to his master but have as their only purpose to "degrade" him further (14). The detailed description of these early brutal floggings (tortures enacted on a body that is between the ages of thirteen and fourteen) pushes a reader to engage in a form of embodied simulation, since Roper's corporeality develops into a material witness against the cruelty of slavery. Indeed, the fact that some copies of the text contain "evidence of countless thumbs" having touched "the unsettling and defamiliarizing" images present even in Roper's first edition suggests that readers did form an embodied, emotional connection to the narrative (Walsh, "Fugitive Slave Narrative").[9] Elsewhere Roper directly encourages his readers to see and feel his bodily and psychological torment. For example, after being beaten and parted from "the *last* relative that [he] *ever saw*" (his grandmother), he remarks that "the reader must judge by what would be his own feelings, under similar circumstances" (39); he urges a reader to imagine his (or her) own mental state in such a situation in order to apprehend Roper's suffering and move toward empathetic understanding.

The narrative encourages parallel empathy and intersubjectivity by never depicting Roper as an abject victim of slavery. Instead, it delineates how he survives corporeal suffering precisely by focusing on its inability to annihilate his human sentience. The physical anguish was not the worst part of many beatings, as the text's representation of the following incident makes clear.

> Mr. Gooch had a female servant about eighteen years old, who had also been a domestic slave, and, through not being able to fulfill her task, had run away: which slave he was at this time punishing for that offence. On the third day, he chained me to this female slave, with a large chain of forty pounds weight round my neck. It was *most harrowing to my feelings thus to be chained to a young female slave, for whom I would rather have suffered one hundred lashes than she should have been thus treated*; he kept me chained to her during the week, and repeatedly flogged us both, while thus chained together. (15, emphasis added)

Roper here narrates being most aggrieved by the treatment of the other slave, which suggests that while his body was being brutalized by the torture, his psyche was not in any way being unmade by it.

Furthermore, after describing this treatment in detail, in which, like Frederick Douglass, Roper may have become both a witness and a participant in the suffering of a female slave, Roper goes on to deny that he has in fact fully described it. In another passage that foreshadows Douglass's 1845 text and Henry Bibb's of 1849 (discussed in chapter 4), Roper writes: "Words cannot describe the misery which possessed both body and mind whilst under this treatment, and which was *most dreadfully increased by the sympathy which I felt for my poor, degraded fellow-sufferer*. On the Friday morning, I entreated my master to set me free from my chains, and promised him to do the task which was given me, and more if possible" (15, emphasis added). Roper's text attempts to shift a reader's horizon of expectations away from the "standing testimony" of the slave's degraded body toward an empathetic understanding of the distress of a man for and with his fellow creature. Wood comments that "slave power . . . was an unending network of torture" that attempted to "break down the personality of the subject/victim" in order to "enforce a consciousness of disempowerment and anti-personality" (*Blind Memory*, 216). Saidiya Hartman phrases this differently when she writes that violence is central to the making of the slave—violence is an "original generative act equivalent to the statement 'I was born'" (*Scenes of Subjection*, 3). Yet a reader can see that Gooch fails to reduce Roper to a nonpersonality governed and made into a slave by torture. Indeed, in Roper's narration of these events, the torture never diminishes him to a state of subjugation. Instead, it increases a sense of empathy for his "fellow sufferer," which is crucial to retaining his idea of his own human subjectivity.

Scarry observes that "in the end the story of *physical pain* becomes as well a story about the expansive nature of human *sentience*, the felt-fact of aliveness . . . just as the story of *expressing* physical pain eventually opens into the wide frame of *invention*" (*The Body in Pain*, 22). A reader is encouraged to understand Roper's sentience and inventiveness explicitly in another passage that follows an escape:

> Mr. Gooch came, and took me back to Chester. He asked me how I got my irons off. They having been got off by a slave, I would not answer his question, for fear of getting the man punished. Upon this he put the fingers of my hands into a vice, and squeezed all my nails off. He then had my feet put on an anvil, and ordered a man to beat my toes, till he smashed some of my nails off. The marks of this treatment still remain upon me, some of my nails never having grown perfect since. He inflicted this punishment, in order to get out of me how I got my irons off, but never succeeded. After this, *he hardly knew what to do with me*; the whole stock of his cruelties seemed to be exhausted. (29–30, emphasis added)

Roper's text underscores that his body acts as testimony to the system of torture that is slavery, and he draws a reader into the sensorium of slave torture and embodied simulation. We can perhaps imaginatively feel the nails being squeezed off hands or smashed off toes, see the marks of the treatment on his body, and hear Gooch's ominous questions. Yet Roper's narration draws a reader away from the sensorium of physical pain into the realm of linguistic resistance by emphasizing that even when tortured, he refuses to divulge the name of the slave who helped him get his irons off, certainly an indication again of his empathy for others and his human spirit.

Theorists of intersubjectivity have argued that our treatment of others always involves a choice: "In every relationship, we may choose to act for the good of the other or we may distance ourselves and act according to our own wishes. We are always locked into this relation of dependence and responsibility" (Johansson, "Empathy or Intersubjectivity?," 35), a point that Roper's text seems to emphasize in his dealings with other enslaved persons as he takes responsibility for aiding and protecting them. In his recital of this event, he models how pain never obliterates his sense of himself as a sentient and moral being in control of his speech and actions and aware of how his actions can affect others, for better or worse. In so doing he may attempt to push a reader toward moral, empathetic actions or behaviors, even if such actions are painful or distressing.

Roper's text narrates his refusal to terminate his attempts to escape from Gooch. In fact, in this competition of wills between Roper and Gooch, Roper appears to prevail. After recounting repeated incidents of torture, Douglass famously comments in his *Narrative*: "You have seen how a man was made a slave; you shall see how a slave was made a man" (68). But torture never signifies that Roper's persona becomes enslaved to his master's will. Indeed, punishment here ultimately signifies a tension point between the master and the enslaved, since it does not succeed in disciplining the enslaved body. Moreover, a temporary inversion of power relations occurs when the master appears to lose control of the technology of punishment over the (enslaved) body and the social regulation that this torture is meant to maintain ("he hardly knew what to do with me; the whole stock of his cruelties seemed to be exhausted"). "Individual correction," notes Foucault, must certify "the process of redefining the individual as subject of law"; ultimately, what correction tries to restore is "the obedient subject, the individual subjected to habits, rules, orders, an authority that is exercised continually around him and upon him, and which he must allow to function automatically in him" (*Discipline and Punish*, 128–29). Roper refuses to portray himself as the obedient subject, the socially regulated enslaved body. In so doing, his narrative scripts forms of opposition to the technologies of power that the master attempts to marshal, and figuratively removes his body from the sensorium of torture.

Torture and the Transfiguration of the Religious Body

By conveying physical torture but also detailing his psychological resistance to it in modes of sentience and empathy, Roper takes charge of the torture and undercuts the passivity and dehumanization sometimes found in transatlantic abolitionist depictions of the slave's body. Moreover, the corporeality subjected to this torture is one that has been retroactively infused with a Christian spirit, a spirit that enables him to transfigure his sufferings as he moves a reader beyond the sensorium of slave torture. Hartman suggests that the re-membering or redressing of the slave's body "is an exercise of agency" directed toward an "alternative configuration of the self" (*Scenes of Subjection*, 77). The text redresses his bodily suffering by transfiguring it so that it becomes part of a conversion experience.

Many African American conversion narratives map traditional African rites of passage onto Christian conversion. More specifically, these narratives are organized around structures of separation, transition, and incorporation (Mbiti, *African*

Religions, 118–29). Keeping in mind as well that the early 1830s saw the revival of a passionate antislavery movement that tracked forms of religious revivalism closely (Clark, "Sacred Rights of the Weak," 477), we can perhaps see a syncretic version of conversion being enacted: Roper is tested, spends time alone, accepts the Christian faith, finds freedom, and then ultimately is incorporated into a (Baptist) religious community. Roper's final escape occurs after he is sold to a man named Mr. Register, who is known for his "savage character." The savage, sadistic, and multisensory experience of slave torture is clearly alluded to here: Roper is placed on "the bare back of a half-starved old horse, which he had purchased, and upon which sharp *surface* he kindly intended I should ride about eighty miles," and forced to ride twelve hours in the pouring rain (38). He thus arrives in Marianna, Florida, starved, soaked, and sore, with the threat of more beatings foremost in his mind. The narrative uses italics to point to the painful kinetic experience of the ride on the bare and "sharp *surface*" of the horse's back for a huge distance—eighty miles. But it is at this juncture, when his body is at its nadir, that he resolves to make his final escape from the sensorium of slave torture (38).

He depicts himself transfiguring and transcending the realm of slave torture via the domain of Christian salvation. During the escape attempt that follows this savage ride, Roper details an experience comparable to Peter's in Matthew 14:29–31: "And when Peter was come down out of the boat, he walked on the water, to go to Jesus. But when he saw the wind boisterous, he was afraid; and beginning to sink, he cried, saying, Lord, save me. And immediately Jesus stretched forth his hand, and caught him, and said unto him, O thou of little faith, wherefore didst thou doubt?" Like Peter, Roper crosses the water in this escape attempt and is (in part) converted by the occurrence:

> I had now to wade through another river to which I came, and which I had great difficulty in crossing, in consequence of the water overflowing the banks. . . . In the midst of the water, I passed one night upon a small island, and the next day I went through the remainder of the water. On many occasions, I was obliged to walk upon my toes, and consequently found the advantage of being six feet two inches high, (I have grown three inches since,) and at other times was obliged to swim. . . . I was, however, dreadfully frightened at the crocodiles, and most earnestly prayed that I might be kept from a watery grave, and resolved, that if again I landed, I would spend my life in the service of God. (42)

The narrative emphasizes to a reader elements of separation (the night on the island) and transition (he appears to move from being an unbeliever to a believer who will "spend [his] life in the service of God"). The text depicts Roper walking in, rather than on, the water, and like Peter, Roper's persona is afraid until he is comforted by the thought of God. Roper is not converted, however, until he attends a Baptist meeting, discovers how to read the Bible, and memorizes "by heart the whole of the last chapter of Matthew" (47). The last chapter of Matthew concerns Christ's arising from the dead and preaching to his eleven disciples to undertake the role of baptism and salvation of other men. In case readers miss this strand of imagery, the text includes a specific allusion to this passage in order to foreshadow his union with the Baptist denomination. Roper ultimately joins the congregation of Dr. Cox, a Baptist, and is integrated into this community (50).

In the representation of the tortured slave's body depicted with particularized specificity in the first part of the narrative, it appears that Roper's faith was retroactively infused into this specific corporeality as a technique to amend the breach between its status as a tortured bestial object and his subjectivity as an empowered and agentive Christian subject. He daringly places slaves in the religious paradigms customarily reserved for white disciples of Christ. Like Paul, they experience a symbolic death but are rejuvenated in Christian faith, or like ex-slaves who described themselves as being "killed dead and made alive in Christ Jesus" ("Autobiography I," 40), they endure phenomena that parallel those of Jesus Christ and his disciples as well as other saints and martyrs.[10] The text encourages his readers to see how his subjectivity becomes reborn within the Christian redemptive body of a community of believers, all of whom are "of one flesh" (50). But unlike Stowe's Uncle Tom (discussed in chapter 5), Roper's religion never makes him passive; in fact, it enables his resistance. He is not the obedient subject of the law that the slave regime endeavors to enact through corporeal punishment and the social regulation of the enslaved body. Instead he scripts a new form of subjectivity for himself outside this domain—a subjectivity as a Christian believer with which a Christian reader might readily empathize. He legitimates his narrative voice by speaking from a position of authorization within a Christian community. Moreover, and most significantly, it is from within this social dominion that he retroactively fashions the text, remending his tortured corporeality so that it is whole and unbroken by torture.

Transfiguring the Illustrated Slave Body

Transfiguration and transcendence of torture in favor of redemptive incorporation into a Christian subjectivity can also be discerned in the text's illustrations, which visually echo the words of the text. Roper's 1837 text and later editions are accompanied by anonymous wood engravings. The first text—the 1837 British edition—contains only two illustrations (and one is very plain); the 1838 and 1839 British editions have four detailed illustrations; and in 1840 a fifth illustration—a frontispiece of Roper—was added. These illustrations elevate the torture of slaves out of the realm of the suffering of animals, as it was sometimes depicted in this epoch, and into the sphere of religious subjectivity.[11] In case nineteenth-century readers did not catch the visual overtones of the illustrations, the text makes abundantly clear through its verbal rhetoric that the illustrations are intended to be read as religious iconography. Because three of the five images use similar layouts —stark vertical and horizontal axes evocative of crucifixes—they create "the relational play of a plurality of interdependent images" (Groensteen, *System of Comics*, 17) crucial to a system of graphic narrative.

The first figure in the 1837 edition represents an object fraught with metaphorical significance, a torture collar designed to keep slaves from running away (see figure 3.1). But it is depicted in a flat and one-dimensional way. Without the words of explanation in the text, it would be difficult to comprehend what this object denotes. Following Scarry, it is evident that the tools of torture here subsume and obliterate the selfhood of the tortured victim. The representation of torture may engage the viewer intellectually ("What is that?"), but it does not evoke anything like a sensory apprehension of torture, nor does it seem to create a diegetic moment in which a reader might enter the text.

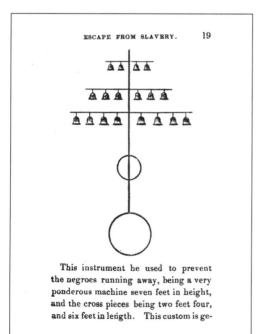

ESCAPE FROM SLAVERY.   19

This instrument he used to prevent the negroes running away, being a very ponderous machine seven feet in height, and the cross pieces being two feet four, and six feet in length. This custom is ge-

FIGURE 3.1 Torture collar, illustration from Moses Roper, *A Narrative of the Adventures and Escape of Moses Roper, from American Slavery* (1837), 19. Wood engraving. Google Books.

In the 1838 British edition and later ones, however, this image is replaced by one that fleshes out the prior illustration by depicting a woman wearing this type of collar (see figure 3.2). Graphic narrative theory argues that the placement of an image on a page, in relationship to text, is as crucial as its content; moreover, the style of lettering of captions, the framing of an image, and its position in relationship to other text are also elements that create meaning. So it is first important to note that like the illustrations in Opie's text, the image is on the same page as the narrative proper. Moreover, the caption—absent from the 1837 text—is centered and neatly balanced with the text above it, which gives the figure a certain kind of harmony. The illustrator thus takes advantage of emerging visual technologies and techniques, which would certainly draw readerly interest to the page. Second, as an image with no formal picture frame but text above it and a caption below it, the illustration segues almost seamlessly between the graphic and the rhetorical levels, and also pulls a reader into the text; as Maurice Samuels notes, unframed artworks tend to "reach out of the text and out to the viewer, who finds herself drawn in, bodily, to the picture" ("Illustrated History Book," 244). The illustration perhaps introduces a pause as a reader tries to understand how the device might function as an "instrument of torture" (18), for the drawing seems somewhat innocuous. And finally, in the passage above the drawing, Roper's narrative has mainly been recounting the torture of a man, yet here is a new and unexplained woman, as the caption boldly proclaims: "A woman with iron horns and bells on, to keep her from running away." Both in the illustration for the caption and in its later description, Roper's text (like those of Opie and Bourne) avoids the dehumanization of language associated with the term "slave," calling this person simply "a woman" (18) or "a young girl that had run away with the above machine on her" (19).

To understand who this woman is and how she is being tortured, a reader must move his or her eyes to the right-hand page and read more than half of it (19). This layout creates both an actual and a symbolic gap: physically, a reader has to read halfway down the next page to get any information about the image, and he or she has to mentally connect the somewhat benign-looking image on page 18 with the torture described on page 19. A reader may have to shift his or her vision back and forth between the two pages, and between the image and its explanation, in order to process the text's meaning, activating semantic systems of the right and left hemispheres of the brain so that they work together to produce a unified comprehension. Because a reader's eyes and brain have to work here to make the pictures and the narrative connect with each other, he or she may more fully enter the diegetic moment described and may feel more empathy. As David Kidd and

18   ROPER'S ESCAPE

the time of his death. Another case, was that of a slave named Peter, who, for not doing his task, he flogged nearly to death, and afterwards pulled out his pistol to shoot him, but his (Mr. Gooch's) daughter snatched the pistol from his hand. Another mode of punishment which this man adopted was, that of using iron horns, with bells, attached to the back of the slave's neck. The following, is the instrument of torture:

A WOMAN WITH IRON HORNS AND BELLS ON, TO KEEP HER FROM RUNNING AWAY.

FIGURE 3.2 "A Woman with Iron Horns and Bells On, to Keep Her From Running Away," illustration from Moses Roper, *A Narrative of the Adventures and Escape* (1838 British ed.), 18. Wood engraving. Google Books.

Emanuele Castano have hypothesized, complex, writerly narratives may mean that an individual's ability to construct a multifaceted representation of another's world (known as "theory of mind") is enhanced ("Reading Literary Fiction," 380).

Readerly intersubjectivity may be enhanced by the fact that this is explicitly not an illustration of an objectified, abject torture victim. Pain, notes Scarry, can obliterate "the contents of consciousness" (*The Body in Pain*, 54), and "torture aspires to the totality of pain" (55). Yet in this illustration, the woman manifests a poise and dignity connoting that the torture has not invaded the entirety of her consciousness. Moreover, the balanced placement of the caption below the text neatens the image on the page, perhaps echoing how the woman neatens the space in front of her with what seems to be a mop. The woman in Roper's text is a figure of calmness despite the outlandish accoutrement with which she is saddled. As Wood has argued, "Any object, every object—bath, chair, bed, sheet, fire, wall, floor, table, spoon—can become a weapon of torture" (*Blind Memory*, 280), and in this illustration we can observe how something as simple as small bells (which often signify joy or pleasure) and wood (which can be employed to keep a home warm) are used to torturous ends. Of course, bells are sometimes put onto animals to notify owners of their whereabouts, so we may here visualize the attempt to break this woman into a subhuman entity through this elaborate headpiece. Yet the calmness of this image—and its close connection with religious iconography—emphasizes not animalization but dignity as she quietly completes her task. It is crucial as well that in this illustration the object of torture—the slave collar—does not obliterate the slave body, as it does in some depictions of slave collars that cover the face or head of the wearer (see chapter 1).

In a brief analysis of this image, Wood remarks that the slave collar is "difficult to read" and that the woman is "drawn small and featureless" with her face "'blacked out'" (*Blind Memory*, 221). This is certainly true, and we cannot tell what this woman is looking at or read an expression on her dark visage. But the narrative text completes the argument that the visual rhetoric as a whole forwards, shifting a reader's horizon of expectations away from viewing this woman merely as a degraded torture victim. In fact, Roper's narrative provides the words with which to understand this woman's character and her insubordinate response to torture:

> Another mode of punishment which this man adopted, was that of using iron horns, with bells, attached to the back of the slave's neck. . . . This instrument he used to prevent the negroes running away, being a very ponderous machine, several feet in height, and the cross pieces being two feet[,] four, and six feet in length. . . . One morning I came up to a man . . . who had caught a young girl that had run away with the above machine on her. She had proceeded four miles from her station, with the intention of getting into the hands of a more humane master. (18–19)

It appears that the torture is unsuccessful: the woman runs *four miles while* bearing a "ponderous machine," a cross that is over six feet in length. Mario Klarer comments that in much British abolitionist visual rhetoric and discourse, images of the torture of enslaved women freeze narration and action ("Humanitarian Pornography," 569, 566), yet we see that this is not the case here: the torture in fact rhetorically produces more action (the flight).

Keeping in mind that visual rhetoric functions through a symbiotic relationship between words and pictures, we might say that when they are read together here, it becomes clear that the woman's poise in figure 3.2 is a type of ruse. She performs a role as a socially regulated and punished subject who has incorporated the automatic functioning of punitive power within her psyche, yet she performs this role just long enough to obtain the chance to run away, indicating that the functioning of power within her psyche is not in fact automatic. Torture is again figured as a point of confrontation and instability rather than as a source of power for the master. The visual rhetoric as a whole shifts a reader's horizon of expectation toward an understanding of an enslaved mode of agency and resistance rather than of passivity and abjection.

Furthermore, by using the words "cross pieces" and "station" in the above description, Roper's narrative verbally alludes to the cross of Jesus, as he does in the ironic and punning phrase, "with the intention of getting into the hands of a more humane master." A more humane master might be God or Jesus. That the cross the woman bears resembles a real crucifix, such as the Greek Orthodox crucifix, which usually includes two additional crossbars, adds to the religious iconography advanced in these images. The distress of this woman under the heavy cross she shoulders is not, of course, meant to displace that of Christ—her suffering parallels Christ's and figures it forth, without the woman becoming crucified. Yet her torment will be revoked only when slaveholders themselves discover a more humane master (God). By designating this woman as a type of active (and running) Christ figure being tortured on the "cross" of U.S. slavery, the text boldly refashions the dominant visual rhetoric through which slavery was conceptualized.

A comparison with drawings of slave collars depicted in this same year in other abolitionist documents further clarifies the radicalism of this first illustration in Roper's text. The front page of the April 1838 issue of the *American Anti-Slavery Almanac* includes an illustration of a man who commits suicide while trapped within a heavy slave collar of bells (see figure 3.3). This wood engraving delineates an incident in Charles Ball's popular, albeit copiously edited, *Slavery in the United States: A Narrative of the Life and Adventures of Charles Ball* (first published in 1836). It is imperative to observe, however, that Ball's 1836 and 1837 editions did not contain illustrations, as the caption on this drawing seems to imply. The abolitionist press seized on a scene of utter pathos, darkness, and despair for its graphic representation of slavery rather than on, for example, the many successful escape attempts that Ball describes. The slave Paul is granted no humanity by this gloomy image, and his only assertion of (mute) resistance seems to manifest in the one act that he can control: suicide. The caption in fact speaks for and about him: "The slave Paul . . . finally hung himself, that he might not again fall into the hands of his tormentor." Yet even in death Paul's body does not escape brutalization, because buzzards appear to be eating his eyes and tearing his flesh. He is also "the slave Paul," rather than a human subject with whom a reader might be encouraged

FIGURE 3.3 *American Anti-Slavery Almanac*, April 1838. Wood engraving.
Courtesy of the Samuel J. May Antislavery Collection, Cornell University.

to feel parallel empathy. Paul does not appear to share what Husserl terms, in his theory of intersubjectivity, the world-experience (*Cartesian Meditations*, 127–28) of the viewing reader.

As is evident from this illustration of the "slave Paul," the image of the woman wearing the slave collar (fig. 3.2) enters into a contemporaneous abolitionist visual context in which enslaved bodies were frequently rendered as silent and abject, passive objects to be read rather than subjects who might manipulate modes of speaking or viewing. This was particularly the case with women's bodies, whose torture (as previously discussed) was sometimes viewed as erotic and sensual (Klarer, "Humanitarian Pornography," 559). It needs to be reemphasized that even staunch advocates of abolition at times engaged in a pornographic and defamiliarizing treatment of women slaves that rendered them as silent, passive, naked, primitive bodies (see figure 3.4; color image 9). This print, attributed to Isaac Cruikshank (father of the artists George and Robert Cruikshank), illustrates an infamous incident of the torture and death of a fifteen-year-old girl on board a slave ship owned by Captain John Kimber. William Wilberforce described the events in an address to the House of Commons on April 2, 1792. Kimber was tried and acquitted, but the incident sparked numerous visual and verbal responses (Klarer, "Humanitarian Pornography," 564). In the illustration, we see not only the tortured

naked woman, but also three other naked women who sit in the background, looking on, and who even appear to be laughing at the shy virgin's modesty and pain.
At least five people in the picture stare at the woman, and the implication is that
they are scrutinizing her scantily clothed genitalia. A reader looking at the picture
perhaps focuses on her naked buttocks or protruding nipple, closing the panopticonic structure of pornographic slave surveillance. The men, on the other hand,
are all fully and elaborately dressed. While the illustration is meant to protest the
treatment of this woman, it replicates familiar binaries common in much British
and U.S. visual rhetoric concerning slavery. The woman's naked and tortured body
clearly becomes the focal point for a viewer, the center of a system of surveillance
and torture, and a reader is implicated in this structure, since she or he must look
directly onto the unmediated naked spectacle of slave brutalization.[12] The woman
herself is portrayed as a mute cipher that silently reflects back the coercive effects
of the master's power on the subjugated body.

FIGURE 3.4 Isaac Cruikshank (attributed), *The Abolition of the Slave Trade. Or the
inhumanity of dealers in human flesh exemplified in Capt. Kimber* (London: S. W. Fores,
April 10, 1792). Etching; hand-colored in some versions. Library of Congress.

The illustrations in Roper's text of enslaved men and women, on the other hand, encourage viewers to read themselves into paralleled bodies that are not unmade by torture. In figure 3.5, Roper is tortured. Again we have an image that lacks a formal picture frame; the narrative text therefore flows easily into the image itself. The caption, however, appears unbalanced, being half as large on the page (four lines) as the narrative proper (eight lines). It focuses mostly on the actions of Gooch, his sons, and his son-in-law rather than on Roper. Furthermore, the action of the image and the caption do not quite correspond. There is a temporal gap: the caption insists that each of the men gave Roper fifty lashes (for a total of two hundred) "at this time" (45), yet the illustration shows Roper before the flogging begins. The caption paradoxically insists on Roper's status as "the author," even though at this juncture in the narrative he has not escaped nor attained literacy. Such temporal disjunctions might be said to haunt many slave narratives, wherein the author appears simultaneously in past, present, and future manifestations of identity (the past-tense self who was tortured, the present-tense subject who is remembering it, and the future-tense individual who will write about it).

Perhaps more importantly, in figure 3.5 a strong vertical and horizontal axis suggestive of a crucifix is again present. For less religiously minded readers who might miss the visual structure that the image invokes, the passage recounting this torture specifically alludes to Christ's suffering on the cross:

> After dinner he took me to a log-house, stripped me quite naked, fastened a rail up very high, tied my hands to the rail, fastened my feet together, put a rail between my feet, and stood on one end of it to hold me down; the two sons then gave me fifty lashes each, the son-in-law another fifty, and Mr. Gooch himself fifty more. When I called for water, they brought a pail-full and threw it over my back ploughed up by the lashes. After this, they took me to the blacksmith's shop, got *two large bars of iron,* which they bent round my feet, each bar *weighing twenty pounds,* and put a heavy log-chain on my neck. (45–46)

Like Christ, Roper asks for water, is beaten, and is weighed down by a heavy burden. And yet Roper, too, arises, escaping from this torture to run away once more. The rhetoric again engages embodied simulation, since a reading viewer might imaginatively feel the weight of *"two large bars of iron"* (and the text's italics graphically help us apprehend this), experience the shock of cold water on a "back ploughed up by the lashes," or hear the call for water. The interaction between text and picture draws readers into the sensorium of slave torture, yet narrative language is ultimately used to iconographize and regulate violence, turning the physical torment into a spiritual or metaphysical matter that transcends the sensorium.

FROM SLAVERY.   45

took me to a log-house, stripped me quite naked, fastened a rail up very high, tied my hands to the rail, fastened my feet together, put a rail between my feet, and stood on one end of it to hold it down; the two sons then gave me fifty lashes each, the son-in-law another fifty, and Mr. Gooch himself, fifty more.

MR. GOOCH STRIPPING THE AUTHOR TO FLOG HIM. HIS TWO SONS AND SON-IN-LAW PRESENT. THEY, AT THIS TIME, GAVE HIM FIFTY LASHES EACH.

FIGURE 3.5
"Mr. Gooch Stripping the Author to Flog Him," illustration from Moses Roper, *A Narrative of the Adventures and Escape* (1838 British ed.), 45. Wood engraving. Google Books.

For example, Roper's text describes not the pain but the linguistic act of calling for water, which resonates with Christ's plea for water on the cross. Hartman reminds us that "the crimes of slavery are not only witnessed but staged" (*Scenes of Subjection*, 17), and in this passage we can perceive Roper's restaging of his torture in a way that configures his body as resistant, verbal, and agentive as well as more than a mere corporeal form onto which the master inscribes meaning.

As mentioned, the illustration represents Roper's figure in a state before torture. Furthermore, although he is being stripped, very little of his naked body is on view—the master's own body blocks this, in effect short-circuiting the pornographic gaze seen in illustrations in Stedman's text (chapter 1, figures 1.2–1.6) and in the one by Cruikshank (see figure 3.4). In figure 3.5, the features of Roper's face are clear, and because his face is centered within the top half of the frame and almost "pointed to" by the horizontal line of the top crosspiece and by the circle of the master's white hat, which mirrors the circle of Roper's white face, Roper's visage seems to become what Wood would call a "compositional hook" of the woodcut (*Blind Memory*, 231). By this structuring, a balance is struck between the implements of torture (the wood pieces and the whip) and the tortured subject. The compositional lines of the woodcut as a whole point upward, in the strong shape of an apex, and Roper's gaze is the highest human focus in the picture. A viewer's eyes are drawn automatically, and first, to his face, and then upward, even before contemplating the figures around him and the implements with which he will be tortured. The apex-like top border of the woodcut, with Roper's face outlined and elevated, highlights Roper's Christlike ability to transcend the torture and rise literally and figuratively above his torturers. It might also forward a process of parallel empathy, since the viewing reader is not allowed to look down onto the viewed object, but must look up to Roper's gaze, which is drawn well above the horizon line of the picture and so pulls a reader's glance toward the top of the drawing.

Moreover, because his features mirror to some degree those of the torturer (and in particular, those of the man who stands to his left), the illustration implies that the tortured body could be anyone—white or black, free or enslaved. And indeed because Roper could and did "pass" for white and because he appears white in this illustration, the notion of a white onlooker voyeuristically gazing upon a black and tortured body may also be short-circuited. In a discussion of W. E. B. Du Bois, Shawn Michelle Smith comments that when the "authorized, surveillant position of a white spectator" is troubled, a momentary recognition or identification "between viewer and viewed" may occur (*Photography on the Color Line*, 142); in short, the distinction between a viewing (white) spectator and a viewed racial object might collapse. A reading viewer of any race is incited to enter the text in this diegetic moment. As noted previously, McCloud contends that physical non-particularity encourages a viewer's projection into an illustration and can function as a "vacuum into which our identity and awareness are pulled" (*Understanding Comics*, 36). Because Roper's visage is drawn with little facial specificity, the illustration may encourage a reader to identify intersubjectively with Roper's persona, project himself or herself into the illustration in a mode of parallel empathy, and move beyond the surveillant position of hierarchical spectator.

The inventiveness of the rhetorical and visual technologies developed within Roper's text becomes clearer from a brief comparison with a sample of images in

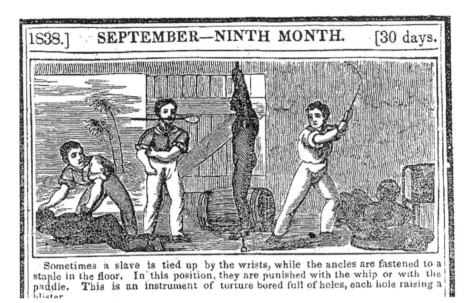

FIGURE 3.6 *American Anti-Slavery Almanac*, September 1838.
Wood engraving of slave torture. Courtesy of the Samuel J. May
Antislavery Collection, Cornell University.

abolitionist depictions of torture in this period. In figure 3.6, for example (another image from the *American Anti-Slavery Almanac* in 1838), the nude slave is barely recognizable as a human being—he looks more like a piece of meat being smoked than a man. The two slaves on the ground, one prone and one supine, appear to be powerless. The caption again speaks for the tortured, debased individual: "Sometimes a slave is tied up by the wrists, while the ancles are fastened to a staple in the floor." Of course, this comparison is not meant to deny that such abolitionist images engaged in effective cultural work. But at what cost? Such illustrations replicate the notion of slave abasement and make the slave the center of panopticonic surveillance as a reader and three white onlookers gaze on the slave body. A viewer may keep a safe distance from identification with the dark form being surveilled and tortured in such a brutal and dehumanizing manner.

The visual rhetoric of Roper's text is designed to transfigure such renditions of passive, objectified, suffering, primitive enslaved individuals common in British and U.S. visual rhetoric throughout the first half of the nineteenth century, as well as to encourage a reader's intersubjective projection into the diegetic universe of the illustrated narrative through a process of parallel empathy. The text's visual and rhetorical configurations grant enslaved corporeality a mode of agency—the agency of religious saints or disciples who use the testing of their body to demonstrate their mastery and transcendence of the body itself. But what is striking as well is that in the most detailed illustrations in Roper's text, the people being tortured often lack racial or physical particularity—they can resemble anyone, even the master. Roper's illustrator seems to realize that the exposure of torture might yield pleasure or indifference, and the wording of the text and its illustrations deliberately impair this process through a certain level of abstraction about whose body, precisely, is being beaten.

Thus, the narrative insistently fosters a new iconography for the reading of the slave's body and, perhaps more importantly, its correlation with other types of corporeality. In figure 3.7, Roper is strung up on a cross-like structure before being buried (or "shut") in a box. Here the almost abstract illustration virtually takes over the page and its narrative text (only a little over three lines of wording are on the page), and the caption ("A cotton screw") is not all that enlightening, since no

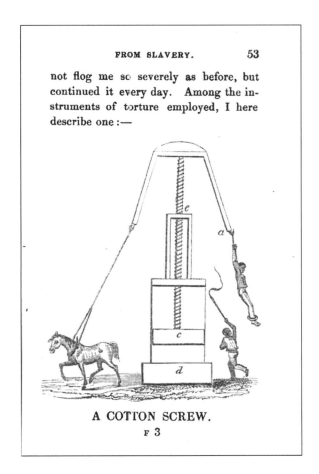

FROM SLAVERY. 53

not flog me so severely as before, but continued it every day. Among the instruments of torture employed, I here describe one :—

A COTTON SCREW.

F 3

FIGURE 3.7 "A Cotton Screw," illustration from Moses Roper, *A Narrative of the Adventures and Escape* (1838 British ed.), 53. Wood engraving. Google Books.

cotton appears to be present and one is hard pressed to understand why a body would be hanging from a cotton screw, in any case. Moreover, the cotton screw, or cotton press, seems to have been remodeled for the purpose of this illustration— actual cotton presses from this time were triangular-shaped, whereas Roper's is more rectangular, so a different structure is being invoked.[13]

Like the other wood engravings in the narrative, the illustration is composed of stark horizontal and vertical lines suggestive of a crucifix, establishing a relational interdependency of images. Should readers fail to notice the connection with religious iconography, Roper's phrasing once more prompts them to formulate this association:

> Among the instruments of torture employed, I here describe one. . . . This is a machine used for packing and pressing cotton. By it he hung me up by the hands at letter a, a horse, and at times, a man moving round the screw e, and carrying it up and down, and pressing the block c into a box d, into which the cotton is put. At this time he hung me up for a quarter of an hour. I was carried up ten feet from the ground, when Mr. Gooch asked me if I was tired? He then let me rest for five minutes, then carried me round again, after which, he let me down and put me into the box d, and shut me down in it for about ten minutes. (53–54)

Like Christ's tormentors, Roper's persecutors shackle him to a cross-like structure and then beat and taunt him before burying him within a tomb-like enclosure. Of course, Roper is secreted in the box for only ten minutes, unlike Christ, who was buried for three days. Roper envisions the slave as a type of Christ figure—an emblem or perhaps emissary of Christ—but not as Christ himself.[14] The narrative provocatively associates the enslaved body with the body of Christ, yet leaves it to the religiously minded reader to make this linkage explicit.

For less religious readers, the text's illustration and descriptions still enable crucial patterns of symbolism to emerge that facilitate intersubjectivity. In figure 3.7, the man "moving round the screw" is not the master, yet the text cleverly obfuscates this fact by repeated use of an ambiguous "he" in this passage, which conflates the driver with the master ("he hung me up . . . He then let me rest . . . He let me down"). By this rhetorical device, the master is equated with the (black) slave driver, who cannot be differentiated from the torturer or victim. It is also imperative to notice that the man beating the slave cannot be substantively distinguished from the slave—the slave and his torturer are everyman forms, almost interchangeable. The panopticonic structure of slave torture is partially undermined by the visual and rhetorical technologies employed here, in which linguistically and imagistically there is a blurring of bodies.

The torture is repetitive and circular (the horse literally moves in a circle), and it is enacted on the body again and again. Hartman notes that "redress is itself an articulation of loss and a longing for remedy and reparation," which may account for "the constancy of [its] repetition" (*Scenes of Subjection*, 77). Redress marks its own failures to contain the violence marked onto the slave body. Perhaps the repetitive quality of the torture in this image and in the text as a whole can be read as insistences that neither words nor pictures adequately explicate or control this violence. But it is crucial once again for Roper's text to substantiate that torture does not function as it is supposed to. After the whipping depicted in figure 3.7, Roper comments: "I stayed with him several months, and did my work very well. It was about the beginning of 1832, when he took off my irons, and being in dread of him, he having threatened me with more punishment, I attempted again to escape from him" (54–55). Wood reads this passage as establishing that the slave becomes "a martyr to his own failure" (*Blind Memory*, 260), yet Roper insinuates that performing his work "very well" and appearing to be defeated by the torture is simply a ruse to get his irons off so that he can attempt "again to escape." Roper depicts himself pretending to be defeated, only to rise again. He refuses to incorporate the automatic functioning of the master's social regulation of the enslaved body into his own corporeality.

Roper's text enunciates a desire for freedom that is never obliterated, signifying an obdurate humanity that cannot be decimated by torture and that is portrayed as posing a threat to the master's own humanity through its assertion of an alternative figuration of the enslaved body. Hartman contends that the slave was "considered a subject only in so far as he was criminalized, wounded body or mortified flesh" (*Scenes of Subjection*, 94). Roper's tortured body is something more than a degraded scaffold on which the torturer founds his own subjectivity. Roper audaciously portrays his body as an instrument for the working of an enslaved will to power as well as an affective textual feature that forwards modes of religious symbolism. Regarding the torturers' subjectivity, Gikandi argues: "As modern subjects, slave masters understood the threat enslavement posed to their own ideas of selfhood. They thus sought to elevate the act of domination to a symbolic level. . . . In slave ships and plantations, so-called medieval forms of punishment that had ostensibly disappeared from European courts were promoted as instruments of exorcizing the idea of freedom out of the slave" (*Slavery and the Culture of Taste*, 89). The detailed description of Gooch's repeated acts of torture indicate that he was testing whether the torture could indeed set him, a free white subject, apart from the enslaved. Yet Roper's text invests the torture with an alternative teleology in which Roper's body is allied with that of a Christian who is tested, tormented, and almost crucified, yet whose spirit remains intact. In so doing, the text attempts to overturn Gooch's imaging of the slave as only a criminalized, wounded body and to present an alternative configuration of identity that might shift a reader's horizon of expectations toward an intersubjective correlation with the viewed slave.

Furthermore, the illustrations in the narrative shift a reader's horizon of expectation toward a configuration of enslaved agency by never showing a naked body stripped of its resistance and power. Each illustration skillfully ruptures the disjunction between a passive, savage object of the gaze who is tortured and enslaved, and an active, free subject who gazes and tortures. Cassandra Jackson has noted that the wounding of black men's bodies in particular "makes visible the liminal space that black men occupy in the culture" as they teeter on the boundary between identity positions such as black-white, masculine-feminine, and abled-disabled (*Violence, Visual Culture,* 4). It is therefore significant that the gaping, bloody wounds seen in other illustrations (such as those in Stedman's text) are absent from the drawings in this narrative. The illustrations in Roper's narrative affirm the text's dominant rhetorical position regarding the enslaved body: it neither lacks agency, nor can it be precisely distinguished from the body of a viewing reader. The spectacular moment is therefore used in tandem with textual rhetoric to produce an argument about modes of enslaved agency and bodily integrity.

Textual illustrations often mirror words from the text quite precisely, and in so doing forward the notion that the enslaved can sometimes craft his or her own social destiny and futurity. For example, an illustration present in the 1838 British edition (but not present in the 1837 edition) closely delineates these lines from the text: "They then called upon me to stop, more than three times, and I not doing so, they fired after me, but the pistol only snapped. This is according to law; after three calls, they may shoot a run-a-way slave" (42–43; see figure 3.8). The caption condenses this action and puts the spotlight on Mr. Anderson's failure to retake "the Author": "Mr. Anderson attempting to shoot the author, after telling him to stop three times, according to the law" (43). The picture itself is filled with speed and energy, and Roper's figure personifies heroism and strength as he exits it, stage left. There is absolutely nothing in the center of this picture except for dark woods; no slave, then, is caught in a web of surveillance. For Western readers who read from left to right, pictures that track this type of movement are natural, and their eyes would likely follow Roper's movement off stage and out of the picture—and they might imagine the space of freedom that Roper (eventually) moves into, which in this particular illustration is a nondiegetic space outside the drawing that can only be envisioned by a reader. Once again, a certain degree of facial nonparticularity may encourage a reader to project himself or herself into the diegetic world and achieve intersubjectivity with the central character, Roper.

FROM SLAVERY. 43

then called upon me to stop, more than three times, and I not doing so, they fired after me, but the pistol only snapped.

MR. ANDERSON ATTEMPTING TO SHOOT THE AUTHOR, AFTER TELLING HIM TO STOP THREE TIMES, ACCORDING TO THE LAW.

This is according to law; after three calls, they may shoot a run-a-way slave. Soon after, the one on the horse came up with me, and, catching hold of the bridle of my horse, pushed the pistol to my side, the other soon came up; and, breaking off several stout branches from the trees,

FIGURE 3.8 "Mr. Anderson Attempting to Shoot the Author," illustration from Moses Roper, *A Narrative of the Adventures and Escape* (1838 British ed.), 43. Wood engraving. Google Books.

One evident implication of the drawings in Roper's text is that the enslaved body is the equivalent of other bodies: it too suffers, can be eradicated, and can exonerate. The illustrations are crucial to this process of promoting an intersubjective projection of a reader into the diegetic world of the text. Wood argues that "it may be a shying away from, or an inability to deal with, the universality of this polluting horror (and *this* is the memory of slavery) which finally lies behind the Western obsession with representing the memory of slave torture through objects" (*Blind Memory*, 280). In other words, objects control the horror of slavery, whereas artworks that feature real bodies can, when appropriately designed, release it, contaminating the spectator with the horror. That the illustrations show an African American woman's body (in figure 3.2) being tortured, as well as a white-looking body (Roper's own in figure 3.5) being tormented, and a body that cannot be distinguished from that of the torturer or the master (in figures 3.7 and 3.8) further adds to this contamination, insinuating that the slave body is every body and any body. In so doing, Roper's text strives to move into a mode of parallel empathy that involves state matching, the idea that the enslaved and the free viewer are more similar than different. And still the narrative implies to its readers that what really matters about the enslaved body is not only the physical matter that composes it, which surely enables the kinetic activity of escape, but more significantly the manner in which this physical body translates torture into a metaphysical or spiritual matter. This "every body" is tortured, but it also is depicted as finding a mechanism to achieve redemption and lift itself into another domain—one that both is, and is not, precisely corporeal.

Conclusion: Identificatory Paths to the "Land of the Free"

Roper's narrative as a whole therefore rescripts the visual and verbal iconography surrounding slave torture, driving and directing the visual rhetoric with which slavery was enshrined within transatlantic abolitionist discourse, as well as a surveillant reader's inscription within this visual culture. In so doing, it shapes new tropes that reconfigure the visual rhetoric of an evolving transatlantic abolition movement. In these new tropes, the slave becomes an everyman who denotes the need for a more humane Master (with a capital *M*)—a godly Master who will replace and, if necessary, rebuke the real masters. Enslaved bodies resist torture and achieve a subjectivity that cannot be challenged because it rests not on a base legal system of masters and slaves but on a higher Master who alone can foresee and grant individual salvation or forgiveness for sins. The visual designs and the lexes of the text operate conjointly to make evident to a reader that the body of the tortured slave, which may become entangled with the free body of the viewer, can withdraw from the sensorium of slave torture through alternative schemas of corporeality that entail spirituality and identification rather than physicality and domination. The power of the master to control the enslaved body is first inverted—the slave comes to possess a corporeal subjectivity of his own—and then dispersed. Power finally is shown to reside with a higher Master.

It is, in fact, a calmly humane spirit, not the brutalized body of the slave, that greets a reader who opens the 1840 text. From 1840 onward, a stylish portrait of Moses Roper was the first image a reader would see before reading a word of text (see figure 3.9).[15] This fine, accurate, and precise engraving shows Roper regarding a reader evenly and patiently, without anger. He seems wise, intelligent, and humane—not the tortured slave of the narrative, but the mature man who has transcended this torture. As an emblem of his literacy, his signature resides below

FIGURE 3.9 Frontispiece, Moses Roper,
*A Narrative of the Adventures and Escape
of Moses Roper, from American Slavery.
With a Portrait,* 4th ed. (1840). Copper
engraving. Google Books.

his image and emphasizes that he has achieved authorship, which was frequently allied in the nineteenth century with a form of advanced subjectivity. Perhaps this image stands in contrast to the social death of slavery, to the specular objectification typically enacted on the body of the enslaved; the portrait explicitly indicates that Roper has survived this social death to become a free subject. A reader is encouraged, I think, to identify and empathize with this benevolent and calm image of him.

In the text's final moments, after pages and pages of torture, escape, and religious transcendence, Roper returns to this benevolent image of himself by refusing to denounce his birth country for its torture of him (107). The text therefore represents slave torture as episodes in the text that do not define the author. He also accomplishes a formidable achievement in this text as a whole, balancing his own assertion of enslaved agency (he repeatedly ran away) against an understanding that his success was also tied to a higher power—not the master's will but God's.

The narrative also facilitates readers' projection into a world where the "deep stain" of slavery and slave torture has been eradicated, and it subtly drives readerly attention toward the creation of such a world. Noting in the final lines of the text the irony that *"The land of the Free"* still contains the mother, the brothers, and the sisters of Moses Roper, not enjoying liberty, not the possessors of like feeling with me, not having even a distant glimpse of advancing toward freedom, but still slaves!" (105–6), Roper uses graphic features of the text—italics, scare quotes, and an exclamation point—to highlight the gap between the country's founding rhetoric and its actual practices. The lettering of the text here functions as an extension of the work's graphic imagery and evokes an affective response—in this case, indignation that Roper's relatives are "still slaves!" in the *"land of the Free."* This indignation perhaps moves readers toward tailored helping behaviors or larger prosocial action: the specific deed of purchasing the text in order to help Roper gain the monetary means to free his mother (106), or the more general action of working for the antislavery movement. As with the other texts discussed in this book, manipulation of emotions is crucial to shifting a reader's horizon of expectations away from spectatorship toward activity and empathy. As one reviewer noted, if the narrative is read by people in the United States, it should have "an effect on their hearts" when they come to feel the "enormities like those practiced on" Moses Roper (*Slavery in America*, "Review," 317).

As William Andrews observes, Roper's narrative "gave the antislavery movement in England and America exactly what it wanted: a hard-hitting tour of slavery as a visitation of hell on earth, conducted by someone who had seen and suffered it all but who had survived to tell his story in a manner likely to evoke both credence and sympathy" (introduction, 5). But critics have failed to notice that Roper's *Narrative* encourages readers to decipher not only the words on the page—which indeed depict the "hell on earth" of U.S. slavery, as Andrews phrases it—but also the interaction between words and pictures, a relationship that might demarcate a nondiegetic realm of freedom outside the space of the text. This nondiegetic space can be distinguished by an active Christian ethos of freedom, agency, and interdependence similar to the one Roper found on the "happy shores of England" (105). Renditions of the suffering of enslaved persons therefore become not only an instrument for the indictment of the system of slavery but also a step toward the creation of a "city of habitation" (107) for everyone, which is indeed the land of the free.[16]

Structuring a New Abolitionist Reading of Masculinity and Femininity

The Graphic Narrative Systems of Lydia Maria Child's
Joanna (1838) and Henry Bibb's *Narrative of the Life and Adventures of
Henry Bibb, an American Slave, Written by Himself* (1849)

Previous chapters of this book established that by the mid-1830s, broadsides, comics, cartoons, caricatures, and illustrated books about slavery had been flowing through transatlantic culture for over fifty years. These print modes functioned as a form of visual rhetoric that made arguments through the symbiotic interrelationship between words and pictures. Yet this visual rhetoric, as we have seen, sometimes was used to support the idea of enslavement (as in Stedman's text). Moreover, abolitionist texts could structure a reading of the enslaved body as always abject and subhuman, which encouraged readers, through a mode of hierarchical empathy, to envision the enslaved as an unfinished, incomplete self in need of pathos and pity, a viewed object rather than a viewing, human subject. The late 1830s saw a renewed recognition of how etchings, comics, and illustrated books functioned as systems of ideology, both for the cessation of slavery and for its perpetuation.[1] Caricature cartoons (with a few exceptions) tended to work against abolition by exaggerating its proposed reforms, while more naturalistic modes (such as those found in painting and in the graphic illustrated books of Branagan, Opie, Bourne, and Roper) tended to be used in antislavery rhetoric.

As has also been argued, the visual rhetoric of some abolitionist texts, and particularly of some graphic illustrated books, attempts to activate a reading protocol in which the line between the viewed, enslaved other and the viewing, free subject is eroded to some degree. This blurring may shift a reader's horizon of expectation and enable a parallel mode of empathy and intersubjectivity to emerge (see the appendix for a fuller description of parallel and hierarchical empathy). This chapter examines how the graphic illustrated books of two abolitionist writers,

Lydia Maria Child and Henry Bibb, attempt to undermine the dominant scopic structure of slavery and in particular its reading of masculine and feminine enslaved bodies. The chapter is also attentive to how Child's *Narrative of Joanna: An Emancipated Slave, of Surinam* (1838), which is an edited version of Stedman's account, and Bibb's illustrated *Narrative of the Life and Adventures of Henry Bibb* (1849) attempt to portray and enact through their citation of previously published visual images of the enslaved a new abolitionist structure of feeling in which the enslaved body is in flux rather than static, active rather than passive, and vocal rather than silent. Some critics view Child's and Bibb's appropriation of illustrations from other texts as only reproductions, but I read them as efforts to create new graphic narrative systems in which ideologies supporting enslavement could be transgressed, and new modes of apprehending enslaved subjectivity forwarded. By appropriating prior images, they appeal to a reader's horizon of expectations, a viewer's desire to see abject, othered slaves. Yet both texts also strive to shift this horizon of expectations through the portrayal of new modes of enslaved power, agency, and subjectivity.[2]

Raymond Williams reminds us that a new structure of feeling precedes the formation of "an alternative ideology" (*Marxism and Literature*, 134), which nonetheless retains "substantial affiliation" with the previous ideology, generating a tension that is at once lived and articulated in new semantic figures (135). The new semantic figure that Bibb and Child attempt to portray for their readers—what we might term an enslaved and gendered figuration of resistance—is meant to promote a substantive mode of feeling in which a reader is encouraged toward parallel empathy and intersubjectivity. Bibb's and Child's modes of storytelling may enhance what neuroscientists call theory of mind—the inference and representations of emotions, beliefs, and intentions of someone else—which is hypothesized to enhance empathy.[3] These new visual-verbal figurations retain vestiges of prior abolitionist ideology even though they attempt to shift toward new empathetic modes for abolitionist viewers. In addition, both writers manifest an awareness that images contain multiple meanings and truths that can be deployed and redeployed within contexts that move closer to an apprehension of not only slavery, but also the uses to which slavery's visual rhetoric could be turned.[4]

Historical Overview: Slavery and Abolition, 1838–1849

The 1830s was the first decade in U.S. history in which abolitionism became a major organized social movement (Upchurch, *Abolition Movement*, 43), and in the late 1830s and into the 1840s, the pressure to end slavery intensified dramatically.

Most importantly for the purposes of this chapter, abolitionism became linked with other reforms such as freedom of speech and women's rights. These associations advanced antislavery causes in radical ways, but also led to profound fissures within the movement. Perhaps this is one reason why Bibb and Child cautiously navigate questions of gender and women's voice or silence in their works.

Freedom of speech became linked to abolition because print activities by abolition societies put political pressure on those who did not favor the end of slavery. William Lloyd Garrison's abolitionist newspaper the *Liberator* began appearing in Boston in 1831, and the first American Anti-Slavery Society (AASS) was established in 1833. The AASS and its affiliated societies across the United States flooded the slave states with illustrated abolitionist literature and lobbied Congress to end slavery (Ruchames, *Abolitionists*, 20). Of course, not everyone embraced the print activities of these antislavery societies, and attempts were made to curtail and control this new mode of political production.[5] In 1835, for example, President Andrew Jackson supported a ban on the mailing of "incendiary" political materials, and Congress in 1840 made permanent the gag rule that automatically tabled petitions for the abolition of slavery. More dramatically, Elijah Lovejoy was killed in Illinois in 1837 while defending his antislavery newspaper from a mob. These attempted suppressions of abolitionist print materials and petitions may have strengthened the abolition movement as a whole. As Aileen Kraditor notes, "Americans who did not feel strongly about slavery began to believe that if abolitionists could be mobbed with impunity and prevented from having their petitions considered by Congress, the rights of all Americans were in danger" (*Means and Ends*, 6–7). Abolition therefore became allied with other social rights, such as freedom of speech and the freedom to petition the government.

Moreover, during this period, abolition became uneasily affiliated with women's political rights. Women had been involved in the antislavery movement from its start, and they organized local antislavery societies for women in Philadelphia (1833), Boston (1833), New York (1836), and other locations (Sklar, *Women's Rights*, 8–9). Yet in the later 1830s, the most active and engaged women abolitionists began to move beyond these local societies; they became, as Sinha has documented, "abolition's most effective foot soldiers" (*Slave's Cause*, 266).[6] For example, in 1837 seventy-one delegates from eight states held the first Anti-Slavery Convention of American Women in New York; they issued publications, formed executive committees, and launched a campaign to collect one million signatures on antislavery petitions. Some women began the scandalous activity of publicly speaking for the cause of abolition and traveling the country in support of the AASS. The most famous of these lecturers were Sarah and Angelina Grimké, who began by addressing all-female audiences but quickly moved to speaking before "promiscuous assemblies"—mixed groups of men and women—exciting great controversy in the process (Kraditor, *Means and Ends*, 43–50; Matthews, *Public Woman*, 112).

Also during this period, African American women became more actively involved in antislavery movements than before. In Boston in 1832, Maria W. Stewart, a black woman, became the first U.S. woman to speak in public to a mixed (male and female) gathering (Sklar, *Women's Rights*, 10–11). Other prominent African American abolition speakers included Sarah Mapps Douglass (who often spoke with the Grimkés in the late 1830s) and Margaretta Forten (who founded the Philadelphia Female Anti-Slavery Society in 1833 and spoke out against slavery in speeches throughout the later 1830s and 1840s). Most famously, Isabella Baumfree took the name "Sojourner Truth" in 1843 and dedicated her life to preaching against slavery. Harriet Jacobs, who had escaped from slavery in 1842, became involved in the abolition movement, working in her brother John's antislavery reading room in New York in the late 1840s (Yellin, *Harriet Jacobs*, 100); Jacobs knew prominent abolitionists such as Frederick Douglass, Amy Post, and (perhaps) Henry Bibb. Such articulate, engaged African American women may have influenced Bibb's portrayals of resistant, vocal women in his 1849 *Narrative*.

Yet there was mixed reaction within the abolitionist movement to the public activities of women, regardless of their race. In New York in May 1840, at the national convention of the American Anti-Slavery Society, a radical majority supported the nomination of a white abolitionist named Abigail Kelley Foster to serve on the convention's business committee. The more conservative abolitionists walked out of the AASS convention and formed the American and Foreign Anti-Slavery Society, which explicitly excluded women from membership (Upchurch, *Abolition Movement*, 44–45). The American Anti-Slavery Society elected Foster to its business committee and named three women (Foster, Lucretia Mott, and Elizabeth Cady Stanton) as delegates to the World Anti-Slavery Convention in London in June 1840. At that convention, however, these women were relegated to seats in a balcony on the grounds that their participation might offend British public opinion. Garrison protested women's exclusion from the convention, and he and other male activists, including Charles Remond, sat with those women who were segregated in the gallery (Cummings, "World Anti-Slavery Convention," 585).

African American and Anglo-American women therefore played a prominent yet controversial role in abolition in the late 1830s and into the 1840s. Crucially and controversially, the right of the enslaved to freedom was ultimately linked by some individuals with the cause of women's rights. Bibb's and Child's texts acknowledge the intersectional nature of oppression—how race, gender, and sometimes class

COLOR IMAGE I

Abolitionist sugar bowl, purchased at the Philadelphia Anti-Slavery Fair
by Josiah Quincy, c. 1836–1861. Courtesy of the Friends Historical Library of
Swarthmore College. Used with permission.

COLOR IMAGE 2
Patch box with abolitionist motif, "Am I not a Man and a Brother."
South Staffordshire, c. 1790. Enamel on copper. Accession number 1987. 212. 3;
International Slavery Museum, Liverpool. Used with Permission.

A Negro hung alive by the Ribs to a Gallows.

London, Published Dec. 1st 1792, by J. Johnson, St. Pauls Church Yard.

COLOR IMAGE 3
William Blake, "A Negro hung alive by the Ribs to a Gallows,"
illustration from John Gabriel Stedman, *Narrative of a Five Years' Expedition* (1796).
Copperplate engraving.

Johnny, Newcome landing in the W.st Indies.   Johnny situated as Clerk of Stores

Johnny on a Country excursion.   Johnny enjoying the sports of the field

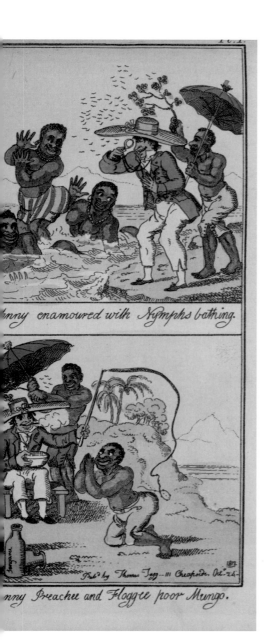

COLOR IMAGE 4

[William Elmes,] "Adventures of Johnny Newcome" (1812), plate 1. Hand-colored engraved cartoon. Courtesy of Yale University.

THE

BLACK MAN'S LAMENT.

THE PETITION FOR ABOLISHING THE SLAVE-TRADE.

—

COME, listen to my plaintive ditty,
  Ye tender hearts, and children dear!
And, should it move your souls to pity,
  Oh! try to *end* the griefs you hear.

SUGAR-CANE.

There is a *beauteous plant* *, that grows
   In western India's sultry clime,
Which makes, alas! the Black man's woes,
   And also makes the White man's crime.

* " A field of canes, when standing in the month of November,
when it is in arrow or full blossom, (says Beckford, in his descriptive
account of the Island of Jamaica,) is one of the most beautiful productions that the pen or pencil can possibly describe. It, in common, rises from three to eight feet, or more, in height; a difference

TORN FROM HIS FRIENDS.

———

From parents, brethren's fond embrace;
 From tender wife, and child to tear;
Then in a darksome ship to place,
 Pack'd close, like bales of cotton there.

STANDING IN LINES, WITH THE DRIVER BEHIND.

They bid black men and women stand
In lines, the drivers in the rear :
Poor Negroes hold a *hoe* in hand,
But they the wicked cart-whip bear.

COLOR IMAGE 8
Amelia Opie, *The Black Man's Lament* (1826), 9. Copperplate engraving and watercolor.
Courtesy of the Lilly Library, Bloomington, Indiana.

COLOR IMAGE 9

Isaac Cruikshank (attributed), *The Abolition of the Slave Trade.*
Or the inhumanity of dealers in human flesh exemplified in Capt. Kimber
(London: S. W. Fores, April 10, 1792). Etching; hand-colored
in some versions. Library of Congress.

COLOR IMAGE 10

Gold-embossed image on the red morocco front cover of the second printing of
Henry Bibb, *Narrative of the Life and Adventures of Henry Bibb* (1849).
Courtesy of the Library Company of Philadelphia. The image also appears
on the back cover of many editions.

COLOR IMAGE 11

Wilmer Wilson IV, 2012, *Henry Box Brown: FOREVER*
(day three, Congress-detail). Copyright Wilmer Wilson IV;
courtesy Connersmith. Used with permission.

COLOR IMAGE 12

Wax figure of Henry Box Brown in the Great Blacks in Wax Museum, Baltimore.
Photograph by the author.

COLOR IMAGE 13

Embossed cover of volumes 1 and 2 of Harriet Beecher Stowe, *Uncle Tom's Cabin* (1852), first book publication. Based on a wood engraving by Hammatt Billings.

COLOR IMAGE 14

Condoleezza Rice, nominee for secretary of state, as Eliza. Illustration by Elliott Banfield,
New York Sun, January 21, 2005. Copyright Elliott Banfield.
Courtesy of the *New York Sun*. Used with Permission.

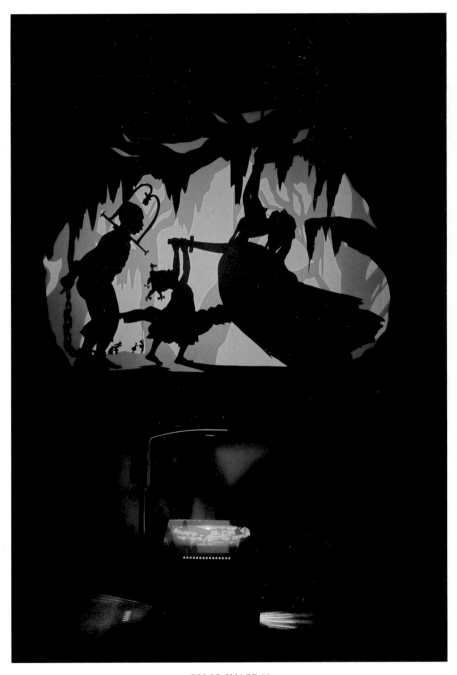

COLOR IMAGE 15

Kara Walker, *Mistress Demanded a Swift and Dramatic Empathetic Reaction Which we Obliged Her* (2000). Cut paper and projection on wall. Collection of Whitney Museum of American Art, New York. Used with permission.

status contributed to women's remaining enslaved, while their male counterparts sometimes achieved freedom. Visually, too, these texts attempt to move beyond the fixation with the enslaved female body as an object of desire and voyeurism, into pictures that illustrate the role of both women and men within these scenes of exchange, commerce, and sexualization.

My So-Called Wife: Visual Rhetoric and the Production of Masculinity and Femininity in Child's *Joanna*

Given this historical backdrop, it is unsurprising that gender plays a role in how male and female abolitionists configured their antislavery rhetoric. According to Anne K. Mellor, prominent male abolitionist writers "tended to attack slavery as a violation of 'natural law,' the argument that all men are born equal and have certain inalienable 'rights,'" whereas female writers "tended to condemn slavery because it violated the domestic affections, separating mothers from their children, husband from their wives, and subjected black women to sexual abuse from their white masters" ("'Am I Not a Woman,'" 315). Child and Bibb, however, strategically deploy both traditionally "masculine" and "feminine" arguments against slavery. Their works explicate how slavery implicates men and women in a system that annihilates basic human rights *and* contravenes masculine and feminine roles within the family structure.

This double focus is particularly evident in Child's republication of Stedman's "Joanna" excerpts in 1838. As discussed in chapter 1, Stedman's narrative recounts his time in Surinam, his affair with an enslaved woman named Joanna (who becomes his concubine), the birth of their son (called Johnny), and his eventual departure from Surinam. For the most part, Child reprints only those parts of the text that concern Joanna and Stedman's affair, but also includes her own editorial comments. This was not the first republication of the Joanna segments in one form or another;[7] indeed, Child had republished them in the antislavery volume *The Oasis* in 1834. But the 1838 book republication contains several new images that appear to have been created specifically for it, as well as revised versions of some of Stedman's illustrations. While positioning Joanna as a virtuous true woman, Child's text attempts to have the last word by transferring the focus onto Stedman's failed masculinity. Some of the new images eliminate Joanna from the picture; in so doing, Child criticizes the abolition movement's scopic and voyeuristic focus on visual representations of enslaved and tortured female bodies. Of course, Child cannot help evoking sentimental spectatorship at times, but her text and its illustrations attempt to transfer focus to the failure of white masculinity within this particular sentimental narrative and to create empathy for Joanna, who is portrayed as being more than a mere object of eroticized pain.[8]

Moreover, by focusing on the narrative of Joanna and Stedman and eliminating all other aspects of Stedman's sprawling travelogue, Child creates a new and discrete story about enslaved women's status and their need for redress. Her text therefore may increase empathy by allowing readers to transport themselves more easily into the famous—not to say infamous—romance of Joanna and Stedman. In scientific studies, P. Matthijs Bal and Martijn Veltkamp have established that reading "will change an individual's empathic skills only when the reader is emotionally transported in a story" ("How Does Fiction Reading"), and Dan Johnson has documented that such transportation fosters "empathic growth and prosocial behavior" ("Transportation into a Story," 154). Child essentially reshapes Stedman's amorphous and morally ambiguous narrative—a narrative that means to ameliorate, rather than end, slavery—into a tight and cohesive love story in which a good and true enslaved woman is harmed by a man who should have treated her more honorably. This remodeling of Stedman's text is meant not only to transport viewers into the story but also to encourage them toward prosocial behavior (abolitionist sentiments and actions) through enhanced identification with Joanna.

Child begins by making evident Joanna's standing as a moral "true woman." The ideology of the true woman held sway in the United States from 1780 to 1860, as numerous critics such as Barbara Welter ("Cult of True Womanhood") and Nancy Cott (*Bonds of Womanhood*) have argued. While contemporary scholars have questioned the reality of this set of beliefs for women's day-to-day lives, there is little doubt that Child strives to use this ideology within her abolitionist fictions, such as "The Quadroons" (1842), to evoke northern women's sympathy for enslaved African American women. But to be converted into a "true woman," the Joanna figure in Stedman's text needed some iconographic refashioning. Child's text initially renovates the visual imagery surrounding Joanna by putting clothing over her naked breast, thereby enhancing a sense of her as beautiful and chaste (see figure 4.1). In addition to covering the bare breast present in the original text, Child's illustration paints over the small image of Joanna and her son Johnny that appeared in the lower-right corner of Stedman's illustration (see figure 1.6; see also Kennedy, "Going Viral," 9). At first this might seem like an abrogation of the cult of true womanhood's focus on women's essential maternal and domestic nature, but we must recall that Joanna is only fifteen when depicted in this illustration; perhaps the image is painted out to enhance a sense of her modesty and innocence. Moreover, a nineteenth-century reader might be able to empathize more

FIGURE 4.1 Frontispiece,
Lydia Maria Child,
*Narrative of Joanna:
An Emancipated Slave, of
Surinam* (1838). Reduced
from a likeness drawn by
John Gabriel Stedman.
Engraved on copper by
G. G. Smith. In the original
illustration in Stedman's
text, Joanna's right breast
is uncovered. HathiTrust
Digital Library.

easily with this young girl than with the rather wanton and more womanly figure that Stedman's text evokes.

The erasure of the smaller image of mother and child has the strange effect of throwing off the perspective of the illustration, since Joanna now seems gigantic in reference to the tiny plant in the foreground and the house in the background. As discussed in chapter 1, the gigantic female figure in Stedman's text is the naked "Female Samboe," so perhaps here Child's revised illustration attempts to compete in some way with this image—Joanna, the (clothed) true woman, is the gigantic figure emblematically hovering over the landscape of slavery, not the tragic (naked) Female Samboe. As in the original text, the pastoral and idyllic qualities of the setting (in a beautiful space in nature) contrast with the harsh fact that this is a girl who essentially will be rented by Stedman to be his sexual concubine and then abandoned.

Perhaps to counteract this fact, Child takes the unusual step of making Joanna the title character of the narrative and, moreover, in the subtitle calling her "An Emancipated Slave, of Surinam." Joanna is never emancipated in Stedman's text; Stedman's friend Mrs. Godefroy buys Joanna, promising manumission. Yet Child's text narrates Joanna's refusal to be freed until "the last farthing of the money should be paid"; Joanna even goes so far as to thank Stedman, with "the countenance of an angel," for her continued but more benevolent enslavement (38–39). How does Joanna's thanking Stedman for her continued enslavement sit with Child's titular enfranchisement of Joanna as "an emancipated slave" and (for that matter) a true woman? If Joanna is "emancipated," then her relationship with Stedman is a chosen one rather than one that exists within the coercive sexual politics of enslavement. For Sharpe, this means that Joanna can become "invested with the political objectives of the antislavery movement"; perhaps it is only "as an emancipated slave that Joanna can speak on behalf" of this cause (*Ghosts of Slavery*, 84). Yet her identification as emancipated in the work's title stands in opposition to the facts of the text, as Child full well knows.

At times Child's text appears to promote the view that Joanna's relationship with Stedman is a type of marriage. Child appends an editorial comment to the narrative in which she notes that Stedman "never calls [Joanna] his wife" (56), even though he refers to himself as having a "wedding" with her and being "as happy as any bridegroom ever was" (15). But as Child was aware, unions between white men and Surinamese women lacked legal protection;[9] moreover, the "marriage" to Joanna does not prevent Stedman from marrying another woman in Holland. Child's text strives to create a niche for Joanna within the realm of marital sexuality and childbirth, and her nomenclature works toward this end. Yet the original text slips away from these legal designations, as Child notes. This leaves Joanna within category crisis, at least from Child's point of view; she both is (and is not) a "wife," both is (and is not) a "married" woman, and therefore both is (and is not) within the sphere of enfranchised maternity and true womanhood.[10]

As a counteraction to Joanna's inscription within Stedman's text, then, the images in the 1838 reprint struggle to reframe Joanna's visual status so that she is placed within the realm of marital sexuality rather than the voyeuristic, scopic extramarital subjugation of the original narrative. In figure 4.1, for example, Child tries to avoid the voyeurism of the original text by covering Joanna with more clothing. She also removes many of the original text's "shocking scenes of cruelty" (47). As chapter 1 demonstrated, many of the most shocking scenes of cruelty involved pornotropic discourses that specifically played upon and over the enslaved, (often) mixed-race, nude, nubile, young female body—pictures that echo the image of Joanna herself in her chains and rings. When Joanna is pictured in Child's text, however, even when she is at auction, she looks like a good, true, virtuous woman. The illustration in figure 4.2, for example, is one of those added to Child's 1838 text. This framed full-page image puts both the auctioned slave (Joanna) and the auctioneer on display. Joanna is the subject of panopticonic surveillance, surrounded on the left by men who stare at her in order to assess her value (sexual and otherwise), and on the right (background) by fellow slaves who look on in shocked horror. Stedman's friend Mr. Lolkens has just stepped into the scene (stage left), and his hand is raised to stop the auction. Joanna is fully dressed in clothing that is more conservative than her attire in figure 4.1; she even wears a modest kerchief on her head. She covers her eyes diffidently and holds her head in her hands, looking away from the viewer. The tight visual composition of the picture gives it a claustrophobic feel, and the perspective line places a viewer on the same footing as Joanna. The horizon (or implied horizon) of the auctioneer's desk means that a reader views the image from a normal eye level instead of looking down on Joanna. About Child's *An Appeal in Favor of the Class Called Africans* (1838), Carolyn Sorisio argues that Child employed techniques that study and manipulate the bodily nature of slavery; she evokes spectatorship to "control

Joanna at the slave market.—See pages 17—18.

FIGURE 4.2 "Joanna at the Slave Market," original illustration from Lydia Maria Child, *Narrative of Joanna* (1838). Wood engraving. HathiTrust Digital Library.

and regulate it" ("Spectacle of the Body," 51). In *Joanna*, Child regulates the bodily nature of slavery by showing how it is negotiated between three bodies: the author, the characters in her story, and a reader, who is challenged with the right to intervene, repeat, or contest the story. In a sense, we can see this readerly challenge in Mr. Lolkens's upraised hand, which seems to urge a reader as well to lift up his or hands against slavery, or at least to contest its story.

As noted in previous chapters, auction scenes were ubiquitous in abolitionist visual rhetoric, but Child's illustrator ironically depicts a scene in which Joanna must be rescued by a man other than Stedman. This scene and the narrative Child excerpts tell us much about Stedman's failure as a husband; although he bewails the fact that he cannot become Joanna's "proprietor" and can imagine her "insulted, tortured, bowing under the weight of her chains, calling aloud for my assistance, and calling in vain" (18), he lacks the money to intercede, so ultimately Mr. Lolkens comes to her rescue. The text's images may encourage parallel empathy with Joanna through several mechanisms, including visually placing her within the circle of true womanhood and within a reader's line of perspective. Yet such an illustration as the auction scene also subtly displaces Stedman from his appropriate masculine role as her "husband" and protector (we do not see him rescuing her).

In another image in Child's text, this one copied from Stedman's narrative with some alterations, Joanna is pictured with Johnny and Stedman in front of their home, The Hope. In the original illustration in Stedman's text, Stedman looks in contented admiration at his home, child, and "wife," and he holds a long, somewhat phallic-looking gun with a sharp tip in one hand (see figure 4.3). The sheep grazing in the foreground suggest bucolic bliss, as does the caption in Stedman's text: "Rural Retreat—The Cottage." Child's illustrator modifies Stedman's image to better focus it on Stedman's failed masculinity. In Child's text, the caption is changed to highlight that the geographic space belongs to Stedman—it is not a generic "rural retreat" (as in the original) but "Capt. Stedman's residence," his domicile (see figure 4.4). The original illustration has a vaster, more panoramic perspective, and details of the landscape are spread out, whereas Child's illustrator moves the figures to the center of the image and crowds a viewer's perspective in close to the figures. In Child's illustration, the figures are placed near the house, which is united with its textual name, The Hope, an appellation the caption ironically foregrounds. The placement of figures near the house in Child's text (the house's roof nearly appears to touch Joanna's head) suggests again the domestic sphere within which the husband or male is supposed to be the protector of the wife or female. The image in Child's text specifically refers to page 41, however, which contains Joanna's statement "If we are separated, I trust it will be only for

FIGURE 4.3 "Rural Retreat—The Cottage," (plate 73, bottom),
from John Gabriel Stedman, *Narrative of a Five Years' Expedition* (1796).
Copper engraving. HathiTrust Digital Library.

FIGURE 4.4 "Capt. Stedman's Residence," illustration
from Lydia Maria Child, *Narrative of Joanna* (1838). Wood
engraving. This print remakes a scene from Stedman's narrative
by giving it a new title and placing both Joanna and Stedman
closer to the cottage. HathiTrust Digital Library.

a time. The greatest proof that Capt. Stedman can give me of real esteem is to undergo this trial like a man"; she then turns "round suddenly" and weeps "bitterly" (41). By the 1830s, readers might have already heard of the famous, incendiary, miscegenational love story of Joanna and Stedman, and if so, the statement that their separation "will be only for a time" would be ironic. There is no hope for this romance at The Hope. In figure 4.4, Child's illustrator cites Stedman's original image, but also re-cites it, remakes it, in a way that highlights the textual themes of both his abandonment of Joanna and her status as a true woman; these themes potentially increases a reader's empathy for Joanna, who seems in Child's text more like a virtuous (if abandoned) true woman than a sexual plaything.

Joanna instructs Stedman to undergo his trial "like a man" (41), but according to Child's augmentation of the story and her illustrations, he fails this task. Editorially, Child introduces these remarks to emphasize his failure: "Such is Capt. Stedman's own account of the beautiful and excellent Joanna. In reading it, we cannot but feel that he might have paid Mrs. Godefroy, and sent for his wife to England, long before 1783. His marriage was unquestionably a sincere tribute of respect to the delicacy and natural refinement of Joanna's character. Yet . . . he never calls her his wife. Perhaps Joanna, with the quick discernment of strong affection, perceived that he would be ashamed of her in Europe, and therefore heroically sacrificed her own happiness" (56). In Child's telling of the love story, Joanna is the perfect domestic saint, sacrificing herself for the unmanly Stedman, but Stedman clearly does not behave as a faithful and genuine man should. The last image in which Joanna and Stedman are pictured together—original to Child's text, and not illustrated in Stedman's *Narrative*—also makes this point (see figure 4.5). Joanna is pictured fully clothed as she comforts Stedman, who seems on the verge of weeping. The rounded-off corners of the framing of many images in Child's text suggests containment within the family compass and might further empathy and intersubjectivity, since readers might feel similarity with the sorrowful "husband" and "wife," Stedman and Joanna. Yet the cozy family circle is violently shattered by Stedman's departure.

In this and other illustrations, Child's text subtly shifts a reader's horizon of expectations away from scopic surveillance of the beautiful Joanna and toward the failure of white masculinity as exemplified by Stedman. Interestingly, the artist places Stedman, not Joanna, in the center of this illustration, and he is clearly and sharply delineated in his formal uniform. He lacks the long phallic gun held in figures 4.3 and 4.4, or any weapon for that matter, perhaps indicating his disempowerment and impotency. His son is held by another woman, and clustered around him are several young boys and girls, who touch his arm and appear to

FIGURE 4.5
"Capt. Stedman taking
a final leave of Joanna,"
original illustration from
Lydia Maria Child,
Narrative of Joanna
(1838). Wood engraving.
HathiTrust Digital Library.

be comforting him. The window on the left of the scene casts a good strong light onto it and onto Stedman, as if asking a viewer to take a long, hard look at not only slavery, but also Stedman's actions as a "man" and "husband." Child editorializes elsewhere in the text that "Captain Stedman appears to have been extremely kind-hearted, and strongly prepossessed in favor of the African character. He was often made ill and wretched by the cruelties he witnessed." Yet he still "conjured the English abolitionists not to oppose the continuance of the Slave-trade; lest Holland should make more money than England!" (57). Stedman's 1796 book "conjures" British abolitionists to continue the slave trade, but Child's text attempts another act of conjuration—one that repurposes the original text in the service of a dismantlement of the logic of enslavement and of the construct of masculinity that a relationship to an enslaved woman fosters. Child directly follows up this statement with one about Stedman's hypocrisy: "Alas, for the inconsistency and selfishness of man!" (51).

Furthermore, by placing other children in this illustration of a soon-to-be-broken family circle, Child's text alludes to the fact that Stedman's narrative of familial annihilation is not exceptional. After Joanna's death, Stedman has his son, Johnny, freed and sent to Holland, but such was not the case with other officers in Surinam, as Child shows through her quotation of another part of Stedman's text: "More than forty beautiful boys and girls, the children of my [that is, Stedman's] acquaintance, were left in perpetual slavery, without being so much as inquired after" (50–51). Once again, the figure of the child is employed to produce readerly empathy—in this case, the more than forty abandoned yet beautiful "boys and girls" are supposed to encourage a reader to see similarity with women like Joanna and have empathy for these mothers and their discarded children. By including this sentence (which is incidental to the story of Joanna and Stedman) in her narrative, Child points to the hypocrisy of white men as a group. Stedman constantly blames "fate" (51) for his inability to continue his union with Joanna, but the text as a whole strongly attributes it to a failure of masculinity—that is, an abrogation of Stedman's role as Joanna's husband and protector.

The illustrated, edited text attempts to counteract and reframe the erotic imagery surrounding Joanna in the original text by turning scopic surveillance onto Stedman. In figure 4.6 (also unique to Child's text), Joanna visits Stedman, and even though the illustration is captioned "Joanna visiting Captain Stedman at 'The Hope,'" she (as Bibb later does) appears to have escaped from the visual technologies that should contain her. In the original text, Stedman writes: "I had been [at The Hope] but a short time, when I was surprised by the waving of a white handkerchief from a tent-boat, that was rowing up the river; when, to augment my happiness, it unexpectedly proved to be my mulatto, accompanied by her aunt" (166). This sentence creates a visual synecdoche for Joanna in the "white handkerchief." Yet in Child's text, Joanna is not pictured "waving a white handkerchief"; in fact, she is not discernible at all. If we have been paying attention at all to the images of Joanna and how they function within the diegetic space of the text's illustrations, this absence is surely noteworthy. Joanna no longer seems to be an object of sexual and racial voyeurism, at least visually.

Instead, Stedman is foregrounded on the bank of the river, hailing Joanna. His placement on a tiny spit of land jutting out in front of the cottage suggests just how precarious and endangered his masculinity is. The Hope is a "valuable sugar plantation, on the beautiful river Comewina" (Child, *Narrative of Joanna*, 19), but Child's illustrator does not picture him obtaining power over this landscape. Instead, the illustrator appears to want to plunk Stedman into the beautiful Comewina. Moreover, because Stedman's figure is situated somewhat below the horizon line of the picture, a viewer's perspective line tends to look down on him. The visual technology erodes the binary of white empowered viewing male subject over black disempowered viewed female object, because a viewer has little choice but to fasten his or her eyes (in a slightly downcast glance) on the figure of Stedman, with his upraised, empty, and ultimately impotent hand. The boat has not yet turned to reach the bank, creating a lack of closure in the icon—it seems

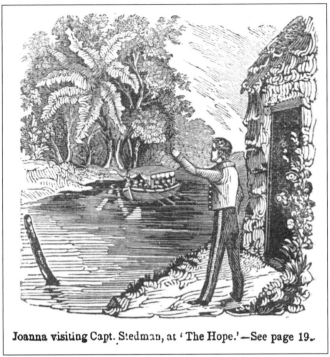

Joanna visiting Capt. Stedman, at ' The Hope.'—See page 19.

FIGURE 4.6 "Joanna visiting Capt. Stedman, at 'The Hope,'"
original illustration from Lydia Maria Child, *Narrative of Joanna*
(1838). Wood engraving. Note that Joanna cannot be seen.
HathiTrust Digital Library.

as if the boat will float right by Stedman. The image itself, then, symbolically presages the severe rupture with Joanna that Stedman will precipitate and foreshadows his failure to protect Joanna from enslavement and (finally) death.

In metatextual moments in the text as a whole, the author draws back from the love story of Stedman and Joanna to editorialize about slavery and Stedman's failure as a man and husband. The black female body often still is caught within the scopic and pornotropic visual order of slavery that is at the heart of Stedman's original text. But the visual rhetoric of Child's text also works toward a critique of this system—and of how empowered white masculinity, in particular, fails to take action to dismantle this system. Worse yet, through acts of "conjuration" and specific failures as husbands and fathers, men like Stedman perpetuate the system, both literally (through the thousands of beautiful children they father and then leave behind) and symbolically, by their failure to recognize their own complicity within it. Even white male abolitionists, by their continuing focus on the scopic pleasure of the viewing of enslaved female bodies, may perpetuate these women's enslavement. Alas, indeed, as Child comments, for the inconsistency and selfishness of *man*.

"But the Horrors of Slavery, He Never Can Trace": Masculinity, Femininity, and the Dangerous Visual Technology of Slavery in *Narrative of the Life and Adventures of Henry Bibb, an American Slave*

In "Narrative, Memory, and Slavery," W. J. T. Mitchell writes that although the public and verbal recounting of a sequence of events may provide an autobiographer with a sense of control over the material of his or her life, such a practice is fraught with danger, especially when visual materials are involved, because it may activate the "mnemotechnique as an uncontrollable technology; the phantom figures in the landscape or memory palace threaten to come alive, to be re-membered and resurrected from the dead as ghosts who act upon the material world and the body of the narrator" (*Picture Theory*, 202). The recalling of events may be so traumatic that it threatens identity itself, leading to a "strategic amnesia, a selective remembering, and thus a selective *dis*(re)membering of experience" (200). "The term slave to this day sounds with terror to my soul," notes Henry Bibb in his *Narrative of the Life and Adventures of Henry Bibb, an American Slave*, written more than eight years after his final escape from slavery; it is "a word too obnoxious to speak—a system too intolerable to be endured" (18). Recounting these occurrences in words or pictures, looking "back with quickened perception at the state of torment from whence I fled," threatens to draw him down into slavery (18). This section reads Bibb's narrative not as an attempt to reconstruct the "truth" or "reality" of his experience as a slave (which might deconstruct his present-tense identity as a free man), but instead as a discursive and visual formation designed to create a distorted, gaping, and broken story of the past—yet one that the narrative persona can actively and consciously perform for both personal and abolitionist purposes. Some cognitive scientists have argued that empathy and theory of mind (the ability to comprehend the complexity of another person's mental state) are enhanced most by complicated, ambiguous stories that propel a reader into a mode of intricate meaning making (Kidd and Castano, "Reading Literary Fiction," 380). Bibb cautiously navigates the line between unfolding a complex, ambiguous, broken story that might compel a reader to comprehend the limits of representation and the need to produce the "truth" of his experiences for antislavery purposes. At times Bibb's graphic narrative even forwards a protean persona that slips free from the text's visual and emotional modes of affect and cognition.

Bibb's narrative as a whole recounts his birth in slavery in Kentucky, his marriage to a woman named Malinda, his many escape attempts with his wife and their child, Frances, and his final decision to escape alone. Many of the twenty-three images in the text are derived from other sources, as Marcus Wood has shown ("Seeing Is Believing"), and they often highlight the gap between the lived and subjective experience of slavery (which is difficult for Bibb to narrate) and the memory of it from another temporal perspective—the more objective standpoint of discursive performance and storytelling. Furthermore, Bibb's radical repurposing of these illustrations upends, distends, and remakes the system of graphic narrative that previously governed antislavery illustrated books. He assembles through bricolage a collective visual-verbal text that gives a reader access to a compendium of experiences that both are, and are not, his own.[11] In what follows, I first consider the general manner in which Bibb manipulates abolitionist visual rhetoric for subversive ends. I then assess how this subversion may allow renovated constructs of femininity and masculinity to be enacted—new icons that create a more active structure of feeling for a reading viewer. These new icons of masculinity and femininity attempt to move beyond the static visual-verbal paradigm of enslaved gender identity present in earlier texts toward a more empathetic mode that uses polyphonic storytelling techniques to enhance intersubjectivity.

Peter John Brownlee has pointed out that print underwent transition in this time period: "Broadsides and letterform signs bearing the marks of newly invented or enhanced 'fat face' letterforms proliferated. . . . They visually 'screamed' at their targeted audiences, assaulting the eyes with letters shaped to combine alphabetical with optical information and to maximize visual effect" ("'The Economy of the Eyes,'" 25). As a publisher and later a newspaper printer, Bibb would have been aware of these developments.[12] Because Bibb's text was self-published, he may have had more control over aspects of its final shape and appearance than other ex-fugitive authors.[13] Indeed, in some versions of the second printing of the 1849 edition of Bibb's text, the frontispiece showily prances a number of print technologies across the page, including fine portraiture, embossment of a flowing signature, and reproduction of an illustration of a cartoonish fleeing slave with an almost comic caption: "Stop the runaway! Where is he!"[14] Of course, "he" (the runaway, Bibb) is expected to be found within the text, and yet Bibb both is and is not there (like Joanna in figure 4.6 above); we get the simulacrum of his life and his visual presence in descriptions and illustrations, yet the "real" enslaved person may escape from the text's visual and rhetorical technologies.

There is no doubt, nonetheless, that the text's visual technologies lure readers in by making them believe that the story of the enslaved man Henry Bibb, his wife,

and his family will be found within its pages. As Wood has noted, some copies
of the first edition of the text had a realistic portrait of Bibb, Malinda, and their
child embossed onto its cover (*Blind Memory*, 14). This image is also embossed on
the front and back covers of many editions that I have examined, such as those at
the New-York Historical Society and the Library Company of Philadelphia (see
figure 4.7; color image 10). Quite literally, then, the image of the enslaved family
was used to sell the text, and was bought and sold like any other market commodity in an economy in which not only books but also people could be purchased.
Compared to the more sedate embossed covers of many other slave narratives
(such as Frederick Douglass's 1845 edition, published four years earlier, which bore
only his name and title, in gold), this cover, when taken together with the frontispiece, visually scream at a target audience, hailing it. But what is the nature of this
interpellation, and what visual argument is being made? Wood claims that many
of the formulaic wood engravings in the text seem to be saying, "Every whipping
is like every other whipping, every failed escape the same. . . . [These images] tes-
tify that there is no pictorial language to do justice to the horror of slave life, only
a series of well-circulated, well-digested stereotypes" ("Seeing Is Believing," 182).[15]
I contend, however, that it is useful to look at images (such as the one on the book's
cover) that are new to Bibb's text, as well as at the way in which the placement,
displacement, and replacement of older images may give them a new currency
within a graphic narrative system.

Like William Wells Brown, who in *Clotel* (1853) reuses many stories from other
abolitionist texts, Bibb reprocesses visuals to create a compilation of slave experience rather than a story that is unconditionally specific and personal to his own
life. "I despair in finding language to express adequately the deep feeling of my
soul, as I contemplate the past history of my life," writes Bibb at the start of his
text (15). He goes on to comment on the limits of visual rhetoric to convey the
horrors of slavery:

> Man may *picture* the bands of the rocks and the rivers,
> The hills and the valleys, the lakes and the ocean,
> *But the horrors of slavery, he never can trace.*
> (18, emphasis added)

Bibb therefore presents his text as an account that is both like and unlike his own
life. For example, he states that at the requests of friends, he has "undertaken to
write the following sketch, that light and truth might be spread on the sin and
evils of slavery *as far as possible*" (xii, emphasis added). There is a telling ambiguity
in the phrase "as far as possible." Is it meant to be a geographic statement (he is

FIGURE 4.7 Gold-embossed image on the red morocco cover of the second printing of Henry Bibb, *Narrative of the Life and Adventures of Henry Bibb* (1849). Courtesy of the Library Company of Philadelphia. The image also appears on the back cover of many editions.

spreading truth and light over the land, as far as possible) or a qualifying one (he is spreading light and truth on slavery, as far as it is possible to do so)? Again and again Bibb appears to tell his story but then undercuts it by indicating that it is in some sense unnarratable (58, 75, 126, 130).

For example, on pages 18–19, Bibb's text takes an image from the *American Anti-Slavery Almanac* of 1838 and adds wide margins and his own words to give it a peculiar visual effect (see figure 4.8). The passage on the left page that accompanies this image emphasizes that the "slave is a human being," but one whose sufferings are "aggravated a hundred fold, by the terrible thought, that he is not allowed to struggle against misfortune, corporeal punishment, insults and outrages committed upon himself and his family; and he is not allowed to help himself" (18). The slave comes close to being an instance of *homo sacer* here, and the image on page 19 contributes to this sense of powerlessness through its framing and placement on the page. Groensteen argues that reframing an image is "not like tailoring a suit out of a single piece of cloth," because "the possibility also exists to enlarge the frame, to add to it one (or several) portion(s)—since this expansion is carried out on one or several side(s) that belong to the virtual off-screen of the previous image" (*System of Comics*, 42). What are we to make, then, of the reframing of this image with wide white margins, and of there being only one sentence of text on the page, above the image? The dark, foreboding, and tattered image is literally buried in the whiteness of a nearly blank page. Bibb states that "the term slave to this day sounds with terror to my soul" (19), and we can perhaps see and feel some of this terror in the placement of the image on page 19, which virtually seems to silence Bibb. The lone sentence (appearing several inches above the picture) alludes to his disempowerment: "This idea of utter helplessness, in perpetual bondage, is the more distressing, as there is no period even with the remotest generation when it shall terminate" (19). It seems as if there is an eternity of space and time on either side of the image, a white grave in which the dark, coffin-shaped picture of "perpetual bondage" is entombed. In other places, Bibb's book crams multiple images onto a page, along with a great deal of text, so here the blankness signifies the terror that the illustration holds for Bibb's narrative persona. The verso side of this page is blank, so a viewer can glimpse a ghostly reversed trace of the engraving glimmering darkly through the blank field of page 20.

Icons of abolitionist visual culture take on additional connotations by their placement within the specific graphic narrative system of Bibb's text, within the story he is telling about his complex relationship to the past, to slavery, and to his own debasement within this omnipresent visual and psychological regime of torture. Yet Bibb also tells the story, at times, of his emergence from this torturous regime.

This idea of utter helplessness, in perpetual bondage, is the more distressing, as there is no period
even with the remotest generation when it shall
terminate.

FIGURE 4.8 Illustration from Henry Bibb, *Narrative of
the Life and Adventures*, 2nd ed. (1849), 19. Wood engraving.
Original source: *American Anti-Slavery Almanac* (1838).

For example, on page 22, an image is placed for which no one has yet detected a source—so perhaps it is original to Bibb's text. It is placed sideways (see figure 4.9). Pages 19 and 22 constitute a type of double page, and must be deciphered as such within what Groensteen terms a "panoptic field" that demands to be "traversed, crossed, glanced at, and analytically deciphered" (*System of Comics*, 19). Perhaps this double page allows a crossing-over from the flat and ghostly living death of the chain gang (page 19) into something like a living, three-dimensional slave community, even as it suggests that the living death of the chain gang haunts every other textual moment and cannot be evaded. This flux and flow characterizes Bibb's narrative as a whole, from silence and abjection into language, from death into living life and back, from slavery to freedom to recapture to another escape.

Bibb's text does not employ these images, which both are and are not within the scopic control of the master, as a form of redress. The image appearing after page 21 matches the words of the text rather specifically; the master orders his slaves to "frolic" on the Sabbath, so the action depicted in this image is quite literally generated by a master discourse. Yet the image breaks the master's discourse because it is reproduced by a fugitive slave who has escaped and written an indictment

" *The Sabbath among Slaves.*"

FIGURE 4.9 "The Sabbath among Slaves," original illustration from Henry Bibb, *Narrative of the Life and Adventures*, 2nd ed. (1849), between pages 21 and 23. Wood engraving. Courtesy of the Library Company of Philadelphia.

of the system. It undermines the master's discourse literally because the picture is inserted midsentence into the text. Page 21 ends abruptly: "The Sabbath is not regarded by a large number of the slaves as a day of rest. They have no schools to go to; no moral nor religious instruction at all in many localities where there are hundreds of" (21). Page 23 picks up the last word of the sentence: "slaves. Hence they resort to some kind of amusement. Those who make no profession of religion, resort to the woods in large numbers on that day to gamble, fight, get drunk, and break the Sabbath. This is often encouraged by slaveholders" (23). A literal break in the sentence occurs, placed between the words "of" and "slaves"; this placement of image interrupts a reader's ability to smoothly process the text's meaning. Having to turn the page sideways, look at the picture, and continue reading the second half of the sentence is distracting, to say the least, to a reader's concentration on the spectacle of the enslaved "frolicking."

Several other images run sideways in Bibb's text, and this orientation has received little critical scrutiny. It is an example of the illustrator taking advantage of print space through use of a panoramic perspective. It may also create a disruptive reading experience, perhaps by forcing a narrative pause when such pictures appear, as well as a spatial sense of disorientation, which is apparent in an image reversing the North and the South (see figure 4.10). The original image (from the *American Anti-Slavery Almanac* of 1840) ran horizontally across the top of the front cover of volume 1, number 5, with this caption: "The slave steps out of the slave-state, and his chains fall. A free state, with another chain, stands ready to re-enslave him." In Bibb's text, the image is rotated ninety degrees to the right, putting "slave state" at the top of the illustration—so in the north spatially— with the "free state" at the bottom of the illustration (geographically, south). This spatial-topographical distortion creates a disorienting reading experience as well as an uncomfortable one; I crook my neck to look at the image, and so experience a physical degree of discomfort and discomposure at this point in the text.

Bibb, the printer, and the text may all use such visuals to encourage a more active reading experience, a process that to some degree asks a reader to reflect on how meaning itself is marshaled and created within visual rhetoric. Groensteen contends that when the arrangement of a graphic narrative is chaotic and irregular, the layout can be transformed into an "ostentatious performance" rather than an "apparently neutral apparatus" (*System of Comics*, 61); this performance can break a reader's "captivity to the rhythm" or natural flow of the text as a whole. The layout of Bibb's text often breaks a reader's ability to process it neatly, smoothly, or comfortably. The unusual visual technologies of the text create gaps, distortions, and holes within the system of meaning surrounding enslavement and abolitionist

FIGURE 4.10 Illustration from Henry Bibb, *Narrative of the Life and Adventures*, 2nd ed. (1849), 71. Wood engraving. Original source: *American Anti-Slavery Almanac* (1840).

discourse, gaps that a reader must struggle to excavate. It is from within these gaps that a new abolitionist structure of feeling might emerge.

Indeed, it is only from within these slips of narrative time or visual space that anything like the "true" story of enslaved experience might be apprehended. It is an oblique and cryptic story at best. One such moment occurs when Bibb's wife, Malinda, gives birth to their second child, who dies. Placed squarely in the center of the text, at the end of chapter 10 (there are twenty chapters), are three terse sentences, isolated from any narrative illustration: "My wife was very sick while we were both living with the Deacon. We expected every day would be her last. While she was sick, we lost our second child, and I was compelled to dig my own child's grave and bury it myself without even a box to put it in" (118). There is no discussion of Bibb's emotion, nor are there are pictures in the text for the space of six more pages, a relatively long pictorial gap. The visual and narrative silence underscores that this loss is profoundly beyond enunciation.[16] This is a story, in short, that Bibb will not tell, and he thereby perhaps forces a reader to use theory of mind to amend or abridge this narrative gap.

Of course, at other times Bibb's text, like many discussed in this book, includes generic images of the torture of enslaved women and men. Sometimes these images are piled into the text without a great deal of narrative commentary beyond the mere fact of the beating itself (see page 118, for example), and sometimes they depict graphic thrashings of half-naked women. Bibb reuses the image captioned "The Flogging of Females" from the *Anti-Slavery Record* of October 1835 (see figure 2.9), which features frontal nudity. The text shows enslaved persons being auctioned off to the highest bidder, an iconographic trope that would have been familiar to his readers.

On the other hand, the text also includes new images that defamiliarize such visual icons. Sometimes they are defamiliarized by running the image on a vertical or landscape axis (rather than horizontal or portrait), which creates more visual space in which to depict enslaved bodies with detail and care (see figure 4.11). This illustration, the last in the text, crafts a representation of how men and women might refuse to be dehumanized under slavery. A viewer can see this in the foreground figures of a parent in chains comforting a weeping child and of a mother hugging one of her children before being sold; the enslaved women's connection with children and family is not erased, even in the face of torture. In this meticulous wood engraving, enslaved persons are sharply and carefully delineated, right down to the cut of their vests or the folds of their skirts, and several hold the supplicating pose of the famous Wedgwood medallion, as if to create an echo in readers' minds of this image.

FIGURE 4.11 Thomas W. Strong, illustration from Henry Bibb, *Narrative of the Life and Adventures*, 2nd ed. (1849), between pages 200 and 202. Wood engraving. Courtesy of the Library Company of Philadelphia.

But even within this traditional mode of representing the supplicant slave, Bibb's text endeavors to shift a viewing reader's horizon of expectations toward a degree of parallel (rather than merely hierarchical) empathy for the enslaved. For example, a circle of men in the background (presumably those who will buy the slaves) mostly appear to look everywhere but at the "merchandise"; by this device, the enslaved figures in the foreground appear to gain a small degree of privacy. The image fits the words of the text and tells a powerful story of family separation, with which a reader might empathize:

> They ordered the first woman [being sold at auction] to lay down her child and mount the auction block; she refused to give up her little one and clung to it as long as she could, while the cruel lash was applied to her back for disobedience. She pleaded for mercy in the name of God. But the child was torn from the arms of its mother amid the most heart rending-shrieks from the mother and child on the one hand, and bitter oaths and cruel lashes from the tyrants on the other. Finally . . . [the mother] was sacrificed to the highest bidder. (202)

From this description (which continues for several more paragraphs), it is apparent that Bibb employs vivid storytelling modes to portray enslaved torment when he chooses to do so, and that he can evoke a reader's pity or sympathy for these abject bodies. On the other hand, he is meticulous in denoting that human beings within family units are tortured by this process, and also in figuring resistance to dehumanization. For example, the persons depicted insist on praying and comforting one another, even while being lashed by the overseer. Referring to the enslaved "mother and child" works to position them as human beings rather than chattel, property, or subhuman entities for whom a reader need feel no care or regard.

The image is signed with an artist's name (Strong, NY), and some editions of the text list Thomas Strong as an engraver. The nineteenth-century engraver and lithographer Thomas W. Strong worked in New York from 1845 to 1851 (Groce and Wallace, *Artists in America*, 611; Peters, *America on Stone*, 377), when Bibb was most likely crafting his narrative. Strong worked in several media, and he later created illustrations for *Uncle Tom's Cabin* such as the lithograph *Perilous Escape of Eliza and Child* (ca. 1853), caricatures of figures in this book, and prints mocking the link between abolition and mesmerism, such as *Professor Pompey Magnetizing an Abolition Lady* (1852) (Peters, *America on Stone*, 378). An extremely talented wood engraver, Strong was fully aware of the modes that visual representations of enslavement could take. That some editions of Bibb's text use this drawing as the frontispiece or as part of a paper wrapper for the volume (similar to a book jacket) to advertise its contents indicate that both Bibb and Strong felt that it had great power.[17]

The panoramic perspective of figure 4.11 shows off Strong's fine skills, yet is also tipped vertically (unlike Bourne's *Auction at Richmond*, which it closely resembles), creating a longer flat space in which to delineate the bodies being auctioned. Goddu has argued that abolitionists adapted slavery's panoramic perspectives for their own ends of scopic control over enslaved bodies ('Antislavery's Panoramic Perspective"). Yet scopic focus is here drawn to the auctioneer, the one figure who stands above the (implied) horizontal line; he stands on the table, at the center of the picture, precariously dangling the infant by its arm. As with Bourne's *Auction at Richmond* (see figure 2.13), frames from windows appear to cast light onto the auctioneer; the top half of the illustration, clean and light, attracts our eyes. If a reader turns the illustration to a horizontal orientation, his or her eyes might be drawn first to the light, top half of the picture and then down to the circle of white men who look on in puzzlement. White figures in the left and right back corners seem to look back at the viewing reader. Directly in the viewer's perspective lines, they seem to ask the viewer to project himself or herself into the picture. The picture does not illustrate as much visual resistance to torture as we find in Bourne's text (as, for example, with K.'s upraised arm; see figure 2.8). Yet certainly it disrupts a reader's scopic viewing of black, abject bodies by presenting a number of figures on which a viewer's eyes might focus and by highlighting not the bodies of the enslaved but that of the auctioneer.

Opposition to the optical reign of slavery is also visually embedded within the text's characterization of enslaved masculinity and femininity. Bibb's text endeavors to create a structure of feeling entailing parallel empathy in which both Bibb and his wife, Malinda, are viewed as active and fluid characters rather than passive and static ones. Malinda in some ways is characterized by the literary stereotype of the tragic mulatto (she does ultimately become her master's concubine),[18] yet it is never really clear how tragic she is. For example, when the family is surrounded by wolves during an escape attempt, she is described as taking "a club in one hand, and her child in the other" in order to help Bibb "fight off the savage wolves" (127); she resembles a heroic character in a story rather than an abject fugitive slave. In addition, Bibb represents Malinda as refusing to be silent about her separation from her husband. Her lamentation is loud and long and ends with words that serve as the caption of an illustration: "'Oh! how shall I give my husband the parting hand never to meet again? This will surely break my heart'" (147). The illustration does not interrupt her discourse, because it is included after she has finished speaking (see figure 4.12). In this less accomplished wood engraving (also signed by Strong), Malinda is sheltered to some extent within the arms of her husband; yet she is the one speaking, and so she gets the last word in the scene, over both her husband and the master. This image is a very small circular drawing placed on

"Oh! how shall I give my husband the parting hand never to meet again."

FIGURE 4.12 Thomas W. Strong, illustration from Henry Bibb,
Narrative of the Life and Adventures, 2nd ed. (1849), 148. Wood
engraving. Courtesy of the Library Company of Philadelphia.

a full page, with massive blank borders surrounding it and no text other than the
caption, which gives her words even more force. It is unframed, and the illustration appears unfinished. The master's face is a masklike structure of brute force; he
looks inhuman, especially in relationship to the kneeling figures of Bibb, his wife,
and the beseeching child, Frances. What stands out from the design are Malinda's
words, spoken in direct discourse—her refusal (at least linguistically) to give her
husband "the parting hand never to meet again." The wounding of the enslaved
body is implied more than illustrated, and verbal and psychological obstruction to
the master's action of separating husband and wife are focalized.

Bibb's text grants outspoken and direct voice to Malinda in another significant
picture, the representation that embellishes the front and back covers of some
editions but also is duplicated within the text on page 81 with the caption "My
heart is almost broken" (see figure 4.13). Bibb's illustrator makes this image, too,
stand out and carry further emphasis by presenting it on a full page, with massive white borders around it. The text on the facing page closely matches what is
shown in the illustration and the caption: "Malinda clasped my hand exclaiming,

'oh my soul! My heart is almost broken,'" at which point she bursts into tears (80). Bibb also refers to taking leave of his "little family" (80), and the illustrator deftly positions Frances within the artwork to echo this phrase. In a text with so many drawings that break sentences, defer information about illustrations, do not connect illustrations with the narrative, or include sarcastic revisions of earlier abolitionist illustrations, we must consider the close correspondence between text and image to matter. This wood engraving grants the nearest approach to the horror of slavery in the text as a whole, and it is an entirely personal one—the psychological trauma of leaving wife and child, which marks these persons as fully human. The language and visual imagery here are sentimental, of course. Yet a viewer's perspective line places the figures at eye level, encouraging participatory observation of the story rather than voyeurism. Moreover, a reader is here given partial access to Bibb's consciousness as a way of incompletely apprehending knowledge about enslavement. "This was *almost* like tearing off the limbs from my body" (80, emphasis added), writes Bibb—almost, but not quite.

Generally, the text uses its visual rhetoric to portray Malinda as possessing a degree of resistance and individuality. In so doing, the text structures an abolitionist

" *My heart is almost broken.*"

FIGURE 4.13 Illustration from Henry Bibb, *Narrative of the Life and Adventures*, 2nd ed. (1849), 81. Wood engraving. Courtesy of the Library Company of Philadelphia.

reading of her that diverges from the dominant rhetoric of mainstream abolitionist visual culture, in which women were frequently portrayed (as has been previously argued) as abject victims of torture, available for the surveillance of a scopic
and even pornographic gaze. The text attempts to move Malinda's characterization beyond the tragic mulatta stereotype, too, and toward a more active form
of African American female heroism, such as that embodied by Maria Stewart,
Sojourner Truth, or Harriet Jacobs. Moreover, unlike Joanna, who dies, it appears
that Malinda lives on, and there is even a hint that she uses a sexual relationship
with her master to gain some degree of power over the circumstances of her life
(189–90). William Andrews reads Bibb's entire narrative as "an elaborate bill of
divorce" (*To Tell a Free Story*, 35), yet surely something more complicated transpires
in Bibb's story of their relationship. Bibb portrays Malinda as attempting to take
control over her life through affiliation with her master. Of course, Malinda is
still a slave and subject to her master's whims, but Bibb's narration of these events
emphasizes a degree of volition on Malinda's part.

The text's visual rhetoric attempts to structure an abolitionist reading of other
enslaved women's resistance. By reusing visual images of enslaved women with
speech balloons that emerge from their mouths, Bibb's visual rhetoric again argues
for women's potential for enslaved agency or voice. Figure 4.14 reproduces a drawing from the *American Anti-Slavery Almanac* from 1840. Wood has criticized
the degradation of the quality of this image over time, which is certainly clear
("Seeing is Believing," 184, 186). But because Bibb's text also portrays women such
as Malinda who are not utterly destroyed by slavery, and who use speech in their
forms of resistance, the image takes on new valence by its placement within a text
that stresses the existence of African American feminine heroism despite grave
oppression. Martin Barker comments, "There is an interaction between the pictures and the verbalness of the speech-balloon, to produce the meaning of sound.
We 'hear with our eyes'" (*Comics*, 11). There are many images of women in the 1840
Almanac that Bibb could have drawn upon, so it is significant that he places an
illustration into his text that attempts to give women voice through the device of a
speech balloon. This placement may also critique abolitionist silencing of women
activists (black and white) at important antislavery meetings and conventions
during this period. It may encourage theory of mind as a reader "hears" (or constructs) this woman's speech with his or her eyes. Empathy is further enabled by
the context for this illustration: it is situated in Bibb's text within a discussion of
women's insistence on being mothers to their children, despite enslavement (118).
Bibb delineates acts that resist dehumanization, such as refusing to be silent or to
abandon a child, even while under the whip, and the words in the speech balloon

FIGURE 4.14   Illustration from Henry Bibb, *Narrative of the
Life and Adventures*, 2nd ed. (1849), 115. Original source: *American
Anti-Slavery Almanac* (1840). Wood engraving. Courtesy of the
Library Company of Philadelphia.

("oh my child, my child") emphasize such a mode of insubordination. This image
does not allow a reader to understand the real horror that is slavery, but it does
allow him or her to come closer to comprehending structures of resistance to the
abasement that enslavement entails.

So too with enslaved masculinity: a reader obtains only a simulacrum of its
function and meaning from Bibb's text, but a simulacrum designed to complicate
abolitionist focus on the passive and static slave and to encourage parallel empathy
by portraying complex and multifaceted representations of enslaved subjectivity.
Bibb details how he is forced to witness his wife and child being tortured (42–43).
Enslaved paternity, in particular, creates a visual landscape of the utmost horror
that again challenges language's expressive capacities: "Unfortunately for me, I
am the father of a slave, a word too obnoxious to be spoken by a fugitive slave.
It calls fresh to my mind the separation of husband and wife; of stripping tying
up and flogging; of tearing children from their parents, and selling them on the
auction block" (44). The recitation of the traumas of enslaved paternity threatens
to overwhelm Bibb as his language breaks apart in a run-on flow of emotion ("of
stripping tying up and flogging"). It is here that he inserts two relatively generic
illustrations of slave floggings (45) from the 1835 issue of the *Anti-Slavery Record*.
These image-texts may allow him to gain mastery over the too painful memories

of his own past; an image is inserted that is both like and unlike what he endured, allowing partial containment of the trauma.

By these verbal and visual mechanisms, Bibb controls the subjective temporality of (enslaved) consciousness and memory and also creates a specific construction of his performance of masculinity. Ultimately, he portrays himself as becoming active in his quest for freedom and crafting a new form of subjectivity. But he initially tries to perform several traditional constructs of masculinity. First, he attempts to configure freedom as an abstract right that men possess, sounding a bit like Patrick Henry: "The voice of liberty was thundering in my very soul, 'Be free, oh, man!'" (47). Such freedom, however, can be pursued only at the expense of his family, as he learns, which interferes with another construct of masculinity, marriage and paternity: "All my flattering prospects of enjoying my own fire-side, with my little family, were then blasted and gone" (62).[19] On several occasions, Bibb tries to escape with his family, but they are retaken, and the illustrations of this part of the text attempt to configure him as a true husband and father, protecting his family (see figure 4.15). As noted, when the wolves attack, Malinda does take a club in one hand, but the illustrator of this image (Strong, again) does not picture this action. Instead, Strong represents Bibb standing up in a manly way to the wolves. Yet Bibb is retaken, and ultimately he must escape alone. This construct of masculinity—men as protecting fathers and husbands—is not available to enslaved African American men, forcing them to seek other avenues for self-definition.

FIGURE 4.15 Thomas W. Strong, illustration from Henry Bibb, *Narrative of the Life and Adventures*, 2nd ed. (1849), 125. Wood engraving. Documenting the American South.

In defiance of such traditional constructions of masculinity, Bibb ultimately portrays himself manipulating a multivalent and even protean mode of identity that finally allows a partial figurative escape from enslaved subjectivity. In one escape, Bibb wears "false whiskers" (56–57), in another he passes for a white passenger on a ship (48), in another he assumes the guise of a body servant (166–67), and in yet another he poses as a white gentleman (168). Passing for white may be a way to blur the binary structure of enslaved torture, which, as noted in other chapters, relies on a configuration of the enslaved as brutalized, viewed, disempowered object and the (white) spectator as free, viewing, empowered subject.[20] Bibb fosters parallel empathy in a white viewer in moments when he equates himself explicitly with white men: "But I ask, if a white man had been captured by the Cherokee Indians and carried away from his family for life into slavery . . . would it be a crime for the poor fugitive, whose life, liberty and future happiness were all at stake, to mount any man's horse by the way side, and ride him without asking any questions, to effect his escape? Or who would not do the same thing to rescue a wife, child, father, or mother?" (163). By using a series of interrogatives, Bibb attempts to put the viewer into the shoes of the enslaved even as he weakens the boundaries between "black" and "white" identities, between free citizens and abject, enslaved others. Over and over again he hails a reader, asking him or her to enter the narrative moment he is describing.

Like Moses Roper, Bibb includes images in which he cannot be distinguished from a white person (see the illustration captioned "Never Mind the Money"). In so doing, he may enhance a parallel empathetic response by entangling his own body with that of a white viewer. Moreover, the text specifically and daringly introduces a reward poster for Bibb's return, but one that has been significantly remade and that does not make his race apparent. At one point in the narrative, Bibb expects to meet, but never encounters, "an advertisement for my person" (166). Instead of placing this advertisement within the action of the text, he introduces a remodeled version of it into the bottom of the double portrait of the frontispiece of the second edition from 1849 (see figure 4.6). The engraving at the top of the page by Patrick Henry Reason depicts Bibb as a serious young man. It is a tasteful and carefully constructed image of Bibb, with a hand resting on a book, which symbolizes his literacy, authorship, and control over the technologies of printing and image making. A well-dressed Bibb confronts a viewer with a direct look from eyes that appear wise but also saddened. Because of Bibb's direct glance, literacy, and tasteful dress, a middle-class reader might intersubjectively enter into what Husserl calls the "world-experience" of Bibb. Simon Gikandi argues for a politics of modern subjectivity that is subtended by the visual presentation of abject black bodies "excluded from the domain of modern reason, aesthetic judgment, and the culture of taste" (*Slavery and Taste*, 5). The tasteful figuration of Bibb—as a reader, a writer, a well-dressed man, and a serious thinker with whom a reader might identify—stands in opposition to such a contrapuntal creation of a modern subject sustained by a premodern and abject (black) object. Its tastefulness closely matches a lithograph of Bibb made in 1847 (see figure 4.17), suggesting that Reason's engraving presents the "real" essence of Henry Bibb.

FIGURE 4.16 Frontispiece to some versions of Henry Bibb, *Narrative of the Life and Adventures*, 2nd ed. (1849), with double portrait. *Top*: copper engraving by Patrick Henry Reason. *Bottom*: wood engraving (artist unknown). Courtesy of the Library Company of Philadelphia.

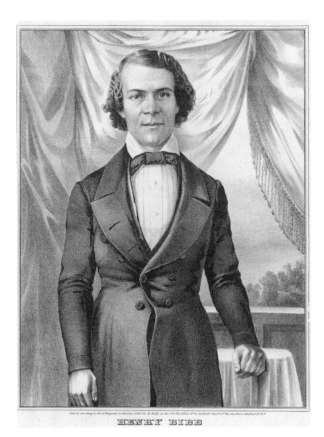

HENRY BIBB

FIGURE 4.17 Henry
Walton Bibb. Lithograph
on paper, 1847, unidentified
artist. National Portrait
Gallery, Smithsonian
Institution.

Does the cartoon image below Reason's engraving provide the realm of abjection out of which Bibb flees, the flight that allows a tasteful construction of himself as a modern self? Gikandi notes that the conceptual separation between modern culture and the world of bondage, premised on a "quarantine" of the modern subject from the "contaminating forces associated with the political economy of slavery and commerce," was continually "haunted by what is excluded or repressed" (*Slavery and Taste*, 100)—which is to say, the fact of slavery or the body of the slave. Bibb's frontispiece represents both the tasteful modern subject and the abject and contaminated realm of enslavement, but it also dismantles the line between these realms by refusing to exclude the ghost or trace of slavery from the formation of the modern subject. It specifically cites, in other words, a connection between the exclusion of the slave (bottom image) from the domain of enlightened subjectivity and the way this exclusion is founded upon an abject "other" who lies, literally and symbolically, beneath the modern subject.

FIGURE 4.18 Detail, frontispiece to Henry Bibb, *Narrative of the
Life and Adventures*, 2nd ed. (1849). Wood engraving. Courtesy of the
Library Company of Philadelphia.

Moreover, the cartoonlike fleeing figure refuses to be contained within the discourse of enslavement. The sarcastic words to the left of the image, "Stop the runaway! Where is he!" seem to indicate that "he" (that is, the escaped slave) cannot be
contained by the discourse (see figure 4.18). At one point, Bibb comments that no
one would buy him because "they saw the devil in my eye; I would run away, &c."
(102). "He" is ultimately a trickster-like figure who amends the breach between
Bibb's status as chattel and as a man, and "he" ameliorates the gap between the
signifier "slave" and his present-tense identity as Henry Bibb through ambiguous
and mutating identities. In the reward poster, it is difficult to tell the race of the
fleeing person; he is caught in a pool of white light, yet not truly caught. There is
a chaotic and ludic quality to the cartoon as Bibb flees with his hands in the air
between rickety houses. Furthermore, because we do not read the advertisement
for Bibb in the text, the image is nondiegetic—it illustrates something that does
not happen in the narrative proper.

And where exactly is Bibb fleeing to in this cartoon? Like Roper, Bibb may be
gesturing to a nondiegetic space outside the text into which he darts—a space
of freedom where he can (finally) articulate his full subjectivity. The flowing line
under his signature describes an elliptical space, a utopian realm of freedom that
the narrative never depicts Bibb reaching. As Lynn Casmier-Paz has noted, author

portraits often operate as paratextual elements that validate racial identity: "The author portraits of slave narratives struggle to evidence multiple icons of realistic, biographical representation available to the period" ("Slave Narratives," 92). Augusta Rohrbach similarly argues that such portraits "locate the physical body" for a readership and to some degree guarantee it a "textual authenticity" (*Truth Stranger than Fiction*, 127). Bibb's frontispiece double portrait both grants his authenticity—he certainly seems real and stable enough in the top image—and undermines it, by mocking the idea that "he" (Bibb) can really be found in the text at all. Placed at the start of the text, this doubled and doubling portrait signals the deconstructive ways that visual and textual rhetoric are employed in the narrative as a whole, and the multivalent character that Bibb fashions to create the objective temporality of discursive performance and re-create his past (tense) self in ways that do not annihilate his present (tense) subjectivity. The double portrait foreshadows his escape from enslavement and movement into authorship, as does the copyright inscription for the text, which reads: "Entered according to the Act of Congress in the year 1849 by H. Bibb"; the inscription makes clear, as Gwendolyn DuBois Shaw notes, "that Bibb possessed himself and his own life story" (*Portraits of a People*, 166). Yet even so, the portrait refuses to locate the space in which this new self-possessed subjectivity is crafted—and Bibb, like Roper, found freedom only outside the geographic realm of the United States.

Bibb's text was popular, making its way into a third edition by 1850, so perhaps the reading public felt that the "real Henry Bibb" was present in the text.[21] Perhaps readers empathized with the man captured to some degree within the text itself, especially in such moments as when he avers that leaving his little family of wife and child "was *almost* like tearing off the limbs from my body." In the above cartoon image, however, "Bibb turned the corner too quick for [his captor] & escaped," in the same way that the real Bibb perhaps escapes from this text as a whole. The central conundrum of Bibb's text is how to tell a story about slavery that will cultivate readerly empathy even as he highlights the unstable nature of both words and images to connote the particular self-deconstructing reality that enslavement entails. The profound double impulse in the frontispiece—to tell the "truth" of enslavement yet be skeptical of visual rhetoric's ability to convey truth—gives the story its tension as a graphic narrative. The illustrations in the text (those that connect with it, and those that do not) allow Bibb's persona to avoid being pulled back into the traumatic memory palace of the past even as they push him forward into a nondiegetic space in the future, where he may obtain control over the subjective temporality of (enslaved) consciousness through the more objective (and controllable) activity of visual representation and rhetorical storytelling.

Conclusion: Moving the Unspeakable into Representation

I have argued in this chapter that Child and Bibb appropriate images from other texts and integrate them within their own graphic narrative systems in ways that allow new meanings to emerge. In so doing, they shift a reader's horizon of expectation away from a representation of the enslaved as completely disempowered by the system of enslavement. For Child, the new messages that her text promotes have to do with the idea that the enslaved are not different from the viewing self (and therefore should be the recipient of a mode of empathy), and for Bibb these new messages concern the resilience, agency, and attempted control of the enslaved over the representation of enslavement. Yet both texts highlight gaps at the center of their stories concerning the subject under representation. The pieces of the story belonging to other people and other texts are incorporated and assimilated not only to tell the story for Bibb or Child, but also to expand questions at each book's center: questions about the meaning of slavery, masculinity, and femininity, and about modes of narration and the way they can fail to uncover certain types of gendered or racialized voices or experiences.

The story that is slavery is full of holes, gaps, fissures, and unspeakable events, events that tear the fabric of language, memory, and identity. In many ways, as critics have noted, the "recovery" of this story is a quixotic project, an act of impossible witnessing, to use Dwight McBride's terms (*Impossible Witnesses*). Yet what is at stake here is not so much the "recovery" of an authentic and true experience that a reader can witness, but rather the writing of something new into these perhaps unrecoverable gaps and fissures. Child's and Bibb's graphic narrative systems concern not so much the uncovering of the past, then, as the imagination of traces of agency and subjectivity that might have been present in these experiences but also are presumed by Bibb and Child to be central to a new story that must be told about enslavement. Perhaps most importantly, they attempt to integrate a reader into the story of slavery through graphic narrative systems that are bricolaged and lacking in closure. In so doing, Child and Bibb compel a reader to live, at least for a time, within the diegetic space of a new type of antislavery illustrated book, a story in which the enslaved have access to a mode of power and are connected with a reader not as object to subject, but as one self to another.

After Tom

Illustrated Books, Panoramas, and the Staging of the
African American Enslaved Body in *Uncle Tom's Cabin* (1852)
and the Performance Work of Henry Box Brown (1849–1875)

In 2012, the African American performance artist Wilmer Wilson IV created three
skins composed of U.S. postage stamps to fit over his body. He walked through
the city of Washington, D.C., asking individuals to mail him to a number of other
locations (see figures 5.1 and 5.2; color image 11). Wilson's performance art was an
homage to the fugitive slave Henry Box Brown, who mailed himself in March
1849 from the South to the North in a large postal crate marked "Philadelphia,
PA; Right Side Up with Care." Incarnations of Brown's extraordinary escape from
his box began just several months later and continue into contemporary times by
way of quilts, films, graphic narratives, opera, performance pieces, and artworks;
there is even a wax sculpture of Brown escaping from his box at the Great Blacks
in Wax Museum in Baltimore, in which Brown's figure is made to wave his hand
slowly at the viewer (see figure 5.3; color image 12). And yet if the name of Henry
Box Brown is mentioned to a person unfamiliar with African American history,
a blank stare will be the likely response. If one alludes to fictional creations such
as Uncle Tom, Topsy, Little Eva, and Simon Legree (who shows up as a *Jeopardy!*
answer from time to time), many more people will catch these references. The
actions of fictional characters portrayed by Harriet Beecher Stowe in her novel
Uncle Tom's Cabin (1852, with six illustrations) have eclipsed the exploits of daring
and heroism by actual persons from this period.

More importantly for the purposes of this book, in the antebellum period, *Uncle
Tom's Cabin* was a huge commercial success that immediately spawned numer-
ous musical shows and panoramas, along with all kinds of memorabilia, in the
United States and Europe, as Sarah Meer has documented extensively in her

FIGURE 5.1 Wilmer Wilson IV, 2012, *Henry Box Brown: FOREVER* (day three, Congress-detail). Copyright Wilmer Wilson IV; courtesy Connersmith. Used with permission.

FIGURE 5.2 Wilmer Wilson IV, 2012, *Henry Box Brown: FOREVER* (day three, Congress-detail). Copyright Wilmer Wilson IV; courtesy Connersmith. Used with permission.

FIGURE 5.3 Wax figure of Henry Box Brown in the Great Blacks in Wax Museum,
Baltimore, 2014. Photograph by the author.

book *Uncle Tom Mania* (2005). Stowe's novel was the most phenomenally popular
and best-selling novel of the nineteenth century on both sides of the Atlantic.
The historian Thomas Gossett estimates that more than a million copies were
sold in England, and in 1852 alone the novel sold three hundred thousand copies in the United States (Riss, "Harriet Beecher Stowe," 34). Moreover, Stowe
was famously lauded by Abraham Lincoln as "the little woman who started the
big war" (Gossett, *"Uncle Tom's Cabin,"* 314). Whether the novel played a part in
the start of the Civil War—and whether it moved readers toward abolitionist
action or any action for that matter—has been debated by historians and literary
critics.[1] It is clear, however, that the archive of both realistic and stereotypical
racist visual materials generated by *Uncle Tom's Cabin*—illustrations, popular cartoons, prints, musical shows, movies, and even decorative plates—expanded until
at least the 1950s. In consideration of this visual culture, Claire Perry writes, "The
impact of *Uncle Tom's Cabin* was such that, for the rest of the century and well
after, its characters served as templates for portrayals of African-Americans in
literature, theater, and the visual arts" (*Young America*, 86). By contrast, Brown's
Narrative of Henry Box Brown, Who Escaped from Slavery, Enclosed in a Box (1849)

and *Narrative of the Life of Henry Box Brown, Written by Himself* (1851) had only moderate success. Furthermore, the moving panorama about slavery that Brown developed to accompany it—*Henry Box Brown's Mirror of Slavery* (exhibited in the United States and Europe from 1850 until at least 1865)—ultimately lost its audience in part because panoramas of *Uncle Tom's Cabin* were of greater interest to the public.

This chapter considers what is at stake in the visual representations of enslavement produced by Brown and Stowe, and why the visual rhetoric of *Uncle Tom's Cabin* (the symbiotic argument made by the interaction of words and pictures) came to dominate the visual landscape of enslavement for more than a hundred years, setting the pattern not only for other illustrated antislavery books of the period, such as Richard Hildreth's revised and updated edition of *The White Slave* (1852) and Solomon Northup's *Twelve Years a Slave* (1853), but also for many later representations of enslavement.[2] I argue that *Uncle Tom's Cabin* frequently deploys a strategy that triangulates empathy between the enslaved, a white person within the illustrated book, and a viewer. This triangulation generally relies on a mode of hierarchical empathy for the sometimes flattened characters, who may not engage a reader to construct the kind of complex representations of their world that would enable a sense of interconnection and interdependence between a reader and the enslaved (see the appendix for a definition of hierarchical empathy).[3] Conversely, representations of Brown within his narrative, panorama, and other performance modes endeavor to shift a viewing reader's horizon of expectations away from the more dominant depictions of enslaved subjectivity visually present in a text such as *Uncle Tom's Cabin*. Brown's multivalent visual persona refuses to be immobilized or pinioned, but rather multiplies itself endlessly in a series of startling transformations. My research demonstrates that Brown at times exhibited his panorama alongside those of *Uncle Tom's Cabin*. Brown may have been laying claim to a resistant and dynamic mode of visual rhetoric—what Marcus Wood terms a "semiotic fluidity" (*Blind Memory*, 114)—as well as to the more stereotypical mode present in a text such as *Uncle Tom's Cabin*. After *Uncle Tom's Cabin*, it seems that no representation of enslaved selfhood—even Brown's—would be unmarked by this pivotal text. Perhaps that was why Brown ultimately turned to magic and mesmerism in his later years, finding a realm where he could carve new routes into and out of the legacy of enslavement through acts of magical performance, transformation, and disappearance.

Historical Overview: Slavery and Abolition, 1849–1859

During the period 1849–1859, tensions concerning slavery grew increasingly divisive and became centered on two issues in particular: the North's role in returning fugitive slaves, and the part that violent resistance to slavery would play in abolition and in the nation as a whole. Undergirding these questions were broader ones about the status of the formerly enslaved in the body politic. Both Stowe and Brown negotiate these historical concerns in their works.

The most significant event influencing the works discussed in this chapter and perhaps this decade as a whole was the enactment of a second, more stringent Fugitive Slave Act, passed by Congress on September 18, 1850.[4] As part of a compromise between southern slave holders and the northern Free-Soil (antislavery) Party, the 1850 act required the return of any escaped slave, once captured, to his or her master, and cooperation with the law by all officials and citizens of the free states, under pain of heavy penalty. It was nicknamed the "bloodhound law" because these dogs often were used to hunt down runaway escapees (Gara, "Fugitive Slave Law," 273). Not coincidentally, Brown refers to bloodhounds in his panorama (which he began performing in 1850), as does Stowe in several crucial incidents in her novel. Stowe alludes to this law specifically in chapter 9, in which Senator Bird, a northern senator who has just voted for it, nonetheless helps his wife shelter and abet Eliza Harris, a runaway slave, on her way to Canada.

The 1850 Fugitive Slave Act was undergirded by a complicated series of issues negotiated by Henry Clay. Their resolution came to be known as the Compromise of 1850, which endeavored to contain hostility between the North and the South over the extension of slavery into the territories. This compromise held until 1854, but mainly "papered over" larger concerns and questions (Waugh, *On the Brink*, 190). Indeed, the passage of the Fugitive Slave Act may have increased tensions, since abolitionists were able to use the law to capitalize on widespread northern sentiment against returning fugitives to slavery and to link the cause of slavery with the idea of civil rights (Gara, "Fugitive Slave Law," 272–73).

As discussed later in this chapter, Brown's and Stowe's texts allude to aggressive confrontations between slaves and slaveholders, or between those who support slavery and those who oppose it. In this sense, their texts foreshadow what happened during the rest of the decade. Despite the Compromise of 1850, states such as New Hampshire, Ohio, Wisconsin, and Vermont continued to pass personal liberty laws that made it difficult to return slaves, and pockets of violence had begun to erupt on both sides of the debate by 1855. The most notable of these— considered by some historians a "mini civil war"—occurred in the Kansas territory in 1855–56, part of a larger conflict that came to be known as Bleeding Kansas (1854–61). Kansas had not been admitted as a state into the Union, and there was enormous debate about whether it would enter as a free or a slave state; potential voters from both sides of the debate flooded the territory in an attempt to influence this outcome. In May 1856, a proslavery group assaulted the antislavery town of Lawrence, destroying and stealing property. In response, the radical abolitionist John Brown and his followers attacked a proslavery settlement at Pottawatomie Creek, killing five men. Violence continued to escalate, and by the end of 1856, nearly two hundred people had been killed, and property worth two million dollars had been damaged or destroyed (Earle and Burke, introduction, 3). Violence over the situation in Kansas even erupted onto the floor of the U.S. Senate. In May 1856, Massachusetts senator Charles Sumner delivered an oration called "The Crime against Kansas," a biting speech in which he attacked slavery and the South, singling out his Senate colleague Andrew Butler of South Carolina for rebuke. In retaliation Butler's nephew, Congressman Preston Brooks of South Carolina, attacked Sumner with a cane on the floor of the Senate, beating him unconscious and causing injuries so grave that Sumner was absent from the Senate for four years (Hoffer, *Caning of Charles Sumner*, 1–3).

While senators squabbled, John Brown and his followers, having escaped from Kansas, began taking matters into their own hands, advocating outright violence to end slavery. In 1859, Brown attempted to take over the federal arsenal at Harper's Ferry in Virginia; his goal was to use the weapons there to encourage a slave rebellion. Brown and his followers were caught and hanged, becoming martyrs for some in the antislavery movement who argued for the immediate end of slavery and endorsed violent methods to reach this goal (Rodriguez, "Chronology," 63). In general, the role of violent self-defense and violence itself grew more heated within U.S. abolitionist circles after 1850 (Stewart, *Holy Warriors*, 150–57).

Perhaps in response to some of these developments and the seeming inevitability of a brutal war that might free the enslaved, the nation as a whole began to debate the future status of this group within (or outside) the body politic of the United States. One argument, concerning African American citizenship, centered on the U.S. Supreme Court's infamous *Dred Scott* decision of 1857. Dred Scott had sued for his freedom in 1846 on the grounds that he had been taken to live in a state that did not allow slavery—Missouri—by his master. The case dragged on for years through lower courts until Chief Justice Roger B. Taney (a southerner) ruled in *Dred Scott v. Sandford* that African Americans were not "citizens" under the Constitution and could therefore claim none of the rights and privileges of citizens of the United States. He added that blacks were "a subordinate and inferior class of beings, who had been subjugated by the dominant race" and therefore "whether emancipated or not yet remained subject to their authority." Before this ruling, a few states had allowed free blacks some state citizenship rights (DeLombard, *Shadow of the Gallows*, 52), but the Supreme Court decision put this status in jeopardy.

Another escalating dispute had to do with colonization. Some abolitionists saw colonization as a way to argue for immediate emancipation of the enslaved, while others believed that "repatriation" might remove from the United States an inferior and non-citizenship-bearing class of people with an inherent criminality (Newman, *Freedom's Prophet*, 203). These debates had been ongoing for a number of years, and from 1821 onward thousands of free blacks had moved to Liberia from the United States. Yet Liberia was not recognized as an independent nation until 1847. This historical development was certainly in Stowe's mind as she began to pen *Uncle Tom's Cabin* four years later; she crafted a space for several of her agentive and near-white former slaves in Liberia rather than in the United States. The novel's visual rhetoric, as will be seen, also works toward a spatial and emotional segregation of a viewing subject from the enslaved black individuals depicted.

Triangulation of Visual Empathy in *Uncle Tom's Cabin*

This section analyzes the visual rhetoric employed in the first edition of *Uncle Tom's Cabin*, published in the United States in 1852 by Jewett and Company. To date, little critical attention has been paid to how the illustrations in this first edition contribute to the text's formulation of a visual rhetoric that entails sympathy, empathy, or sentimental power.[5] In a savvy marketing move, Stowe released this two-volume set (the first with visuals) *before* the novel had finished its serialization in forty-one weekly installments in the *National Era* (June 5, 1851–April 1, 1852). Readers who bought the first published book edition in 1852 therefore were able to read and, perhaps more importantly, to see the last pivotal chapters of the novel before those who had faithfully followed Uncle Tom, Eliza, and Topsy in the pages of the periodical press throughout the prior year (Gates and Robbins, "Harriet Beecher Stowe," xxxvii).

Critics such as Marianne Noble and others have noted that Stowe "sought to make readers feel the pain that slaves felt in order to force upon them an intuitive, experiential approach to the abolitionist question" (*Masochistic Pleasures*, 126). Yet the text's visual rhetoric sometimes undercuts this process. Although Stowe's stated aim, as she says at the end of her novel, is to make every reader understand that "an atmosphere of sympathetic influence encircles every human being" (2:317), *Uncle Tom's Cabin* at times places black characters outside what Husserl has called the world-experience of a reader, and so impedes intersubjectivity (*Cartesian Meditations*). Recent cognitive studies of literary fiction (texts that are "writerly and polyphonic" and "engage the psychological processes needed to gain access to characters' subjective experiences") have argued that such texts can enhance empathy when they force a reader to understand the ambiguity of another's world (see Kidd and Castano, "Reading Literary Fiction," 378, 380; also see Oatley, *Such Stuff as Dreams*). Stowe's characters sometimes are presented through a stereotypical mode in which they lack complex, dense, or polyphonic emotions; as Hartman notes, even Tom's performance in the novel is "embellished with minstrelsy," and blackness as a whole is often "delineated by darky antics—lying, loafing, stealing, and breakdown dancing" (*Scenes of Subjection*, 28). The novel also reproduces sectional, racial, and gendered stereotypes of the time (Sinha, *Slave's Cause*, 443). Empathy for such stereotypical characters cannot be felt directly, but only through a mediational and saintly presence that decontaminates and triangulates a reader's relationship to them.

Triangulation mainly is used here in a visual-spatial sense, but there are psychological overtones to this visual structure as well. Spatially, triangulation is a process of determining a location by measuring angles to it from another known and fixed point on a baseline; in other words, the distance to the unknown point (in this case empathy with the enslaved by a viewer) is not measured directly but proportionally through a "known" angle of a (white) viewing presence within the illustration (see diagram 5.1). The theory of triangulation operates psychologically in the novel as well. Following the work of the Swiss psychiatrist Ernst Abelin, psychological theorists have analyzed how individuals or even entire social organizations fall into a triadic structure of perpetrator-victim-rescuer ("Role of the Father"). Recasting the Oedipal romance of father-mother-child into something

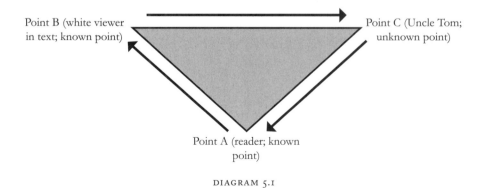

Point B (white viewer in text; known point)

Point C (Uncle Tom; unknown point)

Point A (reader; known point)

DIAGRAM 5.1

like viewer-child-slave, *Uncle Tom's Cabin* uses a figurative white body that takes on the demands of empathy and love. If the reading public, which Stowe envisions as predominantly white, loves this figurative white body, then it too (by way of triangulation) can come to love (or at least sympathize with) the abject slave. But agency is detached from the enslaved body, since the figurative white body takes on the demands of relieving its pain, feeling rightly, and demanding an end to slavery. A reader absorbs this feeling of empathy and demand for justice from the white body (or its surrogates) instead of directly from the enslaved, leaving the enslaved in the contaminated sphere of abjection.

Before moving to the specific strategy of triangulation that *Uncle Tom's Cabin* often employs, I should note that visual rhetoric using a structure of abjection is present from the start of the text, in the image embossed on the covers and used as a title page vignette on both volumes of the 1852 first edition. This image inculcates a visual mode that encourages pity and hierarchal empathy rather than intersubjectivity and parallel empathy (see figures 5.4 and 5.5 and color image 13). In the first edition of *Uncle Tom's Cabin*, this and all other illustrations were created by Hammatt Billings. Billings and Stowe shared abolitionist sensibilities, and she seems to have been pleased with the illustrations, since Billings also illustrated several other editions (O'Gorman, *Accomplished in All Departments*, 47–48). In bold letters, the title page (see figure 5.5) proclaims: "Uncle Tom's Cabin," and then, in the same size font, "Life among the Lowly." The "or" between the title and subtitle implies that "Life among the Lowly" is a type of translation of "Uncle Tom's Cabin," a second titling of the work.[6] In the vignette, Uncle Tom appears in the far background on the left, Aunt Chloe stands in the cabin entrance, and three children (whom Stowe frequently refers to as "woolly headed" in the text)[7] cluster around the doorway to the home. What makes this picture an illustration of "life among the lowly"? Is it that the story will dramatize a destruction of this family through the selling of the father (Tom)? The father (in the background) is literally small and underdeveloped, suggesting his lack of presence and empowered masculinity in the world of the novel.[8] If we follow Freud, the father should break up the Oedipal love dyad of mother and child, but he fails in this enterprise (Tom is in fact sold away from his family). The main action of the illustration is set in the liminal territory of the threshold—between the cultured realm of the home and the natural world of the environment—and perhaps because of this, it has a transitory and even claustrophobic feel. The trees and shrubbery creep into the home, suggesting that the domain of the (slave) home is no genuine home and that it materializes more cogently in the uncivilized region of the natural world. Mandy Reid maintains that this cover illustration incorporates early ideas about

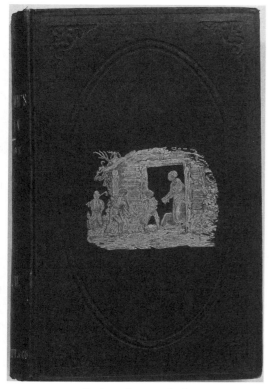

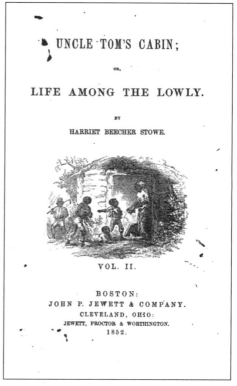

FIGURE 5.4 Embossed cover of volumes 1 and 2 of Harriet Beecher Stowe's *Uncle Tom's Cabin* (1852), first book publication. Based on a wood engraving by Hammatt Billings.

FIGURE 5.5 Hammatt Billings, frontispiece, Harriet Beecher Stowe, *Uncle Tom's Cabin* (1852), vol. 2. Wood engraving.

racial inferiority ("Racial Profiling," 374–75), and the fact that the enslaved cannot be situated in a proper home contributes to this sense of their racial difference.

The illustration stages a central theme of the text—the destruction of the slave family by the failure of males (white and black) to function as effective agents of patriarchy. As the child in the center points at the father coming from the fields to learn that he will be sold, another child looks at the mother. And yet all the figures are diminutive (or perhaps lowly) on the page, crowded small by the title above them and the publishing information below them. Since they mostly are arranged (even the male in the background) below the line of perspective, a reader's glance tends to fall downward onto them. The only figure that stands above the perspective line is the female form, and the illustration thereby enunciates a paradox that the narrative as a whole advances: enslaved women (such as Chloe) appear to have very limited power (she tries to bring Tom back to the Shelby plantation by earning money from her cake making), and that power is always curtailed by larger patriarchal and socioeconomic structures, such as slavery. All the figures are flat and undifferentiated—humble and dark bodies that look away from a viewer, which seems to encourage a type of scopic pity on the part of a (white) reader.

Rhetorically, the novel works in its earliest moments to enforce the notion of lowliness. Stowe alludes to the white "hand of benevolence" that is everywhere "stretched out, searching into abuses, righting wrongs, alleviating distresses" (vi) and to the "unhappy" continent of Africa, which lies "bound and bleeding at the foot of civilized and Christianized humanity, imploring compassion in vain" (vi). Stowe notes that the object of "these sketches"—and by that she means both the illustrations and the novel—is to "awaken sympathy and feeling for the African race, as they exist among us" (vi), yet by this linguistic structure she appears to cordon off the enslaved "African race" ("they") from (presumably white) readers ("us"). This separation breaks down in the case of near-white enslaved persons in the text, who are not necessarily in need of a reader's pity. But in the instance of lowly, fully African bodies such as Tom, the message holds true, and he is often represented with a white (or near-white) hand held out to help him.

Before examining the specific imaging of Tom, I turn to another picture that shows a grouping of bodies, in order to gauge the general function of visual rhetoric within the novel: the ubiquitous image of the slave auction. Linguistically and scopically, the auction scene defines the enslaved as lowly bodies that cannot transcend this status (see figure 5.6). Like Bibb's and Bourne's auction illustrations, scopic focus is to some extent put on the white auctioneer, who stands high above the middle of the visual plane. The illustration is not exactly prurient, as it became in later editions, which made explicit the auction of Emmeline as a commodified and fetishized sexual object (see Reynolds, introduction, xxiii). This is a quieter auction scene, and a viewer's eyes are likely drawn first to the auctioneer, who rises above the midpoint and perspective line of the drawing. A reader's eyes then might follow the line of sight down the auctioneer's phallically placed gavel to land precisely on the head of the slaves. The large figures of white men in the left foreground who look down on the slaves act as focalizing presences, directing a viewer's downward glance to the spectacle of the heap of abject bodies, clustered on the ground, below the perspective line. Compared with Thomas Strong's particularized drawing of enslaved bodies in the auction depicted in Bibb's 1849 text (see figure 4.11), the bodies in Stowe's text seem undifferentiated from one another. The bland caption—"The Auction Sale"— puts little blame on the slave traders and owners who are engaged in the process of selling human flesh. Perhaps most

THE AUCTION SALE.   Page 174.

FIGURE 5.6   Hammatt Billings, "The Auction Sale," illustration from Harriet Beecher Stowe, *Uncle Tom's Cabin* (1852), vol. 1, between pages 174 and 175. Wood engraving.

crucially, the enslaved in this illustration exhibit little scopic or linguistic resistance to the master's control of them. One woman lifts her arm in a half-hearted mode of supplication, but all the other bodies are still and dejected. We do not see anything like the violent lamentation of the mother in Bibb's auction scene, or any enslaved person who stares back at the viewer, as we saw in texts by Bourne and Opie. The illustration denotes the utter powerlessness of the enslaved and eschews delineation of any contestation of the master's regime. This picture manifests what Foucault terms the "obedient subject," the person who has come to allow "authority . . . to function automatically in him" (*Discipline and Punish*, 128–29). A viewer may become part of the structure of scopic surveillance as he or she turns a downward glance onto the slaves, who are surveyed on all sides by white men yet appear to lack what Mirzoeff has called the "right to look."

The three representations of Tom in the first edition likewise enforce a scopic structure of abjection for the enslaved rather than parity or solidarity with a viewer. In many ways, Tom is the hero of Stowe's text—one given the great power to transcend his suffering through his faith, like Roper—yet this transcendence is taught by the figure of a salvific white child: Little Eva. Moreover, unlike Moses Roper, Tom never takes an active role in seeking his spiritual or actual freedom.

Much has been made of the psychological connection between the blond angel child and Uncle Tom,[9] but I wish to examine the visual relationship at play in the text, and the structure of feeling for abolitionist sentiment that it forwards. Little Eva loves the abject blackness that Tom—and for that matter, Topsy—represents; a reader then comes to empathize with figures such as Tom and Topsy through Little Eva's sympathetic and mediational glance.[10] This strategy of using a child to enact abolitionist sentiment is similar in some ways to that used by Opie (see chapter 2), yet in Opie's text the black man ultimately is figured as encouraging readerly identification and intersubjectivity through his own words. Stowe mainly uses Eva as her conduit for hierarchical empathy. Susan Ryan argues that "nineteenth-century benevolent discourse asserted the superiority (racial, regional, moral) of the helper and the otherness of the helped" (*Grammar of Good Intentions*, 150), and this paradigm is apparent in such interactions: the superior figure of Eva is interpolated between a reader and the lowly othered figure, who is always in need of a reader's assistance.

The most famous and frequently reproduced illustration from the first edition is the picture of Little Eva reading the Bible to Tom in the arbor by Lake Pontchartrain (see figure 5.7).[11] Alone, the illustration might be ambiguous—one of Eva's hands rests on Tom's knee in what seems to be a friendly gesture, and

LITTLE EVA READING THE BIBLE TO UNCLE TOM IN THE ARBOR.   Page 63

FIGURE 5.7 Hammatt Billings, "Little Eva Reading the Bible to Uncle Tom in the Arbor," illustration from Harriet Beecher Stowe, *Uncle Tom's Cabin* (1852), vol. 2, between pages 62 and 63. Wood engraving.

her other hand points toward the clouds that hover ethereally above the lake. They could be having an affable dialogue or even a debate about the meaning of a particular biblical passage. Yet the caption here fixes the meaning of the illustration, telling us that the child is "reading the Bible *to* Uncle Tom" (emphasis added). As several critics have noted, enslaved literacy was considered (potentially) revolutionary, yet here the "benevolent white child" works to contain this threat (Ryan, *Grammar of Good Intentions*, 125, 128; Gubar, *Racechanges*, 204). Moreover, the threat is defanged by the fact that Tom's (potential) resistance to enslavement will be curtailed by Eva's vision of an infinite and merciful God who will reward suffering in another world.[12] Tom has already been Christianized, but Eva understands the true meaning of Christianity, and she teaches it to Tom. Eva surrenders herself to the infinitude of God, to an infinite heaven. "'I'm going *there* . . . to the spirits bright, Tom; *I'm going, before long*,'" she tells Tom, pointing to the "new Jerusalem" (1:64) that she sees in the clouds. Apparently "there" is a place where the enslaved do not suffer, because they have been redeemed by a merciful God.

When Tom dies, he follows Eva's vision of heaven's infinity, mercy, and justice. After struggling with his faith and being savagely beaten, he awakens to a sense of God's power: "He that hour loosed and parted from every hope in the life that now is, and offered his own will an unquestioning sacrifice to the Infinite. Tom looked up to the silent, ever-lasting living stars,—types of angelic hosts who ever look down on man; and the solitude of the night rung with the triumphant words of a hymn, which he had sung often in happier days, but never with such feeling" (2:244). Eva's vision of God's infinite mercy and justice is now *in* Tom, and he even replicates her visual gesture of seeing "New Jerusalem" in a celestial object (in this case, the stars in the heavens, whereas Eva sees heaven in the clouds on the lake). Like Eva, Tom sings this knowledge (Tom and Eva are the book's two singers, and they often sing together), in stanzas that were added to John Newton's "Amazing Grace" (Aitken, *John Newton*, 235).

> When we've been there ten thousand years,
>   Bright shining like the sun,
> We've no less days to sing God's praise
>   Than when we first begun.
>   (2:244)

This stanza, the last that Tom sings in this scene, contains an eerie double meaning in that it could imply that even if slavery lasts "ten thousand years," the duration would be irrelevant, because the soul is eternal. Eva's vision allows Tom to achieve transcendence of his suffering and broken body (2:245). Formulating a religious subjectivity that transcends the master's imagining of the enslaved has been crucial to a number of escapes, as noted in previous chapters. But Tom comes to his vision of the infinite after seeing it modeled in Eva, a white child who never suffered enslavement. His vision perpetuates his enslavement by making him pacific and incapable of attempting escape from the horrific circumstances of violence that he finds on Legree's plantation.

The illustration of Eva and Tom in the arbor (see figure 5.7) foreshadows Tom's becoming a type of passive saint, one who models Eva's vision of suffering for a higher cause without attaining her degree of agency. In this drawing, scopic focus is initially drawn to Eva. Her pale and beautiful head, with its luxuriant crop of blond curls, marks the picture's exact center, but she looks at Tom, drawing a viewer's attention secondarily to him. Eva here teaches a (white) viewer how to view Tom lovingly; their eyes meet, and she touches Tom gently. Flowers on either side of the arbor make a natural border for the picture and its circular frame-within-a-frame suggests almost a small and snug love nest. I do not read this as a staging of eroticism (as some critics have), yet it certainly embodies a type of spiritual and physical love that bonds the pair. A viewer is brought close to the image, yet cannot see much of Tom's face; instead he or she may stare at Eva's loving face, which directs its sympathetic gaze to Tom, guiding a viewer to empathize with Tom specifically through Eva's line of vision. Empathy is thus triangulated through Eva's gaze. "I would be glad to die, if my dying could stop all this misery [of slavery]. *I would die* for them [the enslaved], Tom, if I could" (2:84), comments Eva, and in loving and dying for them (the other, the enslaved), Eva enables a viewer to approach empathy with the enslaved specifically through her strong moral presence. She is a Christlike figure that literally points the way to heaven for Tom, who apparently could not fathom this on his own.

Eva's love for Tom and for other slaves is a triangulation of an omnipresent hierarchical structure in the text—one in which a northern and presumably white reader comes to empathize, love, and understand the black enslaved presence and enact action on his or her part through Eva's example. This structure is clearest in the case of Eva's teaching her aunt Miss Ophelia (a northerner with abolitionist sentiments) to have compassion for the seemingly amoral child Topsy. Ophelia tries to teach Topsy some form of appropriate and ladylike decorum, but Ophelia's lessons fall on deaf ears because they miss the one thing the abused and violated enslaved child desperately needs: love. "I've always had a prejudice against negroes . . . and it's a fact, I never could bear to have that child touch me; but, I don't think she knew it," Ophelia tells her brother Augustine St. Clare, who has noted her aversion (2:95). "They *are* disagreeable to me,—this child in particular,—*how* can I help feeling so?" Ophelia queries St. Clare, to which he retorts: "Eva does [love the enslaved], it seems" (2:95). Eva also loves the enslaved physically, kissing them "in a way that Miss Ophelia afterwards declared fairly turned her stomach" (1:238). The physical barrier Ophelia erects here subtends a psychological one: she cannot see herself as like the enslaved, but instead quarantines their (base) bodies from her white one. St. Clare confronts her about this, "You loathe them [the enslaved] as you would a snake or a toad. . . . You would not have them abused; but you don't want to have anything to do with them yourselves. You would send them to Africa, out of your *sight and smell*, and then send a missionary or two to do up all the self-denial of elevating them compendiously" (1:257, emphasis added). Physically, Ophelia would sequester blacks from her own embodied presence. She does not disagree with St. Clare's contention that having missionaries (presumably black ones) attend to them would suit her purposes.

Ophelia ultimately moves beyond this feeling, modeling a process whereby the northern white reader might move toward an empathetic affective intersubjectivity with the enslaved, but only through a mediating and triangulating presence. Eva teaches her aunt to love and touch Topsy through an affective process in which Eva's (dead) body becomes a point in a triangle connecting the northerner and the abused, enslaved child. After Eva's death, Topsy laments that "there an't *nobody* left now" to love her (2:116). At this point, Ophelia touches Topsy, raising her up gently, taking her by the hand, with tears falling from her own eyes, and stating: "Topsy, you poor child . . . don't give up. *I* can love you, though I am not like that dear little child. I hope I've learned something of the love of Christ from her. I can love you; I do" (2:116–17). Perhaps this apparently genuine confession of love for Topsy leads to Ophelia's insistence that St. Clare officially transfer ownership of Topsy to her; this action rescues Topsy from further enslavement when St. Clare dies, because legally Ophelia can take Topsy to the North and free her.

Stowe here points to the ability to genuinely love and touch the enslaved as crucial both to empathy and to antislavery action. More generally, the ability to love the enslaved, Stowe implies, is the only way to shape their destiny and mold their character into upstanding free men and women. From this moment forward, Ophelia acquires "an influence over the mind of the destitute child that she never lost" (2:117). Ophelia learns how to love and make physical contact with Topsy through an empathetic process in which the white individual's psychic distance from the enslaved child is bridged and triangulated through Eva's love for her. Yet this is still a hierarchical mode of empathy that works through the notion of the poor, degraded child needing the mediating presence of the superior angel-child. Moreover, if empathy is based on similarity between subject and object (as numerous researchers have demonstrated), it seems that Stowe's text can never quite bring itself to portray characters such as Tom and Topsy as just like white viewers; there is always emphasis on an aspect of their racial difference that may impede empathetic modes of apprehending them.

I conclude with an examination of the illustrations in the text that feature near-white individuals such as Cassy, Eliza, and George Harris, considering whether they too operate through a triangulated mode of hierarchical empathy or blur the line between bodies to move toward parallel empathy, as seen at times in other graphic illustrated books. The near-white bodies in the text are portrayed as heroic, resistant, and agentive. For example, one illustration features Simon Legree's mistress, Cassy, ministering to a beaten Uncle Tom, at some risk to herself (see figure 5.8). Initially, a viewer might focus on Cassy's figure, which is in the foreground, above the perspective line, and shaded by a light background that draws the eye. A viewer might then replicate Cassy's downward glance to the figure of Tom, on the ground, who has been beaten and yet looks raptly at her. Our eyes might also shuttle between the two figures as we try to understand the action. The caption clarifies what is happening, making clear that Tom is in need of aid, pity, and the "ministering" help that Cassy provides. Tom is drawn here in a flat and stereotypical way, which might discourage readerly empathy with him.

CASSY MINISTERING TO UNCLE TOM AFTER HIS WHIPPING Page 198.

FIGURE 5.8 Hammatt Billings, "Cassy Ministering to Uncle Tom after His Whipping,"
illustration from Harriet Beecher Stowe, *Uncle Tom's Cabin* (1852), vol. 2,
between pages 198 and 199. Wood engraving.

Cassy holds the power to revive Tom, assist him, and direct a reader's gaze toward his misery. She may also function as a triangulating presence: a viewer looking at Cassy ministering to and touching Tom may not feel the need to empathize with Tom directly. Cassy's caring enables a reader's visual care, but the question remains: why can't a reader experience visual empathy directly with Tom, rather than through the mediational presence of Cassy?

Similarly, when Eliza Harris decides to escape from St. Clare's plantation in order to prevent her child Harry from being sold, the illustration of this scene depicts the near-white Eliza as the viewing and active subject, even though Tom and Chloe are also present (see figure 5.9). Eliza is caught midaction, clutching her child, with one foot almost in the air, whereas Tom and Chloe appear to be almost immobilized by the news of Tom's sale; they raise their arms in horror, but their feet are planted firmly on the ground, symbolically suggesting they will not run away, as is indeed the case. The narrative caption guides such an interpretation of Eliza's activity by informing a reader that Eliza has come "to tell Uncle Tom that he is sold" and that she is "running away." Here Eliza exhibits both voice and resistance to enslavement, something Chloe and Tom often lack. Yet again

Eliza comes to tell Uncle Tom that he is sold, and that she is running away to save her child. Page 62.

FIGURE 5.9 Hammatt Billings, "Eliza comes to tell Uncle Tom that he is sold, and she is running away to save her child," illustration from Harriet Beecher Stowe, *Uncle Tom's Cabin* (1852), vol. 1, between pages 60 and 61. Wood engraving.

we view a liminal space, on the border between the natural world and the porch of Uncle Tom's cabin. Spatially, all the characters are far from the large civilized house in the left background; instead, they are made manifest in a realm that is somewhat primitive and unkempt. This depiction fits with a central question of Stowe's text: What will become of the enslaved once freedom is enacted? Will the somewhat "primitive" and lowly conditions under which they have lived mean they will not be integrated properly into the body politic of the nation? The illustration displays uneasiness about the roles that blacks would play in the United States after emancipation.

Not coincidentally, paralleling Stowe's plot, some of Billings's engravings grant agency and resistance to near-white enslaved individuals such as Eliza, Cassy, and George, yet even these bodies are finally cordoned off from the U.S. body politic. For instance, the illustration captioned "The Freeman's Defence" (see figure 5.10) grants George Harris a heroic and violent role in fighting slave catchers who have come to take him back into slavery. George (who can and does pass for white) is in the foreground, and he faces his would-be captors, aided by the Quaker Phineas (further in the background) and a darker-skinned man named Jim (who crouches

THE FREEMAN'S DEFENCE. Page 284.

FIGURE 5.10   Hammatt Billings, "The Freeman's Defence," illustration from
Harriet Beecher Stowe, *Uncle Tom's Cabin* (1852), vol. 1, between pages 284 and 285.
Wood engraving.

behind George). A viewer's glance is drawn to George and his pistol, aimed directly at a white man below him (the slave catcher Tom Loker). Hochman argues that one of Stowe's aims is "to attack the slave system without inciting violence" (*"Uncle Tom's Cabin,"* 53), yet this drawing (which follows the text's narration of the scene), by placing a gun in the hand of a "black" man who points it at a white man, seems to destabilize this objective. This illustration is one of the most radical in the text, in that it portrays the heroic, active, and even violent figure of a fugitive slave, and the audience is certainly meant to applaud the resistance of this insurrectionary character, who ultimately shoots at and wounds a white man.

Perhaps for this reason, this image and the text as a whole must struggle first to remove George from the space of blackness and then to remove him from all of the geographic space of the United States. The image and the surrounding text portray George as manly, intelligent, strong, and basically, for all intents and purposes, white: "If he had been only a Hungarian youth, now bravely defending in some mountain fastness the retreat of fugitives escaping from Austria into America, this would have been sublime heroism" (1:284). This simile explicitly likens George's heroism to that of a white Hungarian youth, making us wonder whether it is precisely George's near whiteness that grants his ability to resist enslavement; indeed, Stowe's novel mainly confines this type of revolutionary behavior to slaves who have strong infusions of what St. Clare refers to as "Anglo Saxon blood" (2:75). The illustration also questions what place such insurrectionary near-white persons would have in a free nation. The jagged dark shading of the rock in the left foreground of the picture connects chromatically with George's outstretched, dark, pistol-holding hand, as well as with the dark hills in the far background, dividing the picture into vertical and horizontal planes and etching out a faraway light but empty space of sky in the picture's center. Perhaps the empty and faraway space of sky marks an absent, nondiegetic realm of freedom for the formerly enslaved man, after emancipation.

Yet the space of possible emancipation within the United States is something that the novel cannot quite imagine. As Sinha comments, "Colonization rather than abolition brackets Stowe's novel," in contradistinction to many abolitionist publications, (*Slave's Cause*, 442). This agenda is made evident in the illustration captioned "The Fugitives Are Safe in a Free Land" (see figure 5.11). The image shows George, Eliza, and Harry Harris, "the Fugitives," safe in a "free land," Canada. A reader looks directly into the picture and onto the spectacle of George dropping to his knees and thanking God for his freedom while Mrs. Smyth (a Quaker woman who has aided them) looks on, turned away from a viewer yet directing our gaze even more firmly to the Harris family. The house in the background on the left and

THE FUGITIVES ARE SAFE IN A FREE LAND. Page 238

FIGURE 5.11 Hammatt Billings, "The Fugitives Are Safe in a Free Land,"
illustration from Harriet Beecher Stowe, *Uncle Tom's Cabin* (1852), vol. 2, between
pages 238 and 239. Wood engraving.

the ship on the right suggest that they have reached a different shore, yet even in
Canada they have not found a home in any sense, and they drop to their knees in
front of a clump of trees. Ivy Wilson maintains that images of African Americans
place them in marginal spaces to depict "the forms of democratic belonging in
the United States" such that "African Americans . . . are precluded from the inner
sanctum of social belonging" (*Specters of Democracy*, 108); moreover, it is rare to see
"depictions of African Americans in the privatized spaces of their interior lives in
nineteenth-century U.S. visual culture" (110). By depriving George and Eliza of a
home of their own, and by placing them constantly in liminal or marginal spaces,
images such as this one foreshadow the plot's ultimate resolution, in which they
will indeed be precluded (visually as well as rhetorically) from social belonging in
the United States.

　　After isolating the potentially disruptive and certainly agentive bodies of
George, Eliza, and (ultimately) Cassy in Canada, the novel removes them even
farther, first to France and then finally to Liberia. In Liberia, George wishes to be
part of a free nation, and in explaining this decision, he becomes Stowe's mouth-
piece (2:300–301). As Elizabeth Ammons comments, Stowe "packs" off to Africa
these "dangerous, ambitious, free American blacks"; in so doing, she demonstrates

that the novel argues for "an end to slavery but not to white supremacy" ("Freeing the Slaves," 238). Resistant bodies such as those of George and Eliza Harris are not folded back into the U.S. body politic; instead, a reading viewer comes to understand that he or she need not achieve intersubjectivity with such bodies, because their main goal will be founding a new nation. Of course, actual fugitive slaves such as Roper, Bibb, and (as we will see) Brown were forced to leave the United States for their own self-protection and to reside in Canada or England. But they did not disown their (potential) U.S. citizenship in favor of a new nationality, as George does. Moreover, Roper, Bibb, and Brown returned to the United States at points in their lives, suggesting a more flexible notion of black citizenship within a transatlantic world than Stowe's text seems to exemplify.

In Stowe's text, moments of seeing enslaved persons such as George, Eliza, and Cassy as rebellious or agentive ultimately are rendered unthreatening by the removal of these possibly insurgent bodies to Africa, far away from the geographic location of many readers.[13] The first edition of *Uncle Tom's Cabin* thereby encapsulates a pattern in which a viewing reader need not see himself or herself in the darker-skinned, abject bodies of the enslaved. Stowe teaches her viewing reader to "feel rightly" for abject others such as Topsy or Uncle Tom—but only through the blond angel-child, Little Eva, who triangulates a relationship to the enslaved other and teaches a viewer to love him or her indirectly, through her mediating angelic presence. Indeed, many early readers did feel sympathy (or perhaps pity) for the enslaved, and some claimed to have been led into abolitionistic sentiments.[14] Yet the novel's visual rhetoric mainly encourages a reader to engage in a hierarchical, triangulated relationship with the enslaved, a form of empathy that rarely moves into intersubjectivity, into a state in which the enslaved other temporarily merges with the viewing self.[15]

Will the "Real" Henry Box Brown Please Stand Up: Polyphonic Performances of Enslavement, Freedom, and African American Identity

This section examines how representations of Henry Box Brown in illustrated books, panoramas, and other performative visual genres trouble abject representations of the enslaved present in a text such as *Uncle Tom's Cabin*. The visual forms associated with Brown—the two narratives about his life, the panoramas he created and exhibited well into the mid-1860s, the portraits of him in various texts, and his stage performances—indicate that as Brown moved through multimedia performative modes (panoramas, singing, acting, mesmerism, and magic shows), he undermined the notion that the enslaved self had been accurately captured or represented. What emerges after consideration of the visual culture surrounding

Brown is a figuration of a man who performs multiple selves in a quest to evade the frame or box that traditional abolitionist visual culture appears to have drawn (both figuratively and metaphorically) around the character of the fugitive slave.

Critics such as Daphne Brooks, Marcus Wood, Jeffrey Ruggles, John Ernest, Cynthia Griffin Wolff, and Suzette Spencer have traced the proliferation of Brown's image and what Brooks calls his "escapology" (*Bodies in Dissent*, 69). Some of these critics privilege Brown's panorama as a subversion of abolitionist visual culture; Brooks, for example, argues that Brown's panoramic exhibition of his life "transcended the discursive restrictions of the slave narrative and redirected the uses of the transatlantic body toward politically insurgent ends" (68).[16] Yet these critics have not fully taken account of the multiple performance modes that Brown created and manipulated well into the late 1880s, including his deployment of panoramas of *Uncle Tom's Cabin*, nor have they scrutinized the other roles he took on as an actor, performer, dramatist, mesmerist, and magician. Archival research indicates that Brown performed avatar-like versions of himself throughout his life.[17] His stage work ultimately fashioned not a transcendence of depictions of enslaved selfhood, but instead rendered them as permeable and open performance terrains—traversable realms and even routes that the fugitive self could enter and exit at will.[18] In so doing, Brown passed into a complex performative mode that perhaps encouraged viewers to use theory of mind—the inference and representations of emotions, beliefs, and intentions of someone else—to create a dense and multifaceted representation of the enslaved, yet also at times risked undermining viewers' empathetic impulses altogether.

Act One: A Man and a Box

Brown's famous escape from slavery transpired in 1849. After Brown's pregnant wife and three children were sold, he made a decision to escape from Richmond to Philadelphia, where slavery was illegal. With the help of a member of his church (a free black man named James Caesar Anthony Smith) and a white contact (Samuel Smith, no relation), Brown used money he had saved from his work as a tobacconist to have himself shipped as cargo to Philadelphia by the Adams Express Company. Labeled "dry goods," the box was lined with cloth and had a hole cut in the top for air; Brown brought an awl to bore additional holes if needed, and water to drink, which he ended up pouring on himself instead because of the extreme heat. After twenty-seven hours of excruciating travel, during which Brown's box was at times turned upside down (placing him on his head), the box finally arrived at the headquarters of the Philadelphia Anti-Slavery Society on March 24, 1849.[19] Brown emerged from the box unscathed, and is reported to have sung a psalm of praise that he had prepared for the occasion. Brown's escape by box rapidly

became a celebrated story, and Brown attained a forceful presence as an abolitionist speaker and singer. Visual and narrative depictions of Brown and his box
appeared almost immediately.

All early accounts agree on the method Brown used to escape, yet they vary as to
what happened when Brown's box was opened. An examination of some of these
variations tells much about tensions within abolitionist visual culture concerning
representations of enslaved subjectivity.[20] For example, one early version of Brown's
story, written by Ann Preston in her illustrated children's book *Cousin Ann's Stories
for Children* (1849), grants Brown a degree of control over his famous exit from the
box: "Quickly the top of the box was knocked off, and Henry stood up. He shook
hands with his new friend, and he was so happy that he hardly knew what to do.
After he had bathed himself and ate breakfast, he sang a hymn of praise, which he
had kept in his mind to sing if he should ever get to a land of freedom in safety" (25–
26). Preston also sees Brown as heroic: "We call people heroes who do something
that is brave and great, and Henry is a hero" (26). In what is the first representation
of Brown exiting his box, the illustration in Preston's book is faithful to this heroic
description by depicting him standing up and shaking the hand of the man who has
opened the box (see figure 5.12). The illustration endeavors to create visual structures
of parity and equality between Brown and the white men who open his box: Brown
stands tall and straight; he looks at the white man and holds out his hand; he is
similar in size to the other figures. Most of his body is above the perspective line of
the illustration, so a viewer would tend to look straight at him rather than casting
a downward glance. Because this is the first image a child would see before reading
the text, it would tend to become a focalizing presence and dovetail with the point
Preston makes at the text's end about Brown's heroism.

The first full version of Brown's escape intended for adults employs a differ-
ent set of visual conventions. *Narrative of Henry Box Brown, Who Escaped from
Slavery, Enclosed in a Box 3 Feet Long and 2 Wide: Written from a Statement of Facts
Made by Himself; With Remarks Upon the Remedy for Slavery* was published just
six months after Brown's escape—in September 1849—with the help of Charles
Stearns, a radical abolitionist. Brown could not write at the time, and most critics
agree that although the text was authorized by Brown, Stearns's voice dominates.[21]
Unlike Preston's text, this one contains no image of Brown exiting his box. Instead,
a drawing of Brown (the man) starts the text, and a drawing of the box ends
it; Brown is therefore visually separated from the innovative mode of escape he
deployed. Stearns's Brown is told by God, "Go and get a box, and put yourself in
it"—a command that Brown does not initially understand: "'Get a box?' . . . 'What
can this mean?'" (59); in this version of the text, Brown lacks the imagination or
intelligence to fashion the scheme himself.

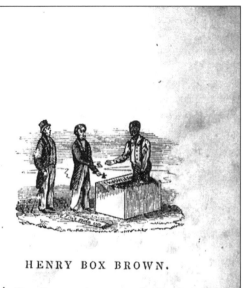

HENRY BOX BROWN.

I will tell you the story of Henry Box
Brown. It is a strange tale, and it is all true.
Henry was a slave in Richmond, Virginia, and
then his name was Henry Brown. He had a
wife and four little children whom he loved
very much.

One night when he went home to his little
hut, his children and their mother, were gone,
and poor Henry found they had been sold to
a trader, and were taken away to Carolina. It
made him almost crazy to hear this dreadful

FIGURE 5.12 Illustration
from Ann Preston, *Cousin
Ann's Stories for Children*
(1849). Wood engraving.
Courtesy of the Historical
Society of Pennsylvania.

In Stearns's text, Brown is a simple man following God's dictates and plan, as
is clear when he exits the box: "At length the cover was removed, and I arose, and
shook myself from the lethargy into which I had fallen; but exhausted nature
proved too much for my frame, and I swooned away. After my recovery from this
fainting fit, the first impulse of my soul . . . was to break out in a song of deliverance, and praise to the most high God, whose arm had been so signally manifest in
my escape" (62–63). Brown faints, awakens, and then humbly praises God; he does
not stand up and shake hands (as in *Cousin Ann's Stories*). He is also, it appears, a
mere servant of God rather than someone taking on the more daring role of being
a Christlike figure who symbolically enacts a death and resurrection.

FIGURE 5.13 Frontispiece, *Narrative of Henry Box Brown, Who Escaped from Slavery* (1849). According to Ruggles, this portrait appears to be an engraving based on a daguerreotype. Documenting the American South.

In keeping with this verbal construction of Brown's identity, the 1849 frontispiece portrays Brown as a somewhat dull, unimaginative creature (see figure 5.13). Brown looks away from a viewer with a vague expression; his eyes are pointed to the right, giving him a rather shifty look. He is dressed in elegant clothing, yet his cravat is poorly tied, and his jacket collar crimped; his vest buttons strain to cover his stomach. In this illustration, Brown looks slovenly and oddly complacent; he also appears a bit foreboding and dangerous. The portrait contains few visual structures that would tend to ask a viewer to engage with Brown intersubjectively or empathetically, and his signature is absent, emphasizing his illiteracy.

In other parts of Stearns's narrative, Brown is visually defined by his box, and his box defines him. In figure 5.14, the final page of the 1849 text, the material artifact of the box encapsulates the figure of Brown; as Brooks states, "Brown is present and yet discursively entombed, forced underground into a manhole of his own making" (*Bodies in Dissent*, 74). Brooks also claims, however, that in ending with the ambivalent space of the box, which resists closure by indicating how slavery continues, the 1849 text forces a viewer into a state of historical meditation and contemplation. Yet to some degree, this illustration and the surrounding text close down the possibility of subversion that the box as an enduring material artifact

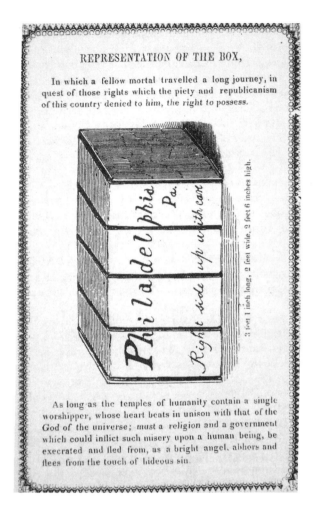

REPRESENTATION OF THE BOX,

In which a fellow mortal travelled a long journey, in quest of those rights which the piety and republicanism of this country denied to him, the right to possess.

As long as the temples of humanity contain a single worshipper, whose heart beats in unison with that of the God of the universe; must a religion and a government which could inflict such misery upon a human being, be execrated and fled from, as a bright angel, abhors and flees from the touch of hideous sin.

FIGURE 5.14 Illustration from *Narrative of Henry Box Brown* (1849), 92. Wood engraving. Documenting the American South.

of slavery raises. In a comment above the illustration, Brown is called merely "a fellow mortal" who "travelled a long journey" in his box; his potential for creativity and agency is again elided. Further, Stearns adds a long, didactic, ornate sentence below the box; in other words, he imposes his message onto the box, thereby turning Brown into a sort of finished moral lesson rather than a hero with a mode of agency and power, or a text that is still being written and rewritten.

Throughout the 1849 text, Stearns strives to create sympathy (or perhaps pity) for Brown. He also tries to use embodied simulation to make a reader *feel* Brown's misery, yet his prose often is so labored and heavy-handed that any such feeling evaporates:

> O reader, as you peruse this heart-rending tale, let the tear of sympathy roll freely from
> your eyes, and let the deep fountains of human feeling, which God has implanted in
> the breast of every son and daughter of Adam, burst forth from their enclosure, until
> a stream shall flow therefrom on to the surrounding world, of so invigorating and
> purifying a nature, as to arouse from the "death of the sin" of slavery, and cleanse from
> the pollutions thereof, all with whom you may be connected. (v–vi)

This sentence starts with the sympathetic tear that should roll freely down the
face of a reader, but as clause after clause is added, it becomes difficult to follow.
Within the text proper, Brown's voice appears to be drowned out by Stearns's;
every forceful sentiment on the subject of slavery is accompanied by so much
tortured syntax that its message is virtually effaced (see, for example, 57–58). The
1849 text ultimately may engender only hierarchical empathy between Brown
and a reader because its images of Brown and his box are somewhat derogatory
and elide Brown's agency in the escape, and because its overly ornate sentence
structure often interferes with comprehension of Brown's suffering, heroism, and
self-fashioning.

Two years later, another version of Brown's story was published—*Narrative of
the Life of Henry Box Brown, Written by Himself* (1851). There is controversy about
whether the text was in fact written by Brown, who may have not yet learned to
write, or whether it was another "as told to" narrative authorized by Brown (who
sold it during performances of his panorama). The 1851 text renovates the 1849
one in several key ways that tend to grant Brown a higher degree of agency and
to portray him as a more complex individual with whom a reader might identify. In a careful reading of the differences between these texts, John Ernest notes
that Brown could not hope to escape from the rhetorical terrain in which he was
enmeshed; in this discourse the terms of enslaved subjectivity were preordained
by abolitionism. Even so, Brown draws from his experiences to reposition himself within that terrain; in so doing, he "revised significantly the terms of agency"
offered by both black and white, slavery and antislavery, discourse ("Outside the
Box," 3).

Perhaps the most significant aspect of this revision entails the way the 1851
text deliberately creates a visual-rhetorical argument in which Brown, like Roper,
is a Christlike figure, killed dead by slavery but made alive in freedom. Brown's
physical unboxing develops into a dramatic metaphor for his death in slavery and
his rebirth into a life of activity and activism: "They soon managed to break open
the box, and then came my resurrection from the grave of slavery. I rose a freeman, but I was too weak, by reason of long confinement in that box, to be able to
stand, so I immediately swooned away. After my recovery from the swoon . . . I

had risen as it were from the dead" (56–57). The 1851 text turns Brown's swoon into a performative action, one that allows him subsequently to arise from the living death of slavery. Moreover, after Brown's "resurrection," he sings a praise song (a remodeled version of Psalm 40) that begins: "I waited patiently for the Lord, for the Lord; / And he inclined unto me, and heard my calling: / ... And he hath put a new song in my mouth" (57).[22] The 1849 text contains this psalm, but constrains it by placing it within Stearns's preface, while the 1851 text gives it back to Brown to sing and perform. It is hard to see how mailing oneself from the South to the North entails waiting patiently for the Lord, yet this text, like Roper's, implies that Brown put his feet in the position of escape while still acknowledging that his fate was in God's hands.

In keeping with this metaphor of death and rebirth that the visual rhetoric of the 1851 text develops, the frontispiece of the second edition has an image of Brown emerging from the box, captioned "Resurrection of Henry Box Brown, at Philadelphia" (see figure 5.15). Brown is not fainting in this illustration, yet he is not standing up, as in Preston's illustration. He appears to be frozen in mid pose, not quite out of the box. Brown is the object of the gaze of all the men in the picture, as well as of a reader, who might tend to look downward onto him as he sits below the horizon line. He seems alert, but he gazes off to the side with an expression that is (again) hard to read. Perhaps this image functions to symbolize his situation in the 1851 narrative as a whole, as Ernest has suggested: Brown finds himself still "boxed in," "seated in the box and gesturing to emerge as the four men around him contemplate his resurrection" ("Outside the Box," 14). On the other hand, the captioning of this image manifests a dominant attempt to guide a reader toward a religious metaphor in which Brown is not a mere abject slave carted from one place to another, but a fully human person who has undergone a spiritual salvation and resurrection through a heroic set of experiences that he crafted. Moreover, while Stearns's account has the boxing scheme coming to Brown from God, in the later text the idea is his own and comes into his mind in its entirety (84); as Ernest argues, the later account grants "Brown greater, and more savvy, agency" ("Traumatic Theology," 20).

A more robust effort is made in this second narrative to deploy cognitive or affective rhetorical structures that push a reader toward intersubjectivity. Like Stowe's novel, the 1851 text appeals to women, and mothers in particular, but it does so in a way that encourages them to feel parallel empathy with the enslaved. At one point, the author of this text writes: "Mothers of the North! as *you* gaze upon the fair forms of *your* idolised little ones, just pause for a moment; how would *you* feel if *you* knew that at any time the will of a tyrant—who neither could nor would

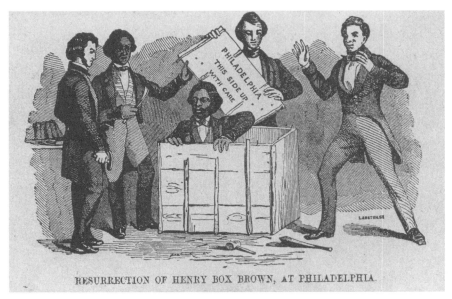

RESURRECTION OF HENRY BOX BROWN, AT PHILADELPHIA.

FIGURE 5.15 Langton, frontispiece to *Narrative of the Life of Henry Box Brown,
Written by Himself* (1851). Wood engraving. Courtesy of the University of Virginia Library.

sympathise with *your* domestic feelings—might separate them for ever from *your*
embrace" (79, emphasis added). This short passage uses "you" or "your" six times to
emphasize parallelism with the enslaved rather than racial difference; the interlocutory structure also aims to compel a reader to engage with the text. An antislavery appeal directly hails women who are mothers and asks them to engage in what
theorists of empathy call state matching and vicarious introspection: a double and
spiraling movement in which a person sees that the pain of another could also be
his or her own pain (see Agosta, "Empathy and Intersubjectivity"). By constantly
using language such as "human beings" or "humans" (i, iii, 16, 25, 29, 42, 50, 79) to
describe the enslaved, the 1851 text encourages a reader to see interdependence and
interconnection between the enslaved self and a viewer.

The 1851 narrative attempts to mobilize a sensory experience—sound—in the
service of its affective appeal to a reader. The narrative's action ends with Brown
speaking and singing before abolitionist audiences (89). Even more strikingly,
Brown becomes a creator of a new musical form that audaciously merges the
melody of a familiar minstrel tune ("Old Ned") with his unique experience of
enslavement and escape. In so doing, he attempts to oscillate his reader's horizon
of expectations away from a minstrel-like image of the enslaved as comic or abject
toward a view of them as fully human and agentive. Brown's chronicle becomes

one that concerns a miraculous and indeed joyful resurrection, and he composes a
song in "commemoration of my fete in the box" (60), which begins:

> Here you see a man by the name of Henry Brown,
> Ran away from the South to the North;
> Which he would not have done but they stole all his rights,
> But they'll never do the like again.

Brown was a talented singer and musician (Ruggles, *Unboxing of Henry Brown*,
14), and he appears to have rewritten the minstrel tune himself. He is described
in this song as a man with rights, not an abased, subordinate noncitizen. The song
chronicles Brown's escape again, and there is no fainting fit in this chronicle. It
also foreshadows the performative role he will undertake as an antislavery celeb-
rity (Ernest, "Outside the Box," 15).[23] Linguistically, visually, and aurally, then, the
1851 text forwards affective and cognitive configurations that might tend to make a
reader empathetic with Henry Box Brown, the heroic man and artist who crafted
his own subjectivity, rather than Henry Brown, the abject slave of the 1849 text.

By this point (1851), Brown was already using music in dramatic spectacles such
as his panorama, which he had begun exhibiting in 1850. Before analyzing the
panorama, I turn to a visual-verbal account of Brown and his box that seems
to undermine the idea that any of the above narratives have captured the "real"
Brown. Writing over twenty years later (in 1872), William Still, a conductor on
the Underground Railroad, claimed that the facts of Brown's escape have "never
before been fully published" and calls Brown "a man of invention as well as a hero"
(83). Still's account focuses more on Brown's individual actions in arising out of
the box:

> Rising up in his box, [Brown] reached out his hand, saying, "How do you do, gentle-
> men?" . . . Very soon he remarked that, before leaving Richmond he had selected for
> his arrival-hymn (if he lived) the Psalm beginning with the words: "*I waited patiently
> for the Lord, and He heard my prayer.*" And most touchingly did he sing the psalm. . . .
> As he had been so long doubled up in the box he needed to promenade considerably
> in the fresh air . . . and while Brown promenaded the yard flushed with victory, great
> was the joy of his friends. (*Underground Railroad*, 83–84)

Still's version does not have Brown fainting, and indeed he portrays Brown glory-
ing in his great accomplishment and promenading the yard "flushed with victory."

In keeping with this more active unboxing narrative, Still reprints a version of
the "resurrection" print in which subtle visual details suggest that Brown is already
rising out of his box, unaided (see figure 5.16). The box is now turned at a slight
diagonal, and Brown's hands are placed on either side of him; their angle suggests

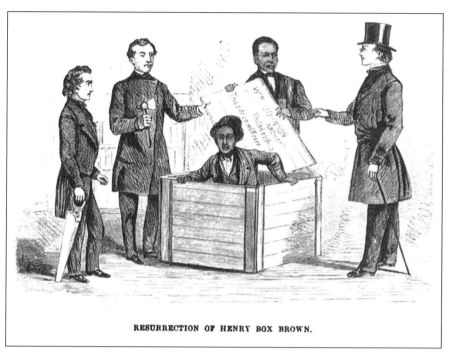

RESURRECTION OF HENRY BOX BROWN.

FIGURE 5.16 "Resurrection of Henry Box Brown," illustration from William Still,
The Underground Rail Road (1872). Wood engraving. Google Books.

that he is pushing himself up and out of the box. The upper half of his torso is
already out of the box, unlike other prints in which only his head and shoulders
appear and in which he seems to be sitting in the box rather than rising out of it.
Perhaps most interestingly, the change in the angle of the box means that Brown
looks at viewers directly, returning their gaze.[24] His expression suggests determination and self-control. Still perhaps chose this image because in it Brown
seems capable of exiting the box on his own, and because Brown's direct glance at
a reader might encourage a mode of parity with this human subject, who sees a
reader at the same moment that she or he sees him.

From 1849 to 1872, then, there were competing visual and narrative representations of the man and his box. Some of these representations tend to elide Brown's
agency and discourage parity with a viewer, while others contain cognitive modes
and affective configurations that attempt to move a reader's horizon of expectations toward a mode of intersubjectivity and empathy. Brown may have contributed to the instability surrounding his enslaved avatar in later years by proliferat-
ing it through performance work. But before discussing this performance work, I
consider the visual rhetoric of the panorama itself.

Act Two: A Man and His Panoramas

As noted above, some critics argue that it was only in his moving panorama, *The Mirror of Slavery*, that Brown found transcendence of the abject visual culture of the slave narrative, a point that is complicated by some archival research that I have uncovered suggesting that he exhibited his panorama alongside panoramas and shows of *Uncle Tom's Cabin*, beginning in 1852. I examine here whether the popular panorama that Brown exhibited from 1850 to at least 1864 initially may have been formulated as a type of visual rhetoric in which Brown could perform as a hero who crafted his own freedom narrative and song. In the late 1840s, moving panoramas, consisting of multiple scenes painted onto rolls of huge canvas that were gradually unfurled, were extremely popular. Unlike panoramic paintings, moving panoramas generally featured a narrator (often known as the "Delineator"), who described the action in each painting as it was unrolled.

Brown's panorama was popular when it premiered in Boston on April 11, 1850.[25] It contained forty-nine scenes, probably eight to ten feet in height, painted on a canvas scroll; Josiah Wolcott (an ornamental sign painter who had contributed to other abolitionist efforts) seems to have been the primary artist creating most of the images for it (Ruggles, *Unboxing of Henry Brown*, 93, 75). Brown and the black man who had helped him escape from slavery—James C. A. Smith—exhibited the panorama throughout the summer in New England and later in England. Brown later had a falling-out with James Smith and then performed the panorama on his own. The panels of the show have been lost, but descriptions of them in the press have been pieced together by Ruggles and Brooks. Judging from the titles of some scenes, the panorama drew a great deal of its visual material from several antislavery illustrated books, including Charles C. Green's *The Nubian Slave* (1845) and Bibb's *Narrative of Henry Bibb* (1849).

The panorama shared many of the themes evident in antislavery illustrated books as well, such as the civility of Africans, the emotional torment of torture, and the heroism of the enslaved who attempt escape. In so doing, it might have encouraged a form of empathy based in similarity and familiarity rather than focused on pity for an abject other. Yet the panorama had a particularly repetitive and recursive structure in which each portrayal of escape was followed by reenslavement. Brooks writes that Brown, "in a spectacular act of recovery," likely crossed over "to the other side" of the panorama (that is, he moved from the narrator's position to a spot more like that of an audience member) in order to watch the painted version of his ingenious escape and "to provide an ending in the flesh for his audiences" (*Bodies in Dissent*, 86). Brown also staged his own boxing and unboxing on many occasions, even having himself shackled and swaddled in a Houdini-like fashion in a large canvas sack (Haskins and Benson, *Conjure Times*, 31). In addition, he performed in plays with titles such as *The Fugitive Free* and *The Nubian Captive; or, Royal Slave* (works by E. G. Burton). Such repetitive performances of captivity seem to raise the question of whether the formerly enslaved person could indeed "cross over" to freedom within performative modes that replicated enslavement. The cyclical and literally circular traumatic structure of these types of art may have been a factor in Brown's turn toward a different form of performance work in his later life.

Generally speaking, the themes of the panorama seem to have moved back and forth between modes of visuality that granted the enslaved an agentive form of subjectivity and those that replicated a scopic regime in which the enslaved were abject bodies with whom a viewer might not feel parity or similarity. For example, as in Opie's illustrated book (see chapter 2), one pronounced theme of Brown's panorama was that Africa was a beautiful, refined country and that Africans were a civilized race not substantively different from the white race. This theme was exemplified primarily by borrowings from Charles C. Green's illustrated poem *The Nubian Slave*, which plays up an interest in Egyptology and portrays Africans with noble features, proportions, and habits of behavior. Green considered Nubians to be African; he describes plate 2 as referring to "the African family sitting at the door of their hut" (2). One of the earliest scenes of Brown's panorama was loosely based on the plate "Freedom" in Green's work (see figure 5.17). In Green's book, this scene (set in Africa) is peaceful and even Edenic; the mother (Zerah) works a spindle and distaff while the father (Nilos) fondly looks at one of his children. As

FIGURE 5.17 "Freedom," plate 2 (lithograph) from Charles Green, *The Nubian Slave*. The image was used as the model for scene 2 of Henry Brown's panorama *The Mirror of Slavery*. Courtesy of the American Antiquarian Society.

used and remodeled by Brown's panorama in his second scene, this picture made
the point that freedom for Africans preexisted slavery, and that Africans, contrary
to some racist tracts written by scientists in the 1830s and 1840s, were not a separate, degenerate, or atavistic race. But because Brown did not come directly from
Africa (as the enslaved Nubian family does in the poem), the panel made the point
that not every slave experience was like every other slave experience. *The Mirror
of Slavery* is not a personal reflection of Brown's awareness, but a compendium of
enslaved subjectivity. As a prosthetic viewing apparatus, the mirror is not meant
to reflect or mirror back a singular experience, and perhaps if a viewer sees himself
or herself in *The Mirror of Slavery* in some way, he or she will envision a self that is
plural and constantly forming and re-forming, rather than singular and flat.

On the other hand, the panorama included many scenes of bondage in which
the low, tortured body of the (black) enslaved person was physically separated
from the high, empowered body of the (white) slaver, and a viewer was encouraged
to pity the enslaved. Scene 22 ("The Brand and Scourge"), for example, may have
replicated such a scopic order explicitly (see figure 5.18). In Green's illustration,

THE BRAND AND SCOURGE.

FIGURE 5.18 "The Brand and Scourge," plate 5 (lithograph) from Charles Green, *The Nubian
Slave.* The image was used as the model for scene 22 of Henry Brown, *The Mirror of Slavery.*
Courtesy of the American Antiquarian Society.

the torture is detailed scrupulously, line by line, and the minister standing in the middle of "The Brand and Scourge" makes evident a point articulated frequently in Brown's 1851 narrative: that clergy abetted and aided slavery rather than seeking to end it. No structure of resistance is embedded—no watcher raises a hand to stop the torture, no defiant glance flashes out from the enslaved, and no prosthetic viewing presence seeks to motivate a viewer to action. If these scenes were closely hewn to by Brown's illustrator, they objectified the bodies in order to engage a viewer in pathos and pity. But they did not ask viewers to alter their horizon of expectations and see the enslaved as a fully human subject with whom they might enter into a mode of empathy or intersubjectivity.

Other images did attempt to transform a viewer's horizon of expectations. After intermission, the second part of the panorama began with four tableaux of enslaved life in the South (Ruggles, *Unboxing of Henry Brown*, 100). The first of these scenes—"Sunday among the Slave Population"—is based on an illustration in *Narrative of the Life and Adventures of Henry Bibb* (see figure 4.9). This representation eventually gave way to Thomas Strong's detailed print featuring Bibb's attempted escape with wife and child, scene 41 of Brown's panorama (see figure 5.19). In Strong's print, Bibb looks bold and heroic as he defends his family with his knife upraised; he is the center of focus, and because of the perspective line, he seems almost as tall as the mountains in the background. The picture forwards a structure of violent resistance to reenslavement, and the wolves may metaphorically

FIGURE 5.19 Thomas Strong, illustration for Henry Bibb, *Narrative of the Life and Adventures* (1849). Wood engraving. The image was used as the model for "Henry Bibb Escaping," scene 41 of Henry Brown, *The Mirror of Slavery*. Documenting the American South.

stand in for the men who would seek to capture him (slave catchers were often referred to in animalistic terms). As discussed above, by the late 1840s, when Bibb wrote his text, and the early 1850s, when Brown performed it within the panorama, the question of violent resistance to slavery was at the center of abolitionist debates, so Brown likely meant to forward implicitly such debates about the need for a sometimes violent self-defense. The panorama here may have attempted to shift a viewer toward an understanding not only of the heroism and agency of the enslaved but also of the need for aggressive resistance to enslavement.

Violent resistance is focalized again in "Man Hunting," the next scene of the panorama (scene 42), another one modeled on Green's *The Nubian Slave* (see figure 5.20). In this final montage in Green's book, the family (now in the United States) is assailed by bloodhounds and fired upon by white men, who have shot and killed Zerah. In the left front of the picture, a dog gnaws at the throat of the small child, who beseeches his father for help. In the poem by Green, only the son is recaptured; the mother and father are killed. Scene 42 of Brown's panorama, "Nubian Slaves Retaken" (note the plural here), may correspond in some ways to Green's seventh and final plate in *The Nubian Slave*, but it also substantially remodels it, by implying that two slaves are taken back into slavery (Nilos and his son) rather than showing a husband dying while defending his family. This enhances the

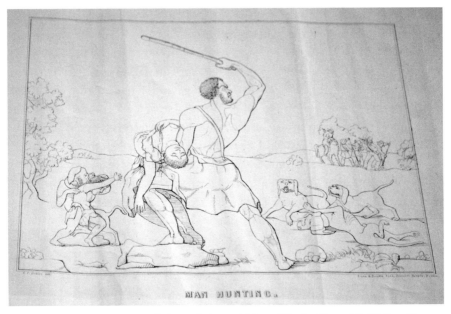

FIGURE 5.20 "Man Hunting," plate 7 (lithograph) from Charles Green, *The Nubian Slave.* The image was used as the model for "Nubian Slaves Retaken," scene 42 of Henry Brown, *The Mirror of Slavery.* Courtesy of the American Antiquarian Society.

panorama's cyclical structure of enslavement-escape-recapture; in Brown's version of the *Nubian Slave*'s narrative, Nilos never escapes from slavery, but is returned, courtesy of the "Bloodhound Act."

Scenes 41 and 42 of *The Mirror of Slavery* evidently featured unsuccessful escape attempts as a way to prepare audiences for the grand and final tableau of the piece (now lost), titled "Universal Emancipation." Preceding these scenes were two more gruesome ones titled "Tarring and Feathering in South Carolina" (scene 43) and "Burning Alive" (scene 45).[26] The latter was based on an incident that occurred in 1836 but was described in the 1840 issue of the *American Anti-Slavery Almanac*. These newspaper accounts chronicle the brutal and violent immolation of black men by mobs; Brown might have used some of these details in his onstage delineation of this picture. Ruggles argues: "*Mirror of Slavery*'s heroes were the slaves. It was positive about their African origins, portrayed their natural state as freedom, and depicted the condition of enslavement as an unnatural imposition" (*Unboxing of Henry Brown*, 104). Yet depictions of gruesome torture such as "Burning Alive," "Man Hunting," and "Tarring and Feathering in South Carolina" might have frozen viewers into inaction or horror. And what would it have been like for Brown, as a formerly enslaved person, to narrate such pictures of gruesome violence? Would he have been pulled back into the trauma that was enslavement?

Successful escape attempts or emancipation were described or alluded to in three of the four final scenes (Brooks, *Bodies in Dissent*, 88; Ruggles, *Unboxing of Henry Brown*, 103). Yet what was the nature of this emancipation? "Promise of Freedom" (scene 46), as Ruggles notes, was "evocative of a number of abolitionist images in which a slave looked heavenward for deliverance" (103). "West Indian Emancipation" (scene 47) showed a distant geographic realm. And the grand finale—"Universal Emancipation" (scene 49)—needed to figure forth (throughout the 1850s and early 1860s) a virtual, unrealized space of U.S. freedom. Indeed, where was liberation for U.S. slaves in Brown's panorama? Brown had to flee the United States in 1850 after his former owner attempted to force him back into slavery. In England, by the late 1850s he was performing for audiences that, influenced by minstrelsy, may have been more interested in confirmation of their own racist or imperialist notions, as Audrey Fisch (*American Slaves*, 73–88) and Hazel Waters have shown (*Racism on the Victorian Stage*, 2, 98).[27] Brooks argues that the panorama as a whole formulates "a chaotic zone that foregrounds the creative agency of the African American activist turned artist" (*Bodies in Dissent*, 83) and transforms "the spectacle of escape into a revolutionary fugitive art" (93). Yet it seems that within the circular and conservative visual-rhetorical matrix of the panorama, which appears to have mainly recycled images rather than creating new ones, the fugitive artist had to keep enslaving, unenslaving, and reenslaving his own body for the edification and entertainment of his audience. The virtual space of freedom was gestured to and imagined, yet remained unreal and perhaps unrealized for Brown.

Brown continued to perform *The Mirror of Slavery* for at least ten years, enacting it more than two hundred times (Ruggles, *Unboxing Henry Brown*, 158). Perhaps Brown became inured to its trauma, which replicated his own in scene 39, "Henry Box Brown Released at Philadelphia," which was based on one of the resurrection prints. Or perhaps the panorama became only a mode of performance for him— something that (as an eventual actor) he could put on and take off with some degree of ease. We do know that Brown voluntarily engaged in acts of reboxing and unboxing on more than one occasion, symbolically reenslaving himself for profit. The following incident, reported in the *Leeds Times* on May 17, 1851, indicates how Brown used the spectacle of his enslavement in a performative mode:

> Great Attraction Caused in England by Mr. Henry Box Brown, a Fugitive Slave who made his escape from Richmond, in Virginia, packed up in a box, 3 feet 1 inch long by 2 feet wide, and two feet 6 inches high. Mr. Brown will leave Bradford for Leeds on Thursday next, May 22nd, at Six o'clock, p.m., accompanied by a Band of Music, packed up in the identical Box, arriving in Leeds by half past Six, then forming a Procession through the principal streets to the Music Hall, Albion Street, where Mr. Brown will be released from the Box, before the audience, and then give the particulars of his Escape from Slavery, also the Song of his Escape. He will then show the GREAT PANORMA OF AMERICAN SLAVERY, which has been exhibited in this country to thousands.[28]

This was no sedate recitation of events like that performed by antislavery orators such as William and Ellen Craft, who toured in England after staging a spectacular escape from slavery in which Ellen (who was very light skinned) passed as white and male, and William (who was darker) passed as her enslaved property. Brown's performance featured a band, a parade, and a spectacular release; Brown then sang the song of his escape, and the panorama of American slavery was shown. As the stage manager, Brown organized and masterminded the show, but he also narrated and performed in it. As Marcus Wood notes: "[Brown] shattered the ceremonial and rhetorical proprieties of the formal lecture hall. He introduced elements of his own art and folk culture and fused them with the visual conventions of the circus, beast show, and pictorial panorama" ("'All Right!,'" 77). In so doing, he challenged the notion of enslaved subjectivity as flat or stereotypical, but may have also turned his own story into entertainment for a public entranced by spectacle and freakery.

Brown's performative modes were also certainly influenced (after 1852) by the popularity of *Uncle Tom's Cabin*, a text that, as argued above, has a scopic order that triangulates a mode of hierarchical empathy for the enslaved through a white viewing subject. Ruggles demonstrates that Brown's show was compared to *Uncle Tom's Cabin*; no doubt Brown was soon aware of what the *London Spectator* termed the "Tom-mania," which was rapidly spreading across Britain (*Unboxing Henry Brown*, 146). By 1853, Brown's panorama had much competition, both from white performers and from those claiming to be ex-slaves, such as Charles Hill.[29] Moreover, some of the advertisements for these shows make clear that slavery had become high entertainment. For example, the *Royal Cornwall Gazette* on May 27, 1853, conjoined a news item about a panorama of *Uncle Tom's Cabin* with the birth of a four-legged chicken. Slavery performance had become a kind of nineteenth-century freakery, accompanied by juvenile brass bands. Panoramas of *Uncle Tom's Cabin*, with their weird characters such as Topsy, may have played into a British voyeuristic curiosity about the savage creatures that slavery was supposed to create.

In the face of this flood of interest in *Uncle Tom's Cabin*, Brown, rather than being threatened by such spectacles, instead capitalized on them. From at least 1853–56, Brown exhibited his panorama in England alongside panoramas of *Uncle Tom's Cabin*. Indeed, the first performance of an entertainment using aspects of *Uncle Tom's Cabin* and Brown's work was in November 1852, when the *Hull Packet and East Riding Times* of November 26, 1852, reported that "Mr. Henry Box Brown, the Proprietor of the Great Moving American Tableaux, or Panorama of African and American Slavery, comprising upwards of one Hundred Magnificent views, representing 'SLAVERY AS IT IS,' painted on 50,000 feet of Canvas, illustrative of many vivid and interesting Incidents depicted in Mrs. Stowe's universally admired Work, 'UNCLE TOM'S CABIN,' will open in the Music-Hall . . . on Monday, Dec. 6th, 1852." It is unclear whether Brown's panorama was using images from *Uncle Tom's Cabin* or whether these were separate panoramas. By May 1853, Brown was performing some sort of program titled "Uncle Tom's Cabin." It was widely reported that he successfully sued James Scott, who booked his services to participate in this entertainment, after Scott refused to pay Brown. As reported in the *Sheffield and Rotherham Independent* on July 30, 1853, Brown entered into an agreement with Scott to perform a show called "Uncle Tom's Cabin" at the casino for two weeks for £34; the sum he was supposed to be paid would be equivalent to about £3,020 today (or $5,129, roughly $427 per performance if Brown performed every day but Sunday, more if he took other days off). Brown must have been considered a star headliner to justify this amount of money, and Scott therefore would have needed to sell a large number of tickets in order to pay Brown this sum. When the entertainment did not generate a large audience, Scott tried to cancel it, but as the newspaper article notes, Brown was savvy enough about the law to "continue to tender his services daily, until the expiration of his agreement," to keep copies of the contract, hire a lawyer, and manage to obtain not only the salary he was supposed to be paid but also fees for his time, his lawyer's, and his witness's. These actions perhaps suggest knowledge not only of reading and writing, but also of contract law.

The nature of the *Uncle Tom's Cabin* show that Brown performed at the Adelphi Casino is unclear, but by 1855 Brown was exhibiting his own panorama side by side with panoramas based on Stowe's novel, as reported in the *Bristol Mercury* on Saturday April 21, 1855: "On Monday and Tuesday April 23rd and 24th, Mr. Henry Box Brown, the celebrated American fugitive slave, will, in addition to his Original panorama of African and American Slavery, exhibit his PICTORIAL ILLUSTRATED PANORAMIC VIEWS OF UNCLE TOM'S CABIN." Moreover, Brown became a master of multimedia, as the following notice placed in the *Isle of Wight Observer* on May 10, 1856, illustrates:

Mr. Henry Box Brown . . . will exhibit his original GRAND PANORAMA of African and American Slavery, the first that ever appeared before the public of this Country. . . . The scenes will be described by Mr. Henry Box Brown, who will give an account of his extraordinary and novel Escape from Slavery. Illustrated Views of UNCLE TOM'S CABIN painted on 50,000 Square Feet of Canvas, and comprising upwards of One Hundred Magnificent Views will also be shown. . . . Mr. H. B. Brown will give a Song descriptive of his Escape, and exhibit the Identical Box in which he made his Escape. . . . Appropriate music will be in attendance. A narrative of Mr. Brown's Life, which has already attained a large circulation, will be sold at the Doors.

Brown used two panoramas (visual modes); songs, singing, and music (aural modes); his own narrative (a print mode); and oral modes (as Brown describes the tableaux). Brown's method of presentation grew increasingly effective at using such multimodal and multimedia forms of communication in one performance space.

By 1857, Brown had taken on a new mode of performance as an actor and a playwright. Notices of his acting roles began to appear in June 1857 in London. The *Era* on June 28 reported that he was appearing in three plays by E. G. Burton: *The Fugitive Free, The Nubian Captive; or, Royal Slave,* and *Pocahontas; or, The English Tar and the Indian Princess*.[30] Just a few months later, he began performing his own work, as notices in the *Era* in September and October 1857 indicate. Whether Brown was successful as an actor is unknown, but it appears that by this time

FIGURE 5.21 Poster from Henry Box Brown's performances in Shrewsbury, England, December 12–17, 1859. Used with permission of the Shropshire Archive.

he had most likely learned to read and write; he went onto the London stage in the "double capacity of dramatist and actor" and as "the hero of one of his own pieces."[31] He was also described as a "hero personifying himself," an actor performing a role that both was and was not the "real" person. That Brown was appearing with "Mr. Charles Rice the well-known comedian" was indicative of the degree to which slavery had become spectacle and entertainment.

This does not mean Brown ended his work with the panoramas. After his marriage to a British woman named Jane Floyd (a former teacher) in 1855,[32] Brown exhibited new panoramas, sometimes with his wife, who had a panorama titled "The Holy Land."[33] Brown paraded through the streets dressed as an "African chief" and gave presents to his audience (see the *Preston Guardian*, May 4, 1861). Posters from this period indicate Brown's contradictory and multivalent personae as both Box Brown and a "Native Prince" (see figure 5.21). Advertisements for this 1859 performance, such as this one in the *Shrewsbury Chronicle*, note that Brown was "born a slave, and as it appears, was packed in a box as luggage and conveyed 350 miles to escape slavery." Brown's name, despite all his accomplishments in the decade since his escape, was still knit up with the "luggage" in which he had escaped.

Newspaper accounts indicate that these shows were relatively popular, but they may have begun to function as entertainment and spectacle rather than as vehicles for viewers' state matching or intersubjectivity. Reviews of Brown's performances indicate that the multiplying of performance modes may have inhibited empathy, because Brown may have been seen as an actor, a performer, and a showman rather than as someone with whom a viewer could identify (Blackett, *Antislavery Wall*, 158–60). Moreover, as Hazel Waters has documented, during the 1850s in England there was a movement away from realistic theater portraying slavery toward minstrelsy and plays that enforced a white viewer's own sense of racial superiority (*Racism on the Victorian Stage*). Brown's panoramas may not have seemed very different from the "thousands of exhibitions of exotic spectacle which crowded Victorian popular culture" and entertained the "hypocritical attention of the English public" (Fisch, *American Slaves*, 83). In the end, some of Brown's antislavery performance work may have fed the desire animating the British public in this period to see abject, entertaining, or foolish black bodies on stage.

Act Three: A Man and His Magic

Perhaps that was why in 1859 Brown undertook a new type of entertainment, one that might symbolically renovate the box, the womb-tomb of slavery, into an open and traversable space. At Brentford, England, in 1859, Brown first performed "with Professor Chadwick" and concluded one of the shows with "several experiments in mesmerism, human magnetism, and electro-biology" (*West London Observer*, Ruggles, *Unboxing of Henry Brown*, 154). Brown continued to exhibit his panorama, yet he increasingly listed his profession in census records as either a "lecturer on America" (1861) or "lecturer in mesmerism" (1864).[34] In this final section, I consider why Brown might have chosen these titles rather than "lecturer on slavery."

As discussed in other chapters, the trauma of enslaved torture remains to a greater or lesser extent outside the realm of language proper. Brown's panorama may have been mere entertainment and spectacle to him after a certain point. He did create new panoramas such as his "Grand Moving Mirror of the American War" (1862), but he also seems to have moved beyond this type of entertainment. Brown had worked with the mesmerist Chadwick, who possessed, according to one account, "A most wonderful influence of all who submitted themselves to his operation: he sent them to sleep, awoke them, made them jump about transfixed to their chairs; at his command they were riveted to the platform, from which they could not move, unless commanded to do so by the operation; they jumped, they danced, they rang imaginary bells, rolled about, held one leg in the air, as long as the mesmerizer choose, and then they were all sent to sleep again" (quoted in Ruggles, *Unboxing of Henry Brown*, 158–59). As late as 1867, Brown was having great success with his lectures on "Mesmerism and Electro Biology."[35] Having been for many years someone who had to "submit" to the authority of masters as well as the public, Brown might have relished using mesmerism to gain control over his audiences' mental and physical powers.

He also began to combine mesmerist shows with magic acts that worked to remodel the visual space of enslavement. Ruggles contends that over the twenty-five years during which Brown performed in Britain, from 1850 to 1875, he appears to have "emancipated himself, in a sense, from his personal history of enslavement" (*Unboxing of Henry Brown*, 159). Yet in all his performance work, Brown still retained the material object he escaped in (the box), which remained part of his persona and his magic act. Rather than escaping the legacy of enslavement, perhaps mesmerism, magic, and conjure gave Brown a type of dominion over the visual culture of enslavement, which had symbolically consigned him to a type of living death. Several recent critics have argued that given the historical legacy of slavery, black subjects are not only marginal to culture but also "share the space the dead inhabit" (Holland, *Raising the Dead*, 6). Abdul JanMohamed argues that death is central to the formation of African American subjectivity; he writes of a "death-bound-subject," formed "from infancy on, by the imminent and ubiquitous threat of death" (*Death-Bound-Subject*, 2). Did Brown's mesmeric acts and magic shows literalize the death-bound trauma of slavery—transform it into art while not abandoning its essential political content?

After returning to the United States in 1875, Brown performed with his wife and daughter, Annie, in a family magic act. Even then, according to Ruggles, Brown continued to "climb into his original box" (*Unboxing of Henry Brown*, 162); advertisements constantly referred to his status as "the original Box Brown." But a poster from this period (first located by David Price) indicates that Brown's tricks used a number of different boxes to make items appear and reappear: "The Programme will consist of the following: destroying and restoring a handkerchief . . . the wonderful Flying Card and *Box* Feat . . . the wonderful experiment of passing a watch through a number of *Boxes*" (see figure 5.22, emphasis added). If the original box—perhaps a replica at this point, more than twenty-five years after Brown's escape—in some way represented the womb-tomb of slavery, these other magical boxes symbolically echoed with it, transforming it into a space that became multiple and open, a space of both destruction and transformation. Samira Kawash argues that "through its various referents . . . the box successively reconstitutes Brown as corpse, as fetus, as first man" ("Fugitive Properties," 229n90), yet it also may have reconstituted him as something magical, as someone who was just slightly more than a mere human being. Act three of Brown's life, as a magician and conjurer, symbolically transmuted the original box into a magical, open, and plural zone of destruction but also transformation.[36]

The original box might also have undergone a form of transmutation to become part of Brown's magic act. Magic acts of the time commonly featured magicians or their assistants climbing into boxes and then disappearing, only to reappear in the box or somewhere else. These magic boxes had trapdoors in the bottom, side, or back from which the magician escaped or seemed to vanish; the magician could then reenter the box through this portal and seem to come back. Sometimes mirrors were placed diagonally to create a "safe zone" within the box so that it merely looked empty; these "Proteus" boxes had to be carefully designed, or else some spectators, as the box was turned, might have seen their reflections in the mirrors (Steinmeyer, *Hiding the Elephant*, 78–79). If Brown used such a magic box in his act, the formerly enslaved man would have seemed to dematerialize and rematerialize, and a viewer might have seen himself or herself momentarily and fleetingly in the sight lines of the magic box, certainly an unsettling situation.

Moreover, whereas the postal crate that Brown made his escape in had only one exit (the top), which was nailed shut (Brown, *Narrative of the Life*, 53) like a coffin and had to be opened by someone else, the protean magic box, if employed by Brown, would have had several exits that the magician controlled. Perhaps, in a spectacular act of symbolic deconstruction and reconstruction, of loss and recovery, Brown literally took the abject, fetishized "original" box and cut holes in its back and side to allow other modes of egress, or added mirrors to create a safe

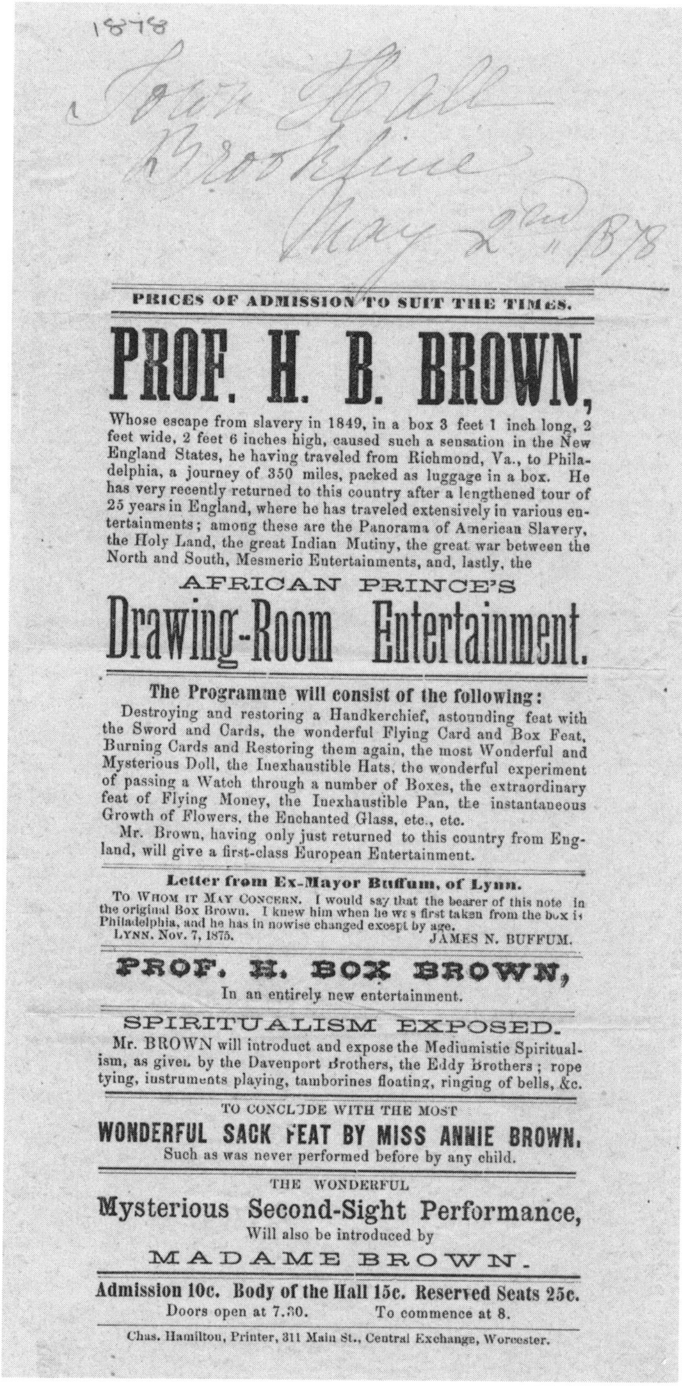

PRICES OF ADMISSION TO SUIT THE TIMES.

PROF. H. B. BROWN,

Whose escape from slavery in 1849, in a box 3 feet 1 inch long, 2 feet wide, 2 feet 6 inches high, caused such a sensation in the New England States, he having traveled from Richmond, Va., to Philadelphia, a journey of 350 miles, packed as luggage in a box. He has very recently returned to this country after a lengthened tour of 25 years in England, where he has traveled extensively in various entertainments; among these are the Panorama of American Slavery, the Holy Land, the great Indian Mutiny, the great war between the North and South, Mesmeric Entertainments, and, lastly, the

AFRICAN PRINCE'S

Drawing-Room Entertainment.

The Programme will consist of the following:

Destroying and restoring a Handkerchief, astounding feat with the Sword and Cards, the wonderful Flying Card and Box Feat, Burning Cards and Restoring them again, the most Wonderful and Mysterious Doll, the Inexhaustible Hats, the wonderful experiment of passing a Watch through a number of Boxes, the extraordinary feat of Flying Money, the Inexhaustible Pan, the instantaneous Growth of Flowers, the Enchanted Glass, etc., etc.

Mr. Brown, having only just returned to this country from England, will give a first-class European Entertainment.

Letter from Ex-Mayor Buffum, of Lynn.

To Whom it May Concern. I would say that the bearer of this note in the original Box Brown. I knew him when he was first taken from the box in Philadelphia, and he has in nowise changed except by age.
Lynn, Nov. 7, 1875. JAMES N. BUFFUM.

PROF. H. BOX BROWN,
In an entirely new entertainment.

SPIRITUALISM EXPOSED.

Mr. BROWN will introduce and expose the Mediumistic Spiritualism, as given by the Davenport Brothers, the Eddy Brothers; rope tying, instruments playing, tamborines floating, ringing of bells, &c.

TO CONCLUDE WITH THE MOST

WONDERFUL SACK FEAT BY MISS ANNIE BROWN,
Such as was never performed before by any child.

THE WONDERFUL

Mysterious Second-Sight Performance,
Will also be introduced by

MADAME BROWN.

Admission 10c. Body of the Hall 15c. Reserved Seats 25c.
Doors open at 7.30.   To commence at 8.

Chas. Hamilton, Printer, 311 Main St., Central Exchange, Worcester.

FIGURE 5.22 Broadside advertising a performance by Henry Box Brown with his family in Brookline, Massachusetts, May 2, 1878. Used with permission of Mike Caveney and the Egyptian Hall Museum, Pasadena, California.

zone in which he was both miraculously invisible and yet still present. Or perhaps more symbolically, he created a new box, a magician's box, that *mirrored* the box used in his first escape, yet was in fact an entirely new entity that allowed him to metamorphose a condition in which he was both present and absent, alive and dead, magical and human.

The formerly enslaved avatar crafted by Brown, although never quite free from the legacy of enslavement, was always in the process of metamorphosing, of becoming something new, even until his death in 1897. Brown's metaphorical corporeality ultimately was alive and dead, visible and vanished, utterly real and completely magical, both physical and metaphysical. In this way, Brown's performative work resisted the idea that the static, flat, formerly enslaved subject belonged only in the realm of abjection, insisting instead on it being plural, multivalent, transformative, and everywhere at once.[37] In so doing, Brown may have attempted to shift a viewer into a radical protocol of spectatorship in which he or she came to understand the instability and transmutability of everything. Proteus, the ever-changing Greek god of the ocean, answered only to someone capable of capturing him. In the end, then, perhaps Brown slipped free from a viewer's gaze, caught and yet not caught in spectacular and protean moments, as with a turn of the box a viewer saw not an abject slave, but fleetingly his or her subjectivity, reflected back in the performative space of enslavement itself.

Conclusion: The Politics of Empathy

I have argued in this chapter that Stowe and Brown used their visual rhetoric to present divergent representations of the enslaved that might move a reader toward empathy or intersubjectivity. The visual rhetoric of *Uncle Tom's Cabin* triangulates empathy by dividing it between a white or near-white viewer within the illustration who loves the abject enslaved body so that the reading viewer does not have to, or sequesters agentive near-white bodies outside the geographic confines of the United States so that they pose no threat to a (white) viewer's physical corporeality or emotional subjectivity. Brown's representations of the enslaved and formerly enslaved, on the other hand, were active, writerly, and polyphonic. They may therefore have engaged theory of mind—the psychological processes needed to gain access to characters' subjective experiences—in order to ask a reader to understand the ambiguity of another's lifeworld. Yet Brown's performances might have dissipated empathy through the multiple visual modes they manipulated, which tended to configure the enslaved as magical, and the space of enslavement as one with many routes in and out. Brown's performative avatars might have finally slipped away from a viewer's modes of cognition and comprehension altogether. Stowe's appeal reached a wider audience and was more popular than any of Brown's performances, and Brown ultimately created panoramas that incorporated *Uncle Tom's Cabin*, suggesting that he may have realized the limits of his performance work in generating both empathy and profit. It seems that after *Uncle Tom's Cabin*, no abolitionist work could ignore the sensation it caused, and that it set the pattern for much visual work to come.

Stowe's *Uncle Tom's Cabin* also seems to have been used by some abolitionists to recruit people into the movement. Ida B. Wells claims that the book was "one of the causes of the abolition of slavery" ("Woman's Mission," 181), and Mary Church Terrell argues that "no author has ever done more with the pen for the cause of human liberty than [Stowe] did" (*Colored Woman*, 282). Martin Delany, Frederick Douglass, and other prominent abolitionists debated the merits of the book; Douglass argued that it was an extremely effective agent of change that would move through the country like fire through "dry stubble," while others criticized its racialist stereotypes or colonization agenda (Sinha, *Slave's Cause*, 443–44).

Information about whether the book in fact caused people to join the abolition movement or free their slaves is hard to come by, but it is clear that the book was widely read. On the eve of the Civil War, in 1860, the book had sold 4.5 million copies in English and been translated into sixteen other languages (Lowance and Pilditch, "Writing the Law," 75). In 1850, there were over three million enslaved people, many of whom knew firsthand the horrors of slavery; but as Stephen Railton points out, for over a million northerners during the 1850s, when the conflicted issue of slavery was becoming more urgent, "Stowe's novel served to define what it was the nation was arguing about" (*"Uncle Tom's Cabin"*). Yet a commonly reported reaction to the book was both tears and laughter at the antics of the enslaved (Meer, "Topsy and the End Man," 131). Stowe's novel also served to structure an overall hierarchical empathetic response that had long-lasting consequences for how the formerly enslaved would be configured within the body politic of the United States. Its strong affective appeal may not have shifted readers away from regarding the enslaved as objects of pity and pathos, in need of white benevolence.

Studies of empathy in a variety of fields have suggested that it can be strongly felt across species, for disabled creatures within the animal world, and for entities that are perceived as weak or childlike (Preston and de Waal, "Empathy," 3). Why is it that even today, appeals for money to improve conditions in any country in the developing world often feature the face of an emaciated child? Some charities eschew such images, instead encouraging someone to buy a chicken so that a man can sell the eggs and feed himself and his family, but the vast majority rely on a mode of empathy that features pity and pathos for those they seek to help, rather than parity and equality. They encourage a viewer (as Stowe does) to feel another's pain, but do not promote the understanding that "another's pain could also be my pain"; that is, they do not lead to introspection about the larger, worldwide forces that have caused this situation and that (but for the luck of being born in the right place to the right family) could have placed the empowered donor in the same space as that of the viewed recipient.

Moreover, it seems that categories such as pity and empathy can easily slide into each other, and that sometimes it is difficult to disentangle a hierarchical empathy that functions like sentimentality—a display of emotion that does not provoke a sense of human connection—from a parallel empathy that attempts to accomplish more than the shedding of tears over another's plight. Perhaps the difficulty of disentangling a mode of pity, sentimentalism, and hierarchical empathy from one of parallel empathy and intersubjectivity ultimately persuaded Henry Box Brown to turn away from this emotion altogether and to engage in sleight of hand, magic, and mesmerism to demonstrate that the enslaved subject could not be caught in the net of ostentatious emotion generated by a weeping reader or viewer. In the end, Stowe's victory over antislavery's foes may have convinced some people that slavery was wrong not because the enslaved person was a self, but because he or she was a crippled, inferior other who needed the ministering hand of the white viewing reader. My epilogue therefore considers modes of visual rhetoric recently used in the portrayal of slavery that attempt to move beyond the vexed politics of empathy, in performance modes that are more ironic than emotional, more distancing and self-reflexive than empathetic.

Epilogue

The End of Empathy, or Slavery Revisited
via Twentieth- and Twenty-First-Century Artworks

Remember that there are parts of what it most concerns you to know which I cannot describe to you;
you must come with me and see for yourselves. The vision is for him [or her] who will see it.
—Plotinus[1]

I have argued in this study that antislavery illustrated books published before *Uncle Tom's Cabin* sometimes contain a radical reading protocol that moves between words and pictures in an attempt to alter a viewing reader's horizon of expectations. The goal is to move a reader beyond spectatorship toward a mode of parallel empathy that entails vicarious introspection in which the viewer comes to realize that the world-experience of the enslaved (in Husserl's terms) could be the viewer's own. This parallel mode of empathy develops what some have called embodied simulation—the "reuse of mental states and processes involving representations that have a bodily format" (Gallese and Sinigaglia, "What Is So Special," 515)—as well as theory of mind, the ability to create a cognitive and emotional map of another's subjectivity and to act with that knowledge in mind. I also contend that some graphic illustrated books use the synergistic interaction between words and images to generate empathy and to represent the enslaved as obtaining a degree of control over narrative and lived experiences, even if these figurations entail a sense that the story of slavery is in many ways untellable, unnarratable, beyond representation itself.

Writing this book in the first part of the twenty-first century, I realized that slavery has again taken precedence in the visual and cultural imagination of the United States. This phenomenon can be seen in popular and award-winning films set in the antebellum era, such as Steven Spielberg's *Lincoln* (2012), Quentin Tarantino's *Django Unchained* (2012), Steve McQueen's *12 Years a Slave* (2013), and Amma Asante's *Belle* (2014). A film currently being cast plays on the popularity of *Django Unchained* and is called *Nat Turner Unchained*,[2] and Nate Parker's film about Turner, *Birth of a Nation*, first shown at the Sundance Film Festival in January 2016, was picked up for distribution by Fox Searchlight for $17.5 million and widely released in the fall of 2016. As I watched *Django Unchained* in Hartford, Connecticut, every time a white person was shot or blown up, the audience cheered or laughed; there was also some applauding when Stephen—the obsequious enslaved African American butler to the slave master Candy—was shot, but it was more muted. As I watched *12 Years a Slave* with students and colleagues from the Institute of Africana Studies at the same movie theater in Hartford, many in the audience wept openly and copiously. Both films were widely released and considered critical successes, and both featured scenes of excruciating torture in which the black enslaved body was once again flailed and broken open, as it was in the pro- and antislavery visual rhetoric of the eighteenth and nineteenth centuries. A commonly intoned phrase used by some to describe local news broadcasts is "If it bleeds, it leads," and it seems that slavery still bleeds. More importantly, just as some accounts of slavery sold extremely well in the nineteenth and twentieth centuries, particularly works such as *Uncle Tom's Cabin*, *Gone with the Wind* (book and film, 1936 and 1939), and *Roots* (book and television miniseries, 1976, 1977, and then remade once more by the History Channel in 2016), slavery still sells well on the small and big screen. It is a bleeding, bloody subject from which we cannot quite unchain ourselves.

Slavery in its most basic form still exists in some parts of the world, a point often ignored while U.S. culture lovingly consumes fact and fiction concerning the past of this "peculiar institution."[3] I might argue that in the wake of "clean" forms of torture such as waterboarding (which leaves no physical marks and was authorized by the U.S. government), some U.S. citizens nostalgically long for depictions of the "dirty" torture of slavery, a torture that was patently wrong and meaningless, in contrast with the "enhanced interrogation techniques" that, after 9/11, some people believe might be useful in producing information about terrorists or would-be terrorists.[4] The pathos of *12 Years a Slave* made some viewers cry, but it also let them feel good that the United States has (in theory) ended such barbaric practices. *Django Unchained* evokes a more ironic response in that the larger-than-life figures and often cartoonish violence are situated in a past that is more imagined than real, as the numerous historical inaccuracies in the film blatantly make a viewer aware.[5] In blurring past and present through historical anachronism and error, Tarantino implies that the past is not past—that it is part of our present and future. Tarantino does not eschew empathy altogether in *Django Unchained*, but certainly his approach to slavery is more ironic and humorous than that of *12 Years a Slave*, in which McQueen tugs at the viewer's heartstrings again and again.

In light of *Django Unchained* and other contemporary artworks that appear to eschew the politics of empathy, we might productively revisit a question asked by Saidiya Hartman in *Scenes of Subjection*. She wonders whether "in making the slave's suffering his own," a white individual "begins to feel for himself rather than for those whom this exercise in imagination presumably is designed to reach." If so, "the denial of black sentience and the obscurity of suffering" are not "attenuated but instantiated" (19). I have proposed that empathy for the enslaved can at times entail a spiraling process of affect that moves between a self and an other, one that does not end in a person merely feeling sorry for himself or herself but instead undermines the conceptual quarantine between the viewer and the viewed. Yet Hartman's point is worth contemplating when considering contemporary visual rhetoric about enslavement and freedom, such as that in *Django Unchained* or in artworks by Kara Walker and Glenn Ligon that directly reference the time period of slavery. My project has delineated diverse modes of empathy within some anti-slavery books, and here I hypothesize that the invocation of an empathetic response on the part of the viewer in visual treatments of slavery has not disappeared, but it has become more ironic, self-reflective, and self-questioning. We might call this new mode meta-empathy, a mode that, even as it promotes forms of identification between the enslaved and a viewing self, turns the viewer toward an examination not of a debased other, but of the politics of empathy as a whole.

Perhaps *Uncle Tom's Cabin* had something to do with this shift into a new mode that asks the viewer to ruminate on empathy. After the phenomenal popularity of this text, it seems that hierarchical empathy (in which the enslaved are viewed as inferior or unlike the white viewing subject) held sway for many years. As Henry Louis Gates Jr. and Hollis Robbins point out, even today, more than 160 years after the novel's original publication, at least 600 editions of it have been published in English and in translation, and at least 150 editions are in print worldwide ("Harriet Beecher Stowe," xlvii). As discussed previously, *Uncle Tom's Cabin* influenced the portrayal of the enslaved in illustrated books that came after it, and also Henry Box Brown's performances of his panorama, which incorporated this pivotal text. Yet the popularity of this novel as a visual sensation did not abate in the nineteenth century. As late as the 1940s, vivid cartoons featuring a manacled Tom replicating the supplicant slave's pose appeared in the classic cartoon illustrated version of *Uncle Tom's Cabin* (see, for example, Classic Comics #15, *Uncle Tom's Cabin*, from 1942).

Moreover, as recently as 1987, the novel was turned into a made-for-television movie on Showtime, directed by Stan Lathan and featuring Avery Brooks, Phylicia Rashad, Edward Woodward, Bruce Dern, and Samuel L. Jackson. Apparently, this melodramatic version of the book still has the power to move viewers, judging by comments made in 2014 when the movie was posted on YouTube: "The movie and book are both sad. When you think of it though it's amazing how Tom's faith set all the slaves free!" (Alicia Rhine) and "First movie that ever make my cry" (Smok Killergold). *Uncle Tom's Cabin* seems to be stitched into the tapestry of U.S. visual culture even today, its images familiar enough that they can be cited without explication. For example, a political cartoon from 2005 portrays Condoleezza Rice (then a nominee for secretary of state) as Eliza running over the ice during her confirmation hearing (see figure 6.1; color image 14). As I have argued, Eliza is one of the more powerful figures in Stowe's novel, yet what does it mean when an influential, intelligent woman such as Rice must be portrayed through the dated iconography of slavery and slave abasement? It may be that *Uncle Tom's Cabin* is still the primary lens that many people use to understand the past of slavery. Modes that invoke pity in regard to enslaved torment are still popular in contemporary culture. Perhaps the authors of earlier antislavery books were wrong to hope that audiences would move beyond this voyeuristic, pitying mode of empathy into one that viewed the enslaved as an equal.

FIGURE 6.1   Condoleezza Rice, nominee for secretary of state, as Eliza.
Illustration by Elliott Banfield, *New York Sun*, January 21, 2005. Copyright Elliott Banfield.
Courtesy of the *New York Sun*. Used with permission.

In the wake of the familiarity and iconicity of the humbled, tortured body of the enslaved, contemporary visual artists such as Kara Walker and Glenn Ligon have tried to remake the politics of empathy in artworks that reflect back this famed imagery through an ironic or minimalist mirror. Indeed, Walker's *The End of Uncle Tom and the Grand Allegorical Tableau of Eva in Heaven* (1995; see figure 6.2) at first glance does not seem to be about Stowe's novel in any way. Like many of Walker's artworks, this tableau features images of enslaved men and women forced to engage in sadistic and sexualized acts rendered within the medium of the seemingly picturesque fashion of the nineteenth-century cutout (or stencil) tradition.[6] This image displays themes manifested in Walker's work as a whole: the brutality of slavery, the strange and weird sexual relationships it fostered, the power that some enslaved women manipulated through their sexuality, and the mundane everydayness of the torture inflicted on the enslaved and embedded in the visual landscape of slavery. The scene is panoramic, and in this way Walker takes control over the visual politics of enslavement. As Teresa Goddu points out, it was often the master's right to take panoramic power over the visual landscape, and here Walker turns this power back on the master, showcasing his barbaric actions, such as sodomizing a young boy ("Antislavery's Panoramic Perspective"). Looking at this panorama, at first a viewer might wonder: Where is Little Eva? Where is Tom? Where is Topsy? Later we might discern the outlines of Eva in the murderous girl who wields an axe in the center of the picture, or of Uncle Tom in the supplicant slave in the picture's far right.[7] But these are vague figures and do not stand out as icons of the novel itself. Perhaps this is Walker's point: these familiar figures have been absorbed into our unconscious understanding of slavery and the past, consumed by us to such a degree that they have become part of our ideology without our being aware of the fact.

Can a viewer feel empathy for any of the figures depicted in this scene? Perhaps, but empathy reflected and refracted through these grotesque figures would have to be rather ironic. In this exhibit, the shadows of the figures reflect darkly onto the polished wooden floor of the gallery. As we walk through these shadows, these remnants of the past, these absent presences, do we become a part *of* them? Or apart *from* them? The panorama is also very large, so a viewer would have to pivot or walk in several different directions to take it all in; the viewer must formulate something of a reading path through it to have it make meaning. Through such mechanisms, Walker leaves it up to the viewer to fashion a relationship to the past, and she may thereby invoke a process of empathy that asks a reader not to absorb the past, but to reflect on it, to ruminate about it, and to understand our physical and mental entwinement with the past in the present-tense moment.

FIGURE 6.2 Kara Walker, *The End of Uncle Tom and the Grand Allegorical Tableau of Eva in Heaven* (1995). Cut paper on wall. Approx. 15 × 35 ft. (4.6 × 10.7 m). Collection Jeffrey Deitch, New York. Used with permission.

In other illustrations, Walker is even more ironic toward the process of empathy under slavery, suggesting that an "empathetic response" is anything but empathetic (see figure 6.3; color image 15). The scene shown in figure 6.3 also features many icons of past enslaved torture, such as the enslaved man on the left in his neck collar and chains, and the tiny image at the bottom left of a naked enslaved woman who has been hung up, either to be tortured or killed. What I find most fascinating about this image, however, is that it does not make clear what performing the titular "swift and dramatic empathetic reaction" demanded by "mistress" actually signifies—and at whom the small child directs her "empathetic reaction." The woman hanging from the tree could be mistress herself; in this case, the "empathetic reaction" of killing her by plunging a dagger into her chest is extraordinarily ironic. Yet the hanging figure lacks the hoop-shaped skirts normally associated with southern slave mistresses in Walker's oeuvre, so she could also be another enslaved woman; in this case, the "empathetic" response might involve an enslaved girl killing an enslaved woman, perhaps to put her out of her misery after great torture. It is also possible that the large dagger is being pulled out of the hanging woman. This would be another hollow gesture of empathy in that it hardly seems likely to stop the hanging woman's torment; if she is not already dead, pulling the dagger out will not save her.

FIGURE 6.3 Kara Walker, *Mistress Demanded a Swift and
Dramatic Empathetic Reaction Which we Obliged Her* (2000).
Cut paper and projection on wall. Collection of Whitney Museum
of American Art, New York. Used with permission.

As a whole, this artwork, like *The End of Uncle Tom*, stages the ambiguity of empathy's ability to cross boundaries and borders or to amend the iconicity and sheer repeatability of the slave's tortured body in the past as well as in the present. Yet Walker has not given up entirely on identification and empathy. This scene is projected onto the wall of the gallery through a wide-lens projector, so a viewer can stand in the artwork (in the beam of the projector, which is part of the installation) as he or she scrutinizes it; a viewer might also cast the shadow of his or her corporeality into it as he or she observes. There is no doubt, as Gwendolyn Shaw notes, that Walker's work reflects upon and offers up for critique, "the problem of the broader culture's inability to come to terms with the past" (*Seeing the Unspeakable*, 6). Yet I would suggest that through such projective mechanisms, Walker implies that we cannot escape an implicated relationship to the historical past, no matter how vexed or fraught this past is. We stand (quite literally) in it.

Glenn Ligon's art makes it even clearer that enslavement of the "past" continues today, integrating his own body into his artworks as the infamous image of the runaway slave (see figures 6.4 and 6.5). Like Box Brown and Bibb, Ligon troubles the politics of identification by portraying himself as multivalent and contradictory: he is both male and female, of the past and the present, a mass of contradictions, "socially very adept, yet, paradoxically, he's somewhat of a loner." He also "talks sort of out of the side of his mouth and looks at your sideways"; perhaps Ligon here alludes to the fact that many images of the enslaved do not directly return the gaze of the empowered viewer. Ligon's figure has also begun referring to himself as "mother," perhaps in an allusion to the absent or lost mothers of slavery, those ancestors (as Hartman notes in *Lose Your Mother*) that can never be reclaimed or, as Toni Morrison notes, called back, because "nobody knows their name" ("In the Realm of Responsibility," 247). Ligon aims for an ironic sense that the body of the enslaved past, both the physical corporeality of the enslaved and the symbolic weight of its visual iconography, remains present in contemporary U.S. culture.

Even more interestingly for the purposes of this book, Ligon alludes to a particular enslaved figure—Henry Box Brown—in specific frames from *Runaways* (see figure 6.6).[8] Here Ligon becomes a version of Box Brown: the picture shows the portrait of Brown from the frontispiece of his 1849 narrative, and the description makes clear that the image is both Brown and Ligon: "Ran away, Glenn." Again we have the sideways glance ("looks at you from the corners of his eyes") as well as an affability that might ensure empathy on the part of the viewer: "When he talks, he usually has a big smile towards you, yet he faces you from a slightly different angle." Most ironic about the image of Brown-Ligon is the way it invokes

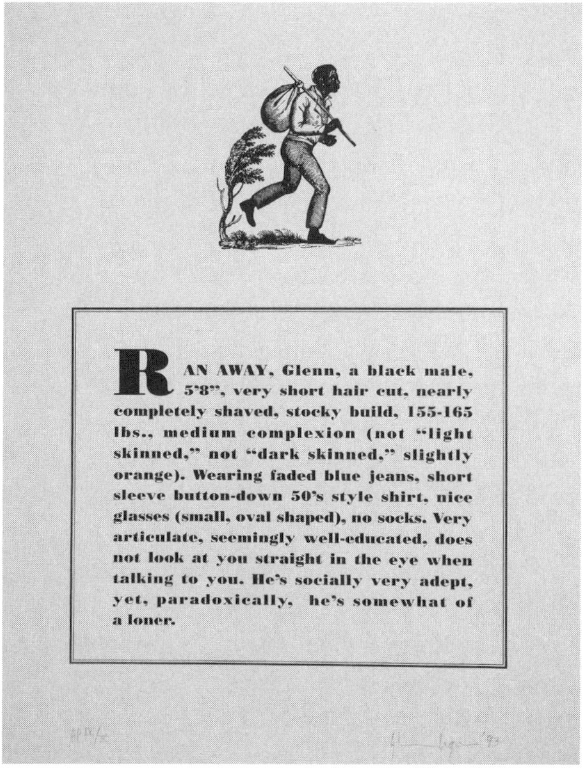

RAN AWAY, Glenn, a black male, 5'8", very short hair cut, nearly completely shaved, stocky build, 155-165 lbs., medium complexion (not "light skinned," not "dark skinned," slightly orange). Wearing faded blue jeans, short sleeve button-down 50's style shirt, nice glasses (small, oval shaped), no socks. Very articulate, seemingly well-educated, does not look at you straight in the eye when talking to you. He's socially very adept, yet, paradoxically, he's somewhat of a loner.

FIGURE 6.4 Glenn Ligon, *Runaways* (1993). Image from a set of ten lithographs, 40.6 × 30.5 cm. (16 × 12 in.). © Glenn Ligon, Courtesy Regen Projects, Los Angeles. Used with permission.

RAN AWAY, a man named Glenn. He has almost no hair. He has cat-eye glasses, medium-dark skin, cute eyebrows. He's wearing black shorts, black shoes and a short sleeve plaid shirt. He has a really cool Timex silver watch with a silver band. He's sort of short, a little hunky, though you might not notice it with his shirt untucked. He talks sort of out of the side of his mouth and looks at you sideways. Sometimes he has a loud laugh, and lately I've noticed he refers to himself as "mother."

FIGURE 6.5 Glenn Ligon, *Runaways* (1993). Image from a set of ten lithographs, 40.6 × 30.5 cm. (16 × 12 in.). © Glenn Ligon, Courtesy Regen Projects, Los Angeles. Used with permission.

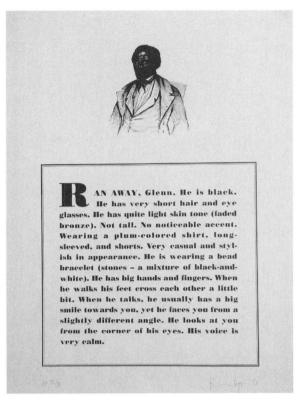

FIGURE 6.6 Glenn Ligon, *Runaways* (1993). Image from a set of ten lithographs, 40.6 × 30.5 cm. (16 × 12 in.). © Glenn Ligon, Courtesy Regen Projects, Los Angeles. Used with permission.

an absent-present voice that could be that of Brown or Ligon. By saying, "His voice is very calm," Ligon cites the struggle for "real voice" seen in both of Brown's autobiographical narratives (which may or may not have been his own words); he also calls up a present-tense Glenn Ligon, who may or may not be speaking in his "true" voice when he uses this tone. Given the high rate of police violence against African American males, an endemic feature of contemporary U.S. society, perhaps this "very calm" voice does not express Ligon's subjectivity, but instead is a verbal mask he wears to protect himself. Yet what other voice does he—or Brown, for that matter—have? Only the voice of his multivalent performance art, which suggests that he both does and does not exist within it.

Ligon also alludes to, yet more distinctly revises, the legacy of Box Brown in his minimalist work titled *To Disembark*, which includes some of the lithographs from *Runaways* (see figure 6.7). Ligon uses direct figurations of Brown's box to explore his relationship to the historical past, but one wonders whether Ligon is implying, as Brown did, that the black self is both nowhere and everywhere: in

FIGURE 6.7 Glenn Ligon, *To Disembark* (1993). Ten lithographs and nine photogravures, nine wood crates with sound, overall dimensions variable. Installation view. Image courtesy Hirshhorn Museum and Sculpture Garden, Smithsonian Institution, Washington, D.C. Photography by Lee Stalsworth. Used with permission.

the box and out of it, in the museum and beyond it, in the past and in the present. Denoting the Middle Passage as well as Brown with the title of the exhibit (*To Disembark*), Ligon embraces (as Christina Knight notes in "Disembarking") the theatricality of the boxes by adding music and sound that suggests actual black bodies, such as the artist reading from Henry Box Brown's narrative, Bob Marley singing his "Freedom Song," Billie Holiday singing "Strange Fruit," and KRS-One's performing their militant anthem "Sound of Da Police." As Knight notes, "This sonic landscape takes us from the 19th century into the late 20th, and it asks us to make connections between the horrors of slave ships and the other kinds of racial violence that the songs evoke." Huey Copeland puts this another way when he argues that Ligon "embarks on a path of representation that interrogates the regimes of viewership that subtend the afterlife of slavery" ("Glenn Ligon," 102). Ligon constantly interrogates the imbrication of the historical past within the contemporary moment of spectatorship, artistic creation, and re-creation. As with Walker, no route through the exhibit is specified, so viewers must create one in order to physically circumnavigate the exhibit or wander through its maze of boxes. Through this mechanism, viewers are asked to reflect on their relationship to this historical past and to create their own story about it.

In such installations, Ligon explores but also counters what Samira Kawash has called the "power of fugitivity." As Kawash explains, neither master nor slave, neither person nor property, the fugitive occupies the space of nonplace, silence, and invisibility ("Fugitive Properties," 279). Ligon notates this place in his minimalist boxes, but also undermines the silence of fugitivity by using sound, music, and voice, turning the silence of fugitivity into a performative oral presence, as Brown himself did. Also, because the boxes in Ligon's exhibit are multiple and closed, it is unclear whether Brown (the fugitive) is inside one or has already escaped. Or perhaps he is within the absent-present space of the magical box that I delineated in chapter 5. The presence of nine boxes suggests that the power of fugitivity lies not so much in its silence or noise, as in its ability to replicate itself in ways that remain potentially unfathomable—there is no way to see inside the boxes, to fathom their contents, to discern whether Ligon-as-Brown is really there—yet highly visual and scopic.

In these artworks, Walker and Ligon turn the debate about empathy in a new direction, one that acknowledges the profoundly unknowable nature of the past and of enslavement. Elizabeth Clark notes that the nineteenth-century United States saw a marked broadening in rights for slaves, women, and children through "the piecemeal growth of protections in common law and by statute, state or private regulation, and constitutional amendment," and that one of the most successful arguments that oppressed people forwarded in this broadening of rights was "I am like that person and so I deserve the same rights." For this logic to triumph, however, the rights-bearing public had to offer an answering embrace to the outsider that brought him or her into the group. According to Clark, empathetic identification—"that person is like me and so she deserves the same rights"—was critical to this response.[9] In the works of Ligon and Walker, we can discern people who are enslaved, and they seem to be real enough. Yet what these people are doing, seeing, thinking, or feeling often remains opaque and just beyond the grasp of the viewer. So we can offer up an answering embrace only uneasily.

By being both familiar and strange or estranging, the works of Ligon and Walker suggest that the person being viewed is both like and unlike the viewer. These artworks may thereby promote a form of empathy that is ultimately more self-reflexive and ironic than straightforward, one that is aware of the ambiguity of the lifeworld of the other and the limits of any process of empathy. This more reflexive mode of empathy acknowledges, in Frederick Douglass's words, that "to understand it one must needs experience it, or imagine himself in similar circumstances" (*Narrative of the Life*, 144) but also the impossibility, on some level, of ever entirely achieving the ability to imagine oneself in the "similar circumstances" of slavery's torturous grasp. In the end, Ligon and Walker engage the viewer in a mode of viewing meant to evoke the horror of slavery's past, but also its denseness, solidity, and (possible) impenetrability. Their illustrated slaves—figured forth in ambiguous shadowy images and (possibly) empty boxes—imply as well that the enslaved presence is everywhere and nowhere in U.S. culture, both seen and unseen, both of the past and of the present, both within the box but also outside, beyond, and ceaselessly escaping from it.

APPENDIX
Hierarchical and Parallel Empathy

HIERARCHICAL EMPATHY	PARALLEL EMPATHY
Enslaved self is a disabled, childlike, endangered other; a partial, open self	Enslaved self is a full conspecific; a finished and closed self
Voyeurism, tears, projection of one's pain onto another	Vicarious introspection
Viewer and enslaved discordant, unmatched	Viewer and enslaved in some degree of concordance; state matching
Viewer placed above the enslaved visually; enslaved portrayed as visually or emotionally different	Viewer and enslaved paralleled visually; visually or emotionally similar
Tears or pity encouraged	Specific, tailored helping actions suggested
Receptivity to another's pain, but no understanding that this pain could also be one's own	Understanding that another's pain could also be one's own
Little understanding of the estrangement of the lifeworld of the enslaved	Understanding the strangeness and ambiguity of another's lifeworld
Unilateral process in which the viewed is always in need of pity, aid, etc.	Reciprocal, back-and-forth process that spirals between the viewer and the viewed

NOTES

Preface

1. There has been debate about the relationship between intersubjectivity and empathy, and whether one precedes the other; see Eva Johansson, "Empathy or Intersubjectivity?," for one summary of this debate. For the purposes of this book, I view intersubjectivity as an achieved *state* in which cognition and emotion are shared, and empathy as a *process* that may move a reader toward this state. These modes certainly overlap at times.

2. I follow András Sajó's argument, in his discussion of abolition and empathy, that the term "sympathy" in the eighteenth and nineteenth centuries was a close equivalent to what is today termed empathy (*Constitutional Sentiments*, 158). See also Suzanne Keen, who argues that aspects of empathy have been described since the days of Adam Smith under "the older term *sympathy*" (*Empathy and the Novel*, 4). The term "empathy" was first discussed in detail by the German philosopher Robert Vischer, who used the term "*einfühlung*" ("in-feeling" or "feeling-into") in contradistinction to "*mitgefühlung*" ("with-feeling") in his doctoral thesis, "On the Optical Sense of Form: A Contribution to Aesthetics," in 1873; see also Theodor Lipps's *Leitfaden der Psychologie* (1903). "*Einfühlung*" can also be translated as "one" or "one-feeling"—sharing the same feeling—rather than sympathy (with-feeling)—viewing from a distance. The term was first translated into English as "empathy" by Edward Bradford Titchener in *Lectures on the Experimental Psychology of the Thought Processes* (1909).

3. For discussion of this point, see Teresa Goddu, "Antislavery's Panoramic Perspective," 12.

4. White writes: "I would use the verb 'enslaved' rather than the noun 'slave' to implicate the inhumane actions of white people. The noun 'slave' suggests a state of mind and being that is absolute and unmediated by an enslaver. . . . 'Enslaved' forces us to remember that black men and women were Africans and African-Americans before they were forced into slavery and had a new—and denigrating—identity assigned to them. 'Enslaved' also nudges us to rethink our ideas about black resistance under slavery" (*Ar'n't I a Woman?*, 8).

Introduction. Visualizing Slavery and Slave Torture

1. Drawings often contain a horizon line (or implied horizon line) running directly through the middle of the picture, which establishes a viewer's line of perspective. When a drawing contains an object situated below an implied middle horizon line, a viewer tends to feel as if he or she is seeing this object from above and looking down on it. When an illustration contains objects situated above an implied horizon line, a viewer tends to feel as if she or he is looking up at it from below. And when an illustration contains objects that are at the line of perspective, the viewer tends to view it as being at a normal eye level. Other aspects of an illustration can amend, transform, or remake the way a viewer's perspective line falls within an illustration.

2. Portraiture was sometimes used to undermine the objectification of enslaved or for-merly enslaved individuals; see Gwendolyn DuBois Shaw, *Portraits of a People*, 27–43.

3. For more on this pamphlet and on Heyrick, see Moira Ferguson (*Subject to Others*, 253–58) and Marcus Wood ("Emancipation Art," 35–36). A similar image, titled "Emancipation in the West Indies," graces the cover of the *American Anti-Slavery Almanac* for 1840, with the following caption: "A free man stands erect upon the whip. A mother caresses her own child. Free children bury the broken chains." What is removed is Heyrick's radical sugges-tion that all men are of one blood and the first-person subjectivity of "I Am a Man, Your Brother."

4. Acts 17:26: "And he hath made of one blood all nations of men for to dwell on all the face of the earth."

5. On the circulation of the Wedgwood image, see Mary Guyatt, "Wedgwood Slave Medallion," and Saadia Lawton, "Contested Meanings." The image was remodeled in the service of a number of other causes (women's rights, debtors' rights, and temperance), and it lasted many years, even being contained today in stationery for Wilberforce House in Hull, England, as Wood has shown (*Horrible Gift*, 35–89).

6. It is important to keep in mind that slavery and abolition were not the only engines driving the production of texts by African Americans, nor were books the only modes through which African American literacy was manifested. For example, as Jeannine DeLombard has established, the antebellum period "saw African Americans participating in other kinds of manuscript and print production, ranging from pamphleteering to diary keeping and the circulation of friendship albums" ("African American Cultures," 362).

7. As Elizabeth Clark has pointed out, abolitionists who used imagery of pain and suf-fering "had feet in many different religious camps," and while there were substantive quar-rels between liberal and evangelical antislavery thinkers, both groups shared a core belief that "the whipping of slaves by masters represented an indefensible exercise of arbitrary agency and that representation of such events should provoke a sympathetic response from right-thinking Christians" ("'Sacred Rights,'" 465). On the subject of abolitionists' religious denominational multiplicity, see Herbert Aptheker, *Abolitionism*, and Lewis Perry, *Radical Abolitionism*.

8. See also Albert Boime's *The Art of Exclusion*, which demonstrates how paintings, prints, and popular art in the nineteenth century often represented African Americans through a system of "visually encoding hierarchy and exclusion" (16).

9. Recent scholarship by Marcus Wood, Kirk Savage, Cassandra Jackson, Jasmine Cobb, Michael Chaney, Radiclani Clytus, Simon Gikandi, Juanita Harper, Maurie McInnis, Maurice Wallace, Teresa Goddu, Shawn Michelle Smith, and others has examined aspects of the visual culture that was slavery, including its photography, painting, caricature, sculp-ture, pamphlet campaigns, and artwork; see the works by these authors listed in the bibli-ography. See also Maurice Wallace and Shawn Michelle Smith, eds., *Pictures and Progress*, a groundbreaking collection of essays on early photography and the making of the African American self. To date, however, the cultural work performed by graphic illustrated books as an antislavery genre has not been examined.

10. I have not found research in the field of empathy that makes this distinction between modes of empathy. One common division is between emotional empathy and cognitive empathy, but that is not the distinction I make here. For a discussion of cognitive versus emotional empathy, see Walter Stephan and Krystina Finlay, "Role of Empathy," 730.

11. For more on how early antislavery graphic work may have been fundamental to the cultural work that Stowe's *Uncle Tom's Cabin* sets out to do, see Clytus, "Envisioning Slavery," 3–7, 129–130.

12. Sajó argues that empathy is a crucial aspect of prosocial action and more specifically examines the role it played in abolitionist movements (*Constitutional Sentiments*, ch. 4). The scientific literature on empathy has a long history, but see, in particular, Stephanie Preston and Frans de Waal, "Empathy," for a good summary of some of these debates.

13. Foucault draws attention to "advances and retreats" (*Discipline and Punish*, 14) in the process whereby the spectacle of public torture and execution was replaced by "the sobriety of the new method" (13).

14. Moses Roper revised his manuscript throughout his life and published it himself in 1840, with no introductory documents. Henry Bibb was a printer who printed his own text. Henry Box Brown, while probably illiterate during the publication of the 1849 narrative, seems to have had a strong hand in shaping the 1851 version of his narrative, which hews closer to his own life experiences than the 1849 version.

15. For an articulation of the reasons behind the refusal to verbally describe beatings, such as the beating of Douglass's Aunt Hester, see Saidiya Hartman, *Scenes of Subjection*; for a rebuttal, see Fred Moten, *In the Break*.

16. The literature on sentimentalism and sympathy is vast, but for some key texts that consider sentimentalism as a potentially progressive political mode, see the works listed in the bibliography by Jane Tompkins, Cathy Davidson, Philip Fisher, Lori Merish, Elizabeth Dillon, and Glen Hendler. For those who are more concerned with how sympathy promotes processes of otherment, see the listed works by Ann Douglas, Nina Baym, Laura Wexler, Shirley Samuels, Marianne Noble, and Karen Sánchez-Eppler. Perhaps most forceful in articulating a middle ground between these approaches is Dana Nelson; in an analysis of Harriet Jacobs's *Incidents in the Life of a Slave Girl* (1861), she writes: "Sympathy ideally should *bridge* the gap of difference between sisters. Yet it neither can nor should *collapse* the differences that it bridges" (*Word in Black and White*, 144). In my interpretation of sympathy and sentimentality within literary texts, however, this mode often focuses on a rhetoric of racial difference and hierarchy that precisely fails to bridge the differences it evokes for the reader. See my reading of *Uncle Tom's Cabin* in chapter 5 for a discussion of how one sentimental text continues to propagate racial divisions, despite its attempt to "feel rightly" for the enslaved.

17. Cognitive processes or structures are defined as "the encoded representations of information in memory" (Kanwar, Olson, and Sims, "Cognitive Structures," 122). More generally, they have been taken to mean the basic mental processes, mental tools, and patterns of thought that people use to make sense of information. Regarding affective responses, I follow Michele Janette's definition of affect as not only emotion but also a transmission

between people: "I here draw on a grammatical distinction between *affect* and its frequent synonym *emotion*. As a noun, *emotion* inclines us towards the individual and the static—towards imagining a self-contained possessor of an identifiable and (however fleetingly) stable feeling. *Affect*, as both a verb and a noun, a process as well as a result or manifestation, insists on intersubjective activity and interactional transmission. Affect must be created and move between actors" ("'Distorting Overlaps,'" 166).

18. In the early nineteenth century, there was also a realization that for some individuals pain might be associated with eroticism and sexual pleasure; see Halttunen, "Humanitarianism and Pornography," 308–9. This association posed a challenge for humanitarian reformers, who wished to use pictures of cruelty in the service of political reforms such as abolition, temperance, and the humane treatment of sailors or convicts, yet were afraid that such images might either awaken or satiate a savage passion for cruelty (330).

19. Stedman's narrative was reprinted numerous times in various languages and formats, and Child's version is not the only reprinting of the Joanna extracts; they went through several other republications in the early nineteenth century, including an earlier one by Child herself in *The Oasis* in 1834 (with two illustrations). However, the 1838 text of *Joanna* contains more illustrations than other U.S. reprints. For a listing of some reprints, see Richard Price and Sally Price, introduction, lxxii–lxxxiii, and Sharpe, *Ghosts of Slavery*.

20. Also see Daphne Brooks, who places Brown's panorama within "mid-nineteenth-century visual entertainment in transatlantic culture" and argues for its "politically revisionist ends" as a work of theater (*Bodies in Dissent*, 83). I am more interested in considering how Brown's performance work as a whole—his narrative and panorama, but also his vocations as an actor, playwright, mesmerist, and magician—attempted to challenge the visual culture of slavery.

21. Jonathan Crary argues that the first decades of the nineteenth century saw a movement away from the concept of eyesight as objective and neutral into a concept of "subjective vision" in which "the human body, in all its contingency and specificity . . . becomes the active producer of optical experience" (*Techniques of the Observer*, 69). Vision became connected with other senses (59), and the "corporeal subjectivity of the observer . . . suddenly becomes the site on which an observation is possible" (69). The notion of "subjective vision" could be an obstruction within a political movement such as abolition, geared toward the presentation of objective facts promoting its main goal: the end of slavery. I test Crary's theories in later chapters, but note here that many of the texts under discussion in this book—especially those written after 1820—do in fact cloud external entities and internal perception; in so doing, they distort boundaries separating the bodies of the enslaved from those of viewing subjects. These works sometimes imply that vision is multisensory and emanates not from an all-seeing objective vantage point but from within the human body. Perhaps the benefits of moving away from the idea of objective vision, then, outweighed the risk; vision itself might become a mode of interrelationship between the enslaved and the free viewer instead of a mode of domination.

Chapter One. Precursors

1. The image of the slave ship *Brooks* first appeared in Plymouth in 1788, and was republished quickly in Bristol, London, and Philadelphia. For a longer discussion of the differences among the various broadsides, see Marcus Rediker, *The Slave Ship*, and Stephen Ferguson, "219 Years Ago."

2. Edwin Wolf attributes the images in the 1794 German document *Sclaven-Handel* to James Poupard ("Sclaven-Handel," 108). I am not convinced by his logic. Christopher Phillips attributes the illustrations to Alexander Anderson ("Epic, Anti-Eloquence," 634), but Anderson was only fifteen when the images first appeared, so it is unlikely that he created them.

3. Some of these images were reused in the condensed children's edition of Equiano's *Life and Adventures* edited by Abigail Mott in 1829, so they circulated for more than thirty-five years (1793–1829).

4. See the appendix for definitions of these terms.

5. The trade continued through smuggling well into the 1820s, and slaves were still held, though not sold, within the British Empire.

6. Facts in this paragraph are taken from David Brion Davis, *The Problem of Slavery*, and Kenneth Morgan, *Slavery and the British Empire*.

7. Napoleon reinstated slavery in France in 1802. The slave trade in France was made a crime in 1830, but even as late as 1848, recently imported enslaved people from West Africa were found on Martinique and Guadeloupe, and Africans were carried to the French West Indies illegally until at least 1870; see Hugh Thomas, *The Slave Trade*.

8. Some countries, such as Brazil and Cuba, continued to allow slavery into the 1880s, and slavery continued in many places well into the twentieth century: Ethiopia did not abolish slavery until 1902; China, 1906; Nepal, 1921; Morocco, 1922; Iran, 1928; Afghanistan, 1923; Nigeria, 1936. But by the second decade of the nineteenth century, a large part of Europe had committed itself to an antislavery future; see Seymour Drescher, *Abolition*.

9. See, for example, Clarkson's unusual 1807 "Map of Abolition" in *The History of the Rise, Progress, and Accomplishment of the Abolition of the African Slave-trade, by the British Parliament*. Of course not all visual materials in this period were pro-abolition. For more on the satirical broadside tradition, see Phillip Lapsansky, "Graphic Discord," 216–18, and Jasmine Cobb, *Picture Freedom*.

10. Stedman's narrative was repurposed by abolitionists, dramatists, scholars, and even contemporary authors such as Beryl Gilroy. For more about these reprints, see Richard Price and Sally Price, introduction; Jenny Sharpe, *Ghosts of Slavery*; and Dustin Kennedy, "Going Viral." Other important readings of Stedman's *Narrative* may be found in the listed works by Marcus Wood (particularly *Slavery, Empathy, and Pornography*), Mary Louise Pratt, Peter Linebaugh and Marcus Rediker, Tassie Gwilliam, Mario Klarer, M. Allewaert, Simon Gikandi, and Helen Thomas. My work differs from that of these critics, who rarely focus on how Stedman's visual rhetoric was part of an evolving flow of images, in both earlier and later abolitionist visual texts, concerning enslaved torture.

11. The spelling of the country's name in English was changed to "Suriname" in 1978.

12. See Richard Price and Sally Price, introduction, l–li, and Helen Thomas, *Romanticism and Slave Narratives*, 126–27.

13. It was not until 1988, when Richard Price and Sally Price reprinted the original text that Stedman sent to his publisher, that the public could see any other edition of the text.

14. For more on the relationship between pain and pornography in the eighteenth and nineteenth century, see Halttunen, "Humanitarianism and Pornography," 314–18.

15. According to the editors of the website of the Blake Archive (Morris Eaves, Robert N. Essick, and Joseph Viscomi), Blake began work on the Stedman plates in 1791. Stedman visited Blake in June 1794, and afterward Blake helped Stedman with business matters. Eaves, Essick, and Viscomi note that "Blake's attitudes towards slavery and colonialism were indebted to Stedman's autobiographical narrative, as is particularly evident in the texts and designs of his illuminated books *Visions of the Daughters of Albion* and *America*, both dated 1793."

16. For other studies taking part in the debate about Blake's illustrations and Stedman's infamous text, see the listed works by Emily Senior, Peter Linebaugh and Marcus Rediker, Anne K. Mellor ("Sex, Violence, and Slavery"), Marcus Wood (*Blind Memory* and *Slavery, Empathy, and Pornography*), and Mario Klarer. In general, a large concern has been the "sentimentalist agendas" (Wood, *Slavery, Empathy, and Pornography*, 95) of Stedman's vivid descriptions of ritualized violence against the enslaved and the ways in which Blake's engravings replicate or complicate these brutal scenes.

17. Unless otherwise noted, my references to Stedman's text are to the one edited by R. A. van Lier. Van Lier does not, however, place the illustrations where they occurred in the 1796 text, so for this I have referred to the edition available through Eighteenth Century Collections Online.

18. Neptune's torture may be modeled on Aphra Behn's *Oroonoko*; see Price and Price's "Editors' Notes," 338.

19. Marcus Wood argues that in Stedman's *Narrative*, "it is the duty of the sympathetic gaze to try to take over the body of the black victim through a supreme empathetic effort" (*Slavery, Empathy, and Pornography*, 103). But the published 1796 text shows the narrator repeatedly *failing* to enter this empathetic mode. Klarer also examines how the text "invites the reader to enter particular scenes by suggesting, on a subliminal level, that they actively participate in the action," even as it allows them to "keep the necessary distance" ("Humanitarian Pornography," 562).

20. See Giorgio Agamben, *Homo Sacer*. In Roman law, a *homo sacer* ("sacred man" or "accursed man") was someone who could be killed without the act being considered murder. Slaves in Surinam could not be killed with impunity, but in other ways they participated in what Agamben has characterized as "bare life." For a longer discussion of the enslaved as examples of *homo sacer*, see Alexander Weheliye, "Pornotropes."

21. Gikandi (*Slavery and Taste*, 186) and Wood (*Blind Memory*, 236) have noted that such images of the torture of women are often sexualized; see also Klarer, "Humanitarian Pornography," and Mary A. Favret, "Flogging."

22. This image, in particular, was reprinted with a number of alterations; see Wood (*Blind Memory*, 238–39). Gwendolyn DuBois Shaw also notes the sexual overtones of this image (*Portraits of a People*, 32).

23. For more on the interracial relationship itself, see the listed works in the bibliography by Sharpe, Gwilliam, Werner Sollors, and Helen Thomas.

24. Johnny, was, however, taken into Stedman's household in Holland; see Kennedy, "Going Viral," 11–15.

25. The vampire bat incident in Stedman's narrative was discussed and reprinted in many journals, including the *Farmer's Repository*, 6 October 6, 1819, 3; *City Gazette*, 9 October 1819, 2; *Berks and Schuylkill Journal*, 23 October 1819, 1; *Providence Gazette*, 23 October 1819, 2; *Freeman's Journal*, 25 October 1819, 4; and *National Standard*, 9 November 1819, 4.

26. Some of these images from the 1793 broadside adapt illustrations present in Clarkson's *Letters on the Slave-Trade* (1791). *Remarks on the Methods* is also deeply intertextual, setting itself within a textual universe of abolitionist writings. For example, it refers specifically and by page number to testimony in *An Abstract of the Evidence Delivered Before a Select Committee of the House of Commons in the Years 1790, and 1791* (1791).

27. The phrase "lay your finger in the wounds" perhaps also recalls Jesus's words to Thomas after the Resurrection: "Reach hither thy finger, and behold my hands; and reach hither thy hand, and thrust it into my side: and be not faithless, but believing" (John 20:27). The broadside may rather audaciously allude to this biblical passage to put enslaved bodies into the realm of a Christlike subjectivity that will convince the readers to be transformed into abolitionists.

28. On the reader becoming a producer of the text, see Roland Barthes, *S/Z*, 4.

29. The broadside is undated, but the publisher, Samuel Wood, is listed at this address in New York City directories from 1805 to 1808.

30. Anderson was extremely fond of decorative, highly elaborate, and highly symbolic borders. See the examples reproduced on the website of the New York Public Library collection "America's First Illustrator: Alexander Anderson": http://digitalgallery.nypl .org/nypldigital/dgkeysearchresult.cfm?word=borders&x=-958&y=-135&c=221&s Scope=Collection+Guide&sLabel=America%2527s%2520First%2520Illustrator%253A %2520Alexander%2520Ander%252E%252E%252E.

31. In all but one of Stedman's illustrations featuring enslaved torture, the white master or overseer is not shown as the torturer, so scopic blame is not placed on white men for the torment of the enslaved, even though they are in charge of the system of slavery. The illustration on page 250 does, however, show a group of black men being driven to market for sale by a white owner holding a whip.

32. Most critics date the images on Anderson's broadside to 1805–7. His scrapbooks list the remodeled images in volume 2 (page 5).

33. For more on Branagan's life, see Mark Thomason, "Colony for Freed Slaves," and Lewis Leary, "Thomas Branagan." The best treatment of Branagan's antislavery views is provided in Beverly Tomek, "'From Motives of Generosity.'"

34. Recently, Phillips, Wood (*Poetry of Slavery*), Tomek, Philip Gould (*Barbaric Traffic*), and Margaret Abruzzo (*Polemical Pain*) have examined aspects of Branagan's work, but they

fail to consider thoroughly how the text constructs a new reading protocol for seeing and understanding these images.

35. The 1805 edition had a different frontispiece—an engraving that takes figure 5 from the 1793 document *Remarks on the Methods* and adds a new top half. Abruzzo attributes this image to Poupard (*Polemical Pain*, 99).

36. Phillips states that this frontispiece was an expensive one, "a copper engraving by David Edwin, the foremost portrait engraver in the United States at the time, based on an original design by Irish American artist John James Barralet" ("Epic, Anti-Eloquence," 615).

37. "There is one thing that every individual can do,—they can see to it that *they feel right*. An atmosphere of sympathetic influence encircles every human being; and the man or woman who *feels* strongly, healthily and justly, on the great interests of humanity, is a constant benefactor to the human race," writes Stowe in *Uncle Tom's Cabin* (299).

38. See, for example, George Cruikshank's famous *The New Union Club* (1819), which bitterly satirizes an abolitionist meeting; the "Bobalition of Slavery" series (ca. 1818–20); Edward Clay's "Practical Amalgamation" series (1839); Thomas Strong's *Professor Pompey Magnetizing an Abolition Lady* (ca. 1845); and Robert Cruikshank's illustrations for *The Condition of the West India Slave Contrasted with that of the Infant Slave in Our English Factories* (1833?). For an assessment of these materials, see Corey Capers, "Black Voices, White Print," and Jasmine Cobb, *Picture Freedom*.

39. Elmes's cartoon is the first in a two-plate series; in the second plate, Johnny marries a (white) plantation owner's daughter (see David Kunzle, *The Early Comic Strip*, 375).

Chapter Two. *"These Loathsome Pictures Shall Be Published"*

1. The description of this plate in Hall's book, *Basil Hall's Forty Etchings*, makes it clear that both individuals are enslaved.

2. For discussion of this political rhetoric, see Abruzzo, *Polemical Pain*, 121.

3. For more on these experiments, see Nicholas Wade and Josef Brožek, *Purkinje's Vision*.

4. For critics who argue that most of these images contribute to a colonial order that in diverse ways keeps the enslaved in the position of the other, see Wood (*Blind Memory* and *Slavery, Empathy, and Pornography*) and Clytus ("Envisioning Slavery").

5. For other pre-1852 books with illustrations of slavery, see Richard Phillips, *A General Description of the People of Africa* (1810); Jesse Torrey Jr., *A Portraiture of Domestic Slavery* (1817); John Augustine Waller, *A Voyage in the West Indies: Containing Various Observations Made during a Residence in Barbados* (1820); Frances Milton Trollope, *Domestic Manners of the Americans* (1832) and *The Life and Adventures of Jonathan Jefferson Whitlaw; or, Scenes on the Mississippi* (1836); Johann Moritz Rugenda, *Voyage Pittoresque dans le Bresil* (Paris, 1835; also published in this same year in German); Jean-Baptiste Debret, *Voyage Pittoresque et Historique au Bresil* (1834–39); John Barber, *A History of the Amistad Captives: Being a Circumstantial Account of the Capture of the Spanish Schooner Amistad* (1840); James Silk Buckingham, *The Slave States of America* (1842), vols. 1 and 2; Charles C. Green, *The Nubian Slave* (1845); Jonathan Walker, *A Picture of Slavery for Youth* (1845), which remodels

Bourne's text, as well as Walker's autobiographical narrative, *Trial and Imprisonment of Jonathan Walker* (1845); and William Spottswood White, *The African Preacher: An Authentic Narrative* (1849). See also John Greenleaf Whittier's *Poems* (1849), with illustrations by Hammatt Billings and others, which uses a few antislavery drawings to embellish the poems.

6. See the introduction and the appendix for explanations of the terms "parallel empathy" and "hierarchical empathy."

7. In the 1820s and 1830s, sympathy became increasingly politicized, both by abolitionists and by those who were proslavery, and was viewed as having a strong visual orientation; see Clytus, "Envisioning Slavery," 14–20, and Abruzzo, *Polemical Pain*, 122, 137–38.

8. Short early illustrated works for children contained limited antislavery content; Opie's appears to be the longest and to have the most illustrations. See, for example, *Clarissa Dormer; or, The Advantages of Good Instruction* (1808), *The Instructive Alphabet* (1809), *An Account of Honest Josiah, an African Youth* (1821), Mary Sherwood's *Dazee, Or, the Recaptured Negro* (1821), and *Juvenile Album: Being a Collection of Poetical Pieces* (1826). Also see Abigail Mott's reprinting of Olaudah Equiano's 1789 narrative for black children in 1828. There are also long and elaborate illustrated books for children with a less clear antislavery stance, such as those by Isaac Taylor, *Scenes in Africa, for the Amusement and Instruction of Little Tarry-at-Home Travellers* (1820) and *Scenes in Africa and America: For the Amusement and Instruction of Little Tarry-at-Home Travellers* (1830).

9. For scholars who place Opie's work within British women's antislavery writers, see Mellor "'Am I Not a Woman'"; Eberle, "'Tales of Truth?'"; and Roxanne Harde, "'The Savage Inscription.'" Of these writers, only Eberle analyzes (briefly) a few of the illustrations in *The Black Man's Lament* and its place within abolitionist visual culture (88–90). I have been unable to find any contemporaneous reviews of this book. Opie's other poems about slavery seem to have been popular.

10. See illustrations for Cowper's poem on the website of the British Library: www.bl.uk/learning/images/makeanimpact/large9018.html.

11. Petition campaigns for the end of slavery or the slave trade were common in the United States and England. In 1792 alone, for example, 519 petitions for the abolition of the slave trade were presented to the House of Commons, the largest number ever submitted to the House on a single subject or in a single session.

12. For more on abolitionist children's literature in the 1830s and later, see Abruzzo, *Polemical Pain*, 129–30; Holly Keller, "Juvenile Antislavery Narrative," 87; and Deborah De Rosa, *Domestic Abolitionism*.

13. As discussed in more detail in chapter 5, triangulation is a geometric process of determining an unknown location by measuring angles to it from two known points; in other words, the distance to a point (in this case, empathy with the enslaved) is not measured directly but through the "known" angles of white viewing presences within the illustration.

14. According to Julia Morton (*Fruits of Warm Climates*), Portuguese traders are thought to have introduced the pineapple plant to the east and west coasts of Africa by 1655. Morton

argues that using them as symbols of hospitality originated in the Caribbean but circulated rapidly to many cultures.

15. For critics who argue that abolitionist women writers used antislavery rhetoric to empower their own subject positions or keep enslaved bodies within the realm of the abject, see Harde, "'The Savage Inscription'"; Deirdre Coleman, "Conspicuous Consumption"; and Sharpe, *Ghosts of Slavery*. For critics who open up the possibility of representations that in some ways undermines this structure, see M. Ferguson, *Subject to Others*; Eberle, "'Tales of Truth?'"; and Sánchez-Eppler, *Touching Liberty*.

16. See also Eberle's point that these lines show the slave as a religious skeptic, similar to the way Heyrick argues, in her 1824 pamphlet, that slaves "could not be expected to embrace a faith practiced by those who enslave and torture them"; therefore, Opie and Heyrick indicate that "only emancipated Africans can be true Christians" ("'Tales of Truth?,'" 91). Dwight McBride argues that the poem "erases the possibility of black rage altogether by enacting a high moral price for it"—"the loss of eschatological fulfillment" (*Impossible Witnesses*, 57, 58). And yet, we do not hear the slave erasing his rage.

17. Biographical details are taken from Theodore Bourne, "Rev. George Bourne," and A. D. Adams, *Neglected Period*. There is little recent criticism of Bourne's *Picture of American Slavery* with the exception of Carol Lasser's essay "Voyeuristic Abolitionism," which does not consider how Bourne's illustrations might undermine the dominant visual rhetoric of enslavement. Maurie McInnis briefly discusses one of his illustrations (*Slaves Waiting for Sale*, 45–46), as does Goddu, "Antislavery's Panoramic Perspective."

18. As Lasser notes, other antislavery writers of the 1830s displayed a similar interest in the sexual sins of slavery ("Voyeuristic Abolitionism," 88), and other scholars—such as Ronald Walters ("Erotic South") and William Freehling (*Secessionists Triumphant*)—have examined what Walters refers to as the "erotic South." Lasser argues that this rhetorical formation, "voyeuristic abolitionism," aimed to channel "outrage at sexual exploitation of slaves into action against the institution of slavery" by "shocking readers into action" (97).

19. In some respects, K. resembles Bourne himself. Bourne's first pulpit, in 1815, was in Virginia, a state where slavery was legal; he was forced out of his job after he made fiery sermons condemning slaveholders and published *The Book and Slavery Irreconcilable* (Whitman, *Challenging Slavery*, 113–14).

20. In the United States, scientific "proof" for the idea of blacks and whites originating in separate races emerged most dramatically in Samuel George Morton's influential *Crania Americana: A Comparative View of the Skulls of Various Aboriginal Nations of North and South America* (1839). Morton argues strenuously that Negroes were created separately to inhabit tropical Africa and that only Caucasians were authentic descendants of Adam. The attempt to demonstrate that blacks were an inferior and separate race from whites, however, can be seen earlier, for example, in scientific works by Georges Cuvier such as *The Animal Kingdom* (1817–30), translated into English in 1832. For more on the emergence of scientific racism in the early nineteenth century, see Kenan Malik, *The Meaning of Race*.

21. The other images in this print feature external views of the jails in Alexandria and Washington, the interior of a jail cell in Washington with an enslaved mother named Fanny Jackson and her children, an illustration of slaves in chains emerging from the slave house of J. S. Neal and Company, a view of a slave ship on the Alexandria waterfront onto which slaves are being loaded, and a drawing of the slave establishment of Franklin and Armfield (in Alexandria).

Chapter Three. Entering and Exiting the Sensorium of Slave Torture

1. The classic essay on enslaved African American struggles toward voice is by Houston Baker. It argues that the enslaved had to write themselves into being out of an ontological void, but they did so only by using the tools and tropes of Western literacy and religion ("Autobiographical Acts," 249). For an astute analysis of how Frederick Douglass struggles in his slave narrative to move from the visual realm to the verbal one, see Jeannine DeLombard, "'Eye-Witness to the Cruelty.'"

2. Olaudah Equiano's *The Interesting Narrative of the Life of Olaudah Equiano, or Gustavus Vassa, the African, Written by Himself* (1789) was drastically condensed, rewritten, and reprinted for children by Abigail Mott in illustrated form in 1829. Because Equiano died in 1797 and his original text did not have illustrations, I do not consider this an illustrated antislavery narrative created by a former slave.

3. For positive reviews, see the one in *Slavery in America* (a British publication), 1 August 1837, and the one in the *Liberator*, 30 March 1838. As Jeffrey Hotz has shown, Roper's narrative was a "trans-Atlantic success" (*Divergent Visions*, 184). Roper estimated in 1844 that he had sold 25,000 copies of the English edition and 5,000 of the Welsh ("Letter"). Gwilym Games substantiates that the narrative went through ten editions and "usher[ed] in an era of slave narratives" ("Roper, Moses," 461). Clearly, then, Roper's work was read and sold in Europe and the United States for at least a decade.

4. The few scholars who have evaluated Roper's text have not viewed it in a positive light. Charles Davis maintains that the experiences depicted "are not placed in a context that has meaning or that demands our greater sympathy" and that "extraordinary horror is succeeded by even more extraordinary Christian compassion and neither is moving" ("The Slave Narrative," 89). Other critics have noted that Roper's "remote narrative voice . . . eschews psychological introspection" (Hotz, *Divergent Visions*, 186) or contended that because he confines himself "to the representation of brutalized bodies," he ultimately turns "black bodies into objects" (Levecq, *Slavery and Sentiment*, 209). Megan Walsh, "Fugitive Slave Narrative," is a notable exception.

5. Roper perhaps deploys a type of religious rhetoric generated during revival movements of the 1830s; as Clark has shown, this type of rhetoric strongly associated conversion to antislavery positions with a religious awakening ("Sacred Rights of the Weak," 477).

6. See my appendix for a description of hierarchical and parallel empathy.

7. Many of these events are contained in an appendix to the 1848 edition (52). It is not known why Roper returned to the United States after 1861. He died alone there in 1891,

with only his dog for a companion. See his obituaries in the *Boston Daily Globe*, 16 April 1891, and in the *New York Times*, 17 April 1891.

8. Unless otherwise noted, all references are to the 1838 British edition of Roper's text.

9. Walsh discusses the thumbprints on the illustration of the cotton press in the 1837 edition held at the Library Company of Philadelphia.

10. See, in particular, Acts 9:13–19, which describes Saul becoming Paul.

11. Wood contends that during the period 1830–50, white abolitionist rhetoric endows slaves with "martyrological suffering" yet presents "no rhetorical structure of celebration, no individual apotheosis, and the slave/martyr never testifies for himself" (*Blind Memory*, 84, 85).

12. See also the reading of this image by Mary Favret in "Flogging."

13. Cotton presses usually had triangular roofs, and they did not look like the one drawn by Roper's illustrator. For an example of a press from this period, see www.djr04.com/norfleet_cotton_press.html.

14. As in the accounts by religious slave figures who came before him, such as George White or John Jea, a reader is pushed to correlate Roper's story with that of Jesus, but Roper stops short of portraying himself as Christ; see Yolanda Pierce, *Hell without Fires*, 32, 38.

15. The frontispiece is dated 1840, so it did not appear in editions published before then. The 1840 British edition is the first to list this portrait in its title.

16. The reference to a "city of habitation" comes from Psalm 107.

Chapter Four. Structuring a New Abolitionist Reading of Masculinity and Femininity

1. I follow Barbara Jeanne Fields's definition of ideology, especially as concerns race: ideology is a "descriptive vocabulary of day-to-day existence, through which people make rough sense of the social reality that they live and create from day to day" ("Slavery, Race, and Ideology," 110); it thus needs to be "constantly created and verified in social life" (112).

2. On Bibb, see Wood, "Seeing Is Believing." On Child, see Bruce Dickson, who views the 1838 text as solely a reproduction of the original Stedman narrative and of the 1834 *Oasis* text (*African American Literature*, 237), and Sharpe (*Ghosts of Slavery*), who discusses one image from the 1838 text.

3. Simone G. Shamay-Tsoory has been the lead researcher on a pair of neuroscientific studies that deal with affective and cognitive theory of mind ("'Affective Theory of Mind'").

4. These texts manipulate the truth of the image without discarding the notion that vision creates a type of truthful apprehension. They therefore do not participate in the "antivisual attitudes" invoked during modernity and postmodernity. On the antivisual turn in the late nineteenth century, see Martin Jay, "Scopic Regimes," 14–15.

5. Both Child and Bibb, who were involved in antislavery print publication beyond the medium of the book, knew of the aggressive role that print modes played in the intensifying of antislavery pressure. Child, for example, wrote short stories for antislavery annuals and edited one, the *Liberty Bell*, in the 1840s; Bibb moved to Canada and began publishing the *Voice of the Fugitive*, the first black newspaper in Upper Canada, in 1851.

6. For more on the role of women in abolition, see Sinha's incisive and thorough discussion (*Slave's Cause*, 179–82, 266–98).

7. Price and Price give a full listing of these reprints in their introduction to Stedman's *Narrative*; also see Sharpe, *Ghosts of Slavery*, 82–83.

8. For discussion of Child's radical abolitionist views, see Sinha, *Slave's Cause*, 273–75, 558–59.

9. For more on this point, see Sharpe, *Ghosts of Slavery*, 58–59.

10. I borrow here Marjorie Garber's construct of category crisis, which she develops to discuss transvestism but believes is applicable to other binary categories (*Vested Interests*, 16). Joanna is therefore (within Child's text) both free and enslaved, wife and not wife, and subject and object.

11. The only treatment of the illustrations in Bibb's *Narrative* that I have located is by Wood ("Seeing Is Believing"; also see his *Blind Memory*, 117–34). Michael Chaney analyzes William Wells Brown's repurposing of these illustrations in his *A Description of William Wells Brown's Original Panoramic Views of the Scenes in the Life of an American Slave* (1850) (*Fugitive Vision*, 136–39). Early criticism of Bibb's narrative mainly focused on its style—see Charles Davis, "The Slave Narrative," 100; James Olney, "'I Was Born,'" 62; and Robert Stepto, "I Rose and Found," 228. More recently, there have been some discussions of masculinity, femininity, and enslaved marriage and family in the text—see Andrews, *To Tell a Free Story*, 152–60; Charles Heglar, *Rethinking the Slave Narrative*, 33–74; and Keith Green, "Am I Not a Husband." Green's discussion of how Bibb reclaims masculinity through "slave incarceration and Cherokee slavery" (36) is a compelling reading of the text, but substantively different from mine.

12. Before publishing *Voice of the Fugitive*, Bibb compiled and printed *Slave Insurrections in Southampton County* (1849); see John O'Farrell, "Bibb, Henry Walton."

13. *Narrative of the Life and Adventures of Henry Bibb* was published "by the author" in New York in 1849. Henry Louis Gates Jr. and William Andrews claim that Bibb made no changes to subsequent editions ("Note on the Texts," 1016), but some editions have different paratextual elements. In some editions, Thomas Strong's auction engraving is used as a frontispiece or end piece, and later editions have letters and reviews that earlier editions lack, as well as the frontispiece portrait of Bibb. There has been some discussion of the role of Lucius C. Matlack, the editor who wrote the introduction (see Olney, "'I Was Born,'" 159), yet Matlack confirms that he corrected only "orthography and punctuation" (Matlack, introduction, ii).

14. Bibb seems to be making fun of actual advertisements for runaway slaves here, such as this famous one placed by the planter Zachariah Booth in 1833: "Stop Mabin!! Runaway from my house in Talbot County, Georgia, on Flint River, on 25th of December last at night a man slave by the name of Mabin, about twenty years old. . . . He will pass for a white man where he is not known" (*Columbus Inquirer*, 9 February 1833; See Proctor, "Slavery in Southwest Georgia," 6). Bibb passes for white several times in his text.

15. Wood does read Bibb's text as an unsettling work that "explodes" many visual and narrative conventions of slave narrative ("Seeing Is Believing," 178).

16. Also see Keith Green, who points out that almost a decade later, "Bibb could not adequately articulate the anguish associated with the dirt-buried child" ("Am I Not a Husband," 28).

17. For editions that appear to have used this image as a frontispiece, see one available from Google Books (the "third stereotype edition," 1849), http://books.google.com /books?id=1_pAAQAAMAAJ. For editions that used it as a wrapper, see the copy of Bibb's narrative housed at the American Antiquarian Society in Worcester, Massachusetts, which has this illustration bound at its end, an indication that it was originally used as a paper wrapper on the rear cover of the book.

18. For an assessment of the stereotype of the tragic mulatta, see Cassandra Jackson, *Barriers between Us*, and Teresa C. Zackodnik, *Mulatta and Politics*.

19. Bibb specifically tells his master (in a letter) that his inability to be a proper husband and father led him to escape (177).

20. Moreover, as Keith Green has pointed out, Bibb places his escape within a familiar genre: that of the captivity narrative ("Am I Not a Husband"). In so doing, he assumes a status as an agentive, non-othered masculine subject rather than an othered, spectated object.

21. Bibb's message appears to have reached its intended audience as well, since both the text and his speaking were popular. One writer notes that some publications reacted with incredulity to the "marvelous stories of cruelty" and the "hair breadth escapes" of the text, yet chides these publications for not recognizing the truth of the story—that there is "no meaner place than . . . the South" (*Wisconsin Free Democrat*, "Servility Rebuked," 534). Bibb's text was considered "a very spicy address to his late master," and at least one writer advised him to "take a lesson from Frederick Douglass, who writes and speaks with more propriety, and more decorum than most of his white associates" (*New Bedford Mercury*, "Eloquence," 1).

Chapter Five. After Tom

1. The literary debate revolves around the use of sentimentality as a mode of social power in *Uncle Tom's Cabin*. The terms of this subject were established by two pivotal texts: Ann Douglas's *The Feminization of American Culture* (1977), which claims that events such as the beautiful death of Little Eva are presented as a protest against slavery but "in no way hinder the working of that system" (12), and Jane Tompkins's *Sensational Designs* (1985), which argues for a powerful and specifically female novelistic tradition that could become a basis for remaking the social and political order (xvii); see as well as Elizabeth Ammons's early argument about how Stowe turns repressive concepts of femininity into a positive and activist system of values ("Heroines," 163). This debate about the text's sentimental power has continued in more recent works by Ammons ("Freeing the Slaves"), Philip Fisher (*Hard Facts*), Shirley Samuels ("The Identity of Slavery"), Joanne Dobson ("Reclaiming Sentimental Literature"), Lauren Berlant (*Female Complaint*), Debra J. Rosenthal ("'I've Only to Say the Word!'"), Noble ("Ecstasies of Sentimental Wounding," *Masochistic Pleasures*), Hartman (*Scenes of Subjection*), Gossett (*"Uncle Tom's Cabin"*), Hochman (*"Uncle*

Tom's Cabin"), Wood (*Blind Memory*, 188–89), and many others. For a good selection of some of these texts, see Rosenthal's sourcebook. But there has been limited consideration of the role that the text's visuals play in its sentimentalism or mode of moving its readers (whether black or white, male or female) toward action.

2. The success of Stowe's novel was an "enabling precondition" for a second, much more lavishly illustrated publication of Hildreth's novel, originally published in 1836; see Nancy Bentley, "White Slaves." Solomon Northup dedicates his narrative, which contains five illustrations, to Stowe, "Whose name, throughout the world, is identified with Great Reform" and calls it "Another *Key to Uncle Tom's Cabin.*"

3. It should be noted that Stowe wrote to people such as Frederick Douglass to ask for information (or other firsthand sources) that would make her picture of slavery "graphic and true to nature" (Stowe, *Life and Letters*, 133). Yet it is also clear that she drew on the stereotypical characters present in the minstrel tradition in her portrayal of some characters; on this point, see Eric Lott, *Love and Theft*, and Sarah Meer, "Topsy and the End Man."

4. The first fugitive slave law was enacted on 12 February 1793. As northern states ended slavery, they relaxed enforcement of the statute, passed laws allowing fugitive slaves a jury trial, and prohibited state officials from helping capture runaway slaves or jailing them. This disregard of the first fugitive slave law led to the passage of the 1850 law; see Junius P. Rodriguez, "Fugitive Slave Act," 301–2.

5. The illustrations in the first edition are discussed in the listed works by Mandy Reid, Barbara Hochman, Jo-Ann Morgan ("Picturing"), Sheila O'Brien, and Paul Gutjahr. My argument differs significantly from that of these critics in that I am concerned with how empathy is triangulated within the illustrations through white or near-white visual figures, a point they do not raise.

6. Stowe's working subtitle for the novel was more ironic: "The Man That Was a Thing." There is little information about why she discarded this subtitle; Susan Belasco speculates that it was because serialized forms, made popular in England by Charles Dickens, were more successful when they focused on multiple characters and subplots ("Writing, Reception, and Reputation," 29–30).

7. See volume 1, pages 40, 46, 47, 64, 67, 71, 102, 298, and volume 2, pages 32, 48.

8. Many critics note the feminization of Tom, but interpretations differ about whether this empowers him; see Ammons, "Heroines," 153; Robyn Wiegman, *American Anatomies*, 116–17; Sánchez-Eppler, *Touching Liberty*, 47; and Noble, *Masochistic Pleasures*, 139.

9. For critics who view the relationships between black and white characters as erotic or homoerotic, see Noble, "Ecstasies of Sentimental Wounding"; P. Gabrielle Foreman, "'This Promiscuous Housekeeping'"; and Hortense Spillers, "Changing the Letter."

10. There has been little consideration of how empathy is triangulated visually in the text. Robin Bernstein comments, "The opening and closing scenes of Tom's life thus triangulate the figures of Tom, George Shelby, and the cabin itself" (*Racial Innocence*, 136), but does not consider how this works in the illustrations. Fisher comments that Stowe "interposes between the reader and the slave, a child" (*Hard Facts*, 98), but does not pursue the visual

ramifications of this. For a sensitive discussion of the uses of sympathy, empathy, and identification in the text, see Hochman, *"Uncle Tom's Cabin,"* 16–18.

11. On the frequent reprinting of this image, see Hochman, *"Uncle Tom's Cabin,"* 71, and
Jo-Ann Morgan, *Uncle Tom's Cabin*, 11, 27.

12. Tom reads by himself, but the threat of literacy—and its connection with black rebellion—is safely contained by the fact that the only thing Tom is ever shown reading is the
Bible. This is a form of what Marcus Wood terms "safe learning"; Tom "sweating over his
Bible" and being taught by a child become iconic images (*Blind Memory*, 188, 186–87). For
more on the meaning of reading within the text, see Hochman, *"Uncle Tom's Cabin."*

13. As Sánchez-Eppler notes, perhaps the most disturbing aspect of *Uncle Tom's Cabin*
is that "the utopian freedom [Stowe] constructs is predicated upon the absence of black
bodies" (*Touching Liberty*, 48).

14. For those who have considered whether the novel did in fact lead readers to prosocial
actions (becoming an abolitionist, joining a boycott, setting slaves free, and so forth) see
the listed works by Abruzzo, Hochman, Jo-Ann Morgan (*Uncle Tom's Cabin*), and Gossett.
Gossett notes, "Emotional responses to *Uncle Tom's Cabin* tended to weaken its antislavery message. . . . A good many readers of the time were more impressed by the scenes in
which Little Eva appeared than they were by the novel's opposition to slavery" (*"Uncle Tom's
Cabin,"* 168).

15. There are, of course, some exceptions to hierarchical structures of empathy within
the text. As Noble notes, Stowe saw the pain of bereavement as a "universal emotion that
cut through cultural difference" and could therefore act as "a unifying force" (*Masochistic
Pleasures*, 129). Stowe is able to depict this emotion when Mrs. Bird persuades her husband,
Senator John Bird, to abet the escaping slave Eliza Harris (chapter 9). But the point I
would make about chapter 9 as a whole is that again empathy for the enslaved (in this case,
Eliza) must be triangulated through a white textual presence (Mrs. Bird); moreover, Mrs.
Bird directs a reader to see Eliza as an object to be pitied by repeatedly referring to her as
"poor child," "poor creature," and "poor thing" (1:123–29). For more on the power of women
in this text, see Tompkins, *Sensational Designs*.

16. See also Cynthia Griffin Wolff's argument that the panorama was a fluid performance
mode that translated Brown out of his status as an object of commodification and allowed
him to craft "an entirely new kind of African American narrative, one that was radically
different from the standard slave's story" ("Passing beyond the Middle Passage," 30–31).

17. Additional information about Brown's later years and his death in Canada in 1897 can
be found in my essay "Will the Real Henry 'Box' Brown Please Stand Up?"

18. I am indebted here to Brooks's figuration of the way gendered or racialized bodies
are able to "traffic in cultural excesses, layering aliases and costumes, devices and genres
atop one another" to demonstrate "the insurgent power of imaging cultural identity in
grand and polyvalent terms which might move outside the narrow representation frames
bestowed on them" (*Bodies in Dissent*, 8). For other extended analyses of Brown's texts, see
Jeffrey Ruggles, *Unboxing of Henry Brown*; John Ernest, "Outside the Box" and "Traumatic

Theology"; Wood, "'All Right!'" and *Blind Memory*; and Wolff, "Passing beyond the Middle Passage."

19. Scholars such as Ruggles (*Unboxing of Henry Brown*), Ernest ("Outside the Box"), and Suzette Spencer ("International Fugitive") date Brown's escape to 23 March 1849. But there is some controversy about this date. In the 1851 *Narrative*, Brown gives the date as 29 March 1849. Yet a letter within the 1851 narrative by James Miller McKim (secretary of the Pennsylvania Anti-Slavery Society and known as McRoy in the *Narrative*) from 26 March 1849, refers to Brown's escape as "Saturday morning last" (ii), which puts the date of Brown's escape at 23 March 1849. I use the 23 March date because other documents (such as letters and telegraphs) that Ruggles has unearthed corroborate it. My thanks to Laura A. Wright for drawing my attention to this discrepancy.

20. The most comprehensive analysis of these images is given in Wood's essay "'All Right!'"

21. For more on the ways in which Stearns's voice co-opts Brown's in the 1849 edition, or for a comparison of the texts, see Brooks, *Bodies in Dissent*, 72–74; James Olney, "'I Was Born,'" 159–61; and Ernest, "Outside the Box."

22. For analysis of the hymn and of music in general in Brown's narrative, see Brooks, *Bodies in Dissent*, 102–4; Wood, "'All Right!,'" 81; Ruggles, *Unboxing of Henry Brown*, 14–22; and Ernest, "Outside the Box."

23. According to Ruggles, the 1851 text appears to have been popular, selling out its first edition of eight thousand copies in two months (*Unboxing of Henry Brown*, 65).

24. There are other images from 1850 and 1851 in which Brown appears to look directly at a viewer; see Ruggles, *Unboxing of Henry Brown*, 82, 114, and 164. But this is the only "Resurrection" print in which the angle of Brown's arms suggests that he is pushing himself up and out of the box and in which part of his torso is already out of the box.

25. According to Christine Ariella Crater, "[The] panorama was a huge success. Large crowds gathered to view Brown's *Mirror*, and newspapers applauded. *The Boston Daily Evening Traveler* named it 'one of the finest panoramas now on exhibition'" ("Brown, Henry Box").

26. Scene 44, called "The Slaveholder's Dream," is "intriguing but difficult to identify by contents" (Ruggles, *Unboxing of Henry Brown*, 102). Some called the 1850 Fugitive Slave Law a "slaveholder's dream" (Christian and Bennett, *Black Saga*, 149), so this scene might have featured a fugitive slave being retaken by northern law officials.

27. In the summer of 1850, Henry Brown was attacked in Providence, Rhode Island; he managed to avoid being taken away in a carriage, but was badly beaten. Brown left the United States for England on 7 October 1850.

28. Unless otherwise noted, citations in this chapter to British newspapers of the period are taken from the website 19th Century British Library Newspapers, Parts I and II.

29. By November 1852, six versions of *Uncle Tom's Cabin* were available on the London stage, and across the country eleven additional stage adaptations plus four pantomimes based on it were being performed (Ruggles, *Unboxing of Henry Brown*, 147; also see

Gossett, *"Uncle Tom's Cabin"*). For more on Hill, see Ruggles, *Unboxing of Henry Brown*, 149–51.

30. See the *Era* (London), 28 June 1857: "Mr. Henry Box Brown, Proprietor of the Great American Panorama, which is well known to have entertained millions of the English Public during the last six years will, in a very short time, make his appearance on the Stage of the London Theater, first appearing in three new Dramas, 'The Fugitive Free,' 'The Nubian Captive; or Royal Slave,' and 'Pocahontas, or The English Tar and the Indian Princess,' all of which Dramas have never yet been brought before the Public."

31. Details in this paragraph are taken from these two notices in the *Era* (London): "Royal Park Theater—Mr. Edgar has secured the services of Mr. Henry Box Brown, the well-known escaped slave and public lecturer, who will make his first essay on these boards as an actor, in a piece written expressly for the introduction of the most stirring scenes in his eventful life. We shall then have the rare occurrence of a hero personifying himself. Mr. Charles Rice the well-known comedian is also engaged for a limited period" (27 September 1857); "Mr. Brown, having established the merits and truth of his exhibition by the unanimous verdict of all the free states of the American [nation], visited this country, and exhibited to Englishmen, with all the adjuncts of scenery and description, the greatest system of crime and tyranny that was ever engulfed of the social status of the world—slavery. But it is not simply as a demonstrator that Mr. Brown comes among us, but in the double capacity of dramatist and actor. He has made his debut on the English stage as the hero of one of his own pieces at the Park Theater, Liverpool, an account of which will be found in its proper column of this day's *Era*" (4 October 1857).

32. As reported in the *Royal Cornwall Gazette* (Truro, England) on 7 December 1855, Brown married "Miss Jane Floyd, late mistress of the National School, Copperhouse" (5); see the website British Newspapers, 1600–1950. According to research conducted by Alan Rice's students in England, in the 1861 census, Brown worked in North Street, Keighley, Yorkshire, as a "lecturer on America etc.," where he lived with his wife Jane Brown, twenty-six, and their daughter Agnes, seven months, who is registered as born in Stockport. In 1864 they had a son named Edward Henry. In the census of 1871, they are registered as living in Cheetham, Manchester; in Manchester that they had another daughter, named Annie. See Shukar Bibi and Rebecca Foss, "Commemorating Abolition & Liberating Sojourn," British Conference of Undergraduate Research, http://bcur.org/journals/index.php/Diffusion/article/viewFile/163/144.

33. See the *Reading Mercury, Oxford Gazette, Newbury Herald*, and *Berks County Paper*, 14 May 1859.

34. See Bibi and Foss, "Commemorating Abolition & Liberating Sojourn," British Conference of Undergraduate Research, http://bcur.org/journals/index.php/Diffusion/article/viewFile/163/144.

35. See the *Cardiff Times*, 12 January 1867, Welsh Newspapers Online.

36. Britt Rusert claims that "Brown's box was likely repurposed as a scientific cabinet, finding a comfortable home alongside the various electrical apparatuses and other

mysterious 'black boxes' that accompanied scientific showmen throughout the period" ("Science of Freedom," 301).

37. Shows by Brown are listed in the *Salem Gazette* in 1875 and in *The Annual Report of the Selectmen and Overseers of the Poor of the Town of Bridgewater for the Year Ending Feb. 28, 1877*; see the website Gale Artemis. The *Bangor (ME) Daily Whig and Courier*, 17 October 1878, lists two performances by Box Brown; see the website British Newspapers, 1600–1950. After this, Brown apparently moved on to Canada, where the *Markdale Standard* (28 September 1882) lists him performing "a dramatic entertainment" on 10 October; see the website Ontario Community Newspapers, OurOntario.ca. Brown also was onstage as a musician in this period; the *Northern Tribune* (Cheboygan, Michigan) lists a performance on 1 December 1883, "under the formidable name of Professor Box Brown's Troubadour Jubilee Singers," and the *Weekly Expositor* (Brockway Centre, Michigan) of 16 August 1883, lists a performance by Brown and the Jubilee Singers; see "Chronicling America" on the website of the Library of Congress. Brown continued to perform with his family until as late as 1889, when an Ontario newspaper reported a performance at Brantford (see Cutter, "Will the Real"). Numerous sources from the time repeat the idea that Brown attended the 1900 Pan-African Conference in England as the Reverend Henry Box Brown, representing the black community in Lower Canada, but this information has not been verified. See, for example, Brent Edwards (*Practice of Diaspora*, 1), Jeannette Jones (*In Search of Brightest Africa*, 98), and Milfred C. Fierce ("Henry Sylvester Williams," 112) for critics who present this view; but also see Marika Sherwood's convincing dismissal of this claim (in *Origins of Pan-Africanism*), and my own research documenting Brown's death in 1897 ("Will the Real").

Epilogue. The End of Empathy, or Slavery Revisited via Twentieth- and Twenty-First-Century Artworks

1. The chapter epigraph is taken from William Inge, *The Philosophy of Plotinus*, 10.

2. See the website for the film, www.natturnermovie.com.

3. I do not allude here to bound labor, child labor, or women and girls pressed into prostitution; these practices constitute a form of slavery and continue today. Instead, I refer to slavery in its more basic, anachronistic sense—lifetime bondage, based on some form of perceived racial difference, passed from parent to child. Mauritania, for example, officially abolished slavery only in 1981, but did not prosecute any slaveholders until 2007. Therefore, as Alexis Okeowo has discussed ("Freedom Fighter"), this practice (although illegal) persists, and the Global Slavery Index estimates that at least 140,000 people are still enslaved there.

4. In the so-called war on terror, the U.S. government practiced torture against U.S. and non-U.S. citizens from at least 2001 (under George W. Bush) onward, and it is unclear whether some of these legalized practices of torture continue today. As recently as 2009, in commenting on the use and effectiveness of various torture methods, including waterboarding, Dennis C. Blair, a former director of national intelligence, wrote that "high

value information came from interrogations in which these methods were used" (Shane, "Interrogations' Effectiveness"). In light of the systematic and legalized torture of prisoners by U.S. military and intelligence operatives at black sites and at the Guantánamo Bay detention camp for more than a decade, U.S. culture may long for something like "dirty torture," a kind of torture from the past that was clearly wrong and bad and that has (evidently) ended—the torture of U.S. slavery.

5. To give just two examples: the movie opens by giving an erroneous date for the start of the Civil War, and closes with a scene in which Django uses dynamite to blows up Candy's plantation—even though dynamite had not yet been invented.

6. Walker has been criticized by the artists Howardena Pindell and Betye Saar for her portrayal of "sado-masochism, bestiality, the sexual abuse of children, infanticide and bizarre acts of procreation" (*International Review of African American Art*, "Extreme Times," 7), and her frequent portrayal of "pickaninnies, sambos, mammies, mandingos, and mulatto slave mistresses" has been much commented upon (see H. Walker, "Kara Walker," 110; Reinhardt, "Art of Racial Profiling," 119). Saar even called for a boycott of Walker's work, which she saw as pandering to white audiences (McEvilley, "Primitivism," 53). Other critics, however, view Walker's work as a "profound act of artistic exorcism" (Henry Louis Gates Jr., quoted in *International Review of African American Art*, "Extreme Times," 5) and a "courageous foray into the dark spaces of the unconscious, made in hopes of illuminating the darkness, and thus, in a manner similar to psychoanalytic theory, straightening out the underlying mental problem" (McEvilley, "Primitivism," 54).

7. For a more specific discussion of these figures, see Shaw, *Seeing the Unspeakable*, 4.

8. For an examination of Ligon's connection with Henry Box Brown, see Marcus Wood, "Slave Narrative and Visual Culture," and Huey Copeland, "Glenn Ligon."

9. Elizabeth Clark, "'Sacred Rights of the Weak,'" 492.

BIBLIOGRAPHY

Abelin, Ernst. "The Role of the Father in the Separation-Individuation Process." In *Separation-Individuation*, edited by J. B. McDevitt and C.F. Settlage, 229–52. New York: International Universities Press, 1971.

———. "Triangulation, the Role of the Father, and the Origins of Core Gender Identity during the Rapprochement Subphase." In *Rapprochement*, edited by R. Lax, S. Bach, and J. Burland, 151–69. New York: Aronson, 1980.

Abruzzo, Margaret. *Polemical Pain: Slavery, Cruelty, and the Rise of Humanitarianism.* Baltimore: Johns Hopkins University Press, 2011.

An Abstract of the Evidence Delivered Before a Select Committee of the House of Commons in the Years 1790, and 1791; on the Part of the Petitioners for the Abolition of the Slave-Trade. London: James Phillips, 1791. Available from the Internet Archive, https://archive.org/stream/abstractofevidenoogrea#page/n1/mode/2up.

An Account of Honest Josiah, an African Youth. Newburyport, Mass.: Gilman, [1821].

Adams, A. D. [Alice Dana]. *The Neglected Period of Anti-Slavery in America, 1808–1831.* Boston: Ginn, 1908.

Agamben, Giorgio. *Homo Sacer: Sovereign Power and Bare Life.* Translated by Daniel Heller-Roazen. Stanford: Stanford University Press, 1998.

Agosta, Louis. "Empathy and Intersubjectivity." In *Empathy I*, edited by Joseph Lichtenberg, Melvin Bornstein, and Donald Silver, 43–60. Hillsdale, N.J.: Erlbaum, 1984.

Aitken, Jonathan. *John Newton: From Disgrace to Amazing Grace.* Wheaton, Ill.: Crossway, 2007.

Allewaert, M. "Swamp Sublime: Ecologies of Resistance in the American Plantation Zone." *PMLA* 123, no. 2 (2008): 340–57.

Ammons, Elizabeth. "Freeing the Slaves and Banishing the Blacks: Racism, Empire, and Africa in *Uncle Tom's Cabin*." In *Harriet Beecher Stowe's Uncle Tom's Cabin: A Casebook*, edited by Elizabeth Ammons, 227–46. New York: Oxford University Press, 2007.

———. "Heroines in *Uncle Tom's Cabin*." *American Literature* 49, no. 2 (1977): 161–79.

Analytical Review. Review of J. G. Stedman, *Narrative of a Five Years' Expedition against the Revolted Negroes of Surinam.* Vol. 24, no. 3 (September 1796). Available from the Internet Archive, https://archive.org/stream/analyticalrevieo5chrigoog#page/n233/mode/2up.

Anderson, Alexander. *Injured Humanity: Being a Representation of What the Unhappy Children of Africa Endure from Those Who Call Themselves Christians.* Broadside in the collection of the American Antiquarian Society, Worcester, Mass.

Andrews, William L. Introduction to *North Carolina Slave Narratives: The Lives of Moses Roper, Lunsford Lane, Moses Grandy, and Thomas H. Jones*, edited by Andrews, 1–19. Chapel Hill: University of North Carolina Press, 2005.

————. *To Tell a Free Story: The First Century of Afro-American Autobiography, 1760–1865.* Urbana: University of Illinois Press, 1986.

Anti-Slavery Alphabet. Philadelphia: Merrihew and Thompson, 1846.

Aptheker, Herbert. *Abolitionism: A Revolutionary Movement.* New York: Twayne, 1989.

"Autobiography I: The Man Who Joined the Yanks." In *God Struck Me Dead: Religious Conversion Experiences and Autobiographies of Ex-Slaves,* edited by Clifton H. Johnson, 24–57. Philadelphia: Pilgrim, 1969.

Avelar, Idelber. *The Letter of Violence: Essays on Narrative, Ethics, and Politics.* New York: Palgrave, 2004.

Azoulay, Ariella. *The Civil Contract of Photography.* New York: Zone, 2008.

Baker, Houston. "Autobiographical Acts and the Voices of the Southern Slave." In *The Slave's Narrative,* 2nd ed., edited by Henry Louis Gates Jr. and Charles T. Davis, 242–61. Oxford: Oxford University Press, 1990.

Bakhtin, Mikhail M. *Rabelais and His World.* Translated by Hélène Iswolsky. Bloomington: Indiana University Press, 1984 [1965].

Bal, P. Matthijs, and Martijn Veltkamp. "How Does Fiction Reading Influence Empathy? An Experimental Investigation on the Role of Emotional Transportation." *PLoS ONE* 8, no. 1 (2013), doi:10.1371/journal.pone.0055341.

Baldwin, James. "Everybody's Protest Novel" (1949). In *Notes of a Native Son,* 13–23. Boston: Beacon, 1955.

Barker, Martin. *Comics: Ideology, Power, and the Critics.* Manchester, UK: Manchester University Press, 1989.

Barnhill, Georgia B. "Transformations in Pictorial Printing." In *A History of the Book in America: An Extensive Republic; Print, Culture, and Society in the New Nation, 1790–1840,* vol. 2, edited by Robert A. Gross and Mary Kelley, 422–40. Chapel Hill: University of North Carolina Press, 2010.

Barthes, Roland. *S/Z.* Translated by Richard Miller. New York: Hill and Wang, 1974 [1970].

Baym, Nina. *Women's Fiction: A Guide to Novels by and about Women in America, 1820–70.* Ithaca: Cornell University Press, 1978.

Belasco, Susan. "The Writing, Reception, and Reputation of *Uncle Tom's Cabin.*" In *Approaches to Teaching Stowe's "Uncle Tom's Cabin,"* edited by Elizabeth Ammons and Susan Belasco, 21–36. New York: MLA, 2000.

Bentley, Nancy. "White Slaves: The Mulatto Hero in Antebellum Fiction." *American Literature* 65, no. 3 (1993): 501–22.

Berlant, Lauren. *The Female Complaint: The Unfinished Business of Sentimentality in American Culture.* Durham, N.C.: Duke University Press, 2008.

Bernstein, Robin. *Racial Innocence: Performing American Childhood from Slavery to Civil Rights.* New York: New York University Press, 2011.

Berry, Daina Ramey. *"Swing the Sickle for the Harvest Is Ripe": Gender and Slavery in Antebellum Georgia.* Urbana: University of Illinois Press, 2010.

Bibb, Henry. *Narrative of the Life and Adventures of Henry Bibb, an American Slave, Written by Himself.* 2nd ed. New York, 1849.

Blackett, Richard J. M. *Building an Antislavery Wall: Black Americans in the Atlantic Abolitionist Movement, 1830–1860.* Baton Rouge: Louisiana State University Press, 1983.

Blair, James R., and Karina S. Perschardt. "Empathy: A Unitary Circuit or a Set of Dissociable Neuro-Cognitive System?" *Behavioral and Brain Sciences* 25, no. 1 (2002): 27–28.

Blair, J. Anthony. "The Rhetoric of Visual Arguments." In *Defining Visual Rhetorics,* edited by Charles A. Hill and Marguerite Helmers, 41–61. Mahwah, N.J.: Erlbaum, 2004.

Blight, David. Comment on "Re: The Use of 'Enslaved.'" *H-Net: Humanities and Social Sciences Online,* February 3, 2010. http://h-net.msu.edu/cgi-bin/logbrowse.pl?trx=vx&list =H-Slavery&month=1002&week=a&msg=RpHYQkUcQJlnFF94KskrSw&user =&pw=.

Boime, Albert. *The Art of Exclusion: Representing Blacks in the Nineteenth Century.* Washington: Smithsonian Institution Press, 1990.

Boston Daily Globe. "Mother Was A Slave; Death of Moses Roper in the City Hospital— Was Suffering from Skin Disease and a Kidney Complaint." April 16, 1891, 1. Available online from ProQuest Newspapers (subscription required).

Bourne, George. *Picture of Slavery in the United States of America.* Middletown, Conn.: Edwin Hunt, 1834. Available from the Internet Archive, https://archive.org/stream /pictureofslaveryoobour#page/n9/mode/2up.

Bourne, Theodore. "Rev. George Bourne: The Pioneer of American Antislavery." *Methodist Quarterly Review* 64 (January 1882): 68–90. Available from the Internet Archive, https ://archive.org/stream/methodistquarter418821meth#page/n5/mode/2up.

Braden, Roberts A. "Visualizing the Verbal and Verbalizing the Visual." In *Seeing Ourselves: Visualization in a Social Context; Readings from the 14th Annual Conference of the International Visual Literacy Association,* edited by Roberts A. Braden and Alice D. Walker, 149–63. Blacksburg: Virginia Polytechnic Institute, 1983.

Branagan, Thomas. *The Penitential Tyrant; or, Slave Trader Reformed: A Pathetic Poem, in Four Cantos.* 2nd ed. New York: Samuel Wood, 1807. Available online from America's Historical Imprints, Readex (subscription required).

———. *Serious Remonstrances: Addressed to the Citizens of the Northern States, and Their Representatives.* Philadelphia: Thomas T. Stiles, 1805. Available from the Internet Archive, https://archive.org/stream/seriousremonstroobrangoog#page/n10/mode/2up.

Brooks, Daphne. *Bodies in Dissent: Spectacular Performances of Race and Freedom, 1850–1910.* Durham, N.C.: Duke University Press, 2006.

Brown, Henry Box. *Narrative of Henry Box Brown, Who Escaped from Slavery, Enclosed in a Box 3 Feet Long and 2 Wide: Written from a Statement of Facts Made by Himself; With Remarks Upon the Remedy for Slavery. By Charles Stearns.* Boston: Brown and Stearns, 1849.

———. *Narrative of the Life of Henry Box Brown, Written by Himself.* Manchester, UK: Lee and Glynn, 1851.

Brownlee, Peter John. "'The Economy of the Eyes': Vision and the Cultural Production of Market Revolution, 1800–1860." PhD diss., George Washington University, 2004. Available online from ProQuest Dissertations and Theses (subscription required).

Bruner, Jerome. *Actual Minds, Possible Worlds*. Cambridge, Mass.: Harvard University Press, 1986.

Canuel, Mark. *The Shadow of Death: Literature, Romanticism, and the Subject of Punishment*. Princeton, N.J.: Princeton University Press, 2007.

Capers, Corey. "Black Voices, White Print: Racial Practice, Print Publicity, and Order in the Early American Republic." In *Early African American Print Culture*, edited by Lara Langer Cohen and Jordan Alexander Stein, 108–26. Philadelphia: University of Pennsylvania Press, 2012.

Casmier-Paz, Lynn. "Slave Narratives and the Rhetoric of Author Portraiture." *New Literary History* 34, no. 1 (2003): 91–116.

Chaney, Michael A. *Fugitive Vision: Slave Image and Black Identity in Antebellum Narrative*. Bloomington: Indiana University Press, 2008.

Charlton, Michael. "Visual Rhetoric: Definitions, Debates, and Disciplinarity." PhD diss., University of Oklahoma, 2008. Available online from ProQuest Dissertations and Theses (subscription required).

Child, Lydia Maria, ed. *Narrative of Joanna: An Emancipated Slave, of Surinam*. Boston: Isaac Knapp, 1838. Available from the Internet Archive, https://archive.org/stream/narrativejoannaoochilgoog#page/n8/mode/2up.

Christian, Charles M., and Sari Bennett. *Black Saga: The African American Experience : A Chronology*. New York: Basic Books, 1998.

Clarissa Dormer, or, The Advantages of Good Instruction. London : J. Harris, 1808. Available from the Internet Archive, https://archive.org/stream/clarissadormeroroolondiala#page/n3/mode/2up.

Clark, Elizabeth B. "'The Sacred Rights of the Weak': Pain, Sympathy, and the Culture of Individual Rights in Antebellum America." *Journal of American History* 82, no. 2 (1995): 463–93.

Clarkson, Thomas. *The History of the Rise, Progress, and Accomplishment of the Abolition of the African Slave-Trade, by the British Parliament*. Vol. 2. London: Longman, Hurst, Rees, and Orme, 1808. Available online from The Making of the Modern World, Gale Cengage (subscription required).

———. *Letters on the Slave-Trade, and the State of the Natives in Those Parts of Africa, Which Are Contiguous to Fort St. Louis and Goree; Written at Paris in December 1789, and January 1790*. London: J. Phillips, 1791. Available online from The Making of the Modern World, Gale Cengage (subscription required).

Clytus, Radiclani. "Envisioning Slavery." PhD diss., Yale, 2007. Ann Arbor, Mich.: UMI, 2007.

Cobb, Jasmine Nichole. *Picture Freedom: Remaking Black Visuality in the Early Nineteenth Century*. New York: New York University Press, 2015.

Cohen, Jane R. *Charles Dickens and His Original Illustrators*. Columbus: Ohio State University Press, 1980.

Cohen, Lara Langer, and Jordan Alexander Stein. Introduction to *Early African American Print Culture*, edited by Lara Langer Cohen and Jordan Alexander Stein, 1–16. Philadelphia: University of Pennsylvania Press, 2012.

Coleman, Deirdre. "Conspicuous Consumption: White Abolitionism and English Women's Writing in the 1790s." *English Literary History* 61, no. 2 (1994): 341–62.

Copeland, Huey. "Glenn Ligon and Other Runaway Subjects." *Representations* 113, no. 1 (2011): 73–110.

Cott, Nancy. *The Bonds of Womanhood: "Woman's Sphere" in New England, 1780–1835.* New Haven, Conn.: Yale University Press, 1977.

Crary, Jonathan. *Techniques of the Observer: On Vision and Modernity in the Nineteenth Century.* Cambridge, Mass.: MIT Press, 1990.

Crater, Christine Ariella. "Brown, Henry Box." Pennsylvania Center for the Book, Pennsylvania State University, spring 2011. http://pabook2.libraries.psu.edu/palitmap /bios/Brown__Henry_Box.html.

Cummings, Amy. "World Anti-Slavery Convention." In *Slavery in the Modern World: A History of Political, Social, and Economic Oppression*, vol. 2, edited by Junius P. Rodriguez, 585–86. Santa Barbara, Calif.: ABC-CLIO, 2011.

Cutter, Martha J. "Revising Torture: Moses Roper and the Visual Rhetoric of the Slave's Body in the Transatlantic Abolition Movement." *ESQ: A Journal of the American Renaissance* 60, no. 3 (2014): 371–411.

———. "Will the Real Henry 'Box' Brown Please Stand Up?" *Common-Place: The Journal of Early American Life* 16, no. 1 (2015).

Davidson, Cathy. *Revolution and the Word: The Rise of the Novel in America.* New York: Oxford University Press, 1986.

Davis, Charles T. "The Slave Narrative: First Major Art Form in an Emerging Black Tradition." *Black Is the Color of the Cosmos: Essays on Afro-American Literature and Culture, 1942–1981*, edited by Henry Louis Gates Jr., 83–119. New York: Garland, 1982.

Davis, David Brion. *The Problem of Slavery in the Age of Revolution, 1770–1823.* New York: Oxford University Press, 1975.

Davis, Mark. "Empathy: Negotiating the Border Between Self and Other." In *The Social Life of Emotions*, edited by Larissa Z. Tiedens and Colin Wayne Leach, 19–42. Cambridge: Cambridge University Press, 2004.

DeLombard, Jeannine. "African American Cultures of Print." In *A History of the Book in America: The Industrial Book, 1840–1880*, vol. 3, edited by Scott E. Casper, et al., 360–72. Chapel Hill: University of North Carolina Press, 2007.

———. "'Eye-Witness to the Cruelty': Southern Violence and Northern Testimony in Frederick Douglass's 1845 *Narrative*." *American Literature* 73, no. 2 (2001): 245–75.

———. *In the Shadow of the Gallows: Race, Crime, and American Civic Identity.* Philadelphia: University of Pennsylvania Press, 2012.

De Rosa, Deborah C. "Amelia Anderson Opie." In *Into the Mouths of Babes: An Anthology of Children's Abolitionist Literature*, edited by Deborah C. De Rosa, 1–3. Westport, Conn.: Praeger, 2005.

———. *Domestic Abolitionism and Juvenile Literature, 1830–1865.* Albany: SUNY Press, 2003.

Dickson, Bruce D. *The Origins of African American Literature, 1680–1865.* Charlottesville: University of Virginia Press, 2001.

Dillon, Elizabeth Maddock. "Sentimental Aesthetics." *American Literature* 76, no. 3 (2004): 495–523.

Dobson, Joanne. "Reclaiming Sentimental Literature." *American Literature* 69, no. 2 (1997): 263–88.

Dooley, Patricia L. "The Missouri Compromise, 1819–1820." In *The Early Republic: Primary Documents on Events from 1799 to 1820*, edited by Patricia L. Dooley, 349–52. Westport, Conn.: Greenwood, 2004.

Douglas, Ann. *The Feminization of American Culture*. New York: Avon, 1977.

Douglass, Frederick. *Narrative of the Life of Frederick Douglass, an American Slave, Written by Himself*. Boston: Anti-Slavery Office, 1845. Available from Documenting the American South, University of North Carolina at Chapel Hill. http://docsouth.unc.edu/neh/douglass/douglass.html.

Dred Scott v. Sandford. 60 U.S. 393 (1856).

Drescher, Seymour. *Abolition: A History of Slavery and Antislavery*. Cambridge, U.K.: Cambridge University Press, 2009.

duBois, Page. *Torture and Truth*. New York: Routledge, 1991.

Duncan, Randy. "Image Functions: Shape and Color as Hermeneutic Images in *Asterios Polyp*." In *Critical Approaches to Comics: Theories and Methods*, edited by Matthew J. Smith and Randy Duncan, 43–54. New York: Routledge, 2012.

Earle, Jonathan, and Diane Mutti Burke. Introduction to *Bleeding Kansas, Bleeding Missouri: The Long Civil War on the Border*, edited by Jonathan Earle and Diane Mutti Burke, 1–10. Lawrence: University Press of Kansas, 2013.

Eaves, Morris, Robert N. Essick, and Joseph Viscomi. "John Gabriel Stedman, *Narrative, of a Five Years' Expedition, against the Revolted Negroes of Surinam*." The William Blake Archive. www.blakearchive.org/exist/blake/archive/work.xq?workid=bb499&java=no.

Eberle, Roxanne. "'Tales of Truth?': Amelia Opie's Antislavery Poetics." In *Romanticism and Women Poets: Opening the Doors of Reception*, edited by Harriet Kramer Linkin and Stephen C. Behrendt, 71–98. Lexington: University Press of Kentucky, 1999.

Edwards, Brent Hayes. *The Practice of Diaspora: Literature, Translation, and the Rise of Black Internationalism*. Cambridge, Mass.: Harvard University Press, 2009.

Eisner, Will. *Comics and Sequential Art*. Tamarac, Fla.: Poorhouse, 1985.

[Elmes, William]. "Adventures of Johnny Newcome." *Caricature Magazine, or Hudibrastic Mirror*, vol. 3, 1812. Available from the Lewis Walpole Library, Yale University. http://images.library.yale.edu/walpoleweb/oneitem.asp?imageId=lwlpr14615.

Equiano, Olaudah. *The Life and Adventures of Olaudah Equiano; or Gustavus Vassa, the African; From an Account Written by Himself*, edited by A[bigail] Mott. Philadelphia: Samuel Wood, 1829.

Ernest, John. *Liberation Historiography: African American Writers and the Challenge of History, 1794–1861*. Chapel Hill: University of North Carolina Press, 2004.

———. "Outside the Box: Henry Box Brown and the Politics of Antislavery Agency." *Arizona Quarterly* 63, no. 4 (2007):1–24.

————. "Traumatic Theology in the *Narrative of the Life of Henry Box Brown, Written by Himself.*" *African American Review* 41, no. 1 (2007): 19–31.

Fanuzzi, Robert. *Abolition's Public Sphere*. Minneapolis: University of Minnesota Press, 2003.

Favret, Mary A. "Flogging: The Anti-Slavery Movement Writes Pornography." In *Romanticism and Gender*, edited by Anne Janowitz, 19–43. Cambridge, U.K.: Brewer, 1998.

Ferguson, Moira. *Subject to Others: British Women Writers and Colonial Slavery, 1670–1834*. New York: Routledge, 1992.

Ferguson, Stephen. "219 Years Ago: *Description of a Slave Ship.*" *Rare Book Collections @ Princeton* [blog], May 3, 2008. https://blogs.princeton.edu/rarebooks/2008/05/219-years -ago-description-of-a.

Fields, Barbara Jeanne. "Slavery, Race, and Ideology in the Unites States of America." *New Left Review* I/181 (May–June 1990): 95–118.

Fierce, Milfred C. "Henry Sylvester Williams and the Pan-African Conference of 1900." *Genève-Afrique* 14, no. 1 (1975): 106–14.

Fink, Stephen. "Book Publishing." In *American History through Literature, 1820–1870*, vol. 1, edited by Janet Gabler-Hover and Robert Sattelmeyer, 148–54. Detroit: Scribner, 2006.

Fisch, Audrey A. *American Slaves in Victorian England: Abolitionist Politics in Popular Literature and Culture*. New York: Cambridge University Press, 2000.

Fisher, Philip. *Hard Facts: Setting and Form in the American Novel*. New York: Oxford University Press, 1985.

Foreman, P. Gabrielle. "'This Promiscuous Housekeeping': Death, Transgression, and Homoeroticism in *Uncle Tom's Cabin.*" *Representations* 43 (1993): 51–72.

Foss, Sonja K. "The Construction of Appeal in Visual Images: A Hypothesis." In *Rhetorical Movement: Studies in Honor of Leland M. Griffin*, edited by David Zarefsky, 211–25. Evanston, Ill.: Northwestern University Press, 1993.

————. "Theory of Visual Rhetoric." In *Handbook of Visual Communication: Theory, Methods, and Media*, edited by Kenneth L. Smith, et al., 141–52. Mahwah, N.J.: Erlbaum, 2005. Reprint, New York: Routledge, 2013.

Foucault, Michel. *Discipline and Punish: The Birth of the Prison*. Translated by Alan Sheridan. New York: Vintage, 1995 [1977].

Freehling, William W. *The Road to Disunion*, vol. 2, *Secessionists Triumphant, 1854–1861*. Oxford: Oxford University Press, 2007.

Gallese, Vittorio, and Corrado Sinigaglia. "What Is So Special about Embodied Simulation?" *Trends in Cognitive Sciences* 15, no. 11 (2011): 512–19.

Games, Gwilym. "Roper, Moses (1815–?)." In *Encyclopedia of Emancipation and Abolition in the Transatlantic World*, vol. 2, edited by Junius P. Rodriguez, 461. Armonk, N.Y.: Sharpe, 2007.

Gara, Larry. "The Fugitive Slave Law: A Double Paradox." In *Abolitionism and American Law*, edited by John R. McKivigan, 267–78. New York: Garland, 1999.

Garber, Marjorie. *Vested Interests: Cross-Dressing and Cultural Anxiety*. New York: Routledge, 1992.

Garrison, William Lloyd. Speech at the Fifteenth Annual Meeting of the American Anti-Slavery Society, May 29, 1849. Reported in the *North Star* [Rochester, N.Y.], June 1, 1849. Available online from Accessible Archives (subscription required).

Gates, Henry Louis, Jr., and William Andrews. "A Note on the Texts." In *Slave Narratives*, edited by Henry Louis Gates Jr. and William Andrews, 1014–1018. New York: Library of America, 2000.

Gates, Henry Louis, Jr., and Hollis Robbins. "Harriet Beecher Stowe and 'The Man That Was a Thing.'" In *The Annotated "Uncle Tom's Cabin,"* by Harriet Beecher Stowe, edited by Henry Louis Gates Jr. and Hollis Robbins, xxxi–xlvii. New York: Norton, 2006.

Gikandi, Simon. *Slavery and the Culture of Taste*. Princeton, N.J.: Princeton University Press, 2011.

Gillespie, Alex. "The Intersubjective Nature of Symbols." In *Symbolic Transformations*, edited by Brady Wagoner, 23–37. London: Routledge, 2010.

Goddu, Teresa A. "Antislavery's Panoramic Perspective." *MELUS* 39, no. 2 (2014): 12–41.

Goggin, Maureen Daly. "Visual Rhetoric in Pens of Steel and Inks of Silk: Challenging the Great Visual/Verbal Divide." In *Defining Visual Rhetorics*, edited by Charles A. Hill and Marguerite Helmers, 87–110. Mahwah, N.J.: Erlbaum, 2004.

Gossett, Thomas F. *"Uncle Tom's Cabin" and American Culture*. Dallas: Southern Methodist University Press, 1985.

Gould, Philip. *Barbaric Traffic: Commerce and Antislavery in the Eighteenth-Century Atlantic World*. Cambridge, Mass.: Harvard University Press, 2003.

Green, Charles C. *The Nubian Slave*. Boston: Bela Marsh, 1845.

———. "Prospectus." *Liberator*, March 21, 1845, 4. Available online from the African American Newspapers Collection (subscription required).

Green, Keith Michael. "Am I Not a Husband and a Father? Re-Membering Black Masculinity, Slave Incarceration, and Cherokee Slavery in *The Life and Adventures of Henry Bibb, an American Slave*." *MELUS* 39, no. 4 (2014): 23–49.

Groce, George C., and David H. Wallace. *The New-York Historical Society's Dictionary of Artists in America, 1564–1860*. New Haven, Conn.: Yale University Press, 1957.

Groensteen, Thierry. *The System of Comics*. Translated by Bart Beaty and Nick Nguyen. Jackson: University of Mississippi Press, 2007 [1999].

Gross, Ariela. *What Blood Won't Tell: A History of Race on Trial in America*. Cambridge, Mass.: Harvard University Press, 2009.

Gubar, Susan. *Racechanges: White Skin, Black Face in American Culture*. New York: Oxford University Press, 1997.

Gutjahr, Paul. "Pictures of Slavery in the United States: Consumerism, Illustration, and the Visualization of Stowe's Novel." In *Approaches to Teaching Stowe's "Uncle Tom's Cabin,"* edited by Elizabeth Ammons and Susan Belasco, 77–92. New York: MLA, 2000.

Guyatt, Mary. "The Wedgwood Slave Medallion: Values in Eighteenth-Century Design." *Journal of Design History* 13, no. 2 (2000): 93–105.

Gwilliam, Tassie. "'Scenes of Horror,' Scenes of Sensibility: Sentimentality and Slavery in John Gabriel Stedman's *Narrative of a Five Years' Expedition against the Revolted Negroes of Surinam.*" *English Literary History* 65, no. 3 (1998): 653–73.

Hall, Basil. *Basil Hall's Forty Etchings, from Sketches made with the Camera Lucida, in North America, in 1827 and 1828.* London: Simpkin, 1829. Available online from the Library of Congress, https://www.loc.gov/item/02001288.

Halttunen, Karen. "Humanitarianism and the Pornography of Pain in Anglo-American Culture." *American Historical Review* 100, no. 2 (1995): 303–34.

Haney López, Ian F. "The Social Construction of Race: Some Observations on Illusion, Fabrication, and Choice." *Harvard Civil Rights–Civil Liberties Law Review* 29, no. 1 (1994): 1–62.

Harde, Roxanne. "'The Savage Inscription': Abolitionist Writers and the Reinscription of Slavery." *Mosaic* 37, no. 2 (2004).

Harper, Juanita. "In All Good Conscience." PhD diss., Yale University, 2003. Available online from ProQuest Dissertations and Theses.

Hartman, Saidiya V. *Lose Your Mother: A Journey along the Atlantic Slave Route.* New York: Farrar, Straus and Giroux, 2007.

———. *Scenes of Subjection: Terror, Slavery, and Self-Making in Nineteenth-Century America.* New York: Oxford University Press, 1997.

Haskins, Jim, and Kathleen Benson. *Conjure Times: Black Magicians in America.* New York: Walker, 2001.

Heglar, Charles. *Rethinking the Slave Narrative: Slave Marriage and the Narratives of Henry Bibb and William and Ellen Craft.* Westport, Conn.: Greenwood, 2001.

Hendler, Glen. *Public Sentiments: Structures of Feeling in Nineteenth-Century American Literature.* Chapel Hill: University of North Carolina Press, 2001.

Heyrick, Elizabeth. *Immediate, Not Gradual Abolition; or, An inquiry into the Shortest, Safest, and Most Effectual Means of Getting Rid of West-Indian Slavery.* London: Hatchard, 1824. Available from the Yale Slavery and Abolition Portal.

Hirte, Tobias. *Sclaven-Handel.* Philadelphia, 1794. Broadside, available online from America's Historical Imprints, Readex (subscription required).

Hochman, Barbara. *"Uncle Tom's Cabin" and the Reading Revolution: Race, Literacy, Childhood, and Fiction, 1851–1911.* Amherst: University of Massachusetts Press, 2011.

Hoermann, Raphael. "'A Very Hell of Horrors'? The Haitian Revolution and the Early Transatlantic Haitian Gothic." *Slavery and Abolition* 37, no. 1 (2016): 183–205.

Hoffer, Williamjames Hull. *The Caning of Charles Sumner.* Baltimore: John Hopkins University Press, 2010.

Holland, Sharon Patricia. *Raising the Dead: Readings of Death and (Black) Subjectivity.* Durham, N.C.: Duke University Press, 2000.

Horton, James Oliver. "Weevils in the Wheat: Free Blacks and the Constitution, 1787–1860." In *This Constitution: A Bicentennial Chronicle* 8 (Fall 1985): 400–407. Available from the

Internet Archive, https://archive.org/stream/ERIC_ED282814#page/n395/mode/2up /search/weevils.

Hotz, Jeffrey. *Divergent Visions, Contested Spaces: The Early United States through the Lens of Travel.* New York: Routledge, 2006.

Husserl, Edmund. *Cartesian Meditations: An Introduction to Phenomenology.* Translated by Dorion Cairns. The Hague: Martinus Nijhoff, 1931. Reprint, 1960.

Inge, William. *The Philosophy of Plotinus: The Gifford Lectures at St. Andrews, 1917–1918.* Vol. 1. London: Longmans, Green, 1948.

The Instructive Alphabet. New York: Samuel Wood, 1809.

International Review of African American Art. "Extreme Times Call for Extreme Heroes." Vol. 14 (1997): 3–16.

Jackson, Cassandra. *Barriers between Us: Interracial Sex in Nineteenth-Century American Literature.* Bloomington: Indiana University Press, 2004.

———. *Violence, Visual Culture, and the Black Male Body.* New York: Routledge, 2011.

Jacobson, Matthew Frye. *Whiteness of a Different Color: European Immigrants and the Alchemy of Race.* Cambridge, Mass.: Harvard University Press, 1998.

Janette, Michele. "'Distorting Overlaps': Identity as Palimpsest in *Bitter in the Mouth.*" *MELUS* 39, no. 3 (2014): 155–77.

JanMohamed, Abdul R. *The Death-Bound-Subject: Richard Wright's Archaeology of Death.* Durham, N.C.: Duke University Press, 2005.

Jasper, James M. "The Emotions of Protest: Affective and Reactive Emotions in and around Social Movements." *Sociological Forum* 13, no. 3 (1998): 397–424.

Jauss, Hans Robert. *Toward an Aesthetic of Reception.* Translated by Timothy Bhati. Minneapolis: University of Minnesota Press, 1982.

Jay, Martin. *Downcast Eyes: The Denigration of Vision in Twentieth-Century French Thought.* Berkeley: University of California Press, 1993.

———. "Scopic Regimes of Modernity." In *Vision and Visuality*, edited by Hal Foster, 3–23. Seattle: Bay Press, 1988.

Johansson, Eva. "Empathy or Intersubjectivity? Understanding the Origins of Morality in Young Children." *Studies in Philosophy and Education* 27, no. 1 (2008): 33–47.

Johnson, Dan R. "Transportation into a Story Increases Empathy, Prosocial Behavior, and Perceptual Bias toward Fearful Expressions." *Personality and Individual Differences* 52, no. 2 (2012): 150–55.

Jones, Jeannette Eileen. *In Search of Brightest Africa: Reimagining the Dark Continent in American Culture, 1884–1936.* Athens: University of Georgia Press, 2011.

Juvenile Album: Being a Collection of Poetical Pieces Selected by M. M., a Little Girl about Ten Years of Age. New York: Mahlon Day, 1826.

Kanwar, Rajesh, Jerry C. Olson, and Laura S. Sims. "Toward Conceptualizing and Measuring Cognitive Structures." *Advances in Consumer Research* 8 (1981): 122–27.

Kawash, Samira. "Fugitive Properties." In *The New Economic Criticism: Studies at the Interface of Literature and Economics*, edited by Mark Osteen and Martha Woodmansee, 277–90. New York: Routledge, 2005.

Keen, Suzanne. *Empathy and the Novel.* New York: Oxford University Press, 2007.

Keller, Holly. "Juvenile Antislavery Narrative and Notions of Childhood." *Children's Literature* 24 (1996): 86–100.

Kennedy, Dustin. "Going Viral: Stedman's *Narrative*, Textual Variation, and Life in Atlantic Studies." In *Circulations: Romanticism and the Black Atlantic*, October 2011: 1–31. www.rc.umd.edu/praxis/circulations/HTML/praxis.2011.kennedy.html.

Kidd, David Comer, and Emanuele Castano. "Reading Literary Fiction Improves Theory of Mind." *Science* 342, no. 65156 (2013): 377–80.

Klarer, Mario. "Humanitarian Pornography: John Gabriel Stedman's *Narrative of a Five Years' Expedition against the Revolted Negroes of Surinam.*" *New Literary History* 36, no. 4 (2005): 559–87.

Knight, Christina. "Disembarking: Christina Knight on 'Glenn Ligon: America.'" Interview by Alex Freedman. *ART21 Magazine*, April 14, 2011. http://blog.art21.org/2011/04/14 /disembarking-christina-knight-on-glenn-ligon-america/#.V8TacRRZHgU.

Kraditor, Aileen S. *Means and Ends in American Abolitionism: Garrison and His Critics on Strategy and Tactics, 1834–1850.* New York: American Books, 1967.

Kunzle, David. *The Early Comic Strip: Narrative Strips and Picture Stories in the European Broadsheet from c. 1450 to 1825.* Berkeley: University of California Press, 1973.

Lacey, Barbara E. "Visual Images of Blacks in Early American Imprints." *William and Mary Quarterly* 53, no. 1 (1996): 137–80.

Lapsansky, Phillip. "Graphic Discord: Abolitionist and Antiabolitionist Images." In *The Abolitionist Sisterhood: Women's Political Culture in Antebellum America*, edited by Jean Fagan Yellin and John C. Van Horne, 201–30. Ithaca, N.Y.: Cornell University Press, 1994.

Lasser, Carol. "Voyeuristic Abolitionism: Sex, Gender, and the Transformation of Antislavery Rhetoric." *Journal of the Early Republic* 28, no. 1 (2008): 83–111.

Lawton, Saadia Nicoe Teresa. "Contested Meanings: Audience Responses to the Wedgwood Slave Medallion, 1787–1839." PhD diss., University of Wisconsin–Madison, 2009.

Leary, Lewis. "Thomas Branagan: Republican Rhetoric and Romanticism in America." *Pennsylvania Magazine of History and Biography* 77, no. 3 (1953): 332–52.

Levecq, Christine. *Slavery and Sentiment: The Politics of Feeling in Black Atlantic Antislavery Writing, 1770–1850.* Durham: University of New Hampshire Press, 2008.

Liberator [Boston]. "Bourne's Picture." December 8, 1837, 200. Available online from America's Historical Newspapers, Readex (subscription required).

———. "Narrative of Moses Roper." March 30, 1838, 51. Available online from America's Historical Newspapers, Readex (subscription required).

Ligon, Glenn. *Runaways.* Lithograph on paper. Minneapolis: Walker Art Center, 1993.

———. *To Disembark.* Art installation. Hirshhorn Museum and Sculpture Garden, Washington, D.C., 1994.

Linebaugh, Peter, and Marcus Rediker. *The Many-Headed Hydra: Sailors, Slaves, Commoners, and the Hidden History of the Revolutionary Atlantic.* Boston: Beacon, 2000.

Lott, Eric. *Love and Theft: Blackface Minstrelsy and the American Working Class.* New York: Oxford University Press, 1993.

Lowance, Mason, and Jan Pilditch. "Writing the Law: Literature and Slavery in Nineteenth-Century America." *Australasian Journal of American Studies* 27, no. 2 (2008): 66–82.

Malik, Keenan. *The Meaning of Race: Race, History, and Culture in Western Society*. New York: New York University Press, 1996.

Mann, Bruce H. *Republic of Debtors: Bankruptcy in the Age of American Independence*. Cambridge, Mass.: Harvard University Press, 2002.

Marshall, P. J., ed. *The Oxford History of the British Empire*, vol. 2, *The Eighteenth Century*. Oxford: Oxford University Press, 1998.

Matlack, Lucius C. Introduction to Henry Bibb, *Narrative of the Life and Adventures of Henry Bibb, Written by Himself*, i–ii. New York, 1849.

Matthews, Glenna. *The Rise of Public Woman: Woman's Power and Woman's Place in the United States, 1630–1970*. New York: Oxford University Press, 1992.

Mbiti, John S. *African Religions and Philosophy*. 2nd ed. Portsmouth, UK: Heinemann, 1992.

McBride, Dwight A. *Impossible Witnesses: Truth, Abolitionism, and Slave Testimony*. New York: New York University Press, 2001.

McCloud, Scott. *Understanding Comics: The Invisible Art*. New York: Harper, 1993.

McEvilley, Thomas. "Primitivism in the Works of an Emancipated Negress." In *Kara Walker: My Complement, My Enemy, My Oppressor, My Love*, 53–61. Minneapolis: Walker Art Center, 2007.

McHenry, Elizabeth. *Forgotten Readers: Recovering the Lost History of African American Literary Societies*. Durham, N.C.: Duke University Press, 2002.

McInnis, Maurie D. *Slaves Waiting for Sale: Abolitionist Art and the American Slave Trade*. Chicago: University of Chicago Press, 2011.

Meer, Sarah. "Topsy and the End Man: Blackface in *Uncle Tom's Cabin*." In *Harriet Beecher Stowe's "Uncle Tom's Cabin": A Casebook*, edited by Elizabeth Ammons, 131–66. New York: Oxford University Press, 2007.

———. *Uncle Tom Mania: Slavery, Minstrelsy, and Transatlantic Culture in the 1850s*. Athens: University of Georgia Press, 2005.

Mellby, Julie L. "Picture of Slavery." In *Graphic Arts*, blog of the Princeton University Library, February 16, 2010. https://blogs.princeton.edu/graphicarts/2010/02/picture_of _slavery.html.

Mellor, Anne K. "'Am I Not a Woman, and a Sister?': Slavery, Romanticism, and Gender." In *Romanticism, Race, and Imperial Culture, 1780–1834*, edited by Alan Richardson and Sonia Hofkosh, 311–29. Bloomington: Indiana University Press, 1996.

———. "Sex, Violence, and Slavery: Blake and Wollstonecraft." *Huntington Library Quarterly* 58, nos. 3–4 (1995): 345–70.

Mercantile Advertiser [New York]. "Just Published." April 5, 1807, 4. Available online from America's Historical Newspapers, Readex (subscription required).

Merish, Lori. *Sentimental Materialism: Gender, Commodity Culture, and Nineteenth-Century American Literature*. Durham, N.C.: Duke University Press, 2000.

The Mirror of Misery; or, Tyranny Exposed: Extracted from Authentic Documents, and

Exemplified by Engravings. New York: Samuel Wood, 1807. Available online from America's Historical Imprints, Readex (subscription required).

Mirzoeff, Nicholas. *The Right to Look: A Counterhistory of Visuality*. Durham, N.C.: Duke University Press, 2011.

Mitchell, W. J. T. *Picture Theory: Essays on Verbal and Visual Representation*. Chicago: University of Chicago Press, 1994.

———. *What Do Pictures Want? The Lives and Loves of Images*. Chicago: University of Chicago Press, 2006.

Morgan, Jo-Ann. "Picturing Uncle Tom with Little Eva: Reproduction as Legacy." *Journal of American Culture* 27, no. 1 (March 1, 2004): 1–24.

———. *Uncle Tom's Cabin as Visual Culture*. Columbia: University of Missouri Press, 2007.

Morgan, Kenneth. *Slavery and the British Empire: From Africa to America*. New York: Oxford University Press, 2007.

Morrison, Toni. "In the Realm of Responsibility: A Conversation with Toni Morrison." Interview by Marcia Darling. In *Conversations with Toni Morrison*, edited by Danielle Taylor-Guthrie, 246–54. Jackson: University Press of Mississippi, 1994.

———. *Playing in the Dark: Whiteness and the Literary Imagination*. Cambridge, Mass.: Harvard University Press, 1992.

Morton, Julia F. *Fruits of Warm Climates*. Miami, 1987. Reprint, Brattleboro, Vt.: Echo Point, 2013.

Moten, Fred. *In the Break: The Aesthetics of the Black Radical Tradition*. Minneapolis: University of Minnesota Press, 2003.

Nelson, Dana. *The Word in Black and White: Reading "Race" in American Literature, 1638–1867*. New York: Oxford University Press, 1992.

New Bedford (MA) Mercury. "Eloquence." November 2, 1849, 1. Available online from America's Historical Newspapers, Readex (subscription required).

Newman, Richard S. *Freedom's Prophet: Bishop Richard Allen, the AME Church, and the Black Founding Fathers*. New York: New York University Press, 2008.

New York Spectator. "An Atrocious Publication." February 22, 1836, 3. Available online from America's Historical Newspapers, Readex (subscription required).

New York Times. "A Colored Lecturer Dead." April 17, 1891, 1. Available online from ProQuest Newspapers (subscription required).

Noble, Marianne. "The Ecstasies of Sentimental Wounding in *Uncle Tom's Cabin*." *Yale Journal of Criticism* 10, no. 2 (1997): 295–320.

———. *The Masochistic Pleasures of Sentimental Literature*. Princeton, N.J.: Princeton University Press, 2000.

Nodelman, Perry. *Words about Pictures*. 2nd ed. Athens: University of Georgia Press, 1990.

Northup, Solomon. *Twelve Years a Slave: Narrative of Solomon Northup, a Citizen of New-York, Kidnapped in Washington City in 1841, and Rescued in 1853*. Auburn, N.Y.: Derby and Miller, 1853. Available from the Internet Archive, https://archive.org/stream/twelveyearslaveoonort#page/n5/mode/2up.

Oatley, Keith. *Such Stuff as Dreams: The Psychology of Fiction*. Chichester, UK: Wiley, 2011.

O'Brien, Sheila Ruzycki. "'There Is No Arguing with Pictures': Stretching the Canvas of Gender in the Art Portraits, Picture-Language, and the Original Illustrations in *Uncle Tom's Cabin*." *American Transcendental Quarterly* 20, no. 2 (2006): 448–80.

O'Donnell, Kevin E. "Book and Periodical Illustration in America, 1820–1870." In *American History through Literature, 1820–1870*, vol. 1, edited by Janet Gabler-Hover and Robert Sattelmeyer, 144–48. Detroit: Scribner, 2006.

O'Farrell, John K. A. "Bibb, Henry Walton." In *Dictionary of Canadian Biography*, vol. 8. University of Toronto, 1985. www.biographi.ca/en/bio/bibb_henry_walton_8E.html.

O'Gorman, James F. *Accomplished in All Departments of Art: Hammatt Billings of Boston, 1818–1874*. Amherst: University of Massachusetts Press, 1998.

Okeowo, Alexis. "Freedom Fighter: A Slaving Society and an Abolitionist's Crusade." *New Yorker*, September 1, 2014.

Olney, James. "'I Was Born': Slave Narratives, Their Status as Autobiography and as Literature." In *The Slave's Narrative*, 2nd ed., edited by Charles T. Davis and Henry Louis Gates Jr., 148–74. New York: Oxford University Press, 1990.

Opie, Amelia. *The Black Man's Lament; or, How To Make Sugar*. London: Harvey and Darton, 1826.

Painter, Nell Irvin. *Exodusters: Black Migration to Kansas after Reconstruction*. New York: Norton, 1992.

Park, Justin H., Mark Schaller, and Mark Van Vugt. "Psychology of Human Kin Recognition: Heuristic Cues, Erroneous Inferences, and their Implications." *Review of General Psychology* 12, no. 3 (2008): 215–35.

Patton, Sharon F. *Oxford History of Art: African-American Art*. New York: Oxford University Press, 1998.

Perry, Claire. *Young America: Childhood in 19th-Century Art and Culture*. New Haven, Conn.: Yale University Press, 2006.

Perry, Lewis. *Radical Abolitionism: Anarchy and the Government of God in Antislavery Thought*. Knoxville: University of Tennessee Press, 1995.

Peters, Harry T. *America on Stone: The Other Printmakers to the American People*. New York: Doubleday, 1931.

Phillips, Christopher N. "Epic, Anti-Eloquence, and Abolitionism: Thomas Branagan's *Avenia* and *The Penitential Tyrant*." *Early American Literature* 44, no. 3 (2009): 605–37.

"Picture of Slavery in the United States. Original." *Religious Inquirer*, July 11, 1835, 113. Available online from America's Historical Newspapers, Readex (subscription required).

Pierce, Yolanda. *Hell without Fires: Slavery, Christianity, and the Antebellum Spiritual Narrative*. Gainesville: University Press of Florida, 2005.

Polletta, Francesca, and Edwin Amenta. "Second That Emotion? Lessons from Once-Novel Concepts in Social Movement Research." In *Passionate Politics: Emotions and Social Movements*, edited by Jeff Godwin, James Jasper, and Francesca Polletta, 303–16. Chicago: University of Chicago Press, 2001.

Pratt, Mary Louise. *Imperial Eyes: Travel Writing and Transculturation*. 2nd ed. London: Routledge, 2007.

Preston, Ann. *Cousin Ann's Stories for Children*. Philadelphia: McKim, 1849. Available from the Digital Media Repository, Ball State University. http://libx.bsu.edu/cdm/ref /collection/chapbks/id/383.

Preston, Stephanie D., and Frans B. M. de Waal. "Empathy: Its Ultimate and Proximate Bases." *Behavioral and Brain Sciences* 25, no. 1 (2002): 1–72.

Price, David. *Magic: A Pictorial History of Conjurers in the Theater*. New York: Cornwall, 1985.

Price, Richard, and Sally Price, eds. Introduction to *Narrative of a Five Years' Expedition against the Revolted Negroes of Surinam*, by John Gabriel Stedman (1796), edited by Richard Price and Sally Price, xiii–xcvii. Baltimore: Johns Hopkins University Press, 1988.

———. "Editors' Notes." In *Stedman's Surinam: Life in an Eighteenth-Century Slave Society; An Abridged, Modernized Edition of "Narrative of a Five Years Expedition against the Revolted Negroes of Surinam,"* 319–42. Baltimore: Johns Hopkins University Press, 1992.

Proctor, William G. "Slavery in Southwest Georgia." *Georgia Historical Quarterly* 49, no. 1 (1965): 1–22.

Railton, Stephen. "*Uncle Tom's Cabin* and Slavery." *"Uncle Tom's Cabin" and American Culture*, University of Virginia, 1999. http://utc.iath.virginia.edu/interpret/intslav.html.

Rainey, Sue. "Wood Engraving in America." In *Embellished with Numerous Engravings: Works of American Illustrators and Wood Engravers, 1670–1880*, by Sue Rainey and Mildred Abraham. Charlottesville: University of Virginia Library, Department of Rare Books, 1986.

Rediker, Marcus. *The Slave Ship: A Human History*. New York: Penguin, 2007.

Reid, Mandy. "Racial Profiling: Visualizing Racial Science on the Covers of *Uncle Tom's Cabin*, 1852–1928." *Nineteenth-Century Contexts* 30, no. 4 (2008): 369–87.

Reinhardt, Mark. "The Art of Racial Profiling." In *Kara Walker: Narratives of a Negress*, edited by Ian Berry, Darby English, Vivian Patterson, and Mark Reinhardt, 109–29. Cambridge, Mass.: MIT Press, 2003.

Remarks on the Methods of Procuring Slaves, with a Short Account of Their Treatment in the West Indies, &c. Broadside. London: Darton and Harvey, 1793. Availble online from the Houghton Library, Harvard University. http://houghtonlib.tumblr.com /post/143481556406/remarks-on-the-methods-of-procuring-slaves-with.

Reynolds, David S. Introduction to *Uncle Tom's Cabin, or, Life among the Lowly*, by Harriet Beecher Stowe, vii–xxxiii. New York: Oxford University Press, 2011 [1852].

Rice, Alan J. *Radical Narratives of the Black Atlantic*. London: Continuum, 2003.

Richter, Emil. *Prints: A Brief Review of Their Technique and History*. Boston: Houghton, 1914.

Ripley, C. Peter. Introduction to *The Black Abolitionist Papers*, vol. 3: *The United States, 1830– 1846*, edited by C. Peter Ripley, 3–69. Chapel Hill: University of North Carolina Press, 1993.

Riss, Arthur. "Harriet Beecher Stowe." In *The Cambridge Companion to American Novelists*, edited by Timothy Parrish, 32–41. New York: Cambridge University Press, 2013.

Rodriguez, Junius P. "Chronology." In Rodriguez, *Slavery in the United States*, 1:1–75.

———. "Fugitive Slave Act (1850)." In Rodriguez, *Slavery in the United States*, 1:301–3.

———. "Gradualism." In Rodriguez, *Slavery in the United States*, 318–19.

———, ed. *Slavery in the United States: A Social, Political, and Historical Encyclopedia*, vol. 1. Santa Barbara, Calif.: ABC-CLIO, 2007.

Rohrbach, Augusta. "Shadow and Substance: Sojourner Truth in Black and White." In *Pictures and Progress: Early Photography and the Making of African American Identity*, edited by Maurice O. Wallace and Shawn Michelle Smith, 83–100. Durham, N.C.: Duke University Press, 2012.

———. *Truth Stranger than Fiction: Race, Realism, and the U.S. Literary Marketplace*. New York: Palgrave, 2002.

Roper, Moses. "Letter from Moses Roper to the Committee of the British and Foreign Anti-Slavery Society, May 9, 1844." In *The Black Abolitionist Papers*, vol. 1, edited by Peter C. Ripley et al., 134–36. Chapel Hill: University of North Carolina Press, 1985.

———. *A Narrative of the Adventures and Escape of Moses Roper, from American Slavery*. 2nd ed. London: Darton, Harvey, and Darton, 1838 [1837].

———. *Narrative of the Adventures and Escape of Moses Roper, from American Slavery: With an Appendix, Containing a List of Places Visited by the Author in Great Britain and Ireland and the British Isles; and Other Matter*. Berwick-upon-Tweed, UK, 1848.

———. *A Narrative of the Adventures and Escape of Moses Roper from American Slavery, with a Portrait*. London: Darton, Harvey, and Darton, 1840.

Rosenthal, Debra J., ed. *Harriet Beecher Stowe's "Uncle Tom's Cabin": A Routledge Study Guide and Sourcebook*. London: Routledge, 2003.

———. "'I've Only to Say the Word!': *Uncle Tom's Cabin* and Performative Speech Theory." *Legacy: A Journal of American Women Writers* 27, no. 2 (2010): 237–56.

Ruchames, Louis. *The Abolitionists: A Collection of Their Writings*. New York: Putnam, 1963.

Ruggles, Jeffrey. *The Unboxing of Henry Brown*. Richmond: Library of Virginia, 2003.

Rusert, Britt. "The Science of Freedom: Counterarchives of Racial Science on the Antebellum Stage." *African American Review* 45, no. 3 (2012): 291–308.

Ryan, Susan M. *The Grammar of Good Intentions: Race and the Antebellum Culture of Benevolence*. Ithaca, N.Y.: Cornell University Press, 2003.

Sajó, András. *Constitutional Sentiments*. New Haven, Conn.: Yale University Press, 2011.

Samuels, Maurice. "The Illustrated History Book: History between Word and Image." In *The Nineteenth-Century Visual Culture Reader*, edited by Vanessa R. Schwartz and Jeannene M. Przyblyski, 238–49. New York: Routledge, 2004.

Samuels, Shirley. "The Identity of Slavery." In *The Culture of Sentiment: Race, Gender, and Sentimentalism in Nineteenth-Century American Literature*, edited by Shirley Samuels, 157–71. New York: Oxford University Press, 1992.

————. Introduction to *The Culture of Sentiment: Race, Gender, and Sentimentalism in Nineteenth-Century American Literature*, edited by Shirley Samuels, 3–8. New York: Oxford University Press, 1992.

————. *Romances of the Republic: Women, the Family, and Violence in the Literature of the Early American Nation*. New York: Oxford University Press, 1996.

Sánchez-Eppler, Karen. *Touching Liberty: Abolition, Feminism, and the Politics of the Body*. Berkeley: University of California Press, 1993.

Savage, Kirk. *Standing Soldiers, Kneeling Slaves: Race, War, and Monument in Nineteenth-Century America*. Princeton, N.J.: Princeton University Press, 1997.

Scarry, Elaine. *The Body in Pain: The Making and Unmaking of the World*. New York: Oxford University Press, 1985.

Senior, Emily. "'Perfectly Whole': Skin and Text in John Gabriel Stedman's *Narrative of a Five Years Expedition against the Revolted Negroes of Surinam*." *Eighteenth-Century Studies* 44, no. 1 (2010): 39–56.

Shamay-Tsoory, Simone G., and Judith Aharon-Peretz. "Dissociable Prefrontal Networks for Cognitive and Affective Theory of Mind: A Lesion Study." *Neuropsychologia* 45, no. 13 (2007): 3054–67.

Shamay-Tsoory, Simone G., et al. "Impaired 'Affective Theory of Mind' Is Associated with Right Ventromedial Prefrontal Damage." *Cognitive and Behavioral Neurology* 18, no. 1 (2005): 55–67.

Shane, Scott. "Interrogations' Effectiveness May Prove Elusive." *New York Times*, April 22, 2009.

Sharpe, Jenny. *Ghosts of Slavery: A Literary Archaeology of Black Women's Lives*. Minneapolis: University of Minnesota Press, 2003.

Shaw, Gwendolyn DuBois. *Portraits of a People: Picturing African Americans in the Nineteenth Century*. Andover, Mass.: Addison Gallery of American Art, 2006.

————. *Seeing the Unspeakable: The Art of Kara Walker*. Durham, N.C.: Duke University Press, 2004.

Sherwood, Marika. *Origins of Pan-Africanism: Henry Sylvester Williams, Africa, and the African Diaspora*. New York: Routledge, 2011.

Sherwood, Mrs. [Mary Martha]. *Dazee, Or the Re-Captured Negro*. Newburyport, Mass.: Gilman, 1822 [1821].

Sinha, Manisha. *The Slave's Cause: A History of Abolition*. New Haven, Conn.: Yale University Press, 2016.

Sklar, Kathryn Kish. *Women's Rights Emerges within the Antislavery Movement, 1830–1870*. New York: Bedford, 2000.

Slavery in America. Review of *A Narrative of the Adventures and Escape of Moses Roper, from American Slavery*. Vol. 14, August 1, 1837, 316–18. Available from the Internet Archive, https://archive.org/stream/ASPC0001974700#page/n323/mode/2up.

Smith, Adam. *The Theory of Moral Sentiments*. London: A. Millar, 1759.

Smith, Shawn Michelle. *Photography on the Color Line: W. E. B. Du Bois, Race, and Visual Culture*. Durham, N.C.: Duke University Press, 2004.

Sollors, Werner. *Neither Black nor White yet Both: Thematic Explorations of Interracial Literature*. Cambridge, Mass.: Harvard University Press, 1999.

Sorisio, Carolyn. "The Spectacle of the Body: Torture in the Antislavery Writing of Lydia Maria Child and Frances E. W. Harper." *Modern Language Studies* 30, no. 1 (2000): 45–66.

Spencer, Suzette A. "An International Fugitive: Henry Box Brown, Anti-Imperialism, Resistance, and Slavery." *Social Identities* 12, no. 2 (2006): 227–48.

Spencer, Suzette A., Jeffrey Ruggles, and the *Dictionary of Virginia Biography*. "Henry Box Brown (1815 or 1816–1897)." *Encyclopedia Virginia*, August 8, 2016. www.encyclopediavirginia.org/brown_henry_box_ca_1815.

Spillers, Hortense. "Changing the Letter: The Yokes, the Jokes of Discourse, or, Mrs. Stowe, Mr. Reed." In *Slavery and the Literary Imagination*, edited by Deborah E. McDowell and Arnold Rampersad, 25–61. Baltimore: John Hopkins University Press, 1989.

———. "Mama's Baby, Papa's Maybe: An American Grammar Book." *Diacritics* 17, no. 2 (1987): 64–81.

Stallybrass, Peter, and Allon White. *The Politics and Poetics of Transgression*. Ithaca, N.Y.: Cornell University Press, 1986.

Stedman, John Gabriel. *Narrative of a Five Years' Expedition, against the Revolted Negroes of Surinam*. 2 vols. London: Johnson and Edwards, 1796. Available from Eighteenth Century Collections Online. www.gale.com.

———. *Narrative of a Five Years' Expedition, against the Revolted Negroes of Surinam*. Edited by R. A. van Lier. Amherst: University of Massachusetts Press, 1972 [1796].

Steinmeyer, Jim. *Hiding the Elephant: How Magicians Invented the Impossible and Learned to Disappear*. New York: Carroll, 2003.

Stephan, Walter G., and Krystina Finlay. "The Role of Empathy in Improving Intergroup Relations." *Journal of Social Issues* 55, no. 4 (1999): 729–43.

Stepto, Robert B. "I Rose and Found My Voice: Narration, Authentication, and Authorial Control in Four Slave Narratives." In *The Slave's Narrative*, edited by Charles T. Davis and Henry Louis Gates Jr., 225–41. New York: Oxford University Press, 1985.

Stewart, James Brewer. *Holy Warriors: The Abolitionists and American Slavery*. Rev. ed. New York: Hill and Wang, 1997.

Still, William. *The Underground Rail Road: A Record*. Philadelphia: Porter and Coates, 1872. Available from the Internet Archive, https://archive.org/stream/undergroundrailroostil#page/n7/mode/2up.

Stowe, Harriet Beecher. *Life and Letters of Harriet Beecher Stowe*. Edited by Annie Fields. Boston: Houghton, 1898.

———. *Uncle Tom's Cabin*. 2 vols. Boston: Jewett, 1852.

Terrell, Mary Church. *A Colored Woman in a White World*. Washington, D.C.: Ransdell, 1940.

Thomas, Helen. *Romanticism and Slave Narratives: Transatlantic Testimonies*. Cambridge: Cambridge University Press, 2004.

Thomas, Hugh. *The Slave Trade: The Story of the Atlantic Slave Trade, 1440–1870*. New York: Simon Schuster, 1997.

Thomason, Mark. "Colony for Freed Slaves." In *The Louisiana Purchase: A Historical and Geographical Encyclopedia*, edited by Junius P. Rodriguez, 77–79. Santa Barbara, Calif.: ABC-CLIO, 2002.

Titchener, Edward Bradford. *Lectures on the Experimental Psychology of the Thought Processes*. New York: Macmillan, 1909.

Tomek, Beverly. "'From Motives of Generosity, as Well as Self-preservation': Thomas Branagan, Colonization, and the Gradual Emancipation Movement." *American Nineteenth-Century History* 6, no. 2 (2005): 121–47.

Tompkins, Jane. *Sensational Designs: The Cultural Work of American Fiction, 1790–1860*. New York: Oxford University Press, 1985.

Upchurch, T. Adams. *Abolition Movement*. Santa Barbara: Greenwood, 2011.

Vischer, Robert. "On the Optical Sense of Form: a Contribution to Aesthetics." 1873. In *Empathy, Form, and Space: Problems in German Aesthetics, 1873–1893*, translated by Harry Francis Mallgrave and Eleftherios Ikonomou, 89–123. Santa Monica: Getty Center, 1994.

Wade, Nicholas J., and Josef Brožek. *Purkinje's Vision: The Dawning of Neuroscience*. Mahwah: Erlbaum, 2001.

Wahrman, Dror. *The Making of the Modern Self: Identity and Culture in Eighteenth-Century England*. 2004. New Haven, Conn.: Yale University Press, 2006.

Waldstreicher, David. Comment on "Use of 'Enslaved.'" *H-Net: Humanities and Social Sciences Online*, February 15, 2010. http://h-net.msu.edu/cgi-bin/logbrowse.pl?trx =vx&list=H-Slavery&month=1002&week=c&msg=U%2b%2bZ3fVx5emljrSj1XDVP g&user=&pw=.

Walker, Hamza. "Kara Walker: Cut It Out." *Nka: Journal of Contemporary African Art* 11–12 (2000): 108–13.

Walker, Kara. *The End of Uncle Tom and the Grand Allegorical Tableau of Eva in Heaven*. Art installation, 1995. Collection Jeffrey Deitch, New York.

———. *Mistress Demanded a Swift and Dramatic Empathetic Reaction Which We Obliged Her*. Art installation, 2000. Collection of Whitney Museum of American Art, New York.

Wallace, Maurice O. *Constructing the Black Masculine: Identity and Ideality in African American Men's Literature and Culture, 1775–1995*. Durham, N.C.: Duke University Press, 2002.

Wallace, Maurice O., and Shawn Michelle Smith, eds. *Pictures and Progress: Early Photography and the Making of African American Identity*. Durham, N.C.: Duke University Press, 2012.

Walsh, Megan. "Diagram of a Fugitive Slave Narrative." *Common-Place: The Journal of Early American Life* 13, no. 3 (2013). www.common-place-archives.org/vol-13/no-03/notes.

Walters, Ronald. "The Erotic South: Civilization and Sexuality in American Abolitionism." *American Quarterly* 25, no. 2 (1973): 177–201.

Waters, Hazel. *Racism on the Victorian Stage: Representation of Slavery and the Black Character.* Cambridge: Cambridge University Press, 2009.

Waugh, John C. *On the Brink of Civil War: The Compromise of 1850 and How It Changed the Course of American History.* Wilmington, Del.: Scholarly Resources, 2003.

Weheliye, Alexander G. "Pornotropes." *Journal of Visual Culture* 7, no. 1 (2008): 65–81.

Wells, Ida B. "Woman's Mission." *New York Freeman*, December 26, 1885. Reprinted in *The Memphis Diary of Ida B. Wells*, edited by Miriam DeCosta-Willis, 179–82. Boston: Beacon, 1995.

Welter, Barbara. "The Cult of True Womanhood, 1820–1860." *American Quarterly* 18, no. 2 (1966): 151–74.

Wexler, Laura. *Tender Violence: Domestic Visions in an Age of U.S. Imperialism.* Chapel Hill: University of North Carolina Press, 2000.

White, Deborah Gray. *Ar'n't I a Woman? Female Slaves in the Plantation South.* 2nd ed. New York: Norton, 1999.

Whitman, T. Stephen. *Challenging Slavery in the Chesapeake: Black and White Resistance to Human Bondage, 1775–1865.* Baltimore: Maryland Historical Society, 2007.

Wiegman, Robyn. *American Anatomies: Theorizing Race and Gender.* Durham, N.C.: Duke University Press, 1995.

Williams, Raymond. *Marxism and Literature.* 2nd ed. Oxford: Oxford University Press, 1978.

Wilson, Ivy. *Specters of Democracy: Blackness and the Aesthetics of Politics in the Antebellum U.S.* New York: Oxford University Press, 2011.

Wisconsin Free Democrat [Milwaukee]. "Servility Rebuked." July 30, 1851, 534. Available online from America's Historical Newspapers, Readex (subscription required).

Witek, Joseph. "Comics Modes: Caricature and Illustration in the Crumb Family's *Dirty Laundry*." In *Critical Approaches to Comics: Theories and Methods*, edited by Matthew J. Smith and Randy Duncan, 27–42. New York: Routledge, 2012.

Wolf, Edwin, II. "Sclaven-Handel. Philadelphia: Gedruckt für Tobias Hirte, bey Samuel Saur, 1794." In *Germantown and the Germans: An Exhibition*, edited by Edwin Wolf II, 108. Philadelphia: Library Company of Philadelphia / The Historical Society of Pennsylvania, 1983.

Wolff, Cynthia Griffin. "Passing beyond the Middle Passage: Henry 'Box' Brown's Translations of Slavery." *Massachusetts Review* 37, no. 1 (1996): 23–44.

Wood, Marcus. "'All Right!': The *Narrative of Henry Box Brown* as a Test Case for the Racial Prescription of Rhetoric and Semiotics." *Proceedings of the American Antiquarian Society* 107, no. 1 (1997): 65–104.

———. *Blind Memory: Visual Representation of Slavery in England and America, 1780–1865.* New York: Routledge, 2000.

———. "Emancipation Art, Fanon, and 'the Butcher of Freedom.'" In *Slavery and the Cultures of Abolition: Essays Marking the Bicentennial of the British Abolition Act of 1807*, edited by Brycchan Carey and Peter J. Kitson, 11–41. Cambridge, U.K.: Brewer, 2007.

————. *The Horrible Gift of Freedom: Atlantic Slavery and the Representation of Emancipation.* Athens: University of Georgia Press, 2010.

————, ed. *The Poetry of Slavery: An Anglo-American Anthology, 1764–1865.* Oxford: Oxford University Press, 2003.

————. "Seeing Is Believing, or Finding 'Truth' in Slave Narrative: The *Narrative of Henry Bibb* as Perfect Misrepresentation." *Slavery and Abolition* 18, no. 3 (1997): 174–211.

————. "The Slave Narrative and Visual Culture." In *The Oxford Handbook of the African American Slave Narrative*, edited by John Ernest, 196–218. New York: Oxford University Press, 2014.

————. *Slavery, Empathy, and Pornography.* Oxford: Oxford University Press, 2002.

Yellin, Jean Fagan. *Harriet Jacobs: A Life.* New York: Basic Books, 2004.

Young, Michael P. "A Revolution of the Soul: Transformative Experiences and Immediate Abolition." In *Passionate Politics: Emotions and Social Movements*, edited by Jeff Goodwin, James M. Jasper, and Francesca Polletta, 99–114. Chicago: University of Chicago Press, 2001.

Zackodnik, Teresa C. *The Mulatta and the Politics of Race.* Jackson: University Press of Mississippi, 2004.

INDEX

AASS (American Anti-Slavery Society), 70, 87, 105, 139–40

Abelin, Ernst, 182

abjection of enslaved, xvii; and action, 20, 68; departicularizing, 12; dominance in visual culture, 9, 109, 123, 187, 196, 207, 221; refusal of in texts, 19; resistance to, xviii, 19, 63, 122, 158, 162, 171, 221; scopic focus on, 65, 105, 128, 163, 186; and subjectivity, 3, 6, 22, 33, 36, 68, 137–38, 169–70; in visual rhetoric, 183, 186–87, 196; women, portrayal of, 166

abolitionism: and abjection of the enslaved, xiv, 9, 94, 108, 123; and action, 10, 22, 60, 68; and agency of the enslaved, 108, 132, 138, 202; and art, xii, xiv, 22, 212; and children, 70–72; colonization, 181, 194; embodied experience, xv; and eyesight, 15, 85, 242n21; history of, 31–32, 68–70, 138–41, 179–81; immediate versus gradual, 69; and reader, xiv, 12, 24, 105; and man (or woman) in the middle, 12, 72–3, 84; and masculinity, 167; parity with the enslaved, 9, 50, 122; radicalism of, xii; and religion, 8, 20, 117, 240n7; and resistance, 86, 97–98, 153; scopic regime and voyeurism of, ix, 11, 13, 163; and structures of feeling, 8, 160, 187; and torture, 75–77, 86, 115, 122, 128; and women, 77, 79, 94, 139–41, 142, 151, 153, 166; visual culture of, xv, xvii, 3–6, 13, 32, 67, 70, 197–198; violence, 180, 211. *See also* antislavery movements

Abolition of the Slave Trade Act (Britain, 1807), 31–32

Abruzzo, Margaret, 71–72, 78–79

Abstract of the Evidence Delivered Before a Select Committee of the House of Commons, An, 54

active reading/viewing protocols, 9, 16, 20, 21–23, 50–51, 63, 68, 85, 137, 159

"Adventures of Johnny Newcome" (Elmes cartoon), 64–65

affect, structures of, xi, 9, 11, 16, 19, 21, 23, 241–42n17. *See also* intersubjectivity; parallel empathy

African Americans: Christian conversion of, 115–16; citizenship, 39, 69, 70, 92, 95–96, 101, 180–81, 196; feminine heroism, 166; function in visual culture, 102–3, 109, 195; illustrated books by, 8; in literary production, 11–12, 83, 111, 240n6; masculinity/femininity, 27, 168; passing for white, xi, 102, 110, 169, 213; police violence against, 233; as readers, 11–12; women, in antislavery movements, 139–41. *See also* enslavement; *specific narratives*

Agamben, Giorgio, 244n20

agency of enslaved, xvi–xvii, xviii; detachment of, 183; and higher power, 135; in specular moment, 9; visual figuration of, 15, 109–10

Agosta, Louis, 102

"Amazing Grace" (Newton hymn), 98

Amenta, Edwin, 77

American and Foreign Anti-Slavery Society, 140

American Anti-Slavery Almanac, 122, 128, 156, 166, 212, 240n3

American Anti-Slavery Society (AASS), 70, 87, 105, 139–40

"Am I Not a Man and a Brother?" (inscription), 1–3, 5–6, 7, 56

Ammons, Elizabeth, 195–96, 252n1, 253n8

Anderson, Alexander, 17, 25, 29–30, 51–54, 243n2, 245n30. See also *Injured Humanity* (Anderson)

Andrews, William, 136, 166

Anti-Slavery Alphabet, 70

Anti-Slavery Convention of American Women, 139–40